The Grateful Dead Reader

READERS ON AMERICAN MUSICIANS
Scott DeVeaux, Series Editor

The
Grateful Dead
Reader

Edited by David G. Dodd
Diana Spaulding

OXFORD
UNIVERSITY PRESS
2000

OXFORD
UNIVERSITY PRESS

Oxford   New York
Athens   Auckland   Bangkok   Bogotá   Buenos Aires   Calcutta
Cape Town   Chennai   Dar es Salaam   Delhi   Florence   Hong Kong   Istanbul
Karachi   Kuala Lumpur   Madrid   Melbourne   Mexico City   Mumbai
Nairobi   Paris   São Paulo   Singapore   Taipei   Tokyo   Toronto   Warsaw

and associated companies in
Berlin   Ibadan

Published by Oxford University Press, Inc.
198 Madison Avenue, New York, New York 10016

Oxford is a registered trademark of Oxford University Press

Library of Congress Cataloging-in-Publication Data

The Grateful Dead Reader / edited by David G. Dodd and Diana Spaulding.
p. cm. — (Readers on American musicians)
Includes Index.
ISBN 0-19-512470-7
1. Grateful Dead (Musical group).
2. Rock musicians—United States—Biography.
I. Dodd, David G., 1957–
II. Spaulding, Diana.
III. Series.
ML421.G72 G69 2000
782.421660922—dc21
99-32195

Credits appear on page 315, which serves as an extension of this page.

Book design by Adam B. Bohannon

9 8 7 6 5 4 3 2 1
Printed in the United States of America
on acid-free paper

To the Pseudo Brothers: Eugene Grealish, Doug Kaplan,
Michel Welmond, and in memory of John Green.
Thanks for the education!
–DD

To David: For sharing his passion.
–DS

"I know this song it ain't never gonna end."

-Robert Hunter, "Ramble On Rose"

Contents

II. "IF YOU GET CONFUSED, LISTEN TO THE MUSIC PLAY": BACK FROM THE HIATUS, INTO THE EIGHTIES, 1976-1986

Acknowledgments

All of the contributors, for their art and for their generosity of spirit. Alan Trist and Ice Nine Publishing Company for making this book possible. Ed Radcliffe, for the loan of his scanner. Philip Baruth, David Gans, Robert Hunter, Dennis McNally, Alan Trist, George W. S. Trow, Lee K. Abbott, William J. Craddock, and Alice Kahn for waiving their permission fees. Maribeth Payne, Soo Mee Kwon, Jonathan Wiener, Tom Owens, Aimee Chevrette, Sarah Hemphill, Martin Patmos, and Mary Francis at Oxford University Press. Fred Lieberman, for arranging for an academic appointment for David. The Special Collections department of the McHenry Library at the University of California, Santa Cruz, for establishing the first special collection of material relating to the band. Sandra Choron, our agent. Julie Murphy, for arranging the manuscript's mailing while we were in Singapore. All the participants in the Well's Deadlit conference. Steve Silberman, for engraving his vision so precisely in language and passing on his inspiration. Rebecca Adams, for sending a much-needed article and for her advice on the book's final form. Blair Jackson, for his early, accurate criticism of this book's proposed format and for his subsequent advice. Jean Anderson, fellow NWU Local 7 member, for long-distance facilitation and printing help. Don Monkerud and National Writer's Union Local 7. Carol Dodd, for forwarding our mail, taking phone messages, and generally being the most wonderful sister a person could want. Barbara Spaulding Anglin, for long-distance assistance. Eileen Law, for her assistance in obtaining photo permissions. Rob Weiner—my fellow bibliographer, for much help and encouragement. Susana Millman for suggesting additional photographers. Robert Gordon, attorney for the Garcia Estate. Leonard Rosenbaum, our indexer. And Steve Silberman, David Gans, Charlie Haas, and Ed Perlstein for attending our proofreading party.

Editors' Prefaces

"What a long, strange trip it's been."

There. I said it. Spoken plain in that way, alone and out of context, this phrase sums up the entire media perception of the phenomenon of the Grateful Dead. But there's more in this tiny sentence than meets the eye.

First, it's a line from the most autobiographical of Dead songs, "Truckin'," written in 1970 by Robert Hunter and the rest of the band to reflect on what was already a "long" history, making it a legitimate statement *by* the band *about* the band. Years of being on the road—years that were to stretch out farther than anyone could have reasonably predicted at the time—had already begun to seem like an eternity when the band was only five years old.

Second, individual Deadheads may have highly personal associations with the line, so that when sung in a concert situation it could suddenly take on an immensely charged collective meaning or set of meanings. Each concertgoer's long trip, depending on the miles traveled to reach the venue, or the particular substances that listener may have ingested, is evoked. Hearing the line, the listener may think about a particular psychedelic experience or, simply, the course of one's life. It may evoke, for some, the psychedelic era as a whole—the collective post-LSD experience of Western Culture—or, more broadly, the Beat tradition in which the Dead squarely placed themselves (with its continent-crisscrossing narratives), or the twentieth century, or the entire evolutionary history of the planet. All long, strange trips.

The phrase was lifted and used as the title for so many articles and books (and for a greatest hits album of the Dead's music), as well as for many a cleverly turned take-off phrase, during the subsequent three decades, that it is now, truly, a cliché. Hunter himself has been accused of having used a cliché in writing the line! It is, perhaps, the single most widely integrated contribution of the band to the culture at large, corresponding to, say, "To be or not to be."

How many times did the Grateful Dead sing this line in concert over the years? (For it was a collectively sung line, not belonging to any particular vocalist. I can see, in my mind's eye, Phil Lesh stepping to the mike to join in singing this line, even during the late '70s, when he rarely sang at all; and I, ever the romantic, imagine the drummers shouting it from behind their drum sets.) Well, as a matter of fact, that number is probably available by now, thanks to the existence of *DeadBase*, that authoritative statistical handbook of all things Dead. Certainly the song was performed well over 500 times.

But I guess the reason I wanted to start this book with the line is that it represents the power of words to summarize, to really *get at* things that do not readily lend themselves to verbal expression at first take. Song lyrics, in the hands of Robert Hunter, become empty vessels into which the listener can pour personal meanings. Was it Elvis Costello who said that "writing about music is like dancing about architecture," with the implication that such an enterprise was foredefeated? (Remember, Robinson Jeffers pointed out that even those, such as architects, who work in stone are "foredefeated challengers of oblivion.") Perhaps it's true, but there are some wonderful writers who give it their best shot, and who's to say that a talented dancer could not communicate something of the essence of a great building? (Remember Jeffers's grudging admission that "stones have stood for a thousand years / and pained thoughts found the honey of peace in old poems.") The pieces in this book have been chosen for their ability to capture, to evoke, and sometimes even to explain something about the unexplainable phenomenon of the Grateful Dead.

Over the past couple of years, I have tried to read everything written about the Grateful Dead—first, as a means to the end of assembling a comprehensive bibliography of these writings, and second, out of a deep attachment to words and to the music of the Grateful Dead. The bibliography is done, and what remains is the belief in the power and ability of words to communicate, at least occasionally, something of the magic of the Grateful Dead. Some of the magic stems from the music itself, some from the surrounding context, some from the personalities of the band's members, some from the words of the songs they sang, and this anthology is an attempt to serve up the best of the attempts to capture those elements over the past thirty years. The writers range from those celebrated on the main stage of American writing to those known only to the relatively small group of Grateful Dead aficionados, the Deadheads.

There are some unifying characteristics that underlie the writing throughout this book, owing to the writers' efforts to capture the band's performance qualities. First is the use of "randomness," in the sense of mixing up the narrative flow on purpose—note, also, the frequent use of the word *random* throughout the various pieces in the anthology. Another characteristic is the constant search for a metaphor to capture the band's playing. These metaphors range from "like a river" to "like a crazed square dance" to "ground zero in a nuclear explosion" to "the answer to the atom bomb." And last, I would point out the use of the word *meditation* in the titles of several of the excerpts—as well as a general meditative flow to a great deal of the writing. These writers are not just writing about music, they are pondering.

The bibliography I compiled with my co-author, Rob Weiner, comprised entries for well over four thousand individual articles, books, papers, and other written works relating to the Grateful Dead. Here, we present forty. Hard choices had to be made, and there is no way to be certain that what is represented here is necessarily the "best." Indeed, some works of very high quality are left out because they are readily available elsewhere. Some that are readily available elsewhere are here because they are singular in their ability to convey some aspect of the Grateful Dead experience. I suggest that this book be taken as one possible starting point among the many available. Certainly, much more will be written as time goes by and as the band itself fades into dimmer memory—in the words of Robert Hunter, "melt[s] into a dream."

I would venture to generalize that all of the writing about the band falls into three categories: writing from *within* the band itself (this would include everything from liner notes, to press releases, to the lyrics of the songs themselves), writing by mainstream or professional journalists, and writing by Deadheads for other Deadheads. This anthology tries to present some of each but definitely leans toward the work of professional journalists (with the largest representation coming in the form of professional journalists who are Deadheads, such as Blair Jackson and Steve Silberman, but who write for a larger audience).

If the Grateful Dead experience was rooted in the Acid Tests, and in the psychedelic adventures of the early days of the band, so too was the early journalism that chronicled the era. Tom Wolfe's *The Electric Kool-Aid Acid Test* set the standard for writing that embodied, echoed, and embraced the "swirl" of the times. William Craddock chronicled the era in what some say is the "best Hippie book." Ed McClanahan's article for *Playboy*, combined with his examination of the lyrics to "New Speedway Boogie," is an excellent example of gonzo journalism, in which the writer is a primary subject and character in the story.

From the mid to late 1970s, the Grateful Dead were largely ignored by the mainstream rock press, and indeed by the nation at large, while they continued to build their fan base and write songs and record them on albums that sold moderately well while drawing faint-praise-damning or outright hostile reviews.

One way in which the Dead built their core fan base was through a wonderful newsletter that was mailed to the Dead Heads mailing list and that contained poems, stories, and even occasional news about the band, written mostly by Hunter, Garcia, and Alan Trist.

Rolling Stone magazine gave the Dead an occasional blurb in "Random Notes"; but 'round about the late '70s, something happened that made several writers take notice: the Dead were still playing. Amazing. And they seemed to have become a kind of backroad traveling circus, drawing adventurous souls out on the road and continuing to attract new, young fans. Writers like Charlie Haas and Lee K. Abbott wrote about the phenomenon. And in the early '80s, Blair Jackson wrote a book about the band and founded an elegantly produced "fan magazine" (though *The Golden Road*, as it was called, looked nothing like any other fan magazine ever produced, except perhaps *Dance Index*). Other books followed, aimed at the large Deadhead market, while the band that had never had a top-ten hit continued to tour relentlessly.

Then: the unexpected. In 1987 "Touch of Grey," a catchy Garcia/Hunter tune, *did* hit the top ten. A wildly popular video dominated MTV. Deadheads were amazed—this song had been around for *years* before it was finally recorded. What was all the fuss? I recall being gratified at the recognition, but worried at the same time. During my college years, I had been impressed by a bathroom graffito: "Good Deadheads don't proselytize." And now, new Deadheads were crawling out of the woodwork. The crowds grew quickly, and the backroad circus hit the interstate, with the Highway Patrol in hot pursuit. The press coverage swelled, books proliferated, and it became impossible to get a ticket.

The market for Deadhead-oriented writing gave rise to five major fan magazines: *Relix, The Golden Road, Dupree's Diamond News, Unbroken Chain,* and, in England, *Spiral Light.* The most serious of these was *The Golden Road,* which was co-edited by Blair Jackson and Regan McMahon, both professional journalists who produced the magazine as a labor of love. Jackson's writing, in particular, has always been the most clear-sighted, well-informed journalism one could hope for from someone who is a rabid Deadhead.

Upon Garcia's death in 1995, a vast new ocean of ink was spilled, and several good pieces were included in the waves of obituaries, reminiscences, feature stories, and opinion pieces. Several are presented here because of their quality of summing up, of truthfully weighing, the meaning of the artist's life.

For me, and for countless others, a world without Garcia, and without the Grateful Dead, is a world lacking the possibility of ever again experiencing quite the same level of intellectual, emotional, and spiritual ecstasy all at once. Which makes the world a little more difficult to bear. But I am so glad to have been on that ride ...

David Dodd
Capitola, California, and Singapore
1998

For me the Grateful Dead represent a cultural enigma that I will never quite come to terms with. My co-editorship of this anthology was an attempt to understand the wonder that has inspired not just these authors but so many of my friends and acquaintances, and especially my husband David. I suppose the time has come to admit the horrible truth: I am not a Deadhead. There, I said it and it doesn't seem so awful. It was only after meeting David in 1990 that I even went to a show; and I only went to two altogether. Still, I do love the music.

I hope that others who are curious about the band and the subculture or who want to understand what their friends are reminiscing or raving about will pick up this book and become enlightened. Maybe I'll even catch an "Other Ones" concert myself in the years to come.

Diana Spaulding
Capitola, California, and Singapore
1998
Note: Headnotes written by David Dodd.

Introduction: Gathering the Sparks
Steve Silberman

There's a wonderful poem by Denise Levertov that describes a series of religious paintings, each presenting an image of God that differed from all of the others. The poem ends by suggesting that *all* of the artists were accurate, and that only in the presence of *all* of the visions—together—are we closer to comprehending the whole that inspired them all.

I feel that way looking through this book. Writing about music is tricky business. If the music is very good, the writing tends to sound lead-footed and foolish soon after it's written, while the music endures to speak to each generation with a voice that seems perfectly fitted to the times. That's what makes it painful to read the liner notes on the back of old jazz albums—the poor authors are blurred by the myopias of the historical moment they're writing in, while the playing soars above the humble circumstances in which it found itself born into this world.

The best writing in this book, however, sees past its occasion. There was something about the Grateful Dead that made writers want to reach beyond the syntax of their times, to weave of language a ghost trap for something ineffable, something that seemed important. An imperative something that ruled out pretense: "No time for poetry but exactly what is," as Kerouac wrote. The words in these pages are charged with an intensity of purpose that has served the authors well.

Starting from the earliest accounts, it's amazing how much of what the Grateful Dead would be for so many people, through many different eras, was evident from the beginning. From William Craddock's description of Jerry Garcia's "explosion of discord made harmonious by the suspension of time" to Tom Wolfe's utterly strange (and right) image of "a lightbulb in a womb," the Dead's signature juxtaposition of the marvelous and the terrifying, the absurd and the sublime, presents itself.

Sure, the Dead had the misfortune to come of age in interesting times (to paraphrase an ironic Chinese blessing); but even if the entire electric Kool-Aid mythosphere hadn't been spun around them by Wolfe and hundreds of other commentators and footnoters on the Haight-Ashbury "scene," their larger-than-life-ness would still have been hanging around, a side-effect of the scale of the music itself, making it hard to see the Dead as they saw themselves—as working musicians.

It's that tension between what the fans hungered to see and how acutely the musicians were aware of their shortcomings and humanity that makes for some of the funniest moments in this book, especially in the interviews with Garcia and Robert Hunter and in Ed McClanahan's and Charlie Haas's portraits of the band members' facing off with the odd characters who would inevitably find their way backstage. As much as the music could be glorious and subtle (or volcanic and primordial), there was always a whiff of scrofulous, priapic Coyote Old Man malingering behind the altar and guzzling from the communion cup, to keep things from getting too precious.

It's that spirit in these writings that should keep this from being a book to evoke pious nostalgia, a yearning for the time when Ye Olde Grateful Dead trod the boards, plucking the tunes of yesteryear. Deadheads were sent to jail for insisting on freedoms they claimed as their birthright (many are still incarcerated as I write this); the only fitting tribute to the ecstatic moments recorded here is to act with as much hope, as much abandon, and as much faith as possible that, with craftiness and joy, you can build a bridge to an order beyond planning and naming—and love will see you through.

Love.

Near the end of his life, another poet, Ezra Pound, wrote: "What thou lov'st well remains, the rest is dross." The *Grateful Dead Reader* is a chronicle of loving well, whether it's Garcia, falling under the spell of the tale-spinning improvisations of old-time fiddle player Scotty Stoneman ("I just stood there and don't remember breathing"); Jack Britton's friend Carp, rapping about "the swirl" ("the thrill of spontaneous creation and total propulsion into the unknown"); David Gans, transcribing his mindstate at ground zero in the Phil Zone ("now I try to keep moving through the fiery bubble of it, solving riddles and posing thoughts"); Paddy Ladd, releasing his heartbreak and frustration during the Dead's last tours after Brent Mydland's death ("something deeper than music has left with his passing, some elemental reality of the fundamental pain of real life and the possibility of transcending it by facing it, at least onstage"); and finally, Hunter, left alone on Earth, crafting for his best friend a gift of poetry to outlast the dust ("May she bear thee to thy rest, / the ancient bower of flowers / beyond the solitude of days, / the tyranny of hours").

For Deadheads, loving well was one way of participating in the mystery. Or is it the way the mystery participates in us?

For many who danced in that place that the music seemed to reveal, the Dead arrived in their lives with an uncanny familiarity, like a true love. Perhaps love is how we learn to recognize those around us, like Levertov seeing the divine in all those faces of the sacred.

From that fire, these sparks.

Steve Silberman
Brooklyn, New York
October 1998

Six discrete "Grateful Deads" are discernable during the period from 1966 to 1974. The 1966 unit (#1) was the five-man Garcia/Weir/Kreutzmann/Lesh/Pigpen body. Hart was added in 1967 (#2). In 1968-1970, Constanten joined (#3), leaving in 1970 (#2 again). In 1971, Hart dropped out, returning the group briefly to their original lineup. Then Keith Godchaux joined (#4), followed by the addition of Donna Jean Godchaux (#5), followed in turn by the death of Pigpen (#6).

Prior even to the formalization of the Grateful Dead as the Grateful Dead, there were a number of lineups featuring various band members together or separately. But the Warlocks of 1965-1966 were the first true Ur-Dead, with the same lineup as Grateful Dead #1. Other early bands that featured various members included Mother McCree's Uptown Jug Champions (1964-65), the Black Mountain Boys (1963), the Sleepy Hollow Hog Stompers (1962-63), the Zodiacs (1962-63), the Wildwood Boys (1963), the Hart Valley Drifters (1962) and the Thunder Mountain Tub Thumpers (1962).

From 1967 through 1975, the band recorded twelve official albums, including *The Grateful Dead*, *Anthem of the Sun*, *Aoxomoxoa*, *Live Dead*, *Workingman's Dead*, *American Beauty*, *Grateful Dead* (aka *Skull & Roses*, aka *Skullfuck*), *Europe '72*, *Bear's Choice*, *Wake of the Flood*, *From the Mars Hotel*, and *Blues for Allah*.

The early albums, especially *Anthem* and *Aoxomoxoa*, were militantly weird, from the cover art down to the final groove in the vinyl. These and all subsequent albums through *Bear's Choice* were recorded on the Warner Brothers label, after which the band embarked on an experiment with their own record label. It is generally agreed that, with the possible exception of *Live Dead*, none of these recordings (and possibly no recording ever released) captured on disc just what it was that the band was all about, and thus the focus devolved upon the live concert experience, which the band consciously regarded as in the realm of the mystical and spiritual.

And so, from their first official performance as The Grateful Dead in December 1965 (captured, partially, in Tom Wolfe's *The Electric Kool-Aid Acid Test*) through their "final" run of five concerts at Winterland Arena, San Francisco, in October 1974, the band toured relentlessly, building a following the hard way, without benefit of extensive airplay. They attracted a following unlike anything ever seen (one of my proudest accomplishments as a librarian is my role in making the term "Deadheads" an official Library of Congress Subject Heading, a testimony to the unique character of the band's fans). In 1975, the year known as the "hiatus," the band played live only four times.

Tom Wolfe's writing, along with that of Hunter S. Thompson, revolutionized journalism in the 1960s, just as the people they were writing about were changing the face of the arts and of politics. This excerpt from *The Electric Kool-Aid Acid Test*, published in 1968 by Farrar, Straus & Giroux, records the first Acid Test given by Ken Kesey and the Merry Pranksters, and the first gig by the Grateful Dead *as* the Grateful Dead, on December 4, 1965. Wolfe's many books include *The Right Stuff*, published in 1979 by Farrar, Straus & Giroux; *The Bonfire of the Vanities*, published in 1987 by Farrar, Straus & Giroux, and *A Man in Full* published in 1998 by Farrar, Straus & Giroux.

Excerpt from

The Electric KOOL-AID *Acid Test*

Tom Wolfe

Resey had hooked up with a rock 'n' roll band, The Grateful Dead, led by Jerry Garcia, the same dead-end kid who used to live in the Chateau in Palo Alto with Page Browning and other seeming no-counts, lumpenbeatniks, and you had to throw them out when they came over and tried to crash the parties on Perry Lane. Garcia remembered—how they came down and used to get booted out "by Kesey and the wine drinkers." *The wine drinkers*—the middle-class bohemians of Perry Lane. They both, Kesey and Garcia, had been heading into the pudding, from different directions, all that time, and now Garcia was a, yes, beautiful person, quiet, into the pudding, and a great guitar player. Garcia had first named his group The Warlocks, meaning sorcerers or wizards, and they had been eking by playing for the beer drinkers, at jazz joints and the like around Palo Alto. To the Warlocks, the beer drinker music, even when called jazz, was just square hip. They were on to that distinction, too. For Kesey—they could just play, do their thing.

The Dead had an organist called Pig Pen, who had a Hammond electric organ, and they move the electric organ into Big Nig's ancient house, plus all of the Grateful Dead's electrified guitars and basses and the Pranksters' electrified guitars and basses and flutes and horns and the light machines and the movie projectors and the tapes and mikes and hi-fis, all of which pile up in insane coils of wires and gleams of stainless steel and winking amplifier dials before Big Nig's unbelieving eyes. His house is old and has wiring that would hardly hold a toaster. The Pranksters are primed in full Prankster regalia. Paul Foster has on his Importancy Coat and now has a huge head of curly hair, a great curly mustache pulling back into great curly mutton chops roaring off his face. Page Browning is the king of face painters. He becomes a full-fledged Devil with a bright orange face and his eyes become the centers of two great silver stars painted over the orange and his hair is silver with silver dust and he paints his lips silver with silver lipstick. This very night the Pranksters all sit down with oil pastel crayons and colored pens and at a wild rate start printing handbills on 8½ x 11 paper saying CAN *YOU* PASS THE ACID TEST? and giving Big Nig's address. As the jellybean-cocked masses start pouring out of the Rolling Stones concert at the Civic Auditorium, the Pranksters charge in among them. Orange & Silver Devil, wild man in a coat of buttons—Pranksters! Pranksters!—handing out the handbills with the challenge, like some sort of demons, warlocks verily, come to channel the wild pointless energy built up by the Rolling Stones inside.

They come piling into Big Nig's, and suddenly acid and the worldcraze were everywhere, the electric organ vibrating through every belly in the place, kids dancing not *rock* dances, not the frug and the—what?—swim, mother, but dancing *ecstasy*, leaping, dervishing, throwing their hands over their heads like Daddy Grace's own stroked-out inner courtiers—yes!—Roy Seburn's lights washing past every head, Cassady rapping, Paul Foster handing people weird little things out of his Eccentric Bag, old whistles, tin crickets, burnt keys, spectral plastic handles. Everybody's eyes turn on like lightbulbs, fuses blow, blackness—wowwww!—the things that shake and vibrate and funnel and freak out in this blackness—and then somebody slaps new fuses in and the old hulk of a house shudders back, the wiring writhing and fragmenting like molting snakes, the organs vibromassage the belly again, fuses blow, minds scream, heads explode, neighbors call the cops, 200, 300, 400 people from out there drawn into The Movie, into the edge of the pudding at least, a mass closer and higher than any mass in history, it seems most surely, and Kesey makes minute adjustment, small toggle switch here, lubricated with Vaseline No. 6343 diluted with carbon tetrachloride, and they *ripple*, Major, *ripple*, but with meaning, 400 of the attuned multitude headed toward the pudding, the first mass acid experience, the dawn of the Psychedelic, the Flower Generation and all the rest of it, and Big Nig wants the rent.

"How you holding?"

How you holding—

"I mean, like, you know," says Big Nig to Garcia. "I didn't charge Kesey nothing to use this place, like free, you know? and the procedure now is that every cat here *contributes*, man, to help out with the rent."

With the rent—

"Yeah, I mean, like"—says Big Nig. Big Nig stares at Garcia with the deepest look of hip spade soul authority you can imagine, and nice and officious, too—

Yeah, I mean, like—Garcia, for his part, however, doesn't know which bursts out first, the music or the orange laugh. Out the edges of his eyes he can see his own black hair framing his face—it is so long, to the shoulders, and springs out like a Sudanese soldier's—and then Big Nig's big earnest black face right in front of him flapping and washing comically out into the glistening acid-glee red sea of faces out beyond them both in the galactic red lakes on the walls—

"Yeah, I mean, like, for the *rent*, man," says Big Nig, "you already *blown* six fuses."

Blown! Six fuses! Garcia sticks his hand into his electric guitar and the notes come out like a huge orange laugh all blown fuses electric spark leaps in colors upon the glistening sea of faces. It's a freaking laugh and a half. A new star is being born, like a lightbulb in a womb, and Big Nig wants the rent—a new star being born, a new planet forming, Ahura Mazda blazing in the world womb, here before our very eyes and Big Nig, the poor pathetic spade, wants his rent.

A freaking odd thought, that one. A big funky spade looking pathetic and square. For twenty years in the hip life, Negroes *never even looked* square. They were the archetypical soul figures. But what is Soul, or Funky, or Cool, or Baby—in the new world of the ecstasy, the All-one...the *kairos*...

William J. Craddock's novel *Be Not Content: A Subterranean Journal*, published by Doubleday in 1970, achieves the very psychedelic feeling he was chronicling–something only a few writers have been able to do. This excerpt from the book describes an adventurous outing to an Acid Test–held December 18, 1965, at Muir Beach Lodge, in Muir Beach, California, an event that followed shortly on the heels of the first Acid Test. Craddock also wrote *Twilight Candelabra*, published by Doubleday in 1972.

MORGAN'S
Acid Test

Excerpt from

William J. Craddock

I **stayed home alone for two days and practiced doing** nothing, slowing down at last to only a couple of notches past normal, at which time I slept.

On the morning of the third day I woke up to a holy quiet that brought to mind visions of postcard Christmases and gently falling snow. I savored the peaceful hum of silence and almost convinced myself that during the night the end had come and now, outside, the world was reverent and at peace and saved. I heard a diesel on the highway, but it sounded a long way off—droning along slow—an honest, satisfying rumble in the distance like I used to hear them late at night when I was a littler kid, lying awake warm and secure, wondering where they were going, dreaming myself inside the cab driving all night till sunrise on the road in some rough, He-man place like Montana, where I would get out of my truck (named Road Eater—a name I'd heard from a friend whose father was a trucker) at a truck-stop and greet all the men inside, who knew me by my reputation as a hard-drivin-man, and smile my craggy smile at the beautiful Spanish waitress (who also knew me well) and drink my coffee and smoke a slow cigarette while trading stories of Deadman's curve and burned-out brakes with the other hard-drivin truckers before climbing back into my dusty rig to drive a hundred miles an hour all the way to probably Texas or Wyoming. The diesel honked once to say goodbye and I rolled over and put my feet on the floor, no longer a six-year-old hard-drivin man.

Why is it so beautifully quiet? I pulled the heavy curtains aside and looked at a drifting wall of solid cloud. The entire outside world cushioned in thick, white fog. So thick that it even muffled the street sounds. A day made up of nothing but soft edges. Cool and soft.

I dressed in coat and sweater, walked out into Sherlock Holmes' London and strolled along with just my boot-taps for company, pretending that I was on the water-front—a lonely sea captain at home in the fog—actually hearing waves lapping on barnacled hulls and fog-horns calling to one another. With every step I took I could feel the depression that had been sitting like a fat toad on my brain rip itself loose one suction-cup finger at a time—like sinuses opening—until, when I reached Tenth Street, the toad fell off with a final croak of surrender and dismay, and I saw with absolute clarity that everything was fine. Only my own hungup mind that produced conflict and confusion. The universe was in perfect harmony. Everything was fine.

Walking back to my apartment, zigzag and really just wandering glad, having met no one in the miracle-healing fog and having been passed by only two or three cars driving slow and quiet with their lights on, I thought of Adriel who loved the fog and the rain and the wind as much as she loved the sunshine, and who, I realized suddenly, I wanted very much to see again. Adriel with her black hair and wide green eyes, paints and poems, shy smiles and hellos, speaking with a sweet southern drawl when I first met her at seventeen. And then, when I re-met her at twenty, I discovered that she actually had raven-black Spanish-Oriental silk-fine hair that touched the small of her back and shrouded her tiny body when she sat like a sleek Siamese cat, her always bare feet tucked under her beautiful little behind, watching me quietly or just eye-drifting into deep space. Raven-black flashing blue hi-lite hair that agonizingly perfectly circled and framed her pale little-girl face with its huge sad eyes that always looked as though they were on the verge of clear tears even when she was laughing and honestly glad.

So much had happened since I'd seen her last—since she went to Georgia to visit Grandfather and cousins and home where she was born, writing only one strange letter to me in a year: a letter that told about Negroes grown sad as she hadn't remembered them, and sticky heat much hotter than when she was five years old running barefoot through the dust, and people all red-faced and uptight and narrow-minded although they used to be wise and friendly and good. The letter'd rambled on for pages about social reform and the South being so different from the North—written in her lacy feminine hand but sounding nothing like the big-eyed naive little Adriel who used to worry about me dumping my bike or being arrested, whispered "be careful, please" and touched my arm when I'd stop by to see her on my way to a *Night Riders* meeting or headed for a big club-run to somewhere, and who was sincerely sorry for me and my discouragement with the (in my eyes hopeless, in her eyes hopeful) games of life.

A long time since I'd seen Adriel. It seemed much longer than it really was. I felt that I understood and could appreciate so much more of her than I had before.

I wanted to see Adriel, but just then I didn't know where she was and there would be plenty of time to find out and anyway it didn't matter because the universe was in perfect harmony and everything was standing fine and there's my apartment hiding in the slow-flowing white cloud and that's beautiful...and inside, roll a slender symmetrical joint and light it while putting all existing Dylan albums one right on top of the other on the thoughtfully automatic record-player and sit down in front of the glass door with the curtain pulled open to get spectacularly high watching the infinitely deep oh so beautiful swirling white outside while mystical Mister Dylan magically adjusts his music to the fog and its special vibrations and comes on from exactly the right place. Perfect. All the world so strange and multi-level intricate, but so perfect, so beautiful, so fine, so good, so *perfect*. Ah, how can anyone possibly fall into hate or worry or hangups or sadness when all the world's so perfect-fine-beautiful-good? Today I'm so fine-glad-perfect-happy that if the worst of all Hell-sent hideous bads burbled in and grabbed me by the spine I'd be able to smile it into submission. And I *am* Abel. Yessir, I'm Abel and everthing's perfect and gooder'n'good.

I surely do wish I'd been able to hold that state of mind.

Later in the week, a search for acid brought me to Rob Tilding's saggy old brown house on San Fernando. Rob met me at the door in a pair of unzipped wrinkled tan slacks, his wild curly dark hair exploding on his head, eyes all bloodshot and blinky from a long run of book-study and paper-write with black coffee and white bennies and no sleep, two days' stubble on his usually clean-shaven jaw, finger-tips stained orange from a hundred chain-smoked Camels. I followed him to his room where he plopped on a straight-backed wooden chair beside a portable typewriter surrounded by reams of typing-paper in neat stacks and crumpled piles all over the floor. Ashtrays and coffee-cups-become-ashtrays overflowed on his desk in between, under and on top of open textbooks. A truly classic slaving-student scene.

"Mid-terms?" I asked, adding a used cigarette to one of the butt mountains.

"Mid-terms," said Rob, stretching with a groan, rubbing knuckles into eyes. "Four papers due next week and an exam in every class."

"Hey, I'll leave you be, then."

"No. No, I was about to knock off anyway," fumbling through empty cigarette packs for a smoke. "Whattayou been up to, man?"

"Right now I'm lookin for some acid. You still got any of those clear caps?"

Rob yawned and shook his head. "I've got some new stuff though. I was thinking of dropping one tonight myself...blow out some of this mind-clutter I've been diligently accumulating." He got to his feet. "How many you need?"

"Uh...three if you've got em."

"Sure," as he went to the kitchen.

Footsteps sounded on the wooden porch, the front door rattled open and Baxtor strode into the room, leaping back in stylized W. C. Fields surprise when he saw me. "Aha! Abe! What a tiny cosmos it is. I was just on my way to see you." "Baxtor!" glad to see him. "How's your head, man?"

He pursed his lips, shoving his mustache over the tip of his nose. "Ah yas. You mean following that freak-out at Marion's. I'm truly sorry about that scene."

"Hey, don't apologize to me. What happened?"

Shrugging his shoulders and speaking as if I already knew—"I became ensnared in a network of elaborate games. I realized that you were all calling hopefully for my successful death from the entrance to the Void and I foolishly rebelled against the inevitable. It's this ego problem of mine. Yas. It took me a few days to work my way out of the hole I dug...Hiya, Robert," to Tilding, an old friend of Baxtor's from long before I came on the scene.

"Nobody's out for your death, man," said Tilding, smiling and counting out acid caps on a glass-top table.

Baxtor gave me a knowing look. "That's what they all say. But don't worry. I've nearly got it worked out. I won't hold things up much longer." He turned to Tilding and said, "Rob, you'll be interested in this. Ben Morgan is holding an—and I quote 'Acid Test' at Muir Beach tonight."

"I heard about it," said Tilding. "What's the word on that anyway?"

"Ben Morgan. Acid test. That's all I got."

Ben Morgan was a young underground film-maker-artist who'd recently won fame and moderate fortune with a disturbing cinema experiment called *House Rules*—a great film, honest and so totally involving that it was bound to drive you insane at the very least. We all looked to Morgan for big amazing things to come.

"What'll it be like? I mean, a party or what?"

"I can't imagine," said Baxtor, "but it's obviously not to be missed."

I said, "Are you sure we can get into this thing? Morgan doesn't know us from Adam," accepting three caps from Tilding and handing him a five-dollar bill.

Baxtor informed us that, "Steve Lewis who's one of Morgan's crew and an ex-card playing acquaintance of mine, told me this morning that *all* freaks are invited. If we don't fit into that category, then I hardly know who or what does and, if nothing more, it will be interesting to witness a gathering of those who consider themselves invited to an all-freak, organized acid test."

Rob and I both wanted to go, of course, and I phoned around to see who else could be found. Only Brian Kelly was at home and he promised to meet us in San Jose. I was supposed to see Gina that night (a chick I'd dated for some time and wouldn't be ready to appreciate for at least two more years) and I asked her to go along.

"*The* Ben Morgan?" she squeaked. "The same."

"Can you get me a cap of acid?" "It's already got if you want *it.*" "*I* do. Come get *me.*"

We met at Tilding's house where everyone but me (because I'd volunteered to drive and recalled bad experiences driving while acid-stoned) dropped small red caps of brand-new, untested but reported to be deadly acid and piled into the big Galaxie 500 that Rob had borrowed from his brother. Then we were zooming down the freeway, headed for Muir Beach and unknown what.

We'd only gone about ten miles when Baxtor said, "Hmmm. I'd forgotten how *fast* this stuff comes on." The last words he said all night. In time to come, I will often wonder what messages and astounding truths we would have attributed to that statement had it been the last he uttered in his life.

Maybe eight miles from our destination and completely lost-me unfamiliar with the territory and the others too spaced to give directions—when a sign materialized in the beam of the headlights blowing our collective mind. "ACID TEST" it shouted in big red letters with an arrow pointing the way (which was up) tacked to a telephone pole.

"It's a hallucination," said Brian.

"It's for real," said I.

"Now that's what I call having absolutely no fear," marveled Rob, who, like all of us, dropped acid in as much secrecy as possible and in constant fear of being busted by the nebulous "Authorities," although acid wouldn't actually be illegal for another five months.

I know it's a joke of some kind, but I followed the signs ... "ACID TEST"..."CAN YOU PASS THE ACID TEST?"..."THE ACID TEST"...to a lodge-like building, where I parked among an unbelievable number of cars, almost positive that at any second people would pop out of the bushes with cameras, yelling, "Caught ya!" since it was becoming more than obvious that we'd been lured into a trap designed to snare unsuspecting, gullible acid-heads as part of "Operation Clean-up." I even reflected that it was a clumsy and child-ish trap which no one in their right mind would fall for, then realized with a mental groan that five of us just had, and I sighed because the statement was still true.

"Are you *sure* this is the place?" Brian peering over the car door and out the window in disbelief. "There aren't that many acid freaks in the whole world."

"It's the right place," Rob assured us, taking the initiative and leading us, "Come on, Baxtor," single file to the door of the building which is wide open, so inside, look around, and it's a kitchen.

"Hey man, this is somebody's home," I whispered, sure that we were stomping into some poor unsuspecting citizen's beach-house.

"It's okay," said Rob, and he seemed to know, so we followed him down a shadowy hallway, turned a corner and walked into a huge dark room full of what seemed to be hundreds of bodies all sitting or standing in every square foot of available space, watching a movie that was being projected on one entire wall. The movie was now a swirling vortex of vivid color, now a black and white study of a man motioning for us to come forward, now color again—bright—moving—spinning—and a chick is dancing through party balloons and flashing lights while a bleary old derelict ogles her from an oozing rain-bow bed. "There is no real," says a loud, amplified voice, "Only the movie is real and it's certainly not real now is it people? But it's the movie children that must be accepted or else where then there can any of us possibly seek...refuge...in...this...chang...ing...veh...tee...veh...tee...holl...oh and cold-and-lifeless-and-dark-and...ahhhhhh...only in the movie sad people of this sad scene...find joy in the movie...we must get into the movie...we must GET RIGHT INTO THE MOVIE!" and a real chick (distinguished from the chick in the movie) is clawing at the wall, trying to obey the command. The film is sud-denly being projected on the ceiling, then the audience, then the wall again, this time upside-down, now sideways, now rightside-up but the film is run-ning backwards. A dying sun is racing across the walls, "Follow the sun...wheeeeooooooh...follow the sun...wheeeeeoooo..." sang the sound track. The lights flashed on, I blinked, cleared my eyes, looked around me and thought, "Tonight something will be revealed." The room—a huge barn-sized enclosure—was packed to overflowing with freaks. Baxtor, Rob, Brian and I—who couldn't appear on a public street without causing heads to turn and cops to come unglued—were among the more conservative of those assem-bled. A cat in a white jump-suit, his face painted green, was passing out caps of acid from an ornately carved, crystal punchbowl. A midget dressed in a purple cape that trailed along behind him and a top hat that covered the upper half of his head passed by crooning, "I can't follow the sun. I can't follow the sun yet, because it's very fast and my legs are very small and slow. But soon I will be swift. Soon I will be tall and swift. Soon I will be fast enough to catch the sun. Soon I will. Soon I will. Yes I will."

Brian turned to me in astonishment and I could only toss it back to him. "It's happening, man. It's happening for real."

In these days just before Be-ins and the Haight-Ashbury scene to be, a gathering of this size made up almost entirely of ecstatic, painted, long-haired, bearded, beaded, mad-eyed, strangely-dressed, obvious acid-eaters was mind staggering. "This is really it," I thought, resigned to the fact that sooner or later it had to happen, "This is the end of the straight-world. The searching people have been gathered together from the far corners of the earth to witness the end."

Strobe-light. Legendary Neal Cassiday in the center ring, surrounded by worshipers as he dances with a fluorescent skeleton, holding it in front of his fly, asking it riddles that he answers in the same breath, pantomiming all-life with his eighteen-year-old body and thousand-year-old mind. Insane—true—impossible—unquestionably happening right there in the center ring under the flash-flash-flash of strobe-light. "That's Cassiday! That's Kerouac's holy Cassiday!" I say to Rob, unable to believe that I'm really seeing the immortal super-hero, raving-mad and in the living flesh and blood and sweat and action.

"Yes," says Rob. "Yes, they're all here. They're here."

Then five strangest of freaks were on the raised platform at one end of the huge room making thunderous gut-rocking sounds with their electric instruments, moving lights and bodies with their driving sound.

Behind the organ, a massive organist. Shoulder-length black hair, a bandito mustache draped over the corners of his mouth, leather vest over striped T-shirt, a bullwhip coiled on his right shoulder, "I'm gonna WAIT till the STARS come out...Till your LOVE comes tumblin down," he howled, the organ squealing under his thick, fast fingers. An eerie graveyard outerspace wail. Have mercy! Have mercy on the poor keys and on our poor souls. And no mercy is to be had, because there's more to say and we all gotta hear it.

Behind the guitar, a sound-god guitarist. Spanish hair, wild and snarled, red-white-and-blue-banded shirt, black Levi's, work shoes. He chewed gum while his fingers—his whole body—tormented, then caressed, then threatened to kill, than made love to the lightning-powered strings, pushing the sound they made through the music of the souls behind him, driving his pleading-coaxing-wailing-laughing-sobbing-demanding guitar-screams and moans over the intricate patterns of All-sound which He commanded. Winding through it, under it, around it—picking up all the separate sounds and molding them into a sun, then dropping the sun with an explosion of discord made harmonious by the suspension of time, soaring above the scattered music and swooping down to pull it all together again in the nick of time and space to save the world.

Behind the bass, a tall, flame-headed bass-man—confident—in love with his sound. He is the deep, eternal, reassuring vibration of the Source. He tells us that we are already there...already there. Just listen. It's over long ago and happening now.

A rhythm-guitar driven by a crystal-eyed pilot who validates and proclaims the truth and purity and unshakable foundation of even the most incredible prophecies made by the leader. He knows where it's all going. He's got the pattern and he's got the power.

A drummer who controls the heart-beat of the universe they have created to work with in order and dis-order to produce SOUND.

"They're the *Grateful Dead,*" said Brian reverently, getting the information from a small, lost, painted chick swaying in front of him.

"Yes!" A whisper. But a whisper with an exclamation point. True on so many levels. It wasn't until much later that I realized that it was actually the group's name—*The Grateful Dead.*

The walls change color with the music. Liquid-light projections dance and tremble to the sound. A strobe jerks the environment into ragged film action. The Grateful Dead lead the lost souls through purgatory and hell and to the gates of heaven in search of salvation, pointing out the torments and joys and wonders that we pass. Grateful to be dead—grateful to have been shown the truth of the void. "In the Land of the Dark the Ship of the Sun shall be driven by The Grateful *Dead.*" These are the Grateful Dead. *The Grateful Dead.*

I took the cap of acid from my shirt pocket and swallowed it, surrendering myself to the coming of The Final Truth. All possible variables lined up. Nothing left to do. This is it.

We slip into the Now of Then

The Dead end their sound universe with a multi-nova. Houselights turn the scene to day. Freaks begin to move aimlessly—a twisting mass of painted faces, knowing eyes. With a start, I notice that some are not freaks. I see two straight-looking young chicks walking arm in arm across the floor, gritting their teeth and recoiling from the bodies that whirl past them. There's a man in faded coveralls who looks like a patient old farmer. Leaning against a stair-railing is a gangster in anti-sun glasses and a black business suit—digging the action from behind a toothpick wedged between his front teeth. How did *he* get here? And the farmer and the young straight-chicks? They must have accidentally stumbled across the reality-warp. (Ah, how selfish not to mention foolish, Abel, to imagine that only flesh-obvious freaks may participate in the Final Flash.) But still, I wonder if it's strange for them to find themselves among mad freaks? (Not if they've seen the Truth.)

Ralph J. Gleason wrote for the *San Francisco Chronicle* from the late 1940s through the 1960s, producing a column about jazz and popular music that ran several times a week. He is generally recognized to be the first critic to give serious attention to popular music. He was a very vocal supporter of the early psychedelic rock scene in San Francisco, and his enthusiasm helped foster the success of a number of bands, especially the Dead and Jefferson Airplane. The Dead appreciated Gleason's early support and eventually created in his name an annual award sponsored by their charitable arm, The Rex Foundation. The following two excerpts, especially the lengthy interview with Garcia, which appeared in Gleason's book *The Jefferson Airplane and the San Francisco Sound*, published by Ballantine in 1969, reveal how close Gleason was to the band. Gleason's questions lead Garcia adroitly into a fascinating discussion of the band's origins and influences and of the conscious evolution of Garcia's guitar style. The first piece appeared in the *San Francisco Chronicle* on March 19, 1967. Gleason was also the author of *Celebrating the Duke, and Louis, Bessie, Billie, Bird, Carmen, Miles, Dizzy, and Other Heroes*, published by Little, Brown in 1975, and *Great Music Festivals*, published by Hansen in 1971, and was the editor of *Jam Session: An Anthology of Jazz*, published by Putnam in 1958. He co-founded *Rolling Stone* magazine with Jann Wenner in 1967 and wrote for it and for numerous other periodicals until his death in 1975.

Dead Like
Live Thunder

Ralph J. Gleason

an Francisco has become the Liverpool of America in recent months, a giant pool of talent for the new music world of rock.

The number of recording company executives casing the scene at the Fillmore and the Avalon is equaled only by the number of anthropologists and sociologists studying the Haight-Ashbury hippy culture.

Nowhere else in the country has a whole community of rock music developed to the degree it has here.

At dances at the Fillmore and the Avalon and the other, more occasional affairs, thousands upon thousands of people support several dozen rock 'n' roll bands that play all over the area for dancing each week. Nothing like it has occurred since the heyday of Glenn Miller, Benny Goodman and Tommy Dorsey. It is a new dancing age.

The local band with the greatest underground reputation (now that the Jefferson Airplane has gone national via two LPs and several single records) is a group of young minstrels with the vivid name, The Grateful Dead.

A Celebration

Their lead guitar player, a former folk musician from Palo Alto named Jerry Garcia and their organist, harmonica player and blues singer Pig Pen (Ron McKernan) have been pictured in national magazines and TV documentaries. Richard Goldstein in the *Village Voice* has referred to the band as the most exciting group in the Bay Area and comments, "Together, the Grateful Dead sound like live thunder."

Tomorrow The Grateful Dead celebrate the release of their first album, on the Warner Brothers label. It's called simply "The Grateful Dead" and the group is throwing a record promotion party for press and radio at Fugazi Hall.

The Dead's album release comes on the same day as their first single release, two sides from the album—"Golden Road" and "Cream Puff War."

The Dead, as their fans call them, got their exotic name when guitarist Garcia, a learned and highly articulate man, was browsing through a dictionary. "It just popped out at me. The phrase—'The Grateful Dead.' We were looking for a name at the time and I knew that was it."

The Grateful Dead later discovered the name was from an Egyptian prayer: "We grateful dead praise you, Osiris..."

Garcia, who is a self-taught guitarist ("my first instrument was an electrical guitar; then I went into folk music and played a flat top guitar, a regular guitar. But Chuck Berry was my influence!") is at a loss to describe the band's music, despite his expressiveness.

The Grateful Dead draws from at least five idioms, Garcia said, including Negro blues, country & western, popular music, even classical. (Phil Lesh, the bass player, is a composer who has spent several years working with serial and electronic music.)

"He doesn't play bass like anybody else; he doesn't listen to other bass players, he listens to his head," Garcia said.

Pig Pen, the blues vocalist, "has a style that is the sum of several styles," Garcia pointed out, including that of country blues singers such as Lightnin' Hopkins, as well as the more modern, urban blues men.

"When we give him a song to sing, it doesn't sound like someone else, it

comes out Pig Pen's way." Pig Pen's father, by the way, is Phil McKernan, who for years had the rhythm & blues show on KRE, the predecessor of KPAT in Berkeley.

Bill Sommers, the drummer, is a former jazz and rhythm & blues drummer. "He worked at the same music store I did in Palo Alto. I was teaching guitar and he was teaching drums," Garcia said. He is especially good at laying rhythms under a solo line played by the guitars. Bob Weir, the rhythm guitarist, "doesn't play that much straight rhythm," Garcia said, "he thinks up all those lovely-pretty things to do."

The Dead (they were originally the Warlocks) have been playing together for over two years now. They spend at least five or six hours a day rehearsing or playing or "just fooling around," Garcia continued.

"We're working with dynamics now. We've spent two years with loud, and we've spent six months with deafening! I think that we're moving out of our loud stage. We've learned, after these past two years, that what's really important is that the music be groovy, and if it's groovy enough and it's well played enough, it doesn't have to be too loud."

Dance Band

The Dead's material comes from all the strains in American music. "We'll take an idea and develop it; we're interested in form. We still feel that our function is as a dance band and that's what we like to do; we like to play for dancers. We're trying to do new things, of course, but not arrange our material to death. I'd say we've stolen freely from everywhere, and we have no qualms about mixing our idioms. You might hear some traditional style classical counterpoint cropping up in the middle of some rowdy thing, you know!"

The eclectic electric music has won the Dead its Warner Brothers contract, offers of work in films, a dedicated group of fans who follow them faithfully and the prospect of national tours, engagements in New York and elsewhere. But Garcia, who is universally loved by the rock musicians and fans, is characteristically calm about it all. "I'm just a student guitar player," he concluded, "I'm trying to get better and learn how to play. We're all novices."

Jerry Garcia, *the Guru*

Ralph J. Gleason

erry Garcia, the lead guitarist and central figure of The Grateful Dead, has been a musical guru to an entire generation of San Francisco musicians. Just as The Dead's first album was about to be released, this interview was done with him. It is, in several ways, indicative of the roots, the aspirations and influences of San Francisco music. The Dead, like the Airplane, are still intact, the originals and still champions of what we have to come to know as the adult rock sound.

JERRY: Being in a recording situation is really a lot different than playing. A recording situation brings out a special, sort of like another side of creativity. It's something like painting or drawing or anything that you do over a long period of time for a finished product. And so when you get a recording studio you begin to have a different feeling about what you're doing. And that's something we're just starting to get into too. So the first album was essentially a live album. They were going to put that really ostentatious oriental quotation, "Egyptian Book of the Dead" quotation on the top but we...

RJG: Is that where the name "Grateful Dead" comes from?

JERRY: No, it doesn't, as a matter of fact. It came out of a big Webster's dictionary or a New World or an Oxford dictionary. Just opened it and there it was. Just happened to turn to a page that had Grateful Dead on it. When we were looking for a name.

RJG: Where did you get the tunes on the first album from?

JERRY: They came from a lot of different places. Like on the album, the material comes from blues, like some of the material is from blues, recent blues, like the last ten years' blues. Chicago style blues. Like "Good Morning

Little School Girl" is a song that's in the public domain and we left it in the public domain, by the way, we didn't copyright any of this shit, the stuff that's traditional we left traditional. "Good Morning Little School Girl" is a traditional song but it's only as far as I know maybe 10, 15 years old. Not much older than that. Some of the others are much older. "Cold Rain and Snow" is a fragment that I learned from a banjo player named Obray Ramsey. A traditional singer from someplace like Indiana. It's in the same kind of mode as it originally was but the melody is different. And we've added a harmony line and of course it's us, it's our rhythmic structure and our ideas. "Sittin' on Top of the World" is another traditional song that was copyrighted some time not too long ago by some country and western guy but it's still essentially a folk song. There are just two or three verses and they're standard blues verses that turn up everywhere. And again, that's our arrangement.... Most of these things, what we've done is we've taken an idea and just developed it. "Viola Lee Blues," the long one on the album, it's about 10 minutes or 11 minutes or something like that. And the words to that and a certain amount of the phrasing, the way the words are sung, comes from a record by Noah Lewis who used to be the harmonica player in Gus Cannon and His Jug Stompers. Really beautiful lyrical harmonica player, one of the early guys. And this song, a good example of how it used to go when Noah Lewis had it, was the Jim Kweskin Jug Band, they do it almost the same way Noah Lewis does it in terms of the way they sing it. Our way is quite a lot jazzier and it has a newer rhythm and we've also done some things with the bar lengths in it. We've slipped in a half bar where there would normally be a bar.... It's sort of like a 12-bar blues but in this case it's $11\frac{1}{2}$-bar blues, 'cause we left out a half bar to make the phrasing and the background work together. It's pretty interesting. And then of course, we will like improvise with it for a long time and do a lot of things in it. Again it's a framework more than anything else. But the words are real powerful, simple direct things.

RJG: $11\frac{1}{2}$ $11\frac{1}{2}$ $11\frac{1}{2}$?

JERRY: Yeah, right. It goes $11\frac{1}{2}$ $11\frac{1}{2}$ $11\frac{1}{2}$ We also, the way we play our stuff is if we're using changes, like blues changes, we frequently throw in two or three bars of just 'comping before getting into the changes. Or sometimes we eliminate the changes entirely. So the construction of the thing, if you were to write it out, is asymmetrical. It's not ever *quite* $11\frac{1}{2}$ bars and it's not ever a straight 12 bars either. It instead has added bars here and there and tags and so forth. That's the thing that occurs in traditional music and doesn't occur too much in more formalized kinds of music.

RJG: Now, when you play it, do you play it the same way all the time?

JERRY: No, never.

RJG: Do you change that structure?

JERRY: Always. That's the part that's fun about it, because it's like we all have to be on our toes. All of a sudden there's something new entering and we all try and pick up on it. That's when we're playing good; if we're not playing good that doesn't happen. But you know about that, you know. Like sometimes you can do it and sometimes you can't. And in this case, the way we did this was interesting. Each night when we went into the studio we played "Viola Lee Blues." For as long as we wanted to play it and we recorded it. And then at the end of the week we went through them and listened to them and the one that turned us on was the one. So that's the one we used. The one that turned us on. It isn't as good as it *could* have been but it's still okay. It's still okay. It's always like after the fact of the recording I don't want to say too much about it, it's like it's finished and it's sort of in the past. And none of the material we're doing that's on the record is going to be much like the record from now on. Because now we feel we've done it that way. I'm even thinking perhaps there's a possibility of rerecording some of this stuff in the future just for the sake of how much it's changed.

I'll have to explain about the four or five idioms that we work in and our music is more or less idiomatic and we do material for the way it is and the way *we* are kind of comes out through it. Do you know what I mean? So our arrangements differ from song to song and our ideas differ, but because of the way we approach our individual instruments, our individual styles can be picked out. Our way of playing. It's hard to like...I'd say that we'd stolen freely from everywhere! Remorselessly and freely! Our ideas come from everywhere, and we have no bones about mixing our idioms or throwing stuff back and forth from one place to another. So you might hear some very straight traditional counterpoint, classical-style counterpoint popping up in the middle of some rowdy thing. And just because we do whatever is fun or whatever is exciting for us musically.

RJG: Do you come from diverse musical backgrounds?

JERRY: Oh, yes. Diverse isn't the word for it! Like my background in music...My first guitar was an electric guitar and my first love on the guitar was Chuck Berry. He was my guy. When I was a kid I got all his records and I'd just try like crazy to learn how to play them. I got this electric guitar and I didn't know anything about the guitar. I had the guitar for maybe six or eight months without ever knowing how to tune it and I invented a tuning for it and invented a way to play it in this tuning so it worked out pretty well until I got to certain points. I'd listen to a record and I'd try to figure out what the guy was doing and it was virtually impossible to do because of the way I had my guitar tuned! Finally I ran into a guy who showed me how to tune it; he showed me a few of the basic chords and it was just a revelation! Here it was! The real way to do it! So I went for a while into rock 'n' roll, like about two years perhaps and I played more or less unsuccessfully with a few little two-saxophone-and-piano bands and electric guitar and amplifier about this big. Little pea shooter of an amplifier. And then my next change in music was when the whole folk-music thing started happening. And I got caught up into that...I got listening to...when Joan Baez's first record came out I heard it and I heard her finger picking the guitar, I'd never heard anything like it before so I got into that and I started getting into country music, into old time white music. Mostly white spiritual stuff, white instrumental music and I got into finger style, the folk-music-festival scene, that whole thing. And I was very heavy into that for a long time and I sort of employed a scholarly approach and even went through the South with tape recorders and stuff recording blue-grass bands. I spent about three years playing blue-grass banjo, that was my big thing and I almost forgot how to play the guitar during that period of time. And then I got into a jug band, we got a jug band going and I took up the guitar again and from the jug band it was right into rock 'n' roll. And so like my background is essentially very straight musically. The traditional forms of music are mostly musically direct. They have simple changes and simple ideas and the melodic lines are easy and so forth but they have a lot of...the interest is in the form, you know, and like the fine points of the form like flamenco guitar or something.

RJG: You didn't study anywhere?

JERRY: No, just on my own, books and whatever, you know, records. And listened a lot and played a lot. That was about all it amounted to.

Phil, our bass player, is the one who has the longest thing in music. He's been in music for about 20 years. He started off playing violin, classical violin and then he played trumpet. And he played trumpet in the San Mateo College Band, the jazz band. And he wrote a lot of arrangements for them too. Stan Kenton-style arrangements. He played those screechy Maynard Ferguson parts, pass out on the stage! And then he got into more modern music, like through jazz. He was also always interested in classical all through this time. He got into modern forms of music, serial music and 12-tone music, 12-tone composition and finally electronic music and he composed these monster things. He has absolute pitch. He used to live over in Berkeley, I'd come over and he'd have these monster pieces of score paper and he'd be working away, working in pen, the notes are coming out of his head, out on to the paper! These things for like 12 orchestras and whatever!

And the big problem, of course, when you're a serious composer is getting anybody to play your stuff; it's virtually impossible. A young composer? No way! So he studied with Berio over at Mills for a long time and then, the way he describes it is, he suddenly found himself out of that. I mean it was just like he had gone as far as he could go in his own head with that. And he just stopped doing it and he was doing nothing for a while and then he went to see the Beatles! The Beatles movie came out about that time. He went to see the Beatles and it of course blew his mind and he grew his hair long and started going to the early dances. When The Byrds were playing in town and all that was just starting to happen. And he and I had been friends for a long time. He used to work at KPFA, he once recorded me in a folk-music show and he and I had been getting stoned together for years and scheming and plotting but we'd never gotten together musically. We were mutual admirers. And at that time I was just finished with the jug band, just starting the rock 'n' roll band, we had this other bass player, and I talked to Phil. And he said he'd like to take it up so I showed him a few things, two weeks later we played our first job! Him playing bass for two weeks! Never played a fretted instrument before, but his mind is so incredibly musical. So that's his background. He's incredible, really musically articulate. He knows more about music than almost anybody I know, he's fantastic.

Pigpen, his father was the first rhythm and blues guy around here, you know. And he's always heard blues since he was a tiny kid and he played piano for a long time, just simple C blues runs and stuff like that and he'd sing. When I met him, he was about 14 or 15. And he was already a step removed from school and family and everything like that and he was hanging around at the various scenes that were going on in Palo Alto at that time. At that time I was sort of a beatnik guitar player. And he'd come around to these parties and I'd be playing blues and he'd watch very carefully and he'd go home and learn things, all on the sly. And he took up harmonica as well, back in those days and one day he'd been playing harmonica for a long time, he was deathly afraid to play in front of anybody, he'd been playing harmonica secretly, and one time he got up on stage at a folk-music place and I backed him up on the guitar; he played harmonica and sang. And he could sing like Lightnin' Hopkins, which just like blew everybody's mind! Here he was, 15 years old with this shaky voice and all this stuff and he could like improvise endlessly. Just endlessly! He could just make up *millions* and *millions* of verses that were all just fantastic and he's really the master at the shady comment in blues, the blues scene. Whatever it is, really a sort of a complicated thing, but he's into that heavier than anybody I know. And so like his thing is blues, almost nothing but blues, he's got some interest in other kinds of music, but it's mostly blues. Like he listens to Jimmy Smith more on the organ than anybody else. And he's only been playing the organ as long as the band's been together. He doesn't really work at it too hard, not as hard as the rest of us do for example, but he has a good mind for phrasing, he's got real clear ideas. And he's always got a way, he can always make a song nicer by the thing that he plays. He's a real great supporting organist. He hasn't got a real heavy chord background or anything like that but he's got a good mind for lines. And so that's Pigpen.

And Bill, the drummer's interest has been like jazz drumming and he also played with a lot of big James Brown-style bands, that kind of rhythm and blues, very fast. And a lot of heavy drum kicks and that show-band kind of stuff. And he was always the fastest, most heaviest rock 'n' roll drummer in Palo Alto, in that whole scene. And he worked in the same music store that I did. I was teaching guitar and he was teaching drums and we got together quite a bit. Bob Weir, who plays rhythm, did the whole folk-blues coffeehouse thing. That was his thing. And he also played jug and kazoo in the jug band when we were playing. And he's a student, you might say. His musical leader was Jorma. He used to go every time Jorma played when he played in coffeehouses Weir'd go there with his tape recorder, tape the whole show and talk to Jorma extensively and watch him play the stuff and study it all and go home and work it out. Jorma is where he learned a lot of his technique and learned a lot of...his whole approach to guitar playing was like Jorma's essentially. Except he's not as good as Jorma, of course. But his background is that way and in that way and in that folk sort of light blues and a lot of full-voice chords and finger style. That's the big thing he's been into. Like we've all been playing electric instruments for as long as the band's been together, so we're all novices. Like there're guys around that have been playing for ten years, nothing but electric music, like Mike Bloomfield and them have been doing that. We're all new at it. So that like we hung together and we didn't steal too many ideas from records, try to do too many other people's material. Instead we'd listen to anything that was good and pick ideas from that and work at it that way.

RJG: It's an interesting thing to me that the sound that the band makes is instantly identifiable.

JERRY: I know. There's a very typical sound.

RJG: Yeah, it's obviously The Grateful Dead, it doesn't sound like anybody else.

JERRY: I know; I can't describe that, I can only say that that's because after working at it and playing together and that's the thing we like to do, that's the result of it. I don't know anything else more about it except that's what it sounds like now.

RJG: What are you trying to do?

JERRY: Get better! Get better! I mean, like I think of myself as being a student guitarist. I'm trying to learn how to play. That's the way I feel about it. I'm trying to learn more about music, more about my playing music. And what...the direction we're trying to go in as of now, after the record, the first record is completed, it kind of put us in a different place. What we're trying to do now is expand ourselves musically and that means to get into other things that haven't yet been introduced into popular music and we're...we've been working with musical...it's difficult to explain. Our approach so far to all our music has been more or less intuitive. And all the arrangements that are on the record are arrangements that we've arrived at through playing the songs. That's the natural way they go, the sum of us. We have never written out charts or made lead sheets or arranged parts for specific instruments, we've instead just, like, played it. And they've settled into arrangements. Now we're working on arrangements but we're trying also to not arrange our material to death, do you know what I mean? So we're like we're someplace where we don't know that anybody else is in the same place, so we don't know what to, there's no one guiding us at this point and we're just left to our own devices. We realize that the one thing that we have to do is to continue to grow as musicians and to continue to expand our outlook on music, to listen to more music and to just get into it. Keep getting into it heavier and heavier so we can continue to do new things. And that's what we're trying to do is to continue to do new things, I guess.

RJG: One of the things that has interested me in listening to the groups in the last year is the whole role of the drums in the electric bands. The drummer seems to me to be a captive.

JERRY: I'll tell you. I would really like for you to be in a situation where you can hear Bill play. The way he plays...what we're thinking about is, we're thinking, we're trying to think away from solo lines. From the standard routine of *these* members' comp, *this* member leads. We're trying to think of ensemble stuff, you know. Not like Dixieland ensemble stuff, something which we don't yet know anything about. The way Bill plays is he plays a little with everybody. So like if I'm playing a line, he knows enough about my playing and my thinking, since we've been playing together for all this time, that he can usually anticipate the way I'll think a line. And he's a great rhythmic reinforcement for any line that I can play, no matter how it relates to the rest of the time going on. He also plays beautifully with Phil, the bass player. In a standard rock 'n' roll band, the way they work it is the bass and drums generally work together as a unit. Like Motown records are the clearest examples of that. And that's one way of describing the rhythmic situation. What we're trying to do is get out of that into where the rhythm is more implied and less obvious. Where it's there all the time and it's there heavy enough so that you can dance to it, but not everybody is playing on the two and four. So that something else is happening.

And Phil's way of approaching the bass is so utterly different than any other bass players', 'cause he doesn't listen to any bass players. He listens to his mind! And so the kind of lines he comes out with are so fantastic. He's an amazing bass player. He plays with Bill a lot, and because of the way Phil plays, he makes it impossible for Bill to rely on an old pattern, on a standard-type pattern. The problems we're having with all this is because all of us still think so musically straight, really, that it's difficult to get away from that and it's difficult to get used to not hearing the heavy two and four. It's difficult to think rhythmically without having it there all the time but we're starting to develop that sense better. The time thing is the whole big problem, as far as I know.

RJG: When you're on the stage playing, what instrument do you hear the loudest?

JERRY: Mine. Because I'm standing right in front of it.

RJG: Do you hear the drums?

JERRY: I always put myself right next to the drums. I always listen to the drums and I always listen to Phil. And if I move out in front, I can hear Bob. Sometimes we work it so that dynamics drop, so that the bass and organ drop a little so that me and Bob work together. We try it so that we all work together one way or another, any way that it happens. What we're trying to do is free all ourselves from any of us having to 'comp, any of us having to play flat rhythm, do you know what I mean?

RJG: Will you hang that on the rhythm guitar then?

JERRY: No, because Bob doesn't play flat rhythm. He doesn't play hardly any of that kind of rhythm at all. He plays a whole other thing. He plays these other kinds of lines and stuff like...he works out this very lovely kind of stuff most of the time. There's not that feeling of the big rhythm going, because we do a lot of tricks within a bar and one of the tricks that we do is like eliminating the beat entirely and just all of us not playing it. Like we're starting to use the space rather than the time or whatever.

RJG: You imply it.

JERRY: That's what we're trying to do. And yet keep it groovy and yet make it so that people can still move to it. 'Cause that's, I think that we still feel that our function is as a dance band. We feel that our greatest value is as a dance band and that's what we like to do. We like to play with dancers. We like to see it and really, nothing improves your time like having somebody dance. Just like pulls the whole thing together. And it's also a nice little feedback thing.

RJG: And I've heard the people stomping on the floor, I hadn't heard that since the Count Basie bands when they'd take a break and everybody's time was just going right on along. Everybody's in the band!

JERRY: Right. That's the ideal situation. Everybody should be in the band! And when that's happening, it's really something special. It's an amazing thing.

RJG: People get very hung up about the volume.

JERRY: That's true. Because it's very loud! But there's something to that too. There's something to that, too. And the thing that I've found is when I'm at one of the dance halls and a band's playing, it's foolish for me to try to tell any-body anything, or say anything to anybody because they can't hear me. The band's roaring away. And I would just as soon have that. And it's like being in a place where there're no lights. You are less self-conscious if you can't be heard, so you don't mind screaming. And if nobody can see you, you can dance any way you want! It's like that kind of thing, you know. It's just...I think of it as being a sensory overload, or something like that. I don't think it's a bad thing.

RJG: I did in the beginning but I don't anymore; I got used to it.

JERRY: Drives the old folks crazy. Too loud!

RJG: Well, there's different ways of being loud.

JERRY: Right. That's another thing that we're getting into. Like the big thing that we see is how loud everything is. Because that's the big problem we deal with continually. The thing we're working on is dynamics. With electric instruments, dynamics are a little bit tricky. Because it necessitates either turning down your volume or really developing a good touch on an electric instrument. And now we've got...the way our stuff is working now it's starting to develop natural dynamics of its own. This is a new thing, just new. That's why we want to work in the clubs and work in these places so we can develop that. The more we play, the better it gets. In a club we've gotten...like we've spent two years with loud and we've spent six months with deafening! I think that we're moving out of our loud stage.

The whole thing about loud is this, is that when you're in a huge place.... The thing we're thinking about, what happened was, we went to the very first Family Dog show stoned on acid, or maybe it was the second one, the one where the Lovin' Spoonful were. And we came in there. We just had our band going, we'd been playing out in these clubs and stuff and we went in there and we heard the thing. And from the back of the hall you couldn't hear anything. You could hear maybe the harmonica. As you moved around you could hear a little of something, a little of something else, but you could never hear the whole band, unless you were right in front of it and in that case you couldn't hear the vocal. So in our expanding consciousness, we thought, the thing to do, obviously, when you play in a big hall, is to make it so that you can hear everything everywhere. How do we go about this, we thought? And the most obvious thing was, we just turn up real loud. But that's not exactly where it is. We've learned that what's really important is that the music be groovy. And if it's groovy enough and if it's well played enough, it doesn't have to be too loud, if it has the definition.

It's more important that it be clear than loud. It would be nice if it were both loud and clear. That's something you can't do with electric instruments. The volume is a device a lot. And it's a good device if you are able to use it well and it's even musical if you're able to use it well, but it's a problem. It's a problem because of the lack of definition involved. And then there's actual technical problems when you're playing on a stage. Certain frequencies of your instrument are washed out by the same frequencies in other instruments. Other electrical instruments. So that in order to hear yourself play you have to be a little bit louder. And you can see what happens. Everybody starts to turn up a little bit so by the end of the night everybody's creeped up so they're real loud. And these kind of things happen.

There's all kinds of freak stuff that happens electronically. Sound against sound. When you have two notes that are approximately in tune but not quite in tune, this whole other thing starts to happen and that's something else we're getting into. The subharmonic or the harmonic over the...Whenever you play an interval of two notes on two different strings on a guitar you also get the sum of the two notes, either an octave below or an octave above. And depending on how good your equipment is, that's how good you'll be able to hear it. There are lots and lots of books on vibrating-string principles and lots of amazing stuff happens. You can play...I've taken to playing some runs that are in open fifths, parallel fifths. Just the whole run is played that way and that gives me the run an octave below the instrument. The same run. And maybe nobody notices it, but I notice it! And those phenomena are things that really start to get interesting. Like when you get feedback from a fretted note. And the feedback is a strong sustained tone, if you slowly move the string, stretch the string, so that it raises in about quarter-steps or eighth-steps, you can also raise the feedback in quarter-steps and eighth-steps. So that you can slur all the way up to a note, have the sustained note you shouldn't be able to get on a guitar. It's a whole other principle using the sustained.

RJG: This is a whole other instrument you're playing anyway.

JERRY: Really. Really it is. It's like when I pick up a regular flat-top plain old traditional guitar, I can hardly play it. You know my touch is developed for the light responsiveness I like in an electric guitar. And I'm used to the way an electric guitar feels and the way they respond, it's a whole other thing. And even playing the electric guitar without the electricity is not playing an electric guitar. And there's also different responses that you get at different volumes, that's another thing. So like if I want my guitar to have a certain characteristic sound, it won't get it any way except for me to turn up my amplifier to a certain point. Then I know that sound, it'll produce that particular sound. That's part of the stuff that we're dealing with, is the actuality of what happens between the guitar, the amplifier and the speakers. So the stuff that comes out is not always what you expect. It depends a lot on how you have it set; rather than fool with the knobs on my guitar, which I do a lot more for dynamic change than anything else, at a certain volume the tone changes are coming from the amplifier and then it's a matter of my going to the amplifier and turning it up a little or turning it down a little or changing one of the tonal responses a little so that it develops another thing. There's a whole series of feedback cycles where if you play a note and get feedback on it, you get that note an octave lower plus its fifth. Sometimes it pops an octave higher and then another octave higher yet.

RJG: Can you predict it?

JERRY: I'm getting so I can. I can't predict it to the point because it depends a lot like on how old the strings are, you know, and how close I am to the amplifier. And if I'm in a certain field by the amplifier, I can get certain kinds of pickup. Certain kinds of feedback. It's very tricky stuff 'cause there's so many elements involved in it.

RJG: It's a kind of electronic music.

JERRY: Yeah, it really is. It's electronic music in its practical application. The music itself, that's the thing about the studio, see, is that this stuff doesn't happen that much in the studio because you aren't playing the kind of volumes where that kind of stuff will happen, although on the record I was loud enough to get some of that, that feedback pops in here and there. It's a matter now that we have this new thing, these electronic sounds, it's a question of how can you use them in such a way so that they are musical rather than just racket? Because the point is fine. I've been using the feedback stuff instead of for playing lines or for producing a layer of sound which is the thing that happens most naturally. I've been using it by like striking a string and bringing up my volume knob so that there is no attack on the beginning of the note. The note just starts to come out of the air. 'Cause I've already played the string, turn up the volume, the feedback starts. And I stop the string at a rhythmic interval. So that I have...if I were to draw a picture of the tone, it would be just about the reverse of what a guitar tone normally is where you have a heavy attack and then a slow decay. Because it's the other way around, it decays *in* and attacks *off*. So I use it as a rhythmic device more than anything else. In

that particular thing. But you know, the more it happens, the more I know about it and the more ideas I get for it and so forth. It's just a matter of playing more.

RJG: How much do you play a day?

JERRY: We put in about six, seven hours a day. Down at the studio, like going over material, working on new ideas or something like that or just goofing off. And if we're working a gig, then it's the gig. Actually, the best practice there is is playing the gig.

RJG: How much of your material is completely original?

JERRY: I'd say about 40 percent of it. And it's only completely original in that it's our choice of elements. The elements, in terms of their relationships from one to another, are still essentially the same. The relationships are standard kinds of relationships. They aren't too weird. Although we have a few songs that have like tritone relationships and we've even got one now, this is the kind of things we're trying to work into, we have this song called "New Potato Caboose" and it's not on the record or anything, it'll probably be on the next album, it's a very long thing and it doesn't have a form, in that it doesn't have a verse-chorus form. We took it from a friend of ours who's a poet named Bobby Petersen who wrote us this thing. And we just set it and it instead is a whole thing. It has two or three recurring elements, but it doesn't have a recurring pattern, it just changes continually, off of itself and through itself in lots of different ways. Rhythmically and the tonality of it and the chord relationships. There's a lot of surprises in it, a lot of fast, difficult kind of transitions. And there are transitions that musically are real awkward. They're not the kind of thing that flows at all but we're trying to make this happen by trying something that's just jarring and making it not jarring. Making it so that it happens without anybody losing their mind when it happens! And just to see if we can do it. And the thing, as it is, is a little stilted because we aren't yet, we aren't really able to get with it. 'Cause it's all so utterly, so odd. But it has its points and I think that's like one direction that we'll be able to move successfully in.

RJG: What kind of music do you listen to, other than going to places around?

JERRY: Everything. Anything. If it's good I'll listen to it or if it's around I'll listen to it. I listen to anything that turns me on. Or that somebody turns me on to.

RJG: What turns you on?

JERRY: What can I say? Almost anything I listen to. If it's well-played music...I mean if you're a musician, you know when somebody's really playing, and when they're not really playing. If it's well-played music, I like it. If it's anything, country and western music, jazz, I've been listening to a lot of jazz lately. I've been listening to a lot of Django Reinhardt. Mostly for the guitar, you know. But I've learned as much from the violin player in terms of those really lovely graceful ideas. And that's the kind of stuff I like. Anything that, like, is beautiful. Indian music. All the things that people listen to, I guess, I listen to, whatever it is. Soul music, rhythm and blues, old-time blues, jug-band music.

RJG: This whole business of blues. Do you get any heat on the racial question on this?

JERRY: No, we haven't. The places we've played...We've played some pretty hard-edge places, too, we played the Job Corps, where it's all spade kids. We played in a spade show, in fact, like a rhythm and blues show. And we were received, I think we were a shock to them, because the music we were playing was heavy blues, certainly heavier than any of the spade guys were doing, they were doing all the lighter stuff. And we've had different kinds of things, like different people have said different things to us. There are certain guys who are like into the whole black nationalist thing about spade music and about jazz and so forth and they say things like, "Oh, why don't these white boys stop trying to play colored music?" And so forth. But I don't feel, like I don't feel that that's my orientation. And the ideas that I've pulled from blues musicians and from listening to blues are from my affection for the blues which is like since I was a kid. And I've been listening to rhythm and blues as long as there's been rhythm and blues around here, you know. That was one of the first kinds of music I was turned on to.

RJG: How old are you?

JERRY: Twenty-four. I mean, I don't feel unnatural—I don't feel uptight about it, somebody might. But the stuff that we're doing, if you look at it, it's like got those ideas, blues ideas and spade kinds of dance ideas and stuff like that, but really musically, in as far as moving yourself goes, those are some groovy ideas and they turn us on. But a lot of other things turn us on as well. Any kind of well-performed stuff. Whatever it is. Pigpen has his own style, that is perhaps the sum of lots of styles, but it's nonetheless consistently Pigpen. He doesn't, like, flash from James Brown to Smokey Robinson. He stays Pigpen. And that's because his attitude toward the blues is so, it's been so long and slow and it's been a mellowing process, you know. At the very beginning, his big vocal influence was Lightnin' Hopkins. And that's who he used to listen to and he could, like, if he wants to, he can sing exactly like Lightnin' Hopkins. And play the guitar like Lightnin' Hopkins and to the point of being completely irregular about the changes and stuff, just like Lightnin' is. But Pigpen has been into that for such a long time that it's no longer an effort, and it's no longer something that he tries to do. Like when we give him a song to sing, it comes out Pigpen's way. It's not anything else.

RJG: That's a beautiful name. Who gave that to him? You did?

JERRY: Oh, a long time ago. A long time ago. 'Cause back when he was about 14 or 15 he was almost like he is now and he'd be around, kind of slouching around and wearing these old duds. He's really a classical figure.

RJG: It seems to me that there are social implications to this music which haven't really been dealt with. It's not only the volume and the style and so on, but it represents a whole attitude.

JERRY: I know it does, but I'd be hard put to define that attitude. Like, the guys that were over interviewing us the other day were talking serious. They wanted to know about the scene and what our motivation was and what about drugs and so forth like that. And the music is doing something else. It has to do with all these things, yes, but I think that the more important thing than just the music is the whole attitude. The dance thing, the whole fact that there are lots of people getting together. And for all of us, this is the first time we've ever seen lots of people get together. 'Cause we never grew up in where there were like dances or things like that. It was pretty isolated and you did some other, like smaller, more intimate stuff. And now suddenly there are large groups of people getting together. And that seems like the more significant point sociologically.

RJG: The bands are at the center of it, really, as I see it.

JERRY: All I can say is I don't know why.

RJG: Take the band out of it and it all goes to pieces.

JERRY: That's true.

RJG: It's like the Trips Festival. Which was a drag except when the music made it. You can do all these things but it doesn't feel good without the music.

JERRY: I know, I'm not sure why. That's something that I don't think anybody really knows quite for sure why. I think that it might be like an excuse. Here is the reason for being in this place, and there is the reason for moving yourself, because there is this going on. But on the other hand, if we weren't doing this...See, it's all very strange because we all came from such far-out backgrounds into the rock 'n' roll scene together as a band. And all this more or less spontaneously in a very short space of time. I really don't know; I don't know why or how. But suddenly it was the thing to do. It was the right thing to do. And I'm not sure why. I think it might be like Phil was saying the other day. He mentioned that when he had sort of like run out of his musical bag before, his prior bag, Kennedy had just been assassinated. And things were looking pretty down. And then all of a sudden here was the Beatles movie. Which was like the first time there was something funny going on. It was very high and very *up*, you know. And high and up looked better than down and out, really. So high and up was the place to go, I guess. So that like for me, my musical bag had run out as well, there was no, like, people who were really interested in blue-grass music and nobody to play with and so forth and so on. It was like a bankrupt scene. Musically it was interesting but there was nothing going on that was any kind of gratification because you never got a chance to play or anything; you never got a chance to perform the thing. And playing the music is a real immediate, satisfying thing. It's like if it's going good, everybody knows it's going good, everybody in the band and everybody in the audience and there's something going on. It's faster, you know, it's a faster thing. It does-n't have to do with...You don't have to worry about the form or anything. It's like really cleansing somehow.

RJG: That's a good phrase for it. When I saw The Byrds at the...that joint on Broadway, they didn't turn me on there. And I didn't get any feeling that a thing was developing. And it didn't hit me until the Spoonful played Mother's. I went right out of my nut in there, completely. And it was...I don't know what it was, I've been trying. I heard The Byrds maybe under bad circumstances in there, as one of them was sick a couple of nights. It just didn't make it for me. And the people on the floor looked L.A. freaky, as opposed to looking...

JERRY: San Francisco hip.

RJG: Yeah. I don't know what the hell it is. That guy came up with them, that was like their male go-go dancer, Vito, wasn't that his name, he was always on the floor.

JERRY: Right.

RJG: It looked wrong.

JERRY: Right.

RJG: And those bands still do it wrong from L.A. I don't know what the hell it is.

JERRY: They *do* and now why *do* they? Is the question. I mean, what's the difference? What's the difference is what I'm wondering. And why is it that San Francisco is so much groovier of a place? Why has the scene blossomed so fantastically? For one thing, everybody's in it, that has a lot to with it. A band is only a band in the sense that they're on the stage. But really the band is just about...at least, in the early dances, it's changed an awful lot, in the early dances everybody was a part of the band. Everybody was stomping on the floor. And waving their arms around. And that was a good feeling.

RJG: You know, there's other things too, though. Those L.A. bands are all like the Mamas and the Papas, they're thought of in terms of going into the studio and making a record. And they're not thought of in terms of playing night after night for people to dance to.

JERRY: Right. Right. Because they don't have any dance things in L.A. The extent of the dancing in Los Angeles is ten feet off the floor in a glass cage. Everybody watches, like the movies. Except you go to be watched as well. Your car is where you live in L.A. The car radio is where it's at in L.A. Because if you don't have an automobile, you're not even alive in Los Angeles. And their scene is real isolated, you know. They don't have a community in L.A. There is no place. There is nothing down there. And that's the truth. We were down there...For the millions of people down there, there is no place where you can go and cool it and just like be there and not have to worry about what you're doing there. Or worry about someone asking you what you're doing there. They roust you down there. It's really heavy. Nothing like...Well, that's the way the rest of the country is. San Francisco's the only place where you can do that.

I never used to like Bob Dylan until he came out with an electric music. And I'm not sure why I like that more. I sure liked it a lot more. Boy, when *Bringing It All Back Home* came out. Yeah, lovely. Very fine guitar player. It just all of a sudden had something going for it. And Bob Dylan was getting a little less heavy. He was having a little more fun with him. And that was nice. That was a nice change. And I remember another thing that turned me on a lot was when I saw Bob Dylan on television. On the Les Crane show. When he went on there and sang those songs, you know, and just rapped insanely. Beautiful mad stuff. And that like turned us all on, we couldn't believe it. Here was this guy, it was almost like being in the South and seeing a spade on television.

RJG: Where do you think this thing is all going to go?

JERRY: Out. Out to the provinces, out to the rest of the world, I think. I don't see where else it can go. And I think San Francisco is getting very, very outrageous, especially during the summer. Who knows? Who knows where it's going to go? I'm hoping that all this represents another alternative for the world. Like, yeah, let's take it easy and have a good time. It would sure be nice, is all I can say. I don't know where it's going to go, it might all be on the streets of Bombay in the next month. It looks good, is all I can say. In terms that it looks like it's going to get out and it looks like everybody that's into it is into it sincerely. And really intends to do right by the scene in terms of continuing to develop and grow, continue to add to it and continue to, you know, spread the word, whatever.

We decided, when we got together with the band, we were all on our very separate trips, we were all doing our gigs of one sort or another. Surviving one way or another. And we decided at one time or another that we would have to make a total commitment so we, like, just put everything down and hung together. We thought we were either going to make it or not. I mean we're going to do a thing or we're not going to do a thing and the only way we're going to find out is, like, devote our whole attention to it. Maybe the thing, whatever it is that's needed to be able to get into that kind of scene of like surrendering your own little trip for some better trip, maybe, you have to care enough about it or be willing to stop caring about what you've already got, maybe. But I think San Francisco bands hang together through inclination. And, like, we were all friends before we got together as a band. We'd all been into various kinds of weird shit together before. We just thought...why not?

We learned how to behave as a unit. We all like each other. We've done it all through inclination. It's an important thing and somehow we manage to hang together. Like when we went to Vancouver and things got real weird, real fast, when we were up there. We went through a lot of bad scenes and got screwed around one way or another. It was really, like, the five of us hung together just because that's who we are, we're a family more than anything else, you know. Just in our attitudes toward each other. And it works out best that way. It seems to.

RJG: What got you interested in music, really interested in music?

JERRY: It was the music that we heard. And like at the time we didn't realize that it was not very good. Because it *was* good to *our* young ears. It was moving music and it talked about us, the way we wanted to hear about us, apparently. And after a while, once you get into music, you start to hear more about it. As you get out into it...Like getting away from rock 'n' roll, when I was away from rock 'n' roll it was going through that whole, the whole Frankie Avalon, Fabian phase and all this plastic nonsense. And it didn't have much vitality. I sort of lost interest in it 'cause the vitality, the energy in it had gone into other channels. For me, it was in folk music.

RJG: But, Jerry, wasn't that folk-music period in a sense...I mean, there were great folk-music performers, like Pete Seeger and The Weavers are great performers. Wasn't there a way, though, in which that folk-music thing was kind of an attraction for performers to get into because they thought it was what they *ought* to be doing?

JERRY: I think so. Now, I got into it because my intellectual self was growing and I didn't feel that rock 'n' roll music was going to be my vehicle for communication, or whatever. When I got into folk music, I never got into it behind the lyrical content. I never was into the protest songs. I was always into...What first attracted me was the sound of it and those kind of modal changes and so forth and the sound of Joan Baez's voice and the sound of her guitar and then into the more complex forms and finally what I really got into was the instrumental parts. Instrumental traditional music and so forth. Because somehow or another I heard in that, musically, something that was more satisfying to me at that time than, like, rock 'n' roll was. But the more I got into it, the more it became obvious to me that it was kind of a closed circle, you know what I mean? Like, there's a traditional thing going on and at this point in time the traditional thing is largely diffused. There isn't really too many bodies of strong traditional music going on. They've all evolved. Now in the twentieth century the strong forms of traditional music, white traditional music and colored traditional music, essentially, in the United States have gotten into...colored traditional music is jazz and soul music and Chicago blues and so on and the white music has gone into country and western and more heavily charged kinds of that stuff. But still, the same elements are there. It's as strong, all these things are as strong as their roots were. I started out into folk music by listening to the Kingston Trio and so forth and as soon as I realized that I could play better than any of them, I lost interest in them and went on to something else! But then the problem was, who wants to hire Flatt and Scruggs or who wants to hire John Lee Hooker, you know? I mean nobody out here knew about him, there were one or two places. The Cabale would maybe have somebody good once in a long time and it was like really scarce. I'd go way out of my way to see somebody good if they were around.

And it's just one of those things; finally my interest got into it so much that it was getting so esoteric there was *no* way for me to hear the music. Except to go out and spend enormous amounts of money and go through these whole big changes to just get to where I could hear it. And this was the music that I was devoting all my energy to. And the chance to, like, get back to the people is really...It's joy! It's sudden freedom! But all that stuff is still very heavy to a head, I used to listen to all the same stuff as well. It's a funny thing the way the interests have jumped around, but I remember during all that time I'd occasionally turn on the radio to a rock 'n' roll station, there would be this utter pap, terrible, featureless music. And that was really an insult. The rhythm and blues station I wouldn't mind listening to but even in that, the rhythm and blues at that time was going through some kind of sticky changes. It was all very dull; it was before Motown had come out; before Phil Spector had been around. And there wasn't anything exciting going on, there were no new ideas.

The point seems to be to try and communicate something or to be in a position where there is more going on than somebody on a stage. I mean, like, it would be nice if traditional folk music could be taken out of the art form that it's been put into, it's art music now. Joan Baez is an art singer and Judy Collins is and so forth. And it lacks vitality, it lacks the vitality that those people as individuals are loaded with.

Like here on the West Coast, the guys that are into rock 'n' roll music have mostly come up through like I have...like me and Jorma for example...up through folk music and through blues and so forth and stuff like that, these simpler forms. On the East Coast, the musicians who are in rock 'n' roll bands are starting to be some of the young jazz musicians who are getting into it and who are bringing it a different kind of vitality. Musical vitality. But it seems as though the jazz music as a movement has somewhere along the line lost the relationship to the audience. The people can't make it with it unless it's really fantastic. The thing of having Charles Lloyd at the Fillmore Auditorium is really fantastic. And a jazz group can't hardly play at the Fillmore without tearing the place down. When Bola Sete's little trio played there, they just ripped it up. Communication is getting so good, so much music is available on records and it's so easy to hear anything you want to hear that in another 20 years, every musician in the world will be able to play with every other musician in the world with no problem at all. That'd be really great, you know!

Richard Brautigan (1935-1984) ably carried a psychedelic sensibility into his fiction and poetry. This poem refers to the arrest of most of the band, October 2, 1967, on charges of possession of marijuana–a symbolic act of enforcement that was meant, more than anything, to send a message to the Haight-Ashbury community. Brautigan was the author of numerous books of fiction and poetry, including *The Abortion*, published by Simon & Schuster in 1966, and *Trout Fishing in America*, published by the Four Seasons Foundation in 1967.

The Day They BUSTED the Grateful Dead

Richard Brautigan

The day they busted the Grateful Dead
rain stormed against San Francisco
like hot swampy scissors cutting Justice
into the evil clothes that alligators wear.

The day they busted the Grateful Dead
was like a flight of winged alligators
carefully measuring marble with black
        rubber telescopes.

The day they busted the Grateful Dead
turned like the wet breath of alligators
blowing up balloons the size of the
        Hall of Justice.

Though Steve Silberman wrote the following piece for the August 16, 1996, issue of *Goldmine* to herald the release of *Dick's Picks, Volume Four*, it belongs, chronologically, to the concerts recorded on that album, in February 1970. Silberman, who has an undeniable way with words, being something of a jazz improviser with language, captures the atmosphere of the concerts and manages to get to the heart of the music making. Silberman is a prolific writer whose work includes numerous pieces on culture for *Hotwired* and, with David Shenk, the essential Grateful Dead book, *Skeleton Key: A Dictionary for Deadheads*, published by Doubleday in 1994. He is a contributing editor of *Wired Magazine*, and in 1997 was given the Best New Media Reporting award by the National Lesbian and Gay Journalists' Association for his work there.

Primal Dead at the FILLMORE EAST: February 1970

Steve Silberman

The Grateful Dead was a beast that thrived on metamorphosis. Though their core of players—Jerry Garcia, Bob Weir, Phil Lesh, Bill Kreutzmann and (with a three-year hiatus) Mickey Hart—hung tight for over 3000 shows. From San Francisco's Longshoreman's Hall to the Great Pyramid of Giza, the Dead made nightly reincarnation their prime directive.

There was the blues-driven swamp mojo of the early years, with Ron "Pigpen" McKernan at the forefront, provoking the band with swaggering raps that teased fire from the mouth of the dragon that the Dead's brand of "electric Dixieland" (as David Crosby once put it) had become. There was the perpetually touring workhorse of the late '70s and '80s, when songs like "Playing In The Band" and "Scarlet Begonias" evolved into lengthy musical conversations that could be astonishingly intimate, even in huge arenas. There was the sunburst of mature creativity in 1989, when MIDI technology allowed the band to place at the disposal of its muse any sound imaginable—from calliopes, kalimbas and phantom choirs, to bells and bass flutes.

If a workable time machine was put on the market tomorrow, however, there's one run of shows that would be standing room only: the 11th, 13th and 14th of February in 1970, at the Fillmore East in New York City.

What makes this run what the Dead's in-house tape archivist, Dick Latvala, calls "primal Dead"?

Consider "Dark Star," the Jerry Garcia and Robert Hunter composition that became the Dead's signature point of embarkation into zones of free jamming. Performed once each night of the Fillmore February '70 run, each "Dark Star" warped into distinct quadrants of improvisational hyperspace, with the version at the late show on the 13th being many Dead fans' single favorite performance by the band, ever. The early show on the 14th boasted the band's very last performance of one of the two quintessential suites of early Dead music: "Dark Star" followed by "St. Stephen," "The Eleven" and "Turn On Your Lovelight." And the late shows of the 13th and 14th produced two of the Dead's best-loved live albums: the 1973 Warner Bros. release *Bear's Choice*, and the 1995 three-disc set on the Dead's own GDM label, *Dick's Picks Volume Four*.

Consider the fact that at the time of this run, the Dead were at one of the turning points in their evolution, from psychedelic assault unit to country-inflected bards of a gone world: a river of American *mythos*, of miners and last-ditch gamblers, that flowed out of the past, along Robert Johnson's haunted crossroads, and up into the present, to water the roots of Bob Dylan's "115th Dream."

Each night of the run featured an acoustic segment, with Garcia strumming new originals like "Uncle John's Band" alongside Pigpen's gritty, unadorned renditions of Lightnin' Hopkins's "Katie Mae," and the bluegrass and old-time chestnuts Garcia grew up playing in coffeehouses south of San Francisco in groups like Mother McCree's Uptown Jug Champions. With songs like "Dire Wolf," "High Time" and "Black Peter" (all of which would appear on the album the Dead began recording the month they played them at the Fillmore, *Workingman's Dead*), Garcia and Hunter made that turf their own, penning Old West miniatures that will be the folk songs of the 21st century.

Factor in the monster jam at the late show on the 11th, when the Dead were joined from "Dark Star" onward by members of the Allman Brothers Band (who were still virtually unknown in New York), along with "rattlesnake" blues guitarist Peter Green, whose journeyman gig was replacing Eric Clapton in John Mayall's Bluesbreakers, before joining Fleetwood Mac.

And consider the fact that the Dead were just beginning to build a fire on the East Coast, especially in the Big Apple, which was proving to be acutely receptive to their kind of alchemy. In 1970, the Dead played at the Fillmore

East (or other local venues, like Port Chester's Capitol Theater and the gym at the State University of New York at Stony Brook) nearly every other month. Said former *Goldmine* editor Jeff Tamarkin, whose second Dead show was one of the February Fillmore concerts, "There was a missionary sense among the early New York Deadheads that this couldn't be kept a secret, the word had to be spread—you wanted all of your friends to be there with you to experience what you'd experienced. By the end of the year, your little group of five had expanded to 25; all of the freaks from your neighborhood had become Deadheads."

Though canonizing any one incarnation of the Dead as *the best* would be as misguided as trying to choose "the best" Miles Davis session, the Fillmore run of February '70 gives us the Dead in the full flourishing of their powers, playing shows that lasted until dawn reddened the snow-dusted sidewalks of Second Avenue, a poignant setting for the winding-down of a psychedelic journey catalyzed by Owsley's pharmacological artistry.

And who was manning the Dead's soundboard for these shows?

Owsley Stanley himself, a.k.a. the "Bear" of *Bear's Choice.*

"Primal" indeed.

Part of the magic of this run had to do with the vibes of the Fillmore itself, and the state of freakdom—"hippie" was a loathed term—in New York City at that moment.

The Fillmore had formerly been the Loew's Commodore theater, where, in its heyday, you could trade a nickel for a whole day of features, newsreels and short subjects. By the late '60s, a new community was transforming the neighborhood—which was just then becoming known as "the East Village"—into a bustling center of psychedelic bohemia. St. Marks Place was right around the corner, which was to Manhattan what the Haight-Ashbury was to San Francisco, if edgier. ("Flower power" had a harder time cutting it on the Lower East Side than in Golden Gate Park.)

When Bill Graham bought out Loew's in 1968, he brought in the bands, like Janis Joplin, Jimi Hendrix, Miles Davis, the Doors, CSNY and the Who, and the blockbuster double and triple bills (Neil Young, Miles Davis and Steve Miller made up one evening's entertainment at the Fillmore East; the Who, Chuck Berry and Albert King another), that had made his Fillmore West in San Francisco a cultural landmark.

Washington Post reporter Don Oldenburg went to the first Dead show of his life on the 13th. He remembers that the street outside the Fillmore was "crawling with molecular energy. An unreal streetlight-illuminated scene surrounded by the darkness of that end of town late at night made it like we all were on stage. A guy who looked like Jimi Hendrix, but wasn't [*possibly the legendary dealer Super Spade—S.S.*] walked by murmuring, 'Acid, acid,' in a fog that emanated from him."

As Dead scholar Blair Jackson described it in *Skeleton Key: A Dictionary for Deadheads*, "The scene outside was completely crazed. Everyone was decked out in their counter-cultural finery, and either rapping with each other, or wandering up and down the line."

"When I walked up to the box office," recalled Gary Lambert, the editor of the Grateful Dead Mercantile's affectionate "hometown newspaper," *The Grateful Dead Almanac*, "I was chagrined to find that the Dead seemed to be catching on—I could no longer count on effortlessly copping seats in the first 10 rows. Still, I was somewhere in the orchestra for all three nights. I remember that this was the first run at the Fillmore for which I purchased tickets at the newly inflated price of—$5.50! Believe it or not, this was considered obscenely exorbitant at the time, and brought yet another wave of vituperation from 'the community' toward the resident capitalist, Bill Graham."

Once inside the venue, said Blair Jackson, "You were transported to a magical world that was completely under Graham's control," with the amenities of a golden-age moviehouse, if funkier than it had once been.

"On the ground floor," Lambert recalled, "there was a conventional refreshment stand, serving up the hot dogs, popcorn, sodas and such, that had doubtless been sold at the venue since its days as the Loew's Commodore. But up on the balcony level was the perfect stoned-hippie-food concession, offering up fresh fruit and juices, donuts, bagels with cream cheese, and best of all, Dannon Yogurt, in a wide selection of flavors. Yogurt never tasted so good! Even now, a quarter-century later, a mere spoonful of Dannon sets loose a Proustian torrent of Fillmore memories."

Dead shows at the Fillmore even gave off their own distinctive aroma, a heady mixture of patchouli oil, incense and diverse smokables—including pungent Moroccan hash—all blending with the building's own antique mustiness.

Unlike the Fillmore West, back in the black neighborhood of San Francisco that gave both halls their name, there were seats at the Fillmore East, rather than an open floor, in front of the stage. Cartoons (trippy Max Fleischer films were a favorite) were shown during the breaks between sets to keep people in their seats, because the lobby was small. But the electricity in the room was similar to the lysergic intensity the Dead were used to navigating through in the dancehalls back home.

As Richard Kostelanetz, in his memoir *The Fillmore East*, described the regulars, "The audience seemed a microcosm of a new society that was free of both race prejudice and class prejudice, free of middle-class inhibitions about pleasure, free of censorship, acutely sensitive to political and social evil."

A significant boost to the hallucinogenic vibe was provided by the Joshua Light Show, throbbing across a translucent screen 20 feet tall by 30 feet wide behind the performers as they played. The Joshua Light Show was the *creme de la creme* of light shows, with eight carousel slide projectors wired for 1200-watt bulbs, three overhead projectors fitted with dishes of swirling fluids, and two film projectors running simultaneously, beaming floods of color and hyp-nagogic imagery onto the screen in time to the music. The light show staff was paid $1000 a week for their art, which drew crowds of students from the NYU film school next door.

Augmenting the light show was the band's "pyrotechnician," Boots, appearing at peak moments in the music to catapult insanely bright, now-you-see-it-now-you-don't fire signs toward the ceiling, throwing neon afterim-ages behind every dilated pupil in the room.

Part of the legendary status of this run in the oral lore of Deadheads is attributable to the fact that high-quality recordings of the late shows have been available in trading circles for years. For many Deadheads who came of age in the '70s and '80s, low-generation dubs of 2/13 and 2/14/70 were a Holy Grail that could be acquired, with a reasonable effort. The odyssey of these tapes offers a fascinating perspective on how tape trading can influence the perceived history of a band.

As the sound crew set up for the first show on the 11th, Bear patched in his Sony 770-2 to record the performance on 7-inch reels. Though taping Dead shows became *de rigueur* for hundreds of people a decade later, Bear, who had acted as the band's patron in the Acid Test days, was one of the first to realize that a band that jammed with such invention each night would be worth taping *every* night.

There was another patch into the sound-board those nights, but only the Fillmore crew knew it. John Chester, who ran the house PA, was feeding a sec-ond deck, a Revox with 15-inch reels, through the "snake" running under the apron of the stage.

One of the men on Chester's crew was a 24-year old stage technician with a background in the traditional theater named Alan Mande. "I got hired because I knew how to move things around in the dark quick," said Mande. Mande would play a significant role in Deadhead history by dubbing Chester's reels after the run, and giving copies to one of the key figures in the nascent Dead tape trading scene, a collector named Bob Menke, a couple of years later.

The copy of the 13th was on a half-track reel, and the 14th was on low-grade cassette. Dubs of those tapes trickled out for years afterwards, with copies of copies crisscrossing the globe by mail and backpack, converting casual fans into full-fledged Deadheads wherever they went.

"The run in February of 1970 provided the quintessential snapshot of the Grateful Dead at their finest," said John Scott, editor of the grand compilation of the band's 30 years of set lists, *DeadBase*. "There are several defining stands in Grateful Dead history, but none is as notorious as this, and none is more deserving of the attention, providing showcase versions of almost all the Dead's important songs. Even after 27 years, these shows have not lost their power to surprise and amaze."

One of the people surprised and amazed by the tapes was Dick Latvala, who was one of the first generation of Dead tape traders years before he was hired as the band's official archivist. Latvala was so impressed by the Dead's performance on the 13th (which Latvala hails, with characteristic hyperbole, as "one of the most intense nights in the history of the planet, almost!") he sent an ad in to *Relix*, one of the first of the tape-traders' journals, offering anyone who had been to the February run free rent at his house in Hawaii for a month.

Twenty years later, by the time Latvala had gotten the job of selecting historical performances for official release, the Fillmore run had become so highly regarded by Heads who had heard hissy copies of the Chester reels, that Latvala was deluged with postcards requesting the release of the master tapes on CD. "2/13/70—IT'S TIME!" read one, and Latvala didn't argue.

There were, however, gaps on the master reels Bear had made, where the tapes had to be flipped during extended jams. It turned out to be a good thing that the hidden deck had been running 15-inch reels. To create a complete master for *Dick's Picks Volume Four*, Jeffrey Norman of the Dead's studio was able to digitally patch in music recorded on the Chester deck to mend the gaps.

The two different source tapes also explains why some Deadheads have believed for years that there was only one show each night (*DeadBase* lists only one). The Fillmore crew hadn't taped the early shows, which had to end at 11 p.m. each night. There was too much stage work to do in a limited time to worry about tapes. The copies in circulation were dubs of Chester's reels.

"One day at the studio about eight years ago," said Latvala, "Bear found a box of stuff, and he came up to the vault and said, 'These should probably be upstairs with the Dead's stuff.' He opens this box, and there's 2/11, 2/13, and 2/14/70! I just about had a heart attack." (There were also master reels of the Dead's celebrated 5/20/70 performance at Binghamton, New York's Harpur

College in that box, featuring one of the warmest acoustic sets of the Dead's career, with harmonies by the New Riders of the Purple Sage.)

The rediscovery of the early shows was a bombshell to John Scott and his fellow collectors, much as if a second, forgotten disc of *Sergeant Pepper's Lonely Hearts Club Band* had turned up in the basement of Abbey Road Studios. "The effects will ripple through the Deadhead community for years to come," declared Scott, "as stunning proof that there are still major archeological finds to be uncovered in the world of the Dead."

The bottom line, of course, is the music.

The first night, after a set by Love, Arthur Lee's pop-folk confection from the Sunset Strip which had taken a Hendrix-like turn, the Allman Brothers played a raging set that included "In Memory Of Elizabeth Reed," "Hoochie Coochie Man" and an extended "Mountain Jam," a cheerful theme borrowed by the Allmans from the Dead, who had themselves lifted it from Donovan's "There Is A Mountain." (The Allmans' performances at the Fillmore shows have recently been slotted for release.)

The Dead's late show begins with a strangely dispassionate introduction by Keeva Krystal, an old waiter friend of Bill Graham's from Graham's days working as a busboy in the Borscht Belt: "Ladies and gentlemen, San Francisco men and their music, the Grateful Dead."

The Dead launch into the first "Dark Star" of the run, and it's a strong version. During this era of the Dead, Phil Lesh's bass was fully a co-lead voice with Garcia's guitar, weaving melodic counterpoint around Garcia's probing lines, rather than metronomically keeping the beat. ("Phil Lesh is either the best bass player in the world, or the worst," Graham Nash once observed. "I mean, it's not like he *keeps time*.") Classically trained keyboardist Tom Constanten had left the band two weeks earlier, which left new space in the music for the sinewy, stripped-down power of electric guitars.

More and more instrumental voices are added into the mix, until "Dark Star" evolves into a rolling ocean of electrified strings and chittering percussion, punctuated by Duane Allman's down-home slide voicings and Peter Green's barbed-wire twang, that surges into a more bluesy mode than one usually associates with "Dark Star."

Then magic happens. Weir begins strumming a theme he lifted from a horn line on Gil Evans's "Solea," from Miles Davis's haunting 1960 masterwork, *Sketches of Spain*. (Dead fans know this theme as "Spanish Jam." Weir introduced it to the band at rehearsals at San Francisco's Potrero Theater in late 1967, and they played it periodically, often as a guitar duet out of "Space," until Garcia's death. A version of it from the early '80s may appear on *Dick's Picks Volume Six* late this year.) The *duende*-saturated changes are a perfect setting for the multiple guitarists, who add their own stinging accents to Weir's moody theme.

The jam shifts abruptly into a marathon workout on Bobby "Blue" Bland's "Turn On Your Lovelight," with Gregg Allman interjecting somewhat super-fluous "Can you feel it, baby!" amens to Pigpen's roadhouse praises of his superhuman lover, who's "Nine foot tall, six foot wide, and wriggles like pigs fightin' in a sack." Alan Mande recollected that, while the other members of the Dead clustered around an octopus of hoses leading to a nitrous oxide tank in the upstairs dressing rooms, Pigpen held court in the sound shop in the basement, "with a bottle of Jack Daniels, and at least six gorgeous women."

By the time "Lovelight" winds up, bass duty has shifted from Lesh to the Allmans' Berry Oakley, and there are over 13 people on stage for the raucous conclusion. (Tragically, both Duane Allman and Berry Oakley would die in separate road accidents, in 1971 and '72, respectively.)

Two nights later, after the Allman and Love sets, and an early show that featured a high-energy "St. Stephen" segueing into the Buddy Holly anthem that the Dead made their own, "Not Fade Away," the Dead played a late show boasting acoustic versions of the spooky traditional ballad "Little Sadie" and Jesse Fuller's spirited "Monkey And The Engineer," as well as the medley of the Everly Brothers' "Wake Up Little Susie" into "Black Peter" that was released on *Bear's Choice*.

One of the delights of the whole run was hilarious stage banter, often at the expense of Bear and the stage crew. During a tune-up for "I've Been All Around This World," Weir warned the audience that you could lose a finger using a "Bill Russell double-action capo," and glanced over at Garcia, who, of course, was minus a finger, accidentally chopped off during his childhood.

The early show on the 14th features this episode of stand-up comedy Dead style:

Weir: We're going to investigate this here crackling sound.
Garcia: Everybody hold your breath.
Weir: Ahh! It just went away. Hey, could we have more monitors? I want to shout and scream.
Garcia: Yeah, we need more monitors here.
(feedback)
Weir: Not much of an improvement. It ain't like it was last night. I WANT IT LIKE IT WAS LAST NIGHT! (more feedback) The swamp's fightin' off the alli-

gators.
 (Garcia plays the opening notes of "Dark Star.")
 Weir: I hope none of you heard that.
 Garcia: Seen any good movies lately?
 (more feedback)
 Pigpen: I got mice in my guitar.
 Garcia: Let's wait until this passing squeech goes by.
 (blast of piercing feedback)
 Weir: We're gonna hang out up here and bleed up your ears.
 Garcia: That's nice, very nice, euphonious, you might even say.
 Weir: Put a spotlight on the PA man.
 Lesh: He deserves a spotlight. The narrow-beamed spotlight focuses.
 Weir: He's responsible for our loss of high-frequency hearing, did you know that?
 Lesh: Yes, it's hard for us to discern spoken words in quiet rooms.
 Weir: Sibilances and such.
 Lesh: Consonant [inaudible]. Are we through now?
 Garcia: Jeez, we just started, man.
 Woman in the audience: Yeah, man!
 Weir: Usher, eject that chick!
 Garcia: 'Yeah, man.' This is outta sight, really, man. Nothing's weirder than coming to New York.
 Lesh: (Counting off "Dark Star") 1, 2, 3, 4...

Right after one of the acoustic interludes on the 14th, Garcia can be heard looking for "the microphone guy." The crew member in question was young Mande, who had other things on his mind at that moment: "Everything went fine on the 13th, but on the 14th, I got totally Owsleyized. When I heard them calling for me to come back onstage to set stuff up, I was tripping out of my mind, laying on my back in one of the aisles."

On the 14th, a spotlight swept down on the legendary WNEW-FM DJ Zacherle (known by many as the ominous voice of "Chill-l-l-l-e-r-r-r Theater"), who introduced himself as "Jonathan Schwartz" (WNEW's morning DJ) before giving the Dead the punchiest intro of their career: "The Grateful God-damned Dead!"

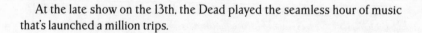

At the late show on the 13th, the Dead played the seamless hour of music that's launched a million trips.

"Dark Star" unfolds with a glorious, stately majesty. Theme after impro-vised theme circulates among the players like shapes in water. Listening intently to one another, responding to the minutest gestures, the band reaches a level of subtle empathy equaled only by, say, the Bill Evans Trio with Scott LaFaro and Paul Motian. Then all at once, the "Dark Star" theme yields to the bright cascade of chords Deadheads call the "Feelin' Groovy Jam," one of the most purely life-affirming melodies the Dead ever played. (The "Dark Star" on the early show of the 14th was much more angular, shunning the fluid transitions of the night before in favor of space-age chaos, a demonstration of the band's determination to reinvent their music from set to set.)

The dynamic range—as the band moves through "Dark Star," "That's It For The Other One" and into "Lovelight"—modulates from the barest rustling to liquid thunder, touching on every emotion from buoyant joy, to volcanic dis-sonance that roars like a force of nature. Time seems infinitely elastic, the band accelerating and decelerating together, breathing music, as if the sounds being generated were the thoughts of a single, flowing harmonious consciousness.

There are no other words for music like this: it's Grateful Dead music.

It was at one of those moments that Alan Mande paused behind an amp to look out into the Fillmore, at all the faces illuminated by the phantoms play-ing on the screen behind the stage.

"I'd spent these years in the theater helping to maintain a fragile suspen-sion of disbelief," Mande recalled, "knowing that if I just stepped out onstage, it would totally break the illusion. I looked out at that moment and saw all these people in ecstasy, and I knew that if I walked onstage, it wouldn't matter at all. I said, 'This is where it's at. This is real power.'

"My life turned around 180 degrees that night," Mande continued, "I'll always be thankful, because Jerry came and got me, and took me there. And I stayed there, on the bus, until August 9th, the day he died."

Since the original publication of this article, Owsley "Bear" Stanley as come forward to dispute the notion that the Dead played two shows each night at the Fillmore East in February of 1970. Bear says that the band instead played one "long, split set of two to two-and-a-half hours of music with a short break, as was their style in those days." The tapes that surfaced shortly before this article was written, he explains, had been kept in his personal collection at home, rather than in the Dead's vault. Bear's account differs from those of the people I interviewed for this article, notably the band's late archivist, Dick Latvala. Memories of ecstatic experiences 25 years past are notoriously unreliable. The power and grace of the music played on those nights remains inarguable.–SS

There's just something about a *New Yorker* article. This one ran, anonymously, on April 17, 1971, in the "Talk of the Town" section and describes the concert of Tuesday, April 6, 1971. Trow is the author of *Bullies: Stories,* published in 1980 by Little, Brown, *The City in the Mist: A Novel,* published in 1984 by Little, Brown; and *Within the Context of No Context,* published in 1981 by Little, Brown.

PURPLE
Lights

Grateful Dead
Dance Marathon
at the
Manhattan Center

George W.S. Trow

e sent a correspondent to the final night of the Grateful Dead Dance Marathon, held three nights last week at the Manhattan Center, on West Thirty-fourth Street. This is his report:

"When I arrived, there was not much dancing at the Grateful Dead Dance Marathon. The promoter, who tipped off a neat five dollars a ticket, had oversold the hall, so that while there was room in some parts of the room for rhythmic breathing, dancing was rarely a possibility. In any case, there was no tinsel or glitter anywhere, and since a proper dance marathon requires a certain amount of tinsel and glitter, the whole dance-marathon hype turned out to be a little bit embarrassing—at least, if you stopped to think about it, which, probably, nobody much did. Everyone was waiting for the Dead, and thinking about them. There is a lot of talk just now about the Death of Rock and the Death of the Alternate Culture, and this talk is just as tiresome in its way as the talk around a while ago about the Triumph of Rock and the Birth of the Alternate Culture, but it is true that there are very few groups playing now in America who can really move an audience in the old way, and the Grateful Dead are probably the most impor-

tant and accessible of these groups. They have worked a route back into country music and early rock-and-roll, and they have very heavy acid-rock creden-
tials, so they cover a lot of ground and they mean a lot to a lot of different
people. No one minded waiting for the Dead.

"The Manhattan Center has aquamarine walls and bad murals on social
themes. The legend under one of the largest of these murals reads, 'For the
Furtherance of Industry, Religion, and the Enjoyment of Leisure.' The Grateful
Dead Dance Marathon fell, presumably, under the heading of leisure,
although there was a religious angle there somewhere. In any case, the managers of the Manhattan Center were sensitive to the leisure habits of their
young patrons and made sure that no one was offended by any evidence of
middle-class material comfort. There are two enormous balconies at the Manhattan Center, and both were crowded with people pushing to the rails. From
the floor, these balconies looked like the decks of a huge foundering hippie
cruise ship. The iron Art Moderne balcony rails were the nicest details in the
hall.

"Everyone was dressed in the New Mufti, if you know what I mean. Very little freakiness. Very few silks and satins and top hats and doorman uniforms.
Most people were wearing layers of T-shirts and sweatshirts and flannel
shirts and Army jackets. Overalls were prevalent. This stuff is a kind of finery,
as people are very selective about which T-shirts and sweatshirts and overalls
they wear. There were several T-shirts with 'Cocaine' written on the front in
Coca-Cola script, and there was one that said 'Holland Tunnel.' The freaky,
tense, expectant atmosphere of a couple of years ago was gone. People knew
what was coming, and they waited to get excited until it did come. There was
a pleasant low-key trust around. People lay on the floor, for instance, and were
not trampled, and the coat checkroom had no coat checker and was run on
sound anarchistic principles. There was, however, no self-conscious celebration of this low-key trust. I didn't hear anyone say 'Oh, wow!'

"The stage was bathed in lights of many colors, but mostly purple. The
Dead came on. They did a lot of songs other people have done—'Me and
Bobby McGee' and 'In the Midnight Hour' and 'Oh Boy,' Buddy Holly and the
Crickets' old song. Bob Weir and Jerry Garcia, the leads, were in good form,
and they received the response they are used to. By the time they got into
some of their own stuff, like 'Casey Jones,' people were, in fact, dancing,
although there was no room to dance. On the first balcony, ten guys danced in
a circle, and then were joined by about twenty other people and set off down
the balcony in a snake. They mumbled the lyrics of 'Casey Jones' until they
reached the 'high on cocaine' part, at which point they shouted the lyrics.

Downstairs, a black guy (one of the very few black guys there) danced flat out. It was a very complex thing. I asked him if there was any kind of name for his dance. 'I'm just dancing, man,' he said. 'The last time I did a dance with a name, it was the tenth grade, I think. I guess that was the bug-a-loo. The bug-a-loo's a long time ago.'"

Ed McClanahan came out of the same creative writing program, the Wallace Stegner Fellows at Stanford, which produced Ken Kesey, Robert Stone, Larry McMurtry, and many others. The main body of the following piece appeared originally, in slightly different form, in *Playboy* magazine in March 1972 and won an award from the magazine for outstanding nonfiction. It was subsequently reprinted in *Playboy's Music Scene*. Interwoven into the original *Playboy* article, McClanahan's "A Brief Exegesis of Certain Sociophilosophical Themes" in Robert Hunter's Lyrics to 'New Speedway Boogie'" appeared originally in a joint publication of *The Realist* and *The Last Supplement to the Whole Earth Catalog* in 1971, though he originally conceived of the piece as a part of what became the article for *Playboy*. Here the two pieces are presented as a unified whole, reworked by McClanahan for his *My Vita, If You Will: The Uncollected Ed McClanahan*, published by Counterpoint in 1998. In the course of the article, McClanahan refers extensively to the *Live Dead* album and also focuses on much of *Workingman's Dead*. But the highlights of the article are the extensive interview segments with Garcia and the brilliant way in which McClanahan captures the band's live performance, in particular Pigpen's stage persona. McClanahan is also the author of *The Natural Man*, published by Farrar, Straus & Giroux in 1983; *Famous People I Have Known*, published by Farrar, Straus & Giroux in 1985; and *A Congress of Wonders*, published by Counterpoint in 1996.

GRATEFUL DEAD *I Have Known*

Ed McClanahan

If you've got it all together,
what's that all around it?
Inscribed on my bathroom wall by Ken Kesey,
who attributes it to Brother Dave Gardner

bright Sunday afternoon in August 1971, just one week after Bill Graham closed the doors of the Fillmore West forever and ever, and I'm sitting in the living room of Jerry Garcia's new house on the headlands above a coastal village an hour north of San Francisco (a very nice house, by the way, not luxurious or anything, but altogether nice enough to reflect the Grateful Dead's rising fortunes during the past couple of years); and if I were to glance over my shoulder, I could see beyond the picture window all the way down the tilting rim of the continent to the shimmering Pacific. Only right this minute, I'm not into scenery at *all*; right this minute I'm deeply engaged in being paranoid about my tape recorder, just sort of *stroking* the treacherous little bastard before I entrust to its tape-eating maw the wit and wisdom of Jerry Garcia, lead guitarist and chief philosophical theoretician of what some claim is the greatest rock-'n'-roll band in the world—Captain Trips, they call him.

Jerry, meanwhile, is doing exactly what he always does—playing it as it lays, which right now means sitting there beside me in his rocking chair, gazing benignly out the window, beaming within the dark nimbus of his hair and beard like a stoned-out John the Baptist, waiting.

"What I'd like to do," I'm prattling, rather desperately trying to fill with the sound of my own voice the void my incompetence has created, "I'd like to feel free to take as many liberties with this interview as I've been taking with the rest of the material, to, uh, interpolate and rearrange things here and there when it seems...But maybe you...?"

"Sure," Jerry says cheerily, waving aside my question. "You're gonna lie a little, you mean. Sure, you can say I said anything you feel like. I don't give a shit."

"Good deal! Because what I'm planning to do, see, is to take this interview and sort of write myself out of it, my own voice, I mean, so that what's left will be just *your* voice, disembodied, just rapping out loud. Like, for instance, did you happen to read John Sack's interviews with Lieutenant Calley? Do you remember how Sack himself isn't really a *presence* there, how it comes down as if it were just Calley alone, telling his own story? That sort of thing. And then I'll just take your voice and weave it through the piece, probably in italics or something, just lacing it in and out wherever it seems..."

Jerry grins and says, *"Sure, feel free, whatever. Only the erroneous assumption in that, see, is that a guy like Calley might ever volunteer any information at all. Or me, for that matter. I mean, nobody ever hears about some of the shit that comes out in interviews unless somebody asks me, you know what I mean? In fact, it's like the basis of the reality from which you write, because you wouldn't write this thing if you'd never talked to any of us, would you? I mean, you know what I mean? If you weren't interacting in there, the story would never have occurred. So it's like you can include yourself or not, but either way, it's all you..."*

Ok, then—*me*, by God:

So there I am in September 1970, early morning, and I'm hurrying home to California to write about the Grateful Dead after a three-week hiatus back East, barreling along in my big Dodge camper all alone through the everlasting vasty reaches of central Iowa, on a back road forty miles in some direction or another from Cedar Rapids, and it's raining like a cow pissing on a flat rock, a cold, driving rain that chills me even with the camper's heater ramming hot air up both pants legs; and beside me on the hump of the engine's housing are spread my Official Accuracy Reporter's Notebooks filled with overwrought three-week-old scribblings (garcia missing 2 joints midl. finger rt. hand!—phil lesh leanness *lincolnesk!*—sam cutler rd. mgr. look like capt. hook!!—bob weir billy the kid!!—john mcintyre bus. mgr. *elegant*, look like yng. *rich widmark!!!!*), and several yellowing copies of *Rolling Stone* featuring articles about the Dead, and my little portable stereo tape recorder and five cassettes of the Dead's albums, and—here comes the weird part—on my head I'm wearing, Buck Rogers-like, an enormous pair of superpowerful stereo headphones plugged into the recorder, and the volume is turned up full blast, and the Dead's "Turn it *on!* Turn it *on!*" is crashing into my eardrums, and I'm bouncing ecstatically in my seat and hammering the heels of my hands on the steering wheel to Bill the Drummer's surging nineteen-to-the-dozen rhythms, while the guitars scream as loud as locomotive whistles; and now an image swirls to mind and shapes itself: the interior of my skull has somehow become the interior of the Fillmore West, San Francisco's onetime Carousel Ballroom, this cavernous old relic of a pleasure palace amid whose tawdry grandeur our forebears forbore Guy Lombardo and Shep Fields and His Rippling Rhythms that we might live to dig the Dead, my throat and tongue the Fillmore's threadbare maroon-carpeted lobbies and stair wells and my teeth its curlicuing rococo plaster balustrades and my brainpan the grand ballroom itself, my medulla oblongata its vaulted ceiling festooned with heavily sagging billows of silvery-gray asbestos damask, and there are three thousand dope-crazed Dead fans crouched haunch to haunch in the darkness on the immense dance floor of my mind, while at the far end of the great chamber, onstage, dwarfed beneath the high, curved, bleached-white band shell that is the inner surface of my forehead, the Grateful Dead are getting it on, a demon-driven suicide squad of assassins under the harsh command of the archbrigand Pigpen ("*turn* it on! jes a leetle bit hi-eee-yer!"), a murderous little band of renegades, savages, tartars in cowboy mufti, angels of death armed not with three supercharged guitars and a set of traps but with three choppers and a mortar, mercilessly laying waste to the shrieking, writhing mass of defenseless supplicants spread beneath them, and against the backs of my eyeballs the giant light-show screen behind the bandstand is ablaze like the night sky above a battlefield with the garish lightning of their fusillade; it is more than just a massacre, it is a by-God *apocalypse* hurtling along right here inside the fragile eggshell of my skull at seventy miles an hour through the Iowa monsoon, the incredible cacophony of it thrumming in my blood and beating wildly against the backs of my eyes, mounting and mounting and mounting until it peaks out at about eleven million megadecibels, and Pig screams *"Yeeeeeeeeeeee-o-o-o-o-o-o-o-o-o-o-owwwwwwwwwwww!"* and barks, "And *leave* it on!" and within the headphones there descends an abrupt and wondrous stillness, a silence made infinitely deeper and more profound by the absence not merely of the Dead's righteous racket but of *all* sound, the headphones baffling out even the engine's roar along with the slap-slap-slap of the wipers and the steady suck of tires on the flooded roadbed, as if the whole wet world were inexplicably and without warning stricken mute, and as the wipers streak the veil of water on the windshield, I see, standing stalwart by the lonely Iowa roadside like heaven's own herald, an enormous billboard, sky blue with great, thick, square white letters proclaiming, for no good reason at all,

TIME ENDS
ETERNITY WHERE

and even as the wind blown water sheets the glass again, blurring, then fracturing the image beyond all intelligence, I hear Jerry Garcia begin the next song on the tape, his voice rising sweet and clear and plangent into the silence:

"You know Death don't
Have no mercy
In this land..."

≈   ≈   ≈

"I mean, everybody who's makin' a big thing about the closing of the Fillmore, that's a crock of shit, actually. Because, you know, what'd they do before there was a Fillmore? I mean, there's always been a musician scene, musicians have always traveled around, and you could always hear music. And that's gonna happen no matter what. In most places, see, there isn't any Fillmore. And that doesn't affect anybody except, you know, the Fillmore freaks. I think the end of the Fillmore is just the beginning of different space."

≈   ≈   ≈

"The first time I saw Jerry Garcia," my young friend Harry (who is said to be a genius in molecular physics, his major at Stanford, but nonetheless retains a certain charming innocence in matters of the spirit) was telling me the other day," was in the Straight Theater up in the Haight in '67. I'd never even *heard* the Grateful Dead except on the radio; I was just beginning to find out about the head scene in those days. But I just loved their music. And when they came on that night—I remember the light show was all these yellow, swirling things going all the way up to the ceiling; it was like *sunshine*—I went up to the front by the stage and stood there lookin' up at Jerry, and I was thinkin' how I'd just never *seen* anyone like this before, this far-out, mellow dude just playin' that rock 'n' roll, the notes so clear and uncluttered, a beautiful, sparkling thing, you know? And so I looked up at Garcia, and I just couldn't *help* but smile, it was just that...the *calm* on his face, it was like a Buddha, you know, like you can see where the Buddha is *at*, Nirvana, you know...and Jerry saw me lookin' at him, saw me smiling, and *he* smiled at *me!* And that just blew my mind! It was so *different*; this dude was just so *different*. I mean, before that I could *never* have smiled at a rock musician; they were all guys who were just showing off. 'I'm the big stud,' you know. It was all just a big *pose* kind of trip with them, showing off for their chicks and the audience, being tough guys. But *this* dude—I mean, you could relate to him *directly*, with just your *eyes* that way..."

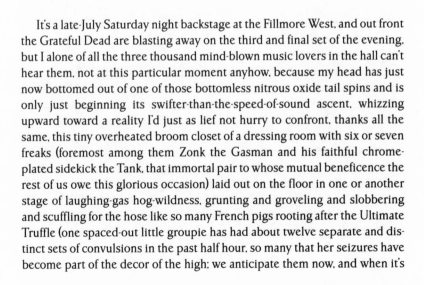

It's a late-July Saturday night backstage at the Fillmore West, and out front the Grateful Dead are blasting away on the third and final set of the evening, but I alone of all the three thousand mind-blown music lovers in the hall can't hear them, not at this particular moment anyhow, because my head has just now bottomed out of one of those bottomless nitrous oxide tail spins and is only just beginning its swifter-than-the-speed-of-sound ascent, whizzing upward toward a reality I'd just as lief not hurry to confront, thanks all the same, this tiny overheated broom closet of a dressing room with six or seven freaks (foremost among them Zonk the Gasman and his faithful chrome-plated sidekick the Tank, that immortal pair to whose mutual beneficence the rest of us owe this glorious occasion) laid out on the floor in one or another stage of laughing-gas hog-wildness, grunting and groveling and slobbering and scuffling for the hose like so many French pigs rooting after the Ultimate Truffle (one spaced-out little groupie has had about twelve separate and distinct sets of convulsions in the past half hour, so many that her seizures have become part of the decor of the high; we anticipate them now, and when it's her turn to toke on the hose, we observe her as coolly as if her drooling rictus and spasmodic shudderings have been provided by the management for our amusement between our own tokes), and up there in the real world, where this particular gas flash is about to surface, I'll be obliged to open my eyes again and deal with the dismal fact that the Dead's final set is well under way and I have yet to really listen to a note they've played all evening, not to mention the equally onerous fact that my tape recorder and my brand-new Official Accuracy Reporter's Notebooks are lost somewhere amid the melee at my feet (I've somehow succeeded, by the way, in commandeering the only chair in the room, an overstuffed old number that's just right for doing nitrous oxide in, since it's so thoroughly rump-sprung I can't possibly fall out of it), and sooner or later I'm going to have to dig them out—the ignominious tools of this ignoble trade, I mean—and Get Down to Bidness, fall by the nearest phone booth and slip into my Front-Page Farrell suit so that when the Dead have wrapped up this set, I'll be all primed and cocked to zap them with the ole five W's, the way Miss Parsons taught us in high school journalism (Who-What-Where-When-Why-and-sometimes-How-are-you, Grateful Dead?), when suddenly my head pops through the surface of my consciousness like the bobber on a fishing line that has just been gnawed in two by the Big One That Got Away, and the sound of the Dead catches up to me all in one great roaring rush, the voice of Jerry Garcia amplified to boiler-factory rumbustiousness yet still somehow as sweet and gentle as the purest babbling branch water chiding me:

"Please don't dominate the rap, Jack
if you got nothin' new to say..."

Oh well, I tell myself happily, settling back into the welcoming embrace of my armchair, probably Jerry's got the right idea there; probably I'd better just have me one or two more tastes on them there noxious gases, just to clear my head, and then I can go out there nice and fresh, all primed and cocked to...

SCENE: *The Dead's business office in San Rafael, where* BOB HUNTER *the Dead's lyricist, has just been telling everybody about a friend recently returned form a trip to Cuba. Enter* RAMROD, *one of the band's equipment handlers.*

HUNTER: Hey, you know who so-and-so talked to? Fidel Castro!

RAMROD: Yeah? Far out! How'd he get his number?

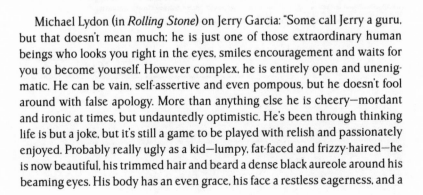

Now, the first time *I* ever saw Jerry Garcia was in midwinter 1965, in Ken Kesey's house up in La Honda. I'm lounging around Kesey's living room, see, and this extraordinarily curious-looking party comes shuffling through. In point of fact, he's the very first true freak I've ever laid eyes on, this somewhat rotund young man with a hairdo like a dust mop dipped in coal tar, and after he's gone, Kesey says, that was Jerry Garcia; he's got a rock-'n'-roll band that's gonna play with us this Saturday night at the San Jose Acid Test. Their name is the Warlocks, but they're gonna change it to the Grateful Dead.

At the time, to tell the truth, I wasn't exactly galvanized with excitement by this bit of news; after all, only a few Saturday nights before that, I'd attended what I've since come to regard as the Olde *Original* Acid Test, a curiously disjointed but otherwise perfectly ordinary party at Kesey's house featuring nothing more startling than an abundance of dope and a drunken Berkeley poet who kept loudly reciting Dylan Thomas and, at midnight (hours after I'd gone home, adept as ever at missing the main event), the ritual sacrifice and subsequent immolation of a chicken.

But what I didn't know then was that four hundred people would turn up for the San Jose Acid Test, which begat the Palo Alto Acid Test, which begat the Fillmore Acid Test, which begat the Trips Festival, which begat Bill Graham, who (to hear him tell it, anyhow) begat Life As We Know It. Still, like I said, I couldn't possibly have known that at the...

Michael Lydon (in *Rolling Stone*) on Jerry Garcia: "Some call Jerry a guru, but that doesn't mean much; he is just one of those extraordinary human beings who looks you right in the eyes, smiles encouragement and waits for you to become yourself. However complex, he is entirely open and unenigmatic. He can be vain, self-assertive and even pompous, but he doesn't fool around with false apology. More than anything else he is cheery—mordant and ironic at times, but undauntedly optimistic. He's been through thinking life is but a joke, but it's still a game to be played with relish and passionately enjoyed. Probably really ugly as a kid—lumpy, fat-faced and frizzy-haired—he is now beautiful, his trimmed hair and beard a dense black aureole around his beaming eyes. His body has an even grace, his face a restless eagerness, and a gentleness, not to be confused with 'niceness,' is his manner. His intelligence is quick and precise and he can be devastatingly articulate, his dancing hands playing perfect accompaniment to his words."

*   *   *

"The thing about us, I guess, is that we're not really layin' anything on anybody. I mean if you're tellin' people directly how to 'be right,' how to act, how to do, if you're talkin' to people on that level, then the kind of feedback you get is gonna be more of, like, 'You promised me this, man; now, where is it?' It's the I-demand-to-speak-to-John-Lennon-personally syndrome. Like, one time this guy came into our office, this fucked-up guy, just walked right up and started staring at me in this intense way, man, and he was so heavy, it was as if he was about to say something really important, you know, really urgent; he looked like he was on the verge of exploding or something, and finally he says, 'Listen, when are you guys gonna get it on, man? Because you know scientology's got a good head start!' But it's just the price you pay for standin' up in public; you get stuff comin' back at you, and if you're a little fucked up yourself, you get fucked-up feedback, that's all."

*   *   *

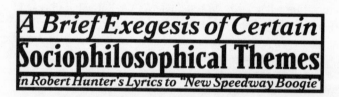

A Brief Exegesis of Certain Sociophilosophical Themes
in Robert Hunter's Lyrics to "New Speedway Boogie"

Ed McClanahan

The Grateful Dead were deeply involved in planning the Rolling Stones' disastrous Altamont concert—they were the ones, according to most sources, who suggested that the Hell's Angels be employed to police the area around the stage—and Robert Hunter's lyrics to "New Speedway Boogie" may properly be regarded as their "official" public statement about the meaning of the grisly events of that unhappy day.

First, then, the lyrics, as sung by Jerry Garcia on the album *Workingman's Dead*:

Please don't dominate the rap, Jack
if you got nothing new to say
If you please, don't back up the track
This train's got to run today

Spent a little time on the mountain
Spent a little time on the hill
Heard some say: better run away
Others say: better stand still

Now I don't know but I been told
it's hard to run with the weight of gold
Other hand I heard it said
it's just as hard with the weight of lead

Who can deny? who can deny?
It's not just a change in style
One step done and another begun
in I wonder how many miles?

Spent a little time on the mountain
Spent a little time on the hill
Things went down we don't understand
but I think in time we will

Now I don't know but I been told
in the heat of the sun a man died of cold
Do we keep on coming or stand and wait
with the sun so dark and the hour so late?

You can't overlook the lack, Jack
of any other highway to ride
It's got no signs or dividing lines
and very few rules to guide

Spent a little time on the mountain
Spent a little time on the hill
I saw things getting out of hand
I guess they always will

I don't know but I been told
if the horse don't pull you got to carry the load
I don't know whose back's that strong
Maybe find out before too long

One way or another
One way or another
One way or another
this darkness got to give
One way or another
One way or another
One way or another
this darkness got to give

The song is, on the one hand, an expression of apprehensiveness and confusion and, on the other, an exhortation to a new order of wisdom, a higher and truer vision. However, unlike the authors of most of the journalistic post-mortems on the Altamont debacle (especially those handwringers and breast-beaters who insist on "dominating the rap" even though they "got nothin' new to say"), Hunter is not of the Altamont-as-Armageddon persuasion, and he does not agree that the quest after salvation—the voyage that began in the Haight-Ashbury and carried us all the way to Woodstock—has dead-ended at last in the molten yellow hills of California just fifty miles east of where it started, impaled on the point of a Hell's Angels rusty blade, skewered there like one of those suicidal Siamese frogs that travel great distances only to fling themselves upon the spikes of some rare thornbush. Rather, the poet suggests, the journey has only just begun, and the way is long and arduous and fraught with peril: Altamont is but one dark moment in...

⚡   ⚡   ⚡

Another summer Sunday afternoon and I'm driving up to Marin County to see a softball game between—get this—the Grateful Dead and the Jefferson Airplane, and just before I get on the Golden Gate Bridge, I pick up this most remarkably scroungy, stringy-haired, snaggletoothed hippie hitchhiker—"Wheat Germ," he called himself, I swear he did—who says he is bound for

Sausalito, and in the slow Sunday bridge traffic I fire up a doobie and rather grandly offer him a hit, all the while coming on (I admit it, I'm freakdom's own Major Hoople) absolutely shamelessly about the Great Moment in Sports that the editors of a certain Nationally Known Publication have prevailed upon me to cover for them this afternoon, and Wheat Germ coolly takes his toke and lays a fat smoke ring against the windshield and then goes for the inside pocket of his ragtag old Goodwill Bargain Basement tweed hacking jacket and outs with...gasp!...a badge? a *gun?* No, just a saddle-soap tin, the kind that's about twice as big around as a Kiwi can, which he extends to me the way one might proffer a tin of lozenges, and I see that it's full of these little purple tablets, *thousands* of them, tiny lavender pastilles that slither around inside the can like collar buttons when Wheat Germ shakes them gently, saying, through a sudden spray of spittle so dense that as his excitement rises, I can sometimes almost make out a rainbow in it, "Serve yourself, dad. Go on, take some. Shit yeah, all you want. Me and my brother Yogurt's got a factory up in Sausalito puts out seven hunnert of these tabs an hour. It's good acid, man. I mean, I've moved over six million dollars' worth of dope in the last three years and nobody's got burnt yet!"

Yogurt? Six million?

"Shit yeah, over that. And that don't even *count* the shipload of hash the Interpol narcs shot out from unner us down at Yucatán last month! Them Interpol pigs, man, they're all a bunch of Commies or somethin'. Fifteen hunnert keys, man, straight to the bottom of the Pacific!" (The Pacific? Uh, say there, Wheat Germ, Yucatán is...) "Shit, yeah. I mean they tar-*petered* the mother, man! But I don't give a shit. I got me a crew down there right now, divin' for it. I mean, I'll get the bastid back, fucking-A dig it, dad. I deal for all the *big* people, see, the really *heavy* dudes. I mean Janis and me was just like *that*, dig, and whenever I need anything done, I just...I mean, I got people all over the fuckin' country workin' for me, man, in my organization. The Syndicate, me and Yogurt call it, hee-hee-hee. Listen, man, are you *sure* you can't use a hit of this acid? Because I was just thinkin', you know, I wouldn't too much mind doin' a little dealin' to them guys, the Dead and the Airplane." He pauses long enough to glance down at the array of Official Accuracy Reporter's Notebooks spread between us on the engine housing, and adds, "Reporter, huh? I can dig it. What are you, dad, a sportswriter or somethin'?"

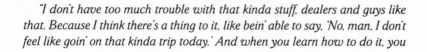

"I don't have too much trouble with that kinda stuff, dealers and guys like that. Because I think there's a thing to it, like bein' able to say, 'No, man, I don't feel like goin' on that kinda trip today.' And when you learn how to do it, you

just don't find yourself in those situations very often. And it's not necessarily to be putting somebody down or even to be turning down some kind of energy exchange or whatever; it's just learning to assume that everybody can understand everything and just tryin' to communicate with that principle always in mind. So I don't have too much trouble with those guys, actually."

Anyhow, I didn't go to the San Jose Acid Test. But a few Saturday nights later I did make it over to a ratty old nightclub called Ben's Big Beat, in the mudflats beside the Bayshore Freeway, for the Palo Alto Acid Test; and the what's-their-names, the Grateful Dead, they were there, too, Jerry Garcia plucking strange sonic atonalities out of his Magic Twanger, backed up by a pair of cherubic-looking boys named Phil Lesh, on bass guitar, and Bobby Weir, on rhythm guitar, and a drummer—Bill Kreutzmann—who looked so young and innocent and fresh-faced that one's first impulse was to wonder how he got his momma to let him stay out so late, and mainly, this incredibly gross person who played electric organ and harmonica and sang occasional blues vocals—Pigpen, someone said his name was—beyond a doubt the most marvelously ill-favored figure to grace a public platform since King Kong came down with stage fright and copped out on the Bruce Cabot show. He was bearded and burly and barrel-chested, jowly and scowly and growly, and he had long, Medusa-like hair so greasy it might have been groomed with Valvoline, and his angry countenance glowered out through it like a wolf at bay in a hummock of some strange, rank foliage. He wore, as I recall, a motor-cyclist's cap, crimped and crumpled Hell's Angel style, and heavy iron-black boots, and the gap between the top of his oily Levis and the bottom of his tattletale-gray T-shirt exposed a half-moon of distended beer belly as pale and befurred as a wedge of moldy Jack cheese. Sitting up there at that little spindly-legged organ, he looked enormous, bigger than life, like a gorilla at a harpsichord. But the ugly mother sure could *play!* To one as dull of ear as I, who'd always pretty much assumed that the only fit place for organ music outside of church was the roller rink, those ham-fisted whorehouse chords he was hammering out seemed in and of themselves to constitute the most satisfying sort of blasphemy. And sing? The way this coarse-voiced ogre snarled his unintelligible yet unfathomably indecent talkin'-blues phrases would make a serial killer's skin crawl; fathers of teenage daughters must have shuddered in their sleep as far away as Burlingame that night. Verily, he was wondrous gross, was this Pigpen, yet such was the subtle alchemy of his art that the more he profaned love and beauty, the more his grossness rendered him lovable and beautiful. "Far *out!*" the teeny-boppers and their boyfriends in Ben's Big Beat kept exclaiming while Pig worked. "Isn't he far fuckin' *out!*" It was an expression I'd not run into before, but even at first hearing, it seemed destined, if only for its commodious inexactness, to be with us for a good long while. In any case, it accommodated Pigpen very nicely; he was indeed one far-out gentleman, no doubt about it, none at all.

Summertime, midmorning, and I'm sitting in the living room of what was then Jerry Garcia and Bob Hunter's house, under the redwoods up a canyon in Larkspur, fifteen or twenty miles north of San Francisco, sitting there in an old easy chair reworking my notes on last night's three sets at the Fillmore ("An Evening with the Grateful Dead," the show is titled, and Jerry played all three sets, straight through from 8:30 until nearly 2:00 A.M., two sets with the Dead and one with their country-cousin stablemates, the New Riders of the Purple Sage, and will do the same tonight and again tomorrow night; yet while he's playing he looks as if he could happily go on forever). While I'm sitting there, Jerry, yawning and stretching and scratching like a freshly dehibernated bear, is puttering around the stereo in search of a record by a vocalist he's so far identified only as "my favorite girl singer," and Jerry's lady, Mountain Girl (a great, gorgeous creature, an Amazon's Amazon, a Valkyrie with raven tresses, the sort of awesome, Venus-of-Willendorf beauty who inspires me to pure press-agent flackery, the "160-pounds-of-eye-poppin'-pulchritude" school of prose)...ahem...and as I was saying, Mountain Girl is banging around in the kitchen fixing breakfast for me and Jerry and Hunter (who is right now standing in the doorway blinking myopically behind his enormous, sleep-frazzled Pecos Pete mustache), and Hunter's lady, Christy, is out back playing with Jerry and Mountain's two kids, and Jerry, dark eyes suddenly aglint behind his dandelion-yellow-tinted glasses, hollers "Eureka!" or "Aha!" or whatever and plunges his hand wrist-deep into a disordered stack of albums and comes up with...no, no, not Joplin, not Grace Slick, not Joni Mitchell or Joan Baez or Laura Nyro, not even Tina Turner or Big Mama Thornton, but...Dolly *Parton*?

Who'da thought it? Who'd ever have supposed that the favorite girl singer of the spiritual leader of the Heaviest Rock-'n'-Roll Band in the Known World would turn out to be *my* favorite girl singer...Dolly Parton, the fairest wildflower that ever bloomed in Tennessee, the best female country vocalist since the prime of Kitty Wells? Far—how do you say?—*flung!* Far fuckin' flung!

Jerry's at the turntable now, flipping switches and adjusting dials, blowing invisible dust off the record with French-maid fastidiousness, delicately plucking up the tonearm, catching it the way one might pick up a small but outraged serpent, with two fingers just at the base of the skull, gingerly almost to the point of reverence, and a moment later the room is filled with the exquisitely melancholic strains of Dolly Parton's mourning-dove-with-a-broken-wing voice, keening:

> "In this mental insti-too-shun,
> Looking out through these arn bars..."

It's her beautiful "Daddy, Come and Get Me" about a girl whose husband has had her committed ("to get me out of his way"), and when Dolly comes to the lines "It's not my mind that's broken / It's my heart," Jerry Garcia, standing limned in soft morning sunlight before the arched front window, turns to me and—remember now, this is *the* Jerry Garcia, Captain Trips himself, the same Jerry Garcia who only twelve hours earlier utterly blew out three thousand of the most jaded, dope-devastated heads ever assembled even at the Fillmore (Dead fans are notorious in that regard)—*that* Jerry Garcia turns to me and clasps his hands to his breast and rolls his eyes after the goofy, ga-ga fashion of a lovesick swain and utters an ecstatic little moan and swoons into the nearest chair...and for the next half hour, while our breakfast turns cold in the kitchen, he and Hunter and I sit there in the living room tokin' on a taste of Captain Trips' morning pipe and groovin' on Sweet Dolly's bucolic threnodies about lost loves and dying lovers and stillborn babes, and by the time her last words ("O Robert! O Robert!") fade into silence, I swear to God there's not a dry eye in the room.

It is, I suppose, my unhappy destiny to be eternally numbered among the Last of the First; 'twas ever thus, even in 1966. For, by the time I arrived, stoned to the eyeballs, at the Longshoremen's Hall in San Francisco for the final night of the Trips Festival, it had somehow got to be one or two or three o'clock in the morning, and the Dead were packing up their gear and nearly everybody had gone home. Some late-lingering hanger-on was fiddling with a slide projector, running through old slides that one of Kesey's Pranksters had shot in the La Honda woods, and even as I walked into the vast, almost empty hall there flashed, purely by cosmic coincidence—the *synch*, Tom Wolfe named it—on a giant screen above the bandstand, a gargantuan medium-close-up of...right...of *me*, slapped up there on the wall behind the stage like some kind of weird wallpaper, head and shoulders in monumental proportions, my eyes masked behind a twelve-foot span of impenetrably black wrap-around shades and my nostrils as big as manholes and my tightly pursed mouth, a furrow the length of the grave of a good-sized dog, fixed in what I must have intended to resemble a pensive attitude but that now seemed fraught with nameless apprehensions (to tell the truth, for all the time I put in hanging around the edges of the La Honda scene, I never did quite manage to shake off that vague, stranger-in-a-strange-land uneasiness that is the special affliction of us day-trippers); and dwarfed by my looming monolithic visage, the Grateful Dead and their equipment crews slouched about at their assorted chores, a shadowy platoon of climbers grouping to scale a one-man, two-dimensional Mount Rushmore. All in all, it seemed as appropriate an image as any to remember the Trips Festival by, so I turned on my heels and split as quickly as I'd come. And that was the very last time I sought out the company of any rock-'n'-roll stars whatsoever, the very last time until...

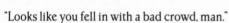

"Looks like you fell in with a bad crowd, man."

Huh? Hoodat said dat?

Jerry Garcia, that's who; Jerry Garcia wading through the jackstrewn corpses carpeting the floor wall to wall, Jerry Garcia grinning down at me, his face swimming slowly into focus, his hairy aspect droll, almost elfin, Jerry Garcia reaching for the guitar case he'd stashed behind my chair about seven centuries ago when this night was young and so was I. All of which means, lemme see now, all of which means...

Son of a bitch, it's *over!* Three sets, three whole sets of the Sweetest Sound this Side of Pandemonium, five solid hours I've been cuddled up back here in icy congress with a cold tank while out front the Dead were raising a rumpus loud enough to wake the Living and set a multitude to boogalooing, and I've scarcely heard a sound all evening long, save the nitrous oxide whistling through the empty chambers of my mind...I mean great *Scott*, Front Page, you've got a *story* to write, fella, you can't be loafin' around back here on your dead ass when...

Prodded at last by my long-dormant conscience, goosed by good intentions, eyeballs bulging maniacally with the effort to Pull Myself Together, I am halfway to my feet when Jerry, who by now has retrieved his guitar case and made his way back to the door, turns and halts me with an upraised hand.

"What's your hurry?" he says, still grinning. "The tank's not empty yet, is it?"

I blink as this highly relevant bit of intelligence illuminates my socked-in consciousness, and when I look again Jerry is gone, vanished like the Cheshire cat, leaving just the memory of his grin hanging in mid-air to mark his passing. And the next thing I know I'm back in my chair, and somehow the hose is rising magically, like a fakir's cobra, from the writhing turmoil on the floor to meet my outstretched hand, and I am thinking, "Yeah, right, just another l'il toke or two for the road, and then I'll get a good night's sleep so I can come back tomorrow night all primed and cocked to..."

"An Evening with the Grateful Dead," Fillmore West, first set: the Acoustic Dead lead off, Bill the Drummer and the three guitars (all acoustic, no electronic augmentation) and Pig, his electric organ temporarily supplanted by an old upright piano—they open w. "Cumberland Blues," much fine bluegrassy gittar pickin', good downhome lyrix like "a lotta po'man got de cumberlan' bloooze / he cain't win for looo-zin'"—sounds like it came straight out of Appalachia (didn't tho; Hunter wrote it)—Jerry sings it *just* rite, his husky tenor a power-thru-gentleness sort of trip, almost unnaturally soft but with a kind of lilting gulp that makes me think of Lefty Frizzell or the way Hank Williams sings "Honky Tonk Blues"—JG's voice's sweetness belies its tuffness and is in perfect counterpoint to the uncompromising pessimism of Hunter's lyrix—seems to me the Dead are carrying their years in this meatgrinder racket really well, aging gracefully—Bobby Weir *still* has the face of a debauched Renaissance choirboy, beautifully modeled features, there are moments when he looks like a dissolute twelve-yr-old—when he does backup vocals for JG (or solo, as on "Truckin'" and several others) he sings in a voice not quite his own, the kind of voice that skims across the top of the glottis and comes out sounding like it never plumbed the depths of the throat at all—Pig's piano has that fine country-honkie-gospel kind of plinking barrelhouse gait that's perfect for the back-to-the-roots thing the Dead are into these days—Pig has somehow shed fifty, maybe seventy-five pounds in the five years since that night at Ben's Big Beat, and now stands revealed as what he was all the time beneath that S. Clay Wilson-ogreish exterior, a fierce-looking *little* guy in cowboy funk, boots and low-slung Levis and oily leather sheepherder's coat, a battered Stetson with its rolled brim cocked so low over his eyes that his tough, pinched little face is barely visible above his scraggly goatee, Gabby Hayes with teeth—Phil Lesh almost never surfaces in the group but is always working behind everybody else, providing substance on bass, fleshing out vocals, clowning, goofing around with little hippy-dippy mouth-breather mugging trips, he looks to be the loosest of them all onstage—Bill Kreutz- mann is darkly handsome, dour, brooding, solemn, looks "deep" and plays the same way, hunches possessively over his traps and seems almost to lose him- self in his own rumbling-hoof-beats-in-the-middle-distance rhythms—he is *never* flashy; his drumming is as steady as the drone of a tamboura, a fixed point around which the guitars work their airy filigrees; tonight's the first time the Dead have tried a strictly acoustic set on the Fillmore audience, and when "Cumberland Blues" is over, a scattering of old-line Dead fans, missing the electronically amplified bedlam of yesteryear, holler "Play louder! Play louder!"—but Jerry, smiling beatifically, steps to the mike and cools them out by explaining, very gently, "No, no, man, you don't understand, this is the part where we play *soft*, and you *listen* loud!"—then they do "New Speedway Boo- gie", "Dire Wolf (Don't Murder Me)," "Candyman" and two or three others, mostly from the *Workingman's Dead* album, then finish off the set with a rev- erently beautiful and altogether decorous rendition of that All-Time Number- One Sike-O-Deelik Space-Music Golden Oldie, "Swing Low Sweet Chariot," everybody *loves* it, crowd really gets off behind it—a fine rousing set, looks like a *good* night.

"I just play the way I play; I play what I like to hear. I don't really think about guitar players anymore, I think about music; I like music, you know what I mean? When I buy records, I don't buy guitar players, I buy...music. Because all those guys, they're just learning to play the guitar, just like I am, and I don't listen to them much, because that'd be like learning from me. You know? They've derived all their shit from the same shit I've derived all my shit from. No, I listen to the real shit if I'm lookin' for ideas musically, guitarwise and so forth; I go to the masters, not to the other students. Like Django Reinhardt or B.B. King, you know, guys who really play. But the main thing is that I play music because I love music, you know, and all my life I've loved music, and I've gotten more and more into lookin' at the whole overall thing. And that's where I am now, doin' that."

Altamont is but one dark moment in the community's *total* experience, the first installment of the dues that we must pay for our deliverance. On the Big Trip, the poet warns, the pilgrims will encounter suffering as well as joy, and those who have no heart for the undertaking would do well to stand aside, because "this train's got to run today." The song's thrice-repeated refrain, "Spent a little time on the mountain, / Spent a little time on the hill," bespeaks the poet's (or, if you will, the singer's) modest claim to have made a private, careful consideration, *hors de combat*, of the enlightened person's obligation in a time of public turmoil;* in fact, we *must* seek guidance within ourselves, since public advice—"Heard some say: *better run away* / Others say: *better stand still*"—is likely to be hysterical and paralyzingly contradictory. And in the next quatrain that contradiction blooms into a full-blown paradox:

> Now I don't know but I been told
> it's hard to run with the weight of gold
> Other hand I heard it said
> it's just as hard with the weight of lead

Metaphorically, these lines describe and define the two equally seduc-tive—and equally treacherous—temptations that beguile the truth-seeker, the Scylla and Charybdis between which he must thread his perilous course: on the one hand, Fortune, represented at Altamont in the opulent persons of the Stones, seen here as listing dangerously beneath the "weight of gold"; and on the other, Violence, the way of the Angels, burdened as they are with chains and helmets and Iron Crosses and all their weaponry, that hardware of their sullen calling. Then too, of course, there is the more literal reading of the pas-sage, in which the relative subtlety of the metaphor is overridden by the omi-nous, code-of-the-West caveat to the effect that he who is so foolish as to make off with his brothers' gold may end up carrying their hot lead as well, cut down by the heavy-handed irony of a Fate which any admirer of *The Treasure of Sierra Madre* could have warned him of right from the start.

Nor may we shrug off the events at Altamont as harbingers of a mere "change in style"; rather, the minstrel contends, the change is *substantive*, and the death of Meredith Hunter signals that when the pilgrimage arrived at Altamont it entered new and hostile territory, the twilight of its own dark night of the soul. Yet "one step done and another begun," and so the song, even as it grieves one emblematic death and dreads the miles and trials ahead, directs us to turn our eyes to the changes yet to come. For, the next verse reminds us, "Things went down we don't understand / But I think in time we

---

* A very literal interpretation of the refrain might also make reference to the fact that the Dead, scheduled to go on after the Stones, never actually played that day; thus they had ample opportu-nity to climb "the hill" overlooking the scene and see for themselves that things were indeed "gettin' out of hand."

will"—that is, however weary we are of mistakes and wrong turns and, most of all, of the terrible burden of our desperate longing for the destination, we can only comprehend the meaning of present events—and of the judgments they pass—from the perspective of the next change.

And now, with the following quatrain—

Now I don't know but I been told
in the heat of the sun a man died of cold
Do we keep on coming or stand and wait
with the sun so dark and the hour so late?

—an almost *literal* shadow sweeps across the trackless yellow landscape of the song, the specter of some nameless thing so unspeakably awful that its very shadow casts a deadly chill, a pall from which no escape is possible, no matter whether we "keep on comin' or stand and wait." It is, of course, the specter of our own inhumanity, our selfishness, our passionless indifference, and now at last the lesson of the song—and of Altamont—is clear: the Angels are the dark aspect of ourselves, reflections of the beast that skulks behind our eyes; we created them as surely as we created the Rolling Stones, fashioned them all of the mute clay of our need for Heroes and Villains as surely as we created Altamont itself that fateful day. Thus we can no more excise the bloody-handed Angels from our midst than we can cut away some vital part of our own psyche, lobotomize ourselves.

Nonetheless, that hard lesson learned the hard way, our course remains set, fixed by the iron resolve of destiny, and there can be no turning back; we can only face up to "the lack.../ of any other highway to ride," and as R. Crumb puts in, "keep on truckin'." True, we travel this treacherous road at our own risk; but...

BOB WEIR: "If you want something for nothing, go jerk off."

Among the habitués of the performers' lounge backstage at the Fillmore is this tall, rangy, loose-limbed, spacy-looking young freak—the Sunnyvale Express, they call him—who, during the breaks, is never far from Jerry Garcia's circle of friends and admirers, usually toying idly with a guitar, just noodling, picking out disconnected phrases and fragments to underscore whatever conversation is going on around him, nothing special, here a bit of bluegrass, there a snippet of flamenco or a rock riff or what have you, anything at all, apparently, that comes to mind. It's obvious he's a Garcia fan, but there is about him none of that earnest innocence and humility that can do so much toward making even us hero worshippers a tolerable lot; rather, the Sunnyvale Express's whole bearing and manner bespeak the languid arrogance of a coxcomb, and a couple of times I've spotted him eyeing Jerry with a look of ill-disguised envy.

He is here again tonight with his old lady, an impossibly beautiful but otherworldly looking redhead named (brace yourself) the Burning Bush, who paints her eyelids dead black like Theda Bara and wears antique crushed-velvet vamp costumes, the two of them lounging in an old threadbare armchair near the couch where Jerry sits talking animatedly to a rock-magazine interviewer. As I cross the big room toward them, the Sunnyvale Express disentangles himself from the Burning Bush, rises slowly from his chair, takes up his guitar, props one foot on the arm of Jerry's couch and announces, in a voice as somnolent with dope as a sleepwalker's, "Now I'm 'onna play jus' like ole G'cia, here."

And with that he launches into what has to be accounted, at least on the face of it, one of the most dazzling virtuoso performances I've ever heard, clawing great fistfuls of sound off the bass strings even as he picks the high notes off with blinding music-box precision and delicacy, playing, as far as I can determine, no particular song but rather a kind of collage, a mosaic—all right, a *medley*, then—of those staccato riffs that are almost a Garcia signature, not chords but swift, rushing runs of single bass notes in which each note is sonorously deep yet somehow clear, sharp, *bright*, never murky or muddy. Closing my eyes, I can at first almost make myself believe it is Jerry himself who is swathing my mind like a swami's turbaned head in layer upon layer of silken sound, but after a minute or so I begin to sense that for all its resonant vibrancy, the Sunnyvale Express's playing desperately wants the quality that Jerry's is richest in—call it density or warmth or even, if you must, soul—and the only ingredient the Express can replace it with is a sour mix of envy and insolence and sullen mockery. His playing is technically perfect but as devoid of human feeling for the music as a player piano tinkling away on an empty stage; one whose prime interest was in listening to the real thing had as well attend a concert featuring Sammy Davis, Jr., playing "Danny Boy" on the Jew's harp.

So it is no surprise to discover, when I look again, that the same old Sunnyvale Express is playing still. Just behind him, leaning forward in her chair, sits the Burning Bush, her dark-ringed eyes glazed with rapture, her right hand lost to the wrist between her lover's parted thighs, cupping and fondling his crotch in the upturned palm. And around them, on the couch and in the other chairs, Jerry and his friends sit listening and watching, their faces stonily impassive. When, after he's played for maybe five minutes or so, the Express senses at last the chilly indifference with which his efforts are being received, he abruptly stops playing, favors his implacable audience with an elaborately phlegmatic shrug and turns and drifts off toward the far end of the room, the Burning Bush floating along beside him, her busy hand now wandering aimlessly, crablike, across his narrow rump.

"Whew, that guy," says Jerry wearily, rising to go out front for his set with the New Riders. "He's like my own personal psychic bedbug." Then, brightening, he adds, "But you know, I *need* guys like him around, everybody does. I mean, they keep us honest, you know what I mean?"

PHIL LESH: The Grateful Dead are trying to save the world.

"I don't think of music as a craft, see. Like, when I'm writing songs, I don't sit down and assemble stuff. Because music to me is more of a flash than a craft, so that somethin' comes to me and that's the thing I'll bother to isolate, you know, the stuff that nudges its way out of the subconscious and you sorta go, 'Oh!' and suddenly there's a whole melody in your head. And it happens just often enough to seem like a, you know, like a flow. I mean I recognize the mechanism; I know what it is as opposed to everything else. And that ends up to be the stuff I can live with a long time, and that's a thing I think about a lot, too."

So here we are, me and ole Wheat Germ, smack in the middle of your typical sunny Sunday afternoon in a small, semirural suburb in upper Marin County, and well under way is your typical softball game in your typical small-town municipal ball park: chicken-wire backstop, rickety wooden bleachers along both base lines, scrofulously barren infield, shaggy outfield— in short your regulation government-issue I-see-Amurrica-playing scene as it

is enacted every summer Sunday not just here in Marin County but from sea
to shining sea, lots of good cold beer and good fellowship and good-natured
umpire baiting...and here today among these particular devotees of the
national pastime, an abundance of good vibes and good karma and the
world's own amount of goooooood dope.

Because the curiously coiffed fifty or sixty fans in the stands here today
are not your common, ordinary, garden-variety bleacherites, those dulcet-
toned, undershirted cigar chompers and their frumpy Cowbell Annies who
customarily attend to the umpire baiting on these occasions. Such under-
shirts are in evidence this afternoon are brilliantly tie-dyed, and the ladies in
the crowd, for all their electrified bride-of-Frankenstein hairdos, are almost
unanimously pretty, not a frump in sight. No more do those improbably
befurred gents manning their posts upon the field of combat bear more than
a passing resemblance to the Mudville Nine's anonymous opponents, nor is
that the Mighty Casey at the bat.

No, sports fans, the awful truth (may J.G. Taylor Spink, up there in the
Great Press Box in the Sky, be spared it!) is that the freaks afield are Jefferson
Airplanes to a man; and the big-wigged fellow who just struck out, the one
who looks like John the Baptist, that's Jerry Garcia, guitarist extraordinaire
but a banjo hitter if ever there was one. And the umpire just now being baited,
that scowly little dude with the scraggly chin whiskers and the red-white-and-
blue backwards baseball cap, is either Augie Donatelli or Pigpen McKernan,
choose one.

So far, seen as I am seeing it through the blue haze of all those joints that
keep coming my way, it's been a genuine pisscutter of a ball game—which
appraisal has, as the Great Scorer is reputed to have written, naught to do
with who's winning (the Airplane, by about eleven to about six, nobody seems
to know exactly) or losing, but solely with How They're Playing the Game. For
if the Great Scorer ever looked in on this contest, He'd probably take His ball
and go home; because these weirdos are simply having much more fun than
this moldy old sport was ever intended to provide. Most of them play like the
guys who always made the second string in high school but never actually got
in a game: lotsa hustle, lotsa chatter on the benches and base paths, no end of
hot-pepper razzle-dazzle when they're chucking the old pill around the
infield, but complete and utter panic when they somehow get themselves
involved in an actual honest-to-God *play*. The Airplane, for instance, has a
beautiful, big-bearded guy wearing bib overalls in the outfield who circles
frantically under pop flies like a man with one leg shorter than the other hollering "Me! Me! Me!" and waving his arms as though besieged by a swarm of
bees, but who, to my admittedly none-too-reliable recollection, has yet to lay a

glove on the ball. And Jerry Garcia cavorts very impressively around the Dead's hot corner until he sees the ball headed in his direction, at which point he instantly goes into such gleeful paroxysms of excitement that he can't possibly execute the play.

What they lack in skill, though, they more than make up for in élan, jawing at Pig and guzzling beer in the on-deck circle and squawking "Whaddaya waitin' for—*Christmas?*" at batters who don't choose to swing at every pitch within bat's length of the plate. So that when, along about the fifth inning, Mickey Hart, sometime second drummer for the Dead, bounces one out of the park over the low fence in deep left field, and a furious hassle ensues along the third-base line over whether or not Pig should have ruled it a ground-rule double instead of a homer—both teams storming up and down the base paths and gesticulating wildly and turning the air yet another shade of blue with good old-fashioned cussing plain and fancy—one understands immediately that behind all their histrionics, the players are taking enormous delight in burlesquing these hoary old rituals, and at the same time one senses, too, that behind *that* is profound and abiding respect—*reverence*, even—for the very traditions they are pretending to make light of. Which in turn goes a long way toward explaining how it is that the Dead, who not long ago were plunging ever deeper into the howling wilderness of electronic exoticism, are now working almost exclusively within the relatively strict, fundamental forms of stay-at-home country music and blues. It may even help explain why Mickey Hart, after he has negotiated the knot of wrangling dialecticians around Pigpen and tagged the plate, trots directly over to where I'm sitting with my ubiquitous notebook spread upon my knee and says, grinning proudly, "Listen, man, I don't give a shit what you write about my drummin', but you be *sure* and put that fuckin' homer in, OK?"

Anyhow, all those heady speculations aside, there remains one more disconcerting little distinction between today's contest and your run-of-the-mill Sunday softball game—to wit: that unwashed young chap over there, furtively but eagerly proffering first this freak, then that, something or other from the small round tin he's palming, is no peanut vendor. As a matter of embarrassing fact, he's none other than the noted Wheat Germ, my very own millionaire millstone, and judging from the withering scowls his attempts to peddle his wares have been drawing all afternoon, business is bad, exceeding bad. Evidently the Dead's and the Airplane's respective rooting sections prefer their tradesmen to come on—if at all—considerably cooler than Wheat Germ, who, his self-advertised six million dollars' worth of experience in these affairs notwithstanding, has already forgotten the cardinal precept of his chosen profession: *Nobody* loves a pushy pusher. Poor old Wheat Germ; even from where I sit, in the bleachers down near third, it's apparent that he's trying way too hard, buttonholing fans while they're trying to watch Paul Kantner strike out Jerry Garcia, spraying them with the humid spindrift of his enthusiasm, generally conducting himself in a manner likely to get him a reprimand from the Dealers Association's Ethical Practices Committee if the word gets around.

Which is all the same to me, actually, except that as I ponder the obdurate sales resistance his cheapjack wheedling seems to be eliciting in the market place, it begins to occur to me that it just might not be in my best interest to associate myself too closely with this pariah in the present company. After all, despite the unarguable fact that it was my vainglorious boasting of Connections in High Places that brought him here in the first place—thereby making Wheat Germ in a sense the corporeal embodiment of my vanity, my alter ego incarnate—Oh, Christ, here he comes now, heading straight for me, wearing the rueful hangdog look of a man who's just suffered putdown upon putdown; everybody'll see that he's with me and I'll never get within hollerin' distance of the Dead again and...it positively *behooves* me to maintain at all costs my credibility in the eyes of these subjects of my report to my vast readership; one might almost say I owe it to my public to cook this albatross's goose somehow, to sneak away from him or pretend I don't know him or offer to drive him to the bus station or...

We need guys like him; they keep us honest. Jerry Garcia's own true words echoing up from some lost recess of my memory, and even as I hear them, I hear, too, my own voice saying, aloud and straining to convey the heartiness I'm trying hard to feel, yet in a kind of secret harmony with Jerry's words, "Hey listen, Wheat Germ, the New Riders are playin' at the Family Dog tonight, and I've got an extra ticket. You want to come along?"

And as his snaggle-toothed grin chases the despair from Wheat Germ's unlovely countenance, I am smote by yet another Cosmic Axiom, this one more or less of my own making: One man's pain in the ass is the next man's psychic bedbug. Dig it, dad, you never know when you might need one.

⚡   ⚡   ⚡

PIGPEN: Hey, Magazine, y'wanna know the secret of m' success?
ME (eagerly): Yeah, sure, hell yes!
PIG (*growling sotto voce behind his hand, mock furtive as a Disneyland Foxy Loxy*): Take 35 percent off the top and *split*!

⚡   ⚡   ⚡

"*Well, I think the Grateful Dead is basically, like, a good, snappy rock-'n'-roll band. I mean, that's its basic character. So when we do country stuff, for instance, people sometimes tend to think we've suddenly gotten very pure, very direct. But we don't actually do it very purely or directly at all, compared to, like, Roy Acuff, say. And if we're talking about country music, we have to compare it to those kind of guys. I mean, when we play it, it's still us.*"

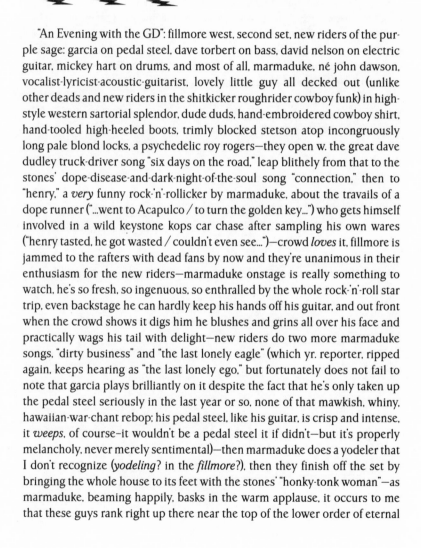

"An Evening with the GD": fillmore west, second set, new riders of the purple sage: garcia on pedal steel, dave torbert on bass, david nelson on electric guitar, mickey hart on drums, and most of all, marmaduke, né john dawson, vocalist-lyricist-acoustic-guitarist, lovely little guy all decked out (unlike other deads and new riders in the shitkicker roughrider cowboy funk) in high-style western sartorial splendor, dude duds, hand-embroidered cowboy shirt, hand-tooled high-heeled boots, trimly blocked stetson atop incongruously long pale blond locks, a psychedelic roy rogers—they open w. the great dave dudley truck-driver song "six days on the road," leap blithely from that to the stones' dope-disease-and-dark-night-of-the-soul song "connection," then to "henry," a *very* funny rock-'n'-rollicker by marmaduke, about the travails of a dope runner ("...went to Acapulco / to turn the golden key...") who gets himself involved in a wild keystone kops car chase after sampling his own wares ("henry tasted, he got wasted / couldn't even see...")—crowd *loves* it, fillmore is jammed to the rafters with dead fans by now and they're unanimous in their enthusiasm for the new riders—marmaduke onstage is really something to watch, he's so fresh, so ingenuous, so enthralled by the whole rock-'n'-roll star trip, even backstage he can hardly keep his hands off his guitar, and out front when the crowd shows it digs him he blushes and grins all over his face and practically wags his tail with delight—new riders do two more marmaduke songs, "dirty business" and "the last lonely eagle" (which yr. reporter, ripped again, keeps hearing as "the last lonely ego," but fortunately does not fail to note that garcia plays brilliantly on it despite the fact that he's only taken up the pedal steel seriously in the last year or so, none of that mawkish, whiny, hawaiian-war-chant rebop; his pedal steel, like his guitar, is crisp and intense, it *weeps*, of course–it wouldn't be a pedal steel it if didn't—but it's properly melancholy, never merely sentimental)—then marmaduke does a yodeler that I don't recognize (*yodeling*? in the *fillmore*?), then they finish off the set by bringing the whole house to its feet with the stones' "honky-tonk woman"—as marmaduke, beaming happily, basks in the warm applause, it occurs to me that these guys rank right up there near the top of the lower order of eternal

verities: rock-'n'-roll stars may come and go, but there'll *always* be the Sons of
the Pioneers.

Backstage again and I've retreated to the remotest corner of the lounge to
work for a few minutes on my notes on the New Riders' set. I'm just getting
fairly deep into it when I begin to feel that creeping uneasiness that signals
another presence, close at hand and watching me intently. I lift my eyes reluctantly from my notebook and find myself face to face with a small child, just a
toddler, a little boy about a year old, standing there right next to the arm of my
chair, his wide blue eyes fixed on my moving ballpoint. He has rust-red hair,
brushed nearly flat, and a round, fair face upon which has settled an expression as solemn as a judge's. And he very definitely does *not*, let it be said here
and now for reasons that will momentarily become apparent, resemble Jerry
Garcia in any way, shape or form.

"Hi, sport," I greet the boy, offering him the pen. "You wanta write something?"

"Oh, Lord, baby, don't go bothering people that way, sweetheart. Is he bothering you?"

The mother, presumably: a tall, slender blonde, very pretty in a sort of pale,
bloodless way, oddly brittle-looking somehow, a china figurine off some Vic-
torian parlor's whatnot shelf, or perhaps, with her plaid wool skirt and cardi-
gan sweater and plastic barrettes and silk stockings and penny loafers,
Andrew Wyeth's Kristina. She seems, in every sense that the phrase can con-
jure, out of time.

"No, he's fine," I reassured her, flipping a page in my notebook for the boy
to leave his mark on. "Let him write; he probably understands it all better than
I do, anyhow."

"Are you writing something about the band?" she asks. I own up to it and
name the magazine I'm doing it for. "Oh," she says, "that's very interesting.
Because Jerry Garcia, well, he's, you know," she rolls her eyes significantly
toward the kid, who by now is assiduously inscribing his hieroglyphic autograph in my notebook, "he's little Jerry's father."

Uh, beg pardon, ma'am, but heh-heh, I could've *sworn* you said...

"His true father, I mean. He's his true father."

My first flash is to those two lines from Jerry's song "Friend of the Devil,"
the ones that go "Got a wife in Chino, babe / And one in Cherokee..." But then
I cop another quick peek at the weanling at my knee, with his sober delft-blue

eyes and that red hair, and instantly the next lines of the song come to mind: "First one say she got my child, / But it don't look like me." Which is to say either that the girl is some kind of shakedown artist or that she is, as the quaint old phrase so delicately had it, bereft of reason. Because if this kid is Jerry Garcia's offspring, then I am Walter Winchell.

"And you know what?" she hurries on. "I came all the way out here from Stockton on the Greyhound, just so he could see little Jerry, and I paid my way in tonight just like everybody else, and I talked the door guy into letting me come backstage and *everything*, and then when I said hi to Jerry and held up the baby to him and all, he acted like, you know, like he didn't even *know* us. Which I just don't understand what's *wrong*. I mean, I sure hope it's not because of something I've, you know, *done* or anything..."

True father indeed. But this time I can plainly hear, through the rush of words, the faint rattle of hysteria that bespeaks a screw loose somewhere.

"I just hope he's not, you know, *mad* at me or something," she adds, bending to scoop up little Jerry and clutch him defensively to her breast, as if to demonstrate that nothing in the living world terrifies her quite as much as the thought of Jerry Garcia in a snit. "Because I certainly don't know what I could've, you know, *done*..."

My pen slips from little Jerry's moist grasp and clatters to the floor. Rising to retrieve it, I offer her what meager reassurance I can muster. "I wouldn't worry too much if I were you," I tell her lamely. "Jerry's pretty busy these days. He probably just didn't..."

"I mean, we're *very close*, me and Jerry are. Like, you take the last time I saw him, last April I think it was, why, I just walked right up to him, right on the street outside this building, and said, you know, 'Hi!' And he said Hi back and *smiled* and sort of patted the baby on the *head* and *everything*. And that's why I'm afraid he must be mad about something. Because this time he just, you now, walked right on by like he didn't even *see* us!"

The girl is beginning now to look as distraught as she sounds; her cheeks are flushed and several strands of hair have pulled loose from the barrettes to dangle limply at her temples, and her pale eyes well with tears. She is, as they say, Going All to Pieces, and as her fragile composure shatters I can read in the crazed web of striations a case history of her delusion that if not altogether accurate in every detail, will answer almost as well as if it were:

Two years ago she was a carhop in a Stockton A&W root-beer stand, and that night, summer before last, when she got herself knocked up, the red-headed Stockton College dairy-and-animal-husbandry major who took her and two six-packs out on the levee in his Mustang played the Grateful Dead on his eight-track stereo while he pumped drunkenly atop her in the back seat, and she heard, in midzygote as it were, not the redhead's sodden grunting but a true dream lover's voice, his honeyed lips just at her ear whispering what somehow seemed—even though she didn't exactly, you know, *understand* it—the sweetest, tenderest, loveliest thing anybody had ever said to her, ever in her life:

> "Lady finger, dipped in moonlight,
> Writing 'What for?' across the morning sky..."

Jerry Garcia, of course, ready, as always, with the right word at the right moment. And since from that night forward she never once saw or heard from the redheaded dairy-and-animal-husbandry major ever again, whereas she could hear from Jerry Garcia any time she wanted to, merely by playing a Grateful Dead album on the $29.95 Victor portable stereo she'd bought on sale at the discount store with her first week's wages from the root-beer stand, we-e-e-lll...

"I mean," she whimpers wretchedly, "we don't *want* nothing from him, not one thing. But you'd think he could've at least reckanized his own flesh, and, you know, *blood*..."

Well, it occurs to me to observe, there are an awful lot of people around here tonight, most likely he really *didn't* see you. But then it also occurs to me that she is already quite clear on that technicality and that as far as she is concerned, it's altogether beside the point; according to her lights, a man is *obliged* to see and recognize the fruit of his own loins in *any* crowd, he *is*.

And anyhow, before I can utter the first word, the girl suddenly squeaks, "Oooo! There he *is!*" and takes off for the other end of the room, leaving me standing there dumfounded in a leftover cloud of her tooty-frooty dime-store perfume, still biting the air and trying to think of something to say. She is headed, as you might expect, for Jerry Garcia himself, who stands at the far end of the lounge talking to Pigpen and Phil Lesh and Zonk the Gasman's handsome wife Candace and Bob Weir's beautiful, Garboesque girlfriend, Frankie; and as she makes for them, I see, over her shoulder, those great blue eyes of little Jerry's gazing back at me, grave as a lemur's stare.

The girl marches resolutely up to Jerry and thrusts the baby at him and announces herself—I can't hear what she says, but it's doubtless some such commonplace pleasantry as "Allow me to present your own flesh and, you know, *blood*—" And Jerry looks at her with an expression so blankly devoid of recognition that for an instant I'm afraid some hideous little slice-of-life drama is about to happen, that any second now she's going to whip out a .44 and start blazing away at Jerry or herself or Candace and Frankie or whomever a lady in her frame of mind might settle on as a fit target for her ire.

But when at last Jerry's countenance lights up with that fabled beatific smile and he says hello or whatever and bends to peer closely at the baby, then at her, and, still smiling, shakes his head, there is even in his denial of them such a palpable quantity of gentleness and generosity that she is utterly disarmed and undone. She blushes and shies and smiles back at him, and after a moment she shoulders the baby once more and goes on out, restored, into the main ballroom. As the door closes after her, Jerry turns back to the others and delivers himself of one of those exaggerated, palms-upturned, beats-the-hell-out-of-*me* shrugs, and that's it, it's over, good karma has triumphed once more over bad, and playing lead guitar for the Grateful Dead is still quite as safe a calling as, say, being Eddie Wakefield and playing first base for the Philadelphia Phils in 1949.

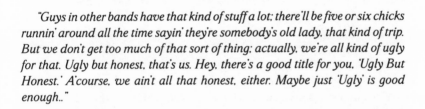

"Guys in other bands have that kind of stuff a lot; there'll be five or six chicks runnin' around all the time sayin' they're somebody's old lady, that kind of trip. But we don't get too much of that sort of thing; actually, we're all kind of ugly for that. Ugly but honest, that's us. Hey, there's a good title for you, 'Ugly But Honest.' A'course, we ain't all that honest, either. Maybe just 'Ugly' is good enough.."

"an evening with the gd," fillmore, third set, full complement dead (garcia, weir, lesh, pig, kreutzmann, hart), full electronic amplification—they open w. "dancing in the streets," a motown-style rocker, follow that w. merle haggard's tender honky tearjerker "mama tried," then "it's a man's world," with pig doing a very creditable james-brown-in-whiteface, then buddy holly's "not fade away," working through their repertory the way a painter might put together a retrospective, displaying their influences, putting the audience through the same changes the dead themselves have been subject to—it is eclecticism in its very best and highest sense, and the audience, already thoroughly jacked up by the first two sets, is flashing strongly to it—the upturned faces near the stage, awash with the splashover of swirling colors from the light show, seem to glow with enthusiasm and delight, and each time the band takes up a different song there arises from out there in the dark a wild chorus of voices, dozens of them from even the farthest corners of the hall, whooping and howling and yipping like coyotes baying at the moon, aa-ooo-aa-ooo-aaaa-ooooo, a savage, animal, tribal thing one knows instinctively they do *only* for the dead, in *honor* of the dead—a christian missionary would get gobbled up in seconds in such a scene as this—now bob weir, looking like a full-color, slick-paper idealization of billy the kid on a dime-mag cover, sings "truckin'," hunter's leisurely, laid-back ramble about the vicissitudes of life on the road with the dead ("busted / down on bourbon street / set up / like a bowlin' pin..."), puts me in mind of those old-timey toddlin' tunes like "side by side," only with more substance, gene kelly and donald o'connor with soul—they follow that with two more hunter songs, "uncle john's band" and "casey jones," and by the time casey ("drivin' that train / high on cocaine..."), is highballing down the track toward that fateful encounter with train 102, the crowd is on its feet and chugging up and down, it *is* the train, a great joyous surging mass of energy hurtling headlong into the uncharted darkness of the future—and it doesn't stop when the song ends but charges right on into "love light" with just the scantest pause to catch its breath, pig taking the throttle now, strutting around onstage with his tambourine whirring in his hand and his hat cocked low and mean, *dangerous*, snarling and fierce ("i don' want it all! / i jes wanna leetle bit!"), his exhortations as raw and lewd and laden with insinuation as a carnival kootch-show pitchman's hype ("git yo' hands outta yo' pockets and turn on yo' *love* light!"), and every now and then i seem to hear a line of such brazen unbounded lickerishness ("dew *yew* lak ta fu-u-u-uckkkk?") that i start and blink and wonder did he really *say* that?—and the whole thing builds and builds, ten minutes, fifteen, twenty, and now the audience is clapping to keep time, they have joined the dead en masse as one enormous synchronized syncopated single-minded rhythm section, taking up the beat from bill the drummer's tom-tom and making it their own, insisting on it, demanding it, and the dead are delightedly handing it over to them, one by one laying down guitars and drumsticks and leaving the center of the stage to pig and jerry, first weir, then hart and lesh, then even bill the drummer, leaving their posts to join the crew of groupies and quippies and buddies and wives and old ladies at the rear of the stage back against the light-show screen among the throbbing blobs, greeting friends and accepting tokes on whatever gets passed their way, beer or joints or coke or ripple, and just jerry and pig and the audience are left to mind the music, jerry's guitar weaving incredible intricacies in front of the rhythmic whipcrack of applause, pig chanting his unholy litany ("...so come awn bay-beh, baby please, / i'm beggin' ya bay-beh, and i'm on my knees...") like a man possessed by a whole mob of randy, rampant demons, and now jerry too puts down his guitar and leaves, and it's just pig up there along with his tambourine and his snarl ("...turn on yo' *light*, all i *need*...") and his three-thousand-member rhythm section keeping time, *keeping* time, i've never before considered ("... huh!...") what that expression really means, the crowd has undertaken to tend and cherish the beat until the band comes back ("...i jus' got to *git* sum, it's all i *need*...") and resumes its stewardship, the whole arrangement amounts to a very special kind of trust, we are ("...huh!...") not just audience but keepers of the flame, we are *of* the grateful dead, *with* them ("...got ta keep pooshin', all i *need*...") and *for* them and *of* them...

BLAM!

It's the crack of doom or the first shot of the revolution or, anyhow, a cherry bomb that Pig has somehow set off just at his feet. A cloud of dense gray smoke still boils up around him; no longer any doubt about it, he is plainly a satanic manifestation. And without my noticing them, the other Dead have stolen back to their places and taken up their instruments, and at the signal of the cherry bomb the song blasts into life again, the decibel count is astronomical, the crowd is shrieking in one hysterically ecstatic voice and the volume of the music is so great it swallows up the very shriek itself; by a single diabolic stroke, a multitude of three thousand strong has suddenly been struck dumb. The din is enough to wake even the moldering spirits of those moribund old poots who once set myriad toes a-tapping in the hallowed hall. I can almost see them now: Vaughn Monroe and Wayne King the Waltz King and Clyde McCoy and Ginny Sims and the Ink Spots and Frankie Yankovic and Ralph Flanagan and the Hilltoppers and Kay Kyser and His Kollege of Musical Knowledge and Horace Heidt and His Musical Knights...a whole host of phantoms, troupers to the last, crawling out of this old wormy woodwork and rising up from the rankest, dankest depths of the memory of man to join the living Dead for one last encore. Just *listen* to the racket. Bill the Drummer's heavy artillery is pounding at my temples and Mickey Hart is laying into his four great shimmering gongs until the pandemonium itself is all atremble with their clangor and my back teeth taste of brass, and Lesh and Weir are ripping furiously at the faces of their guitars, and the crowd is screaming as if that enormous palpitating blood-red blob of light behind the band were the flaming dawn of doomsday, and Jerry's guitar is winding out a shrill silvery coil of sound that spirals up and up and up until, whining like a brain surgeon's drill, it bores straight through the skull and sinks its spinning shaft into the very quick of my mind, and Pig, a rag doll buffeted by hot blasts of ecstasy gusting up from three thousand burning throats, flings himself into a

demented little St. Vitus' dance of demonic glee and howls the kamikaze cry
of one who is plunging headlong into the void, the last word beyond which *all*
sound is rendered meaningless as silence...
YEEEEEEEE-

O-O-O-O-OOWWWWWWWWW!

True, we travel this treacherous road at our own risk; but could we ever
have supposed it might prove otherwise? And if the absence of "signs" and
"dividin' lines" and "rules to guide" guarantees a hazardous journey, it also
promises times when this heaven-bound ride is indescribably wild and sweet
and free: things *will* get "out of hand"—"*always*"—but even that inevitability
has its compensations, so long as we are among friends.

Still and all, "if the horse don't pull you got to carry the load"—that is, if the
communal vehicle and the full power of the community's combined energies
will not bear one safely through, then the whole burden of care and growth
must rest upon oneself. And, the minstrel cautions, it may well be that none of
us is capable of that effort, that the whole enormous enterprise will come to
nothing. But this is a time of testing, of pitting our strength against all the
forces that oppress us—our guilt and our despair, our selfishness, our failures
and our fear of failure—for, "one way or another," relief *must* come, these
gloomy times *must* pass, the darkness *will* give.

This "New Speedway Boogie" is at once a sober—if highly subjective—
study of a violently traumatic moment in the course of human events, a desperate prayer for deliverance, and a hymn of hope. And when those final
fervent lines—

One way or another
One way or another
One way or another
this darkness got to give

—come echoing and reechoing down like "Excelsior!" from the heights, it
also becomes an anthem quite as stirring, in its own somber, introspective
way, as "Onward Christian Soldiers."

"*When I talk about musicians, I'm talkin' about people who make music, not
just people who are technically perfect. Music bein' That Thing Which Gets You*

Off, I mean that's just my definition of that word. And when you're playin', and really Gettin' Off that way, it's like when you're drivin' down a road past an orchard, you know, and you look out and at first all you can see is just another woods, a bunch of trees all jumbled up together, like there's no form to it; it's chaos. But then you come up to a certain point and suddenly—zing! zing! zing!—there it is, the order, the trees all lined up perfectly no matter which way you look, so you can see the real shape of the orchard! I mean, you know what I mean! And as you move along, it gets away from you, it turns back into chaos again, but now it doesn't matter, because now you understand. I mean, now you know the secret."

These cryptic notes accompanied the release of the band's *Europe '72* album, attributed to "The Choirmaster," later revealed to be Willy Legate, a long-time member of the Dead family. The notes point to the band's predilection for wacky pseudo-occultism, a stance perfectly reflected by Legate, who was known as "The Professor" in the studio where he handed out a business card with the moniker "Ideologue" and dispensed sage nonadvice. Legate was the building maintenance manager at the band's Front Street studio and the first archivist of the tape vault.

Liner Notes to
Europe '72

Willy Legate

And the dead were judged by what was written in the books, by what they had done (*Revelation* 20.12)

For example, consider the rise of hypnocracy during April and May of 1972. The 43 persons constituting the Grateful Dead's (latest) European tour apportioned themselves for the most part between two buses which came to be known as the Bolo bus and the Bozo bus. The Bolo bus had a john in it and its seats faced forward. The Bozo bus had a refrigerator and some of its seats were installed facing back, to accommodate four tables. And to look back.

The subtle difference in character and import and atmosphere between the two omnibuses was so profoundly hidden and enigmatic that you could never possibly understand it. The Bozos wore masks, and the Bolos showed their faces. At one time the Bozos staged a raid on the Bolo provisions; at one time the Bolos staged a raid on the Bozo provisions.

One St. Dilbert defected from the Bozos and lived for a season with the Bolos. In view of his subsequent martyrdom, his penitence and reconciliation with the Bozos, it came to be said that he was a true hypnocratic missionary to Bololand. And to look back, it appears evident that Bozo and Bolo knew themselves each the other's raison d'etre. Is hypnocracy not the aspiration to know what it is?

Departure from U.S. was Feast of Fools, 1 April. Arrival in London was Easter Sunday, 2 April. April saw England, Denmark and Germany. May saw France, England, the Netherlands, Luxembourg, Germany and England.

The Band during their European tour, 1972. © Mary Ann Mayer

The following article, a September 28, 1972, contribution by Gleason to *Rolling Stone*, the magazine he co-founded with Jann Wenner, shows the critic's knack for taking the best of that which had become the Grateful Dead "scene" and holding it up as an exemplar for the rock music industry in general.

FULL
Circle
with the Dead

Ralph J. Gleason

short time ago the **Grateful Dead played a four-night** engagement at the Berkeley Community Theater, a hall that seats 3,500 when the orchestra pit is used.

The entire series of four performances—14,000 tickets—was sold out by the end of the second day the tickets went on sale. There was no special advertising campaign, just the usual announcements in the standard Bill Graham ads.

No other group appeared with the Dead on the show and the music began early every night, at seven o'clock and went on until 11 or 11:30 PM. The theater is part of a high school campus, and it is against various rules and regulations of the local and State Departments of Education to run after midnight.

The Berkeley Community Theater is not a dance hall. There is no flat, wide area on which to dance or crash. There are only regular auditorium/theater seats and it was a reserved seat affair with numbered tickets and prices ranging from $3.50 to $5.50.

It was beautiful. Night after night the audiences were warm, friendly, appreciative and enthusiastic. Even the usual Bill Graham Quiz, in which he stands on stage and answers questions ("When is the Airplane coming? September 15 and 16 at Winterland. John Lennon? John Lennon is at Madison Square Garden Saturday night") went down without heckling or antagonism.

The music was superb. The band played straight through each night with only a half-hour intermission long about mid-evening. Of course the Dead are unique and the affair would have been obvious as a Grateful Dead tribal stomp even to a deaf man. All you had to do was to look around backstage and see the women, babies and dogs and it couldn't have been anyone but the Dead.

However, what they did was not the kind of thing which is possible only for one special group. It is possible for a lot of groups and it should be noted and considered by the whole rock & roll world. The standard rock show of today has evolved from two sources. The old original Fillmore dance concerts and the all-star touring show/concerts of the Fifties. At the Fillmore, the concert was three groups: a lightweight, middleweight and a heavy, each playing about an hour and the show generally repeated twice an evening. A light show was standard right from the beginning. The Fifties concert/show with Paul Anka or Fats Domino would include half a dozen groups or singles each doing two or three songs (concluding with their hit) and then the star doing about an hour.

But earlier, in the Swing Era of the Thirties and Forties, the big bands drew crowds of thousands to dances with only the one group, themselves, on each show. Count Basie or Benny Goodman would play from eight or nine o'clock until 2 AM with only a ten or 15 minute break every hour or so. Occasionally— and for a very special promotion—another band would be added and it then became "A Battle of the Bands" with, say, Andy Kirk and Count Basie, or Benny Goodman and Count Basie in which each band alternated hour by hour from eight or nine o'clock until, sometimes, four AM. In those days you stood on the dance floor, you didn't sit or crash.

I have never known why it was necessary to sit or stand through two opening groups to hear the band you came for, except as a means of introducing new groups to an audience.

The whole concert style of Goodman, Ellington, Kenton and the rest which became standard operating procedure at the beginning of the Fifties and which set the matrix for the Fats Domino/Paul Anka/ Bill Doggett touring shows which followed, was a combination of the status (ego) involved in playing a concert as opposed to a dance and a method of getting new locations to replace the dwindling dance balls. Also, dance halls could have only one ticket price and concerts could be scaled in various echelons for a bigger gross.

So now we have come full circle. The Grateful Dead can play four nights (and they obviously could have played a week) at a concert hall with absolute artistic and commercial success. Some of the patrons—Graham estimated 20 percent—were repeaters, buying tickets for every night. It reminded me of a big band playing the Roton Point Casino when I was in high school. We'd be there every night. Or Glen Island where we would make it three nights out of five, say.

There were other good things about the Dead's Berkeley series. Because it was for four nights and there was room enough for everybody (ticket swapping was common with Listeners' Personals on KSANFM acting as a bulletin board), there was none of the hysterical meat-market scrum at any of the box offices. There was time enough for us all.

The Dead do not go in for any of the show biz nonsense you see with some Svengali-created groups in which costumes and lighting attempt to create the drama missing from the music. The Dead are very straight ahead in their presentation. To begin with, they are among friends and they know it. And of course it is axiomatic that, being among friends, there is nothing to live up to. Just be yourself.

Aside from the individual virtues of the group, they have mastered the ability to control dynamics to a more consistent degree than any other group I know of except the James Brown band. The Dead can come down to a whisper and still keep it moving, and this is one of the hardest things to do in group music. That they make it appear to be so effortless is a tribute to their ability. That, too, is hard to do, but as everyone knows who has become expert in any field, it's easy when you know how and the Dead sure do know how.

For me, Jerry Garcia was always one of the true original sounds in contemporary instrumental music. Like a very few others (B.B., Hendrix) it has always been possible to pick him out right away. In earlier days he was not a particularly impressive singer. But he has developed into one now. It was evident from the records that he was getting a lot better, but then in the studio it is possible to aid the voice in a way it can't be done in live performance, and now on the concert stage Jerry is a fine singer, again with a highly personal sound.

Phil Lesh (like Jack Casady) has always been a fascinating bassist precisely because he did not play the bass like other bass players but instead made it into a continual counter-melody to Garcia and the song. But Lesh has gotten even better and his bass playing takes over from time to time to become a uniquely dominant voice.

Bob Weir is the personification of the Dead's philosophy of "let it grow." Standing there beside one of the greatest guitarists of his time, Weir has grown. In other circumstances he might have been inhibited, but the Dead's ambience let him be, and he has become a fine singer and an excellent player.

Bill Kreutzmann has mellowed out over the years as a drummer and really swings his ass off. Keith Godchaux who replaced the ailing Pig Pen, plays keyboard which gives an unusual pianistic sound now and Donna Godchaux sings an occasional song in a charming Southern-flavored voice.

All in all the week was pure joy. Now why don't the Band, the Who, Van Morrison, Rod Stewart, and the rest do the same thing? Must we always be prisoners of those amphitheaters?

Robert Hunter's position within the Grateful Dead was that of a band member, though he never set foot onstage with the band, and that position, possibly unique among rock lyricists, is evident in the following poem, which has a fine sardonic, self-mocking edge. It appeared, unsigned, in the newsletter the band mailed in 1972 out to the Dead Heads mailing list, though it was "signed" with an insignia which was later identified as Hunter's. Hunter has published several books of poetry, including a translation of Rilke's *Duino Elegies*, published by Hulogos'i in 1987; *Night Cadre*, published by Viking in 1991; *Idiot's Delight*, published by Hanuman in 1992; *Infinity Minus Eleven*, published by Cityful Press in 1993; *Sentinel* published by Penguin in 1993; and *Glass Lunch*, published by Viking in 1997, as well as his collected lyrics, *A Box of Rain*, published by Viking in 1990 and 1993.

Now That We've GOT A MOMENT TO Stand...

Robert Hunter

Now that we've got a moment to stand
what have we got
do we like it or not?
Kindly King of Light will explain the fine details
in the long run
but for the short run
the usual ambition, greed and just a touch
of goodwill
we put what faith we can muster there
not much and not often
but not Never, this far.
We build a way to get time
We build a way to grab on to chunks of it,
choke on it but would not spit it out
when so much effort has gone into getting
the damned thing half swallowed

(cf: Amoeba That Ate the World by Lefty Lamont)
One day perhaps all ambition will subside leaving only eternity
pipers poets killers and men of state
in one drunken reel
given enough microphones of right impedance
we will record it
thanks for supporting us.

Some *Pretty Basic Tenets of*
HYPNOCRACY

Robert Hunter

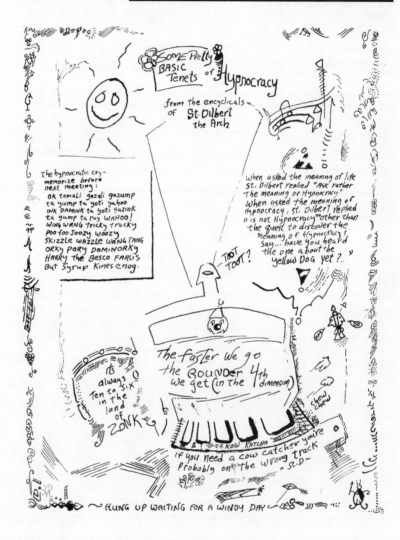

The following two pieces appeared in successive issues of the Dead Heads newsletter. The first is by Alan Trist, who runs Ice Nine Publishing Company, the band's in-house music publishing and licensing arm, and it details the business-side ramifications of the band's steady growth in popularity in the 1970s. The second piece is a collage of responses to the first, from letters sent in by Deadheads. Trist is the author of *Water of Life: A Tale of the Grateful Dead, A Folk Story Retold*, published by Hulogos'i in 1989.

State of the Changes

How the Dragon Urobouros (Giga Exponentia) Makes Us Go Round and Round

Alan Trist

e've received 25,000 letters to date from Dead Heads, telling us your trips, and ideas and questions and comments about ours. Whatever the voyage, the current concerns are at least real, and this newsletter is a report on the state of the ship.

The pursuit of quality presentation of our music, with more and more people wanting to hear it, has led us into larger and larger halls with an ever-increasing array of equipment. St. Dilbert calls this process 'Urobouros':

Configurations of speakers and amplifiers change almost as rapidly as we move from gig to gig. The equipment diagram shown overleaf is a schematic of the set-up at Kezar Stadium, San Francisco, 26 May 1973 (auxiliary PA's and mid-field delay towers to reinforce the sound at the back against wind, are not shown).

You are one million Dead Heads who attend the concerts. In the New York City area, given the space, we will draw some 50,000 people. As your numbers increase in each area, we play larger and larger halls. The apparent alternative to this is a kind of riot. We are musicians.

The physics of sound projection dictate that any given increase in the size of a hall requires an exponential rate of increase in equipment capability to reach everyone in the hall with quality-at-volume.

YEAR	WEIGHT	TRANSPORT
1965	800 lbs	Bill's station wagon
1967	1,300 lbs	Barney's van
1968	6,000 lbs	Metro van
1970	10,000 lbs	18 ft truck
1973	30,000 lbs	40 ft semi

We're growing!—some 30 people now on payroll. We're affiliated with Alembic in San Francisco on design, research and development of equipment and recording. Our rehearsal hall in San Rafael is the center of acoustic enquiry and equipment maintenance/development. Our office here manages, controls finance, accounting, insurance and the like, and Ice Nine Publishing Company (copyrights, licenses, songbooks) and Dead Heads. Out of Town booking agency and Fly By Night travel agency, two outgrowths of our scene, are in the building.

By the nature of the beast, the energies of over a hundred directly enter our endeavour. Urobouros turns his circles. St. Dilbert is a bombast. Let's surface the moon with an electrostatic spherical tidal spatial counter-entropic sound system. Energy spoken here.

On earth, our overhead expense is $100,000 a month. In 1972 we grossed $1,424,543. Here's who ate the pie:

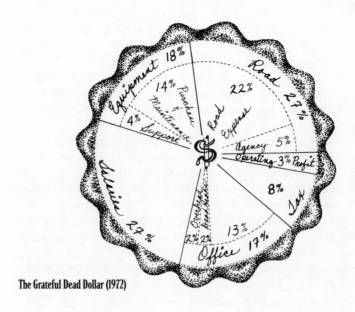

The Grateful Dead Dollar (1972)

70% of this income came from gigs, and 30% from record royalties. Gigs offer the only means to earn more money when it is needed to maintain our operation in all its particulars. We cannot sell more records at will, but we can go on the road, within the limits of energy: so that we must play larger halls, with more equipment, and a bigger organization, requiring more gigs.

St. Dilbert calls this fellow 'Urobouros,' and he's a good trip, but he has a mind of his own:

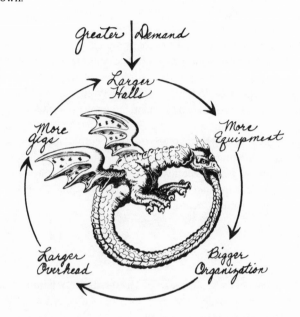

We like a variety of concert situations. Ambiance comes in different sizes. We like a small hall, and so do you, and an outdoor gig in the sun, and a large hall when it can be made to sound good (few halls over 6,000 capacity aren't sport arenas with novel acoustic and environmental puzzles).

Urobouros is hungry. How do we control him? We've planned for a year to form our own record manufacturing and distributing company so as to be more on top of the marketing process, package and promote our product in an honest and human manner, and possibly stand aside from the retail list-price inflation spiral while retaining more of the net dollar (keep a tight ship). If the records cover a larger share of the overhead, then the concert situation becomes more flexible. This is the working future-possible, in the direction we see to go, now. We want this freedom to achieve gig variety, to experiment. We are musicians.

What else might we do? Write and suggest it. Magic ideas welcome. Dead Heads altogether, too—what might we do with it? What might you do with it?

Your mail is an energy input, 400 letters a week that we tack on bulletin boards and read aloud and pass back and forth. The drawings ('DH') in this issue are yours. This flow enters the common pool of plans and theories and ideas and speculations and fantasies and hopes and fears and futures and galaxies and stuff.

To hear from you, furthers.

"Having been born into a world of rather curious values, values apparently unrelated to the direct experience of human truths, the Bozos and Bolos hypnocratically pursue a direction of self-determination in as many ways as interestingly possible, believing that this course will best aid a continuation of integrity and meaning in their music and other life spaces. This has meant that their business activity seeks to be in control of as many areas as become possible, employing their own people to do the work that would otherwise be farmed out to straight business. Thus there is the possibility that the message in the music can be reflected in the manner and purpose of conducting the business necessary to get the music heard."

—St. Dilbert, Bombast

Arbitrary Synopsis of Recent Communications from Dead Heads in Response to Urobouros

Molière, "Man needs nothing so much as the dance...All human unhappiness, all blows of fortune which history reports to us, all mistakes of politics...result from...that the dance is misunderstood."

Is it sad to be one's own enemy?...all that super-star hype. Don't get lost in the shuffle. It sounded like a stock report. If I don't hear the Grateful Dead at least once a day I go into withdrawals. Will you come play our softball team? Have you sold out? Whoever wants to be born must first destroy a world. The egg is the world. Is it a non-profit organization? Concerts are way too big. Their music is hair. We know each other. Remember, the truth hurts! if you got any feelings to begin with. Music to remember innumerable lifetimes. The showboat lifted into a brightening atmosphere—orange sun across numerous heads regathering from muddy drizzle fallen to 2-3 days. In case you are planning to rip-off a starship, I do simple veterinary medicine. What is hypnocracy? Who is St. Dilbert? Cut albums on astrologically auspicious days. Run twice as fast as you can run. I'm doing my best not to be a fan. Am I writing to a computer or real people? Records lots more studio material, and undersell; the more you play the better you'll get. Form a symphony orchestra from Dead Heads to do to classical what the Dead do to rock and roll. Make Coke commercials or an underarm thing. Gibran. "Yet unless the exchange be in love and kindly justice it will but lead some to greed and others to hunger." The physical newcomers can go—cool, cool—but they don't dig the head. Is this bad? I don't know, do you think so? It's impossible to ask any more of any musicians than what you've given us. Release more singles. I love you.

Spiritual forces control events today; the state of conflict in the spirit world parallels conflict on earth. Satan is a liar. You are the only band who still plays for the people, not money. Whatever happened to the music for the common people? Don't call it a revolution, we still have birth and death; keep it clean and honest, we have to try just a little bit more. Annual Dead Heads reunion. The whole must shift. I want to know what's going on. Coupons in albums for concert ticket discount or annual freebie tour. You still do parties or small clubs? I dig chamber music. If the AM and FM DJs won't promote you, whom can you turn to? The police band? Astral project yourselves to everywhere at once. Call it all an Opportunity to Experiment With On-Stage Sound. TV should display Dead form and style so people won't fear what it really represents. Simulcast. Do a screenplay for Dead music. Cuckoo's nest. Play a small hall five days running. Play two small halls a day or two apart. I've some ideas about concert sound. Concert sound has a long way to go. Low-budget 16mm, 35mm feature film; videotape; independent distribution channels, campus screenings, network TV, film-to-cassette. Mobile TV w/SCU individuals, concerts, lots of tight short tunes; blow-up to 35mm for theatres...tight pilot for TV variety series, group talk, films you already have...syndicated prime-access markets...cinema-verité concert/studio/Dead lifestyle footage for art houses, campus...Define yourselves to yourselves. Jam baroque works from Bach, Handel energetic dazzling to mellow moods of Mozart and Ludwig van, new experience in as yet nonsyncretist forms w/ symphonic format and much practice, as country-classical/spacey-acid-jazz-classical/blues-jazz-pop etc. w/ref a multitude's lifestyle. Literally five minutes before you came onstage the sun broke through the clouds, remained the entire show.

Robert Christgau's miniature portrait published in December, 1971 in the *Village Voice*, of the crowd and its behavior at a New York Grateful Dead concert is a telling and sympathetic view from a non-Deadhead rock critic. Christgau is the author of *Any Old Way You Choose It: Rock and Other Pop Music, 1967-1973* published by Penguin in 1973, *Christgau's Record Guide: Rock Albums of the Seventies* published by Ticknor & Fields, 1981, *Christgau's Record Guide: Rock Albums of the '80s* published by Pantheon in 1990, and *Grown Up All Wrong: 75 Great Rock and Pop Artists from Vaudeville to Techno* published by Harvard University Press in 1998.

Dead Heads
Pay Their Dues

Robert Christgau

Grateful Dead concert at the Felt Forum is postflower America reveling in its contradictions, but Dominique was reminded of the Soviet Union, where the queue has not withered away, and elbowing ahead of your comrades is a national pastime. As we pushed on in toward our complimentary third-row seats, the crowd got heavier, and so did the contradictions. The cross section of Dead heads—heavy music proles and suburban folkies and old rock and rollers—is a confusing combination of our fabled new community and the nightmare mob of Ortega y Gasset. Half the audience avoids the crush, but the remainder presses forward, packing the aisles and the front rows, and everyone is up and boogieing. To boogie, you just stand and move to the music, relating to your brothers and sisters no matter how stoned you are because your brothers and sisters are sweating and boogieing on all sides. It isn't a dance, and not just because there isn't room at a concert—even in seat-less halls the floor is always tight up front. Folks do dance with each other in back, but for most the exhilaration of the boogie increases exponentially with the proximity of the musicians, and if Jerry beams his cosmic grin down at someone, he/she will not shriek like a twelve-year-old chickie at the TAMI Show but just boogie harder.

The dismay of the mass-culture theorists and their politely raised offspring is understandable—too many people in too little space, all competing to get to the fore of the hero-worshiping swarm, ignoring the hard-earned wisdom of the fire laws and damaging property that they and their sibling consumers will pay for in the end. Many of the boogiers are usurpers who buy cheap seats and confidently move up or just sneak in to begin with. Despite the love-and-community rhetoric and sacramental joint-passing, the boogiers do discriminate against the weak and the short and the timid—a few always pass out, many more get sick, and eventually someone will die—and a boogieing biker is almost as likely to knock your head off at a Dead concert as anywhere else. Yet when we finally reached our seats, we had no trouble claiming them, and the wallet and cigarettes that Dominique had unknowingly dropped at the other end of the row were passed down a minute later. A girl standing in front of us started to bum out but revived when an orange miraculously materialized. Regulars greeted other regulars, remembered from previous boogies, and compared this event with a downer in Boston or a fabulous night in Arizona.

A lot of people avoid live rock because they can't stand the crowds. In a medium-sized hall where the music can be felt in back, that smacks of the old aristocratic bullshit to me. Rock and roll developed as it did because it was a mass art, and if it can bring us together in a celebration, that's good-club intimacy and living-room privacy are fine, but in the end I am proboogie. The Dead, who played four nights at the Felt Forum instead of filling Madison Square Garden and who arranged a special live broadcast on WNEW-FM to accommodate those who couldn't make it, demonstrate that despite the contradictions, live performances are still a viable form. Ideally, the band radiates fun while a hip, property-oriented tough like Bill Graham, who produced the series, does the work. Someone has to pay, I guess, but anyone clever enough to get past Graham deserves to boogie as much as this reporter. A lot of hassle might be avoided if reserved seats were eliminated—the fanatics should be in front, first-come-first-serve. The risks and the contradictions are real, but the principle seems to be that a good time involves a few dues. That doesn't seem like such a bad principle to me.

Robert Petersen was a long-time friend of the band, a Beat poet whose life, judging from the trail of markers he left via his poems, was spent on the road, largely up and down the West Coast. Several of his lyrics were set to music by Phil Lesh, including "Unbroken Chain." Petersen died in 1987, and his collected poems, *Alleys of the Heart* (Hulogos'i, 1988), were edited and published by Alan Trist. The following eloquent elegy for Pigpen takes its title from a folk song which had been in the band's repertoire.

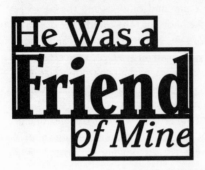

He Was a Friend of Mine

Robert Petersen

weird how it goes
with beginnings
& endings
again
this year
winter's over
end of the loco months
new green
appearing everywhere
sweet lunacy
birds & blue skies
eternal snows
glutting the rivers
brown with earth
whales starting north
with precious
young

& pigpen died

my eyes tequila-tortured
4 days mourning

lost another fragment
of my own self
knowing
the same brutal
night-sweats & hungers
he knew
the same cold fist
that knocked him down
now clutching furiously
at my gut

shut my eyes
& see him standing
spread-legged
on the stage of the world
the boys prodding him
egging him on
he telling all he ever knew
or cared to know

mike hand cocked like
a boxer's
head throwed back
stale whiskey blues
many-peopled desolations
neon rainy streets
& wilderness of airports
thousands maybe millions
loved him
were fired instantly
into forty-five minutes of
midnight hour
but when he died
he was thin, sick, scared
alone

like i said to laird
i just hope he didn't hurt
too much

weird
all these endings
& beginnings
pale voices of winter
faces, rivers, birds, songs
lunacies
i wonder
how many seasons
new green coming once more
to the land
fresh winds turn
bending the long grasses
we'll hear him sing
again

Mt. Hermon, Ca. 1973

Pigpen, 1972 European tour. Photo by Mary Ann Mayer

This letter from Robert Hunter appeared in *Crawdaddy* magazine in January 1975, in response to a request for an interview by *Crawdaddy* writer Patrick Snyder-Scumpy. Hunter uses the format as a convenient way to give considered responses to the typical interviewer questions about lifestyle and the artistic process, while Hunter maintains his generally reclusive stance in terms of his own personality. The time Hunter spent in London was particularly fruitful, resulting in many of the songs on *American Beauty*, *Wake of the Flood*, and *From the Mars Hotel*.

Robert Hunter
Dark Star

Robert Hunter

London
September 23, 1974

Dear Scump,

It occurs to me that I've been doing in-depth interviews for many years now, saying more or less exactly what I wish to say, deciding the topics and spaces I want to explore and telling more about myself than I realize until years later. Why anyone would want to know any more about me than I lay out in my songs is a puzzle to me.

No, that sounds a little naive. As soon as I state something in an interview, the opposite occurs to have just as much merit. Trying to know myself aloud in someone else's terms is a particular form I've shied away from and hence have little skill at it. I hit upon the idea of a written interview because I don't exactly like the idea of turning requests for them down and there's no real point to making enemies in the trade. Also, I don't dig being dissected in public, although that is a due which most artists must pay to achieve recognition. I give the best of me in my work and the rest is just my life and there is little point to having your roots above ground. I have several lives, in fact. Half the time I live in London and half in the Bay Area. I go back and forth about every 2-3 months. I don't know many people in London and have about zero social life here. It is a place to work, practice, relax and think. To retreat and recoup. I live on the surface of an ice Möbius strip upon which I skate, sometimes on the inner, sometimes on the outer surface. The inner surface I can tell about.

The outer surface is a continual puzzle and yet they are one and the same in a Möbius strip.

The kind of fame which comes from interviews and such self-promotional activity is a drag and a farce. The fame which comes from a solid body of work is a comfort and a delight to the heart; one realizes that some part of what exists here will continue to exist when what is was, and there is a motivation and a call to hard work and study of preceding forms and an attempt to base one's work on traditions. This assures that the traditions not die and that there is a solid ground with which to relate and occasionally solo. I don't mean to say that I'm not as hot for fame as any other half-baked jerk-off, but discrimination amongst the modes of fame could save a lot of grief. Popular fame demonstrates the "bigger are the harder they fall" phenomenon, which my grandmother was fond of impressing on me, along with a distaste for shellfish and an unshakable conviction that "only crazy people talk to themselves" (which I on occasion find myself doing).

The interviewer asks you what *he* wants to know, rather than what you'd be half interested in saying. Most interviews show more about the interviewer than about the subject. The written interview, based freeform around a couple of questions (which make it an interview rather than an essay), allows me to ignore the questions which I don't care to answer or find fruitful and to concentrate more fully on the areas where I really don't mind saying a thing or two and, incidentally, to practice my prose with some motivation. An occasional flap at prose gets a lot of garbage out of my head and frees up my lyric flow. Lyrics is a form which demands great economy and striving for succinctness (sp?) of image or statement. Also, it must be metrically interesting and musically pleasing. I write a good deal of prose as a vacation from lyrical work and it is always refreshing. Mostly, I just put it away in folders and consider it exercises. I don't expect I'll write anything very worthy for many years in the field of prose. I'm too young to have all the co-ordinates of style, experience and dedication which go towards making a fine essayist or novelist. My mid-forties will do for that, I think, though it may all come together next year. Meanwhile, the written interview is one good way to practice.

You ask me how fame has affected my friends in their heads and in their attitudes. A few years ago I had a flash that the energy pouring through the Grateful Dead would strengthen strong characters and destroy weak ones. It is the particular test which has accrued to us, and a hot one it is, too. It is too early to tell. Each of my friends has been on the down side of it and has once in awhile risen to the challenges it presents.

I saw your picture in the magazine with the advertisements and the rock and roll queens; you blew the words and called it soul, but we all fall a little short of Rock and Roll. The way they lay you get just one chance, you can pick it up and maybe learn to dance. You can go for gold, you can go for broke, you can go for dreams that go up in smoke. Love's to love and not to hold, been said before but it's never been told. You can say it right, you can say it wrong, but it's *got* to be the heart of a Rock and Roll song.

You ask about major themes and world views that run through my songs. In the last analysis, you probably could answer that question better than I. I live there and am pretty subjective about it all, but you have the body of work to walk around and judge objectively. I don't know. Am I good looking? My mother thought so, though not as good looking as my brother, and I thought he was real ugly. Here's that dastardly interview syndrome.

My major themes are an intercourse between the heart and the head and a pointing to possibilities of some kind of semi-human interaction between the two. I consider hate to be misguided and prejudiced interpretations of another's actions. There is no place for it. One may have contempt for and despise the actions of another without despising the person and there, I think lies an important kernel for contemplation.

I like to write songs with crow quill and ink, as you get into an entirely different flow than with the tappity tap-space of typewriters. But I usually use a ball point, though when nothing else is available I'm not above using a burned match. I've got to write it down when it occurs to me. I've learned that from sad experience; a fantastic couplet vanishes as easily as it comes. My method is to write a lot. I try to write every day, if only letters. I answer all the letters which come to me, and take great delight in doing so. Nothing pleases me more than getting mail, and when I don't have a letter or two my day is severely blackened. I sleep rather later in California than I do here as my California mail comes at eleven, where here it arrives at 7.

You ask if any other poets/prose or songwriters influenced or affect my work and if so, how? I try to keep abreast of the field and listen a lot. I find much guidance in what not to say and how to not say it, to be frank. With the exception of the obvious genius gone into lyricism in the decade, it's like the Oklahoma Territory in the eighteen-hundreds. There's room and plenty for anyone who wants to make a life of it. The formula demands of the pop market, as indicated by the charts, keep everybody running after one will-o'-the-wisp or another and not many settle down to express what it is they really experience as up and against what they think the public would like to hear. Some of Marty Balin's stuff around the *Surrealistic Pillow* days contains some of the sweetest and most potent statements in the idiom. "I'm so full of love I could burst apart and start to cry." I mean, what do you want from a man in the way of laying it right up on the table, vulnerable and undressed? Yeah, I guess that's how I judge a good lyric: vulnerable, unique, universal, graceful and craftsmanly.

You can't be too concerned about whether you are right or mistaken in the things you express; just that you express them completely and allow some possibility of accessibility, however remote. Some writers say things which haven't been said before; the context of the times allows for that. Each one who does liberates areas of poetic territory which then become common property; modes of expression are developed which haven't been heard before and in turn become fertile ground for further exploration. Gradually, in each age, a music and lyric tradition emerge which can be food for the times to come. With proper respect for tradition, one becomes part of a course of spiritual events which is one of the few immortal aspects of this sack of ashes. That, to me, is spirit, and it is not just personal and unique and yet is nothing other than personal and unique. Not only the creator partakes in the charisma of that "entity" but all who are moved, instructed or otherwise diverted by the work, and so on out...

Just got back from a little junket out in the rain down Queensgate and up to Gloucester Road to buy a bottle of wine. Stopped at the bookstore to buy *The Golden Notebook* by Doris Lessing and *The Process* by Brion Gysin. Have been reading Anais Nin and corresponding with her about writing for a literary review I've been fantasizing, which may or may not get off the ground. Most of the writers I have solicited have failed to respond. Nikki Giovanni has offered to help after a raving letter I wrote her, something about a silver bullet in the heart of apathy in the arts. If I don't get the thing published, I'd like it to at least be known that these great ladies were not among those who couldn't be bothered with answering a query from the Rock Division of the College of Unilateral Process.

You ask which comes first: the lyrics or the music, in general. Usually, I sit down with a guitar and write a song. Sometimes I write to changes provided for me, which is the hardest way to do the number. Or, I play a song I've written to a friend, and it is dismantled and put together in a new and often more pleasing fashion. I am a fairly accomplished guitarist and a devotee of the Great Highland Bagpipe, upon which I can play most of the standard tunes and which, incidentally, keeps my lungs in fairly good shape in spite of my tendency to smoke. I can play half of Bach's 1st 2-part invention on the piano by heart—which should tell piano players about exactly where I am on their instrument—and have played the trumpet off and on since I was a kid, never getting particularly good on it, nor too far away from being able to handle it at all. My embouchure is educated enough to play a double high C with no effort, but my endurance is slight. I play bluegrass mandolin well enough, though I'm no Dave Grisman or Frank Wakefield. A little bluegrass banjo and frailing; working on the tin whistle and scheming on picking up a good old wooden piccolo. Guitar is the only instrument I compose on, however.

The Grateful Dead have never required melodies from me (coals to New-castle) and consequently I have a great stock of "Orphan Tunes" in my head which I used to write my lyrics to. My tune writing does not approach the richness and subtlety of Jerry's so I've never felt overlooked and misunder-stood in that area—it was simply not required of me. I've worked some with Weir and think his compositional sense is just amazing, though he does little of it; it takes him a long, long time to fashion one of his tunes. The only song I've written with Phil ("Box of Rain") remains one of my favorites. Keith's head is awash with melody and I look forward to many more good nights of carving out tunes with him and listening to Donna interpret them for us. The actual act of writing a good song with someone I like being around is the closest thing I know to the way things ought to be. It's strange to write tunes with a drummer, but Billy and I were working away at it in Munich last week and he turned me on to some rhythmical possibilities I'd not considered on a song which I've been hammering out called "The Last Flash of Rock and Roll."

The idea of the Grateful Dead "breaking up"—I really don't see how that would come about. After ten years of touring, we've decided to cut that way down. A gig here and there—a solstice or an equinox, perhaps. The physical strain of touring is pretty grueling and we've been on the road for a long, long time. At least a six month's vacation to just cool out and survey what we've been up to. Building and carting that sound system around is, in my head, akin to building a pyramid. It's the world's greatest hi-fi system, and there's no one who would deny that. Recording and practices will go on as usual, but leaving space for diversified personal musical projects.

The Dead is the logical extension of a meeting of energies which you all know more or less about already. If, as you propose, it had not happened, it would have happened anyway. I mean, there was no way that thing wasn't going to happen. My energies were turned to songwriting before there was an "official" G.D., as was every one else's involved in their own peculiar way. If it hadn't been *this* Grateful Dead, it would have been another and if not that one, another yet. Sensible? I suppose not, but just so, nevertheless. I don't mean to get mystical on you, or nothing like that, but there was a question asked in the early '60's which demanded an answer and those who demanded to answer naturally came together and recognized one another. There has never been the slightest doubt in my mind that we would accomplish what we've accom-plished, and it seems too foredrawn that there has never been any need to rush it, promote it or pluck it before it was ripe.

Now you ask me, "what has it been like," "what do you do all day" and do I have any hobbies or pressworthy perversions? Man, life on this planet is a perversion. To write or play or do anything other than live in serenity on a field where you plow and reap and raise your children to do the same is a perversion. So here we are, largely (pygmies excepted) (for which see: "Pygmy Kitabu" by Jean-Pierre Hallet and Alex Pelle) a world of perverts of one persuasion or another, pointing fingers at off-the-wall individual kinkiness and calling *that* perversion...well I mean—how about you, compare—what do *you* see when you turn off the lights?

What do I do all day? I wander about in a dream, answer letters, look for wheels of hansom cabs among the weevily wheat, reflect, reject, patronize, soliloquize; bathe, shave, rave—once in a henhouse, down on my knees, I though I heard a chicken sneeze. Do just about anything except interviews and hang out in R&R circles, but why carry anything to extremes? Bagpipes and essays are my hobbies. I don't collect anything; I tried old war medals once, as I thought a man should try and collect something, but, no matter how hard I applied myself and tried to want those rare old medals, it just didn't work. I gave my Distinguished Service Cross to my brother when he got shot in the leg by a junkie, and gave my gold-edged Blue Max (not to be confused with lesser editions of that great Franco-Prussian war medal for valor) to Paul Foster for spending several months on roller skates rather than shoes.

What has it been like? It's been roses, man. A great thorny field of roses. I don't see how I could be more satisfied with the so-farness of it. I used to keep waiting for the axe to drop. Now it is past, the dropping of the axe; we have children and a creative family with a great deal of mutual respect. The problems have been games and the tragedies instructive. Lives have been lost, new ones born. One of these days I'm going to kick off, too. I hope it's not painful or when something I've started isn't completed, but what the fuck if it is? There's time to consider that in the moment it occurs—and an occasional freak meditation to prepare you for the possibility. When the Dead are playing their best, blood drips from the ceiling in great, rich drops. Together we do a kind of suicide in music which requires from each of us just enough information short of dropping the body to inquire into those spaces from which come our questions. It is partly about how living might occur in the shadow of certain death; and that death is satisfactory or unsatisfactory according to how we've lived and what we yield. The contemplation of death for the unfulfilled is a nightmare, and it is good that it should be. The vision of life without a great deal of responsibility is hollow. Satisfaction in itself is nothing to be sought, it's simply an excretion of the acceptance of responsibility.

But I rave. You asked me if I'm rich and whether that makes a difference. I'm certainly rich by the standards I had two or three years ago. I made about fifty grand last year. I spent half of it making my record and paying the musicians who played on it. So far I haven't been financially forced into buying any property. I try and support a few worthwhile trips. The only thing I have which only money could get me is the ability to fly back and forth from England to the States and to keep my '58 Porsche running (which it would never do, so I traded it in on a '72 Datsun which keeps breaking down. I've no luck with cars). I should make a lot more money next year ('75) and so have thought of investing in a friend's recording studio, rather than pay it all back to the government, but if my record sells well I don't really know how I am to handle it. Probably spend more on recording and make a fancier record. I paid all the costs for my last record out of my own pocket. I try to put what I make out of music back into music.

OK, then. I think I've answered all your questions. I started when I got up and it is turning dark now on your regulation black and wet London summer day. Or wait—equinox today. First day of fall.

Yours etc.,
Robert Hunter

II

"If You Get Confused, *Listen to the Music Play*"
Back From the Hiatus, *Into the Eighties,*
1976-1986

Winterland, March 1977. Photo by Ed Perlstein

The band's lineup from 1975 to February 1979 was Garcia, Weir, Lesh, Kreutzmann, Hart, and Keith & Donna Godchaux. Keith and Donna Godchaux departed in early 1979, and Brent Mydland joined the band in 1979, remaining until his death in 1990.

The Dead's experiment with their own record label ended during the 1975 hiatus, and the band signed with Arista Records, which has remained their label ever since, though they do issue archival recordings on their own label for mail order sales. Their albums from 1976 through 1986 included *Steal Your Face, Terrapin Station, Shakedown Street, Go to Heaven, Reckoning,* and *Dead Set.* The last two were both released in 1981, and both were live albums devoid of new original material, so the final studio album showcasing original songs in this period was 1980's *Go to Heaven.*

During these years, new material was developed on tour. "Touch of Grey," for instance, which, in 1987, was to become the band's one and only top-ten hit, debuted on September 15, 1982, and became a concert staple. (The song's refrain, "I will survive," became particularly poignant when Garcia suffered a diabetic coma in summer 1986, and "Touch of Grey" opened the first concert after Garcia's recovery, in December.) On tour, in fact, was the life of the band and of the Deadheads, as the selections in the following section make plain.

Richard Meltzer's review of *Terrapin Station* from the September 5, 1977, *Village Voice* stands on its own as the most entertaining record review I've come across, ever. *Terrapin* was a controversial album among Dead-heads, drawing fire for its slick production values, a disco version of "Dancin' in the Streets," and the use of an orchestra and chorus on the Garcia-Hunter epic title track. Meltzer is a prolific rock critic and is the author of *The Aesthetics of Rock*, published by Something Else Press in 1970; *Gulcher: Post-Rock Cultural Pluralism in America 1649-1980*, published by Straight Arrow Books in 1972; *Guide to the Ugliest Buildings of Los Angeles*, published by Illuminati in 1986; and *L.A. Is the Capital of Kansas: Painful Lessons in Post-New York Living*, published by Harmony in 1988.

St. Stephen Revisited *and Beyond*

Richard Meltzer

an into **Jerry Garcia a few months ago at the shooting of** this film I was in that y'really oughta go see (*Grand Theft Auto*) while meanwhile him and his band were recording *Terrapin Station* nearby and we were talkin about 1. punk rock (sez to me "It's nice that kids're forming bands and all that but sooner or later they're gonna wanna hear real music") and 2. strings (sez "There's some guys today who really have the string trip together"). Funny cause side two of said album, the 16-or-so-minute title cut (forget about side one, don't even play it once, really no need), is not only THE GREATEST THING THE DEAD'VE EVER (EVER) CUT IN A STUDIO but it's got a helluva lot to do with both 1 and 2 to boot.

Like for all us folks who've been with rock-roll from the goddam beginning and know there's nothin new under the sun no more but still ain't lost the beat for a goddam second cause we're cool (*I* am, Gene Sculatti is, don't know about *you* tho) there's an obvious willing suspension of historic disbelief currently operational in the whole experience, y'know? Y'know like everything's in *some* time warp or other and most of em're so damn *insulated* from the *rest* of history, y'dig? The posing's all so arbitrary but sometimes it's so *super*-arbitrary that it's what you might call pure—in some cases PURE ENOUGH TO BRING GODDAM TEARS TO YOUR EYES. The Dictators, Crime (from San Fran), Tom Petty, lots of neo-punkers and their ilk, some original-punk rockabilly assholes like Colin Winsky and Jerry Sikorsky, etc., etc., but it *ain't* limited to just your punkers cause *Terrapin Station* is as absolutely pure-beyond-belief a reorchestration of the non-heavy-metal post-'67 experience as the Beatles' White Album was to the mid-to-late '60s British-Invasion-unto-psychedelic whatsis, even to the point of thrusting you into the same identify-the-readymades situation the Beatles handed you on a platter back in December '68.

Like you're listening to some surprisingly unmistakable vintage Zappa marimba-band-parody fucking around when suddenly from out of nowhere the Dead leap into a nifty chorus of *Abbey Road* harmonies followed quickly by a dose of Procol Harum. Fast & furious! Then—note for goddam *note*: that orchestra riff from "You Set the Scene" on Love's *Forever Changes*. And plenty else: ELO, Van Dyke Parks, Pink Floyd, "Expecting to Fly," Country Joe, Chicago, Paul Mauriat, Moody Blues, Queen, *Flowers*, the elpee version of "You Can't Always Get What You Want," Quicksilver, Santana, even some tamer BOC. *Lots* of horns & strings and they're fucking *great* but don't think you ain't gettin the vintage Dead (who've been lying semi-dormant since *Workingman's*) cause you're gettin em in *spades*—play *Live/Dead* first and *Terrapin* beats it to fucking *shit* (true). An amazing amalgam that ain't really one at all.

Whole thing might seem a little excruciatingly over-melodious at first but once again the Dead (famous as hell in the past for their official acts of musical courage) have *done* it, journeyed into a genre that was *there* to be stripmined all along only nobody had the balls to tackle the project: kiddie swashbuckler soundtrack music! Reminds me a fucking helluva lot of what it was like to hear the simple-yet-*exciting* soundtrack to *Prince Valiant* back in '54 when I was 9 (fuckin *wow*). *Victory at Sea!* I've played it at least 89 times already and I still ain't got tired of it.

Then there's the lyrics, goddam *waves* of images that hit you across the face between and on top of segments of musical meat. Still ain't figgered all the words out myself but there's shit like "Till things we've never seen will seem familiar," "Counting stars by candlelight," "Faced with mysteries of the last," and "Nothing to believe in, the compass always point to Terrapin." Then there's the whole turtle bizness of the terrapin itself, y'know like which Asian cosmology is it that has the universe resting on a turtle that's resting on another turtle that's resting on...? "I can't figure out...if it's the end or beginning" sings Garcia. Only the goddam Dead could make *that* whole field of eternal mumbo-jumbo suddenly goosepimply again with newborn thrills & chills (*Star Wars* of course helps for spati-temporal/mythic context but the Dead when they wanna be are way beyond all that shit *by definition*: eat yer heart out, Thomas Pynchon! (Coleridge too.)

But there's this one recognizable theme towards the beginning that really *grabs me by the shorthairs*: While the mythic flames of love—etc. burn bright in whatever crypto-mythic locale it's all happening at there's this sailor who once "loved a lady many years ago" and a soldier who "came thru many fights—but lost at love" (one-time winner and an all-time loser). Out of the flames comes this femme fatale type broad who throws her fan into the lion's den and insists they retrieve it ("I will not forgive you if you do not take the chance"). The sailor's dumb enough to do it and she just laughs in his face (soldier's big on "strategy" so he just sits on his ass): Y'CAN'T WIN! Point being: what's a greater REALER-THAN-SHIT LIVING HELL than the irrational challenges of desperate love? Over the fucking cliff! Nothing back on earth is real anyway so fuggin *do* it! Or don't! Either way: burn you sucker BURN! Point *being*: 10 whole years after the Summer of Love what's left for a (non-gay) asshole of the male persuasion to torment himself over anymore but PUSSY(=personal, *non*-universal luv) (Y'know: just me & my heart & dick)?!!!! All this (compliments of those *ace* storytellers the Dead) ON THE EDGE (AT THE CENTER) OF THE UNIVERSE.

The point being: in "St. Stephen/The Eleven" on *Live/Dead* the issue was just the laws of physics and an arrow (Wm. Tell and all that shit) which ain't *nothin* compared to having to *compete* for a bimbo where failure means it's *all over* (been thru it THREE TIMES in the last 12 mos. so oughta know). And like "Friend of the Devil" on *American Beauty* was about this neurotic saddleweary cowpoke who'd've welcomed a goddam *rest* and in this life *many* an ass-blistered muhfuh (like mr. soldier & mr. sailor) will eventually turn his back on all aspects of the "adventure," all that is—except for CUNT (=etc.) (hate to use despicable "sexist" terms but they *are* quite functional!): dicks & hearts have retirement plans of their own! (Like: you stop pissing on the carpet at press parties but you never—?—stop HUNGERING like a fucking starving puppy for Love Object #1, y'know?) (Ain't life funny?) TERRAPIN!

One more observation on this entirely swell second side: the Beatle version of *Satanic Majesties*, or the Stones version of *Magical Mystery Tour*.

New West magazine ran from 1976 to 1981, and its stable of writers was a who's who of California journalism. Charlie Haas's article appeared as a cover story in December, 1979–at a time when little was being written about the band, though Haas probably wrote the story as much as ten months earlier. *Shakedown Street* was released in mid-November 1978. The concerts that Haas writes about happened in December 1978 and January 1979. Between the Pauley Pavilion concert and the two-concert Madison Square Garden run, the Dead closed Winterland on New Year's Eve 1978 in a six-hour marathon reminiscent of the early days. Keith and Donna left the band in February 1979 and were replaced by the keyboards and harmony vocals of Brent Mydland, who debuted in April. Haas performs a rare service: he captures the entire band–each member is vividly portrayed and most interviewed–while also giving insight into the development of the Deadhead scene, the state of the band's performances, and, indeed, into the state of civilization in general! Haas also contributed to *Esquire, The National Lampoon, Mother Jones, Film Comment, The Village Voice,* and other magazines. As a screen-writer, his credits include *Matinee, Over the Edge, Gremlins 2,* and *Tex.*

Still Grateful After All These Years: In Which the Grateful Dead,

Pinup Uglies

of the Haight-Ashbury, Become the House Band of the Age of Certain Doom

Charlie Haas

New Ones Coming As the Old Ones Go

uys in the traditional clown makeup and cardboard stars-and-stripes top hats; a circle of five grinning people gobbling sections of an orange fortified with vitamin LSD; skulls, skeletons and red roses on patches sewn to the breasts of denim jackets and the butts of denim pants; a girl in a garland of red roses like the one worn by the skeleton on the second live album and another girl in a baldy clown mask like the one worn by Garcia in the *Europe '72* photographs; and raiments silk-screened, heat-transferred and appliquéd with every known piece of Dead artwork, from the sperm-shooting skull on *Aoxomoxoa* to the fiddling fright-wigged skeleton on *Blues for Allah* to the skull-and-lightning-bolt on *Steal Your Face*; all of them wafting across the UCLA campus to Pauley Pavilion and most of them getting inside by 7. when the Dead secure the stage and start into "Jack Straw":

We can share the women,
We can share the wine...

—the vocal harmony shakily apportioned among lead guitarist and reluctant hep arbiter Jerry Garcia, bulbous in a blank black T-shirt and extravagantly hairy around Sphinxomatic shades; Donna Godchaux, who plays with the ends of her straight brown waist-length hair during tricky passages; and Bobby Weir in his aviator glasses, the one actual handsome rock star connected with the enterprise. The other Dead—Keith Godchaux on piano, Phil Lesh on bass, Mickey Hart and Bill Kreutzmann on drums—are off to one dark side of the stage, but it's Garcia's attention the Deadheads in the third row want anyway. They're holding up a Charlie McCarthy-sized Jerry Garcia rag doll, a grotesque but accurate little sucker with black shirt and glasses, teeny loose blue jeans and a scarlet rose sticking out of a mouth obscured by a real-hair beard. He doesn't notice it—or, rather, he doesn't acknowledge it; Garcia, they say, notices *everything*—and the doll is down as Weir goes into "Mama Tried" and "Mexicali Blues" short versions without extended solos, because the first 90 minutes or so of the Dead show is prelude, a vigil kept until the vibes reach critical mass so the seance can get under way, so the band and the audience will be available to the magic if it should choose this night to visit.

Ten years after the Haight-Ashbury cashed its food stamps, the Grateful Dead are still selling out halls. The funny thing about tonight's college-campus crowd, though, is that there are very few people of college age. There is a scattering of old people—30 to 35, looking the way they looked at the be-ins, like Japanese World War II soldiers on remote Pacific islands who haven't surrendered yet. These older types are mostly charter Deadheads, who heard them play for free in Golden Gate Park or for $1.50—punch included—at the Acid Tests in '65. They may even have heard the Dead before they were the Dead, as Mother McCree's Uptown Jug Champions in Palo Alto, and then, in the Haight, as The Warlocks "Featuring Ron 'Pig Pen' McKernan," the original scary motorcycle hippie, whose glower was marketed on pinup posters in head shops and who became the first literally dead Dead in 1973. Certainly they recall the Dead's enmeshment in the fatal fiasco of the Rolling Stones' Altamont concert in 1969, and their almost simultaneous departure from weirdly layered improvisations and tone-poem lyrics in favor of folksy story-songs about miners, gamblers and outlaws, songs whose musical structure comes straight out of Carl Sandburg's *American Songbag* but whose lyrics are pocked with the darkest intimations of roller-coastering doom. They may recall tsk-ing Random Notes about the Dead's propensity for being stolen blind by managers or the bath they took when they started Round Records and poured their money into a scheme to laser-encode music on pyramid-shaped software that would make round records obsolete.

But that's the *old* people in the audience. The majority here, and the bulk of the present-day Deadheads, who can buy out a two-night stand at Madison Square Garden without benefit of advertising and who made the Dead's last album, *Shakedown Street*, the fastest-selling record in their history—these Deadheads are mostly fifteen or sixteen years old, which means that in the Summer of Love they were just barely three or four.

And among these Deadheads are some whose involvement with the Grateful Dead far transcends the normal fan-star parameters. They follow a Dead tour as if it were the circus come to town, working their way across the country or down a coast to see twenty shows in succession. Their notions about life and morality rest heavily on the blank-check aphorisms built into Robert Hunter's lyrics for the Dead. Whatever positions the individual Deadheads may take in the endless factional contretemps over the merits of the Spacy Period versus the Pretty Period versus the Post-Round Period, they are all unshakably committed to the chief article of Deadhead faith, as stated on the bumpers of half the cars in the parking structure across the quad from Pauley tonight: THERE IS NOTHING LIKE A GRATEFUL DEAD CONCERT.

A true statement, on several levels. The sound of the Dead is not blues nor metal nor disco, but a loose and sometimes sloppy tumbling along, centered around the guitar of Garcia, whose solos are mercury-bright mutations of the western swing cadences of Bob Wills, and whose virtuosity is conceded even by the many critics who find the Dead boring. The lyrics recurringly catalogue symbols of chance and loneliness ("trains, rain, highways, cats and card games," as Phil Lesh puts it). While the simple dynamics of tension and release supply the cues for the normal rock audience to get excited, the Dead's long jams are after something more elusive. Anyone who says that fifteen-year-olds have no attention span hasn't seen them sit raptly through 40 minutes of Grateful Dead noodling, wordlessly passing joints and mirrors as the quirks, accidents and epiphanies are marshaled in pursuit of a spark. Though the art of shared improvisation is commonplace in jazz, especially since the Parker/Coltrane/Davis dynasties, it's almost absent from current rock 'n' roll, which may be why both the Dead and their fans feel free to toss around concepts like synchronicity and the Group Mind.

A little after 8:30 they strike up "Tennessee Jed," a litany of insults and injuries from *Europe '72*—

Dropped four flights and cracked my spine,
Honey come quick with the i-o-dine...

—and the crowd tangibly starts getting off during a pauseless medley of "All New Minglewood Blues," Chuck Berry's "Promised Land" and Weir's plaintive-ballsy version of "Good Lovin'." It's unlikely that many of the kids now pressing the stage-front barrier remember the Young Rascals' hit of 1966, but it makes a perfect Dead rave-up—standard I-IV-V chords and a straight four time that supplies Hart and Kreutzmann with a playground of ready-made crescendos. Then "Playing in the Band," Weir's rock-star-as-working-stiff credo, and "Shakedown Street," which leads into a long drum duet. The other band members drift off and cop Heinekens as Mickey and Billy's congeries becomes a locomotive third party that can no longer be reasoned with by the time Mickey deserts his kit for a marimba parked upstage and starts a simple melody that grows an architectonic complexity under Kreutzmann's goading, Billy now playing in some diabolical uncountable time signature for a series of ecstatic exchanges with Mickey and then—almost before the Heads can be sure they've seen him and not imagined him—a short, smiling black man in a white robe and turban, carrying a round, flat white drum, comes stage front where Garcia stood earlier and starts bouncing riffs off the drum and chanting in *Arabic*, okay, as six young white men in robes and beards materialize on stage in a semicircle around him. They chant along, hand-clapping, bowing and rising and ritualizing their brains out.

Well. Even those Deadheads who've seen Mickey jam with Ravi Shankar's tabla player have to regroup a little. It's like We Interrupt the Grateful Dead to Bring You Some Wiggy Religious People, or maybe it's a likely enough hallucination in the middle of a Mickey-Billy duet—but then the other Dead start wandering back on. Keith sits at the piano and drops some gospelly chords into the chant; Weir and Garcia pick up their guitars and lay some riffs around it. The little black man—turns out later it's Hamza el-Din, Mickey's very favorite Upper Egyptian drummer, but who knew?—takes his back-up pray-ers off the stage, and the Dead screw around with the residue of the ceremony until Garcia is ambushed by the heraldic, thumping opening riff of "St. Stephen," the vaguely religious puzzler (Hunter is very big on vague religiosity) that debuted on *Aoxomoxoa* in 1969. Garcia works toward his and Weir's vocal entrance at half-speed, a luxurious sexual slowness intended to milk the maximum from the loveliest lyrics and melodic hooks in their repertoire—

Saint Stephen with a rose,
In and out of the garden he goes.

Country garland in the wind and the rain,
Wherever he goes the people all complain

—and Garcia's fat raindrop notes go cascading down the guitar neck, the thunderous drums making it a full-scale storm, and the crowd is hot; a high-speed jam connects "Stephen" to Buddy Holly's "Not Fade Away" with its a cappella chills and Chuck Berry's "Around and Around," wherein Weir jumps and whoops and the lines "No they never stopped rockin' / Till the moon went down" seem to contain all the hoodoo that's been sliding back and forth between the Dead and the Heads all night—all the Americana and Arabica and psychedelia and cokeabilia boiled into four measures like a spoon of 1970 street speed, with Weir airborne for good this time and the audience hysterical, stomping, lighting matches and butanes, screaming almost as loud as the twenty speakers stacked on each side of the stage. *Got* some.

Believe It If You Need It

Les Kippel, 32, manages apartment houses in Bedford Stuyvesant for the New York City Housing Authority. He also publishes *Relix* magazine, using the back room of his Brooklyn apartment as a business office. *Relix*, a 20,000-circulation bimonthly whose principal subject matter is San Francisco-area music, particularly the Dead's, runs articles with titles like "Bring Back the Sixties, Man" and "Where Have All the Hippies Gone?" and carries advertisements for every skull-and-roses *tchotchke* conceivable and rare photographs of Pigpen grabbing Janis Joplin's left breast.

Kippel—earnest mustached face, International Marijuana Wholesalers and Distributors T-shirt—sits down over tea and oranges in his kitchen and says, "The first time I saw the Grateful Dead was in 1970, at Fillmore East. I had recently moved out of my parents' house and traded twenty hits of Orange Sunshine acid for my first stereo. I'd been listening to Vanilla Fudge, Melanie, the Doors, stuff like that, but I was unaware of the Grateful Dead.

"Then a friend of mine said, 'I got tickets,' and I said, 'I'll go.' I sat in seat F122. Amazing, right? To remember your seat number? Well, they played a couple acoustic sets, and then they played electric until dawn, and it was *phenomenal*. I couldn't believe it. 'St Stephen,' 'Dark Star'—the audience was going crazy. In those days, they would open the doors at 11 p.m. and you wouldn't leave until 6 a.m., so you could take an entire trip, mentally and physically, with the Grateful Dead. In '70, '71, I was satisfied with just their local shows, but in '72 I started traveling as far as Philadelphia. In '73, '74, I had my period of total involvement as a fan. My car got stolen and I got $2,000 for that and I just started following the Grateful Dead. I went to Winterland in San

Francisco on New Year's Eve, followed them from Florida to Rhode Island on an entire East Coast tour.

"When I put an advertisement for *Relix* in a program at a Dead concert at Meadowlands in New Jersey, I get coupons back from Ohio, Michigan, Florida, Mexico...we're talking about a whole audience that travels to see the Grateful Dead. 'There's a Grateful Dead concert in Detroit tomorrow night' 'Okay, let's go.' And the Dead won't be *on* every night, and you want to see the best you can. Therefore, travel.

"If you send five people down to get tickets, and they allow you four tickets per person, you'll have twenty people sitting together, and what better place is there to have a party than twenty people together at a Grateful Dead concert? That's the whole concept, Brotherhood. I mean, even enemies will pass joints at Grateful Dead concerts. Even enemies will get into water-gun fights at Grateful Dead concerts. Of course, there's LSD in the water.

"You know that old science-fiction TV show where they said, 'We now return control of your set to you until next week'? The Grateful Dead are like that. When you come to that concert, if you catch the right concert, it's 'Give us control of your senses and at the end of the concert we will give you back control.' That's what they did to me. They took control of my mind and opened it up to music.

"I'm constantly quoting things from their songs and applying them to my personal situations. It's intelligent music. The *thinking* that goes on! The tons of imagery in the lyrics—to understand a song like 'Box of Rain,' you have to sit down and listen to it. It's just making such a *statement* about things—I mean, it's crazy. It's so intense, it all works out so well, Hunter is so intelligent.

"If not for the Grateful Dead, I can see where I'd have been married at 21, narrow-minded and simple-minded, with three kids, working as a statistician at some company and being a Mason. The Grateful Dead saved me from that. The Grateful Dead energy constantly affects everyone, and it's a very catchy energy. If the Grateful Dead are sluggish, everyone else is sluggish. If the Grateful Dead are like *this*"—he snaps his fingers—"moving along quickly, they're an energy center. The musicians on that stage are shooting off energy in all directions, and if the twenty people who are at that Grateful Dead concert say, *'Catch* this fuckin' energy, man; I gotta get my friends here,' then those other people will come and after one concert they'll just be addicted."

Just Like New York City, Just Like Jericho

A couple of weeks after the UCLA date, the Dead come to New York for a pair of sold-out concerts at Madison Square Garden, to be attended by every rowdy fifteen-year-old stoner in the metropolitan area. The shows are makeup dates, this chunk of the tour having been postponed because of Garcia's bad throat, which is acting up again after a couple of cold nights in Philadelphia.

The day before the first show, Mickey Hart goes to visit Arthur Jones, who was his band teacher at Lawrence High School, out on the Island. "I sent him twelve free tickets to the Grateful Dead and I went out to see him," says Hart, whose acute, hungry face and fast speech recall Alan Arkin. "Years ago, when I was starting to play drums, I came into this new high school as a freshman, and I had my sticks, I knew the rudiments, and I wanted to be in the band. Mr. Jones said, 'Mickey, there are 28 drummers in the band, I don't know what I can do. Play for me.' So I play him a couple ratta-tats. Had he said no, I might've gone up on a steeple and shot people, flipped out totally. Given up drumming, at least. He said, 'Okay, you can be in Band II,' and he put a strap on me and I pulled the bass drum in the band, and finally worked my way up through the cymbals, the tenor drum line, and finally snares.

"So he's been 37 years teaching at this high school and I wanted to go back and honor him. I told him, 'Don't tell anybody I'm coming.' But somebody saw me in the parking lot, and when I went into the office of the high school and started talking with Mr. Jones, the kids started leaving their classrooms, and all of a sudden they're in the office with us, yelling, *Grateful Fucking Dead! Grateful Fucking Dead!* The secretaries are moving back to the wall, the kids are jumping over desks, I'm signing autographs, which I never do, and the whole place just went kablooie. Mr. Jones was enjoying the hell out of it. I had no idea. I walk back in the high school and *whooosh.*"

On the other hand, this rheumy kid comes reeling up to Bobby Weir after the first night's show—a show that suffers badly from Garcia's throat problem—and corners him against a wall backstage. "Why don't you just come out and *admit* it?" the kid yells, hysterical.

"Admit what?" Weir says, trying not to incite this Drug Burnout Poster Boy any more than is necessary.

"About your lyrics!" the kid shouts. "Admit that all your lyrics are about the Guru Maharaj Ji! Why don't you just come out and say it?"

So Weir hotfoots it to the limo and back to the Hilton, but he's not safe yet, because in the hotel lobby he's intercepted by a blonde teenage girl who says, "*Bob*by. I was waiting the whole *time*, at the door in the *back*. They didn't know to let me in..." He looks at her blankly. "I'm *Kathy*. From Florida, last week?"

Weir nods, trying to be nice. "Hi, yeah, I'll make sure you're on the list, uh, tomorrow—"

"Where are you going *now*?" Kathy demands.

"Uh...I was just going upstairs and have a...beer and..."

"Can I come?" Weir, cornered again, nods. "Can I go get my friends?"

"Your *friends*?"

"We came all the way from *Flor*ida." It appears that she may cry.

Weir sighs. "Okay." He tells her the number of a suite occupied by the Dead's logistician, Rock Scully. "You can come up in a little while."

The girl nods and runs for the hotel exit doors. Weir, shaking his head, takes the elevator up to Scully's suite, where a half-dozen people are hanging out.

Bill Kreutzmann, the 33-year-old senior drummer, who appears to be in his cups, maybe in his spansules and not inconceivably in his nostrils, is stalking the window, waving his arms and making faces at the street twelve floors below.

"Billy's entertaining the corner of 53rd and 6th," Scully's wife Nicki says. Weir nods, and sits down on the floor between a bed and the wall to talk to an editor from *Saturday Night Live* who's been hanging around with the Dead a little since they appeared on the show a few months ago.

Nicki complains that the room service food hasn't shown up yet. The phone rings. She answers it and talks for a few seconds before Bill comes over and takes it from her. "Hi," he says into the mouthpiece. "How ya doin'? Okay. Look, we're up here in...1219 and we need some sandwiches, about a couple cases of beer and uh, some wine. About enough wine for fifteen people, okay? Thanks." He hangs up and goes back to the window.

"I think maybe I better call room service again," Nicki says.

"Bill just ordered some sandwiches and stuff," I say.

"Yeah, but that was Phil on the phone," Nicki says, dialing. The girl from Florida arrives with two clones and is shown to the back bedroom of the suite. Garcia is sequestered in his room with a humidifier tonight, but there is a mounted black-and-white photograph of him propped on the Scullys' night table. "Did you see this picture of Jerry?" Nicki asks Weir. He nods.

"Boy, that's him, isn't it? I mean, that's really him, don't you think?" says a member of the Dead crew, looking at the photograph.

There's a knock at the door. Bill wheels abruptly from the window and asks, "Who is it?"

"It's *Phil!*" Bill says excitedly. He has just spent four hours on the same stage as Phil. He and Phil used to live in the same house. "How *are* you, Phil?"

"I'm fine, Bill," says the voice on the other side of the door.

"Phil, I'm so sorry that there's this...this barrier between us," Bill says.

"I am too, Bill. Don't you worry, though..." Nicki opens the door and Phil Lesh walks in—a slight, likable man whose intellectual curiosity was not satisfied by a formal education in music and composition, nor by a couple of seasons of dropping acid in the Haight, and who enrolled in the Dead as a kind of protracted graduate study in both of the previous disciplines. He sees Bill confronting the window. "You *can* fly, Billy," he says.

"Phil," says Bill, "that was such a burn about the overtime, man."

"What overtime?" I ask.

"There are—what—57 unions in Madison Square Garden?" Bobby says. "You can't play past 11 or they fine you. Ten thousand dollars for every minute past 11."

"I mean, one minute you're making money and the next minute you're *broke*?" Bill says. "They can't *do* that to us. And you know why they can't? It's because...because when you check in your room here, both the faucets say 'C' on them and..." He turns toward Weir, points at him. "You have to do your paper airplane," he says.

"Oh, okay," Bobby says. He gets up, finds a piece of paper and begins folding it into one of those crafty *Scientific American* jobs. "I was the best at this in high school," he says.

"But I'm gonna make you a bet," Billy says. "I'm gonna bet you that if you throw that airplane out the window it won't stay up for more than 6.457 seconds." He turns to Phil. "Does your watch do three decimal places?"

Lesh looks at his watch. "No, only two."

"*That's* no good," Billy says.

"Well, hell," Lesh says, and takes the watch off and tosses it over his shoulder.

The airplane flirts with an updraft but goes down fast. The food arrives. The girls from Florida leave. Keith Godchaux comes in, sits down in a chair in the middle of all the noise and says nothing—just smiles to himself, falls asleep and wakes up several times in the space of an hour, then gets up and leaves as silently as he came.

Weir is talking about a book that explains how to "walk out of your door naked, with nothing, and just survive on the earth. All the herbs and everything. That ought to be required reading for everybody. I mean, I was born into civilization, and civilization gave me something to do that I'm good at, or I'm getting good at, which is making art in order to make a living. But if I had to make an art *out* of living, I'd want to be able to do that too."

"I have a friend that does all the stunts for Fonzie," Billy says.

"They were searching the kids pretty heavily tonight," somebody says.

"Hey, *let 'em search*," Billy says. "I don't want some freak that likes Kiss coming to a Grateful Dead concert and trying to blow me away. Probably miss and hit Hart anyway."

"Einstein," Bobby Weir is saying to his friend the editor, "believed that an idea, a real original idea, is something that happens to people maybe two or three times in their lives, if they're lucky. So when the *band* comes up with an idea, it's—I mean, we can always take some lick and put a twist on it, but to have a real musical *idea*, well, that's Christmas. In fact, that's the only real Christmas there is."

Drink Down a Bottle and You're Ready to Kill

The Grateful Dead, it is said, once proposed to their record company that they be allowed to record the hot air of the desert and the cold air of the high mountains and mix them together in the studio to see how it sounded. The Grateful Dead are now on their fourth record company.

"They were difficult," says an executive who worked with the group at one of their former labels. "Anything that was in the realm of everyday happenings, they didn't want any part of. They wanted to be different.

"For example, the two-record live set that they did for us was originally going to be called *Skull Fuck*. Now, we felt at the company that that wasn't an appropriate title for getting the album into Sears, say, or the other department stores. However, it was Garcia's feeling that he would settle for 15,000 in sales if the album could go out as...with that title.

"But any decision that concerned them had to involve everybody in the band, and their *families* were involved in the decision as well, and the other people associated with them. So, on that title, it was necessary to hold a meeting with all of them here at the record company, but the record company's conference room wasn't big enough, because the Dead had brought 55 people with them, so we had to rent the conference room at the Continental Hyatt House to discuss the whole *Skull Fuck* question. So they were unique.

"Their music, of course, is incredible. It's fantastic. People who are aware of it are enjoying something that...well, they're sensational live. You get your music fix for the *month* at a Grateful Dead show. They play their asses off and they love it. Just get high and go on and play half the night.

"I remember, I was at the Palladium one evening when they were playing— I think it was fall of '71—and I must have had a Coke or a beer or something, backstage before the show, and a while later I began to feel this total...hallucinating...effect coming on, and—maybe I shouldn't admit this, but I had never taken acid before that point, and that's what it was.

"I had to leave. It was craziness. I'd always been told that when I was around them I should watch what I ate or drank, because they got a kick out of that, but I just forgot and...it was funny the next day, but it wasn't funny at the time, because I had no idea what was happening to me. I mean, they could have *said* something."

I Need a Miracle Every Day

Garcia cannot shake the aura. Knowledge is ascribed to him. Powers. It gives him pause. He never volunteered to be the ayatollah of hip culture, though he never quite ran away from it either—giving out quotes like "In my version of the universe, it's far out: There's more than meets the eyes in every situation" and submitting to an epic interview with Jann Wenner of *Rolling Stone* and Charles Reich, the greener of America, which was published as a book called *Garcia: A Signpost to New Space.*

Nor can he shake the throat trouble. A couple of weeks after Madison Square, his voice, which is rickety even when he's well, is even thinner and wheezier, like taffy with a fine coating of rust. He sits in the San Rafael house occupied by the Dead's booking agency, watching a country music show on color television and coughing. More than one person who works for the Dead has suggested to me that Garcia's throat problem would yield to a cutback from three packs of unfiltered Camels a day, a vacation from central nervous system stimulants, and some sleep. When I ask how he's feeling, he shakes his head and rasps, "I just can't seem to get rid of this thing. Must be some persist-ent...bacteria."

I ask him how it feels to be 37 and have all these new fifteen-year-old fans. "Well," he says, lighting a Camel, "I think there's maybe a certain percentage of people in the population that can dig the Grateful Dead at any given time, and they can dig it for as long as five, six years, maybe longer than that, depending on who they are. It's an additive factor that's useful in some people's lives. Every three or four years there's a whole bunch of new people who can dig the Grateful Dead...but *we* live in a world in which there *isn't* any Grateful Dead, as an experience. Our version is bound to be different from theirs."

And why is the fans' version so crucial in their lives—why all the traveling and lyric quoting and the 9 zillion skulls all over everything?

"That's an interesting question. It can't be solved by examining *our* motives. I've pondered this, man, I'll tell you. And I've always been on the trip of, like, I'd sure hate to mislead anybody with this. It'd be a drag to have people believing weird things because of what we're doing. But our old psychedelic experiences always pointed out the possibility that, like, the best thing you can do is to do what you're doing the best way you can and hope for the fuckin' best. Because psychedelics suggest, I think, that there are bigger and better things as far as human consciousness is concerned. There's someplace to go, something to look for. I think of our audience as people who are out lookin' for something. We've sort of gamely stuck to those initial possibilities and maybe they pick up on that and it gives us some kind of vaaal-idity." He giggles.

"Whereas for us, playing together is what's real. For me, emotionally, if I have a show and it's a bad show. I really don't feel like *any*thing is together. I don't feel like answering questions or signing autographs. I feel like everything that's ever happened has been so we could play this bad set. It's existential. It's an emotional reality I can't avoid; I mean there's no comfort from your past glories or anything like that. The audience fuckin' knows it, they know if we're havin' a good night or if we're struggling, and they can dig it if we're struggling. They know we're going to get off eventually—if not at this gig, then at some other gig.

"As to when we get off...you can't make it happen by acts of will or addressing it in a direct way, so you look for devious ways. It's like dialing a combination: Let's see, I remember that night I had two glasses of brandy, smoked a little hash and took a snort or two, and I felt just perfect and that night the band played beautifully, so maybe if I repeat that combination—but it never works that way, so that automatically keeps it interesting, because it isn't a matter of will. The fact that things work out as well as they do as often as they do is like on the level of miraculous; I mean it's way outside of chance.

"There are times when I spend the whole night thinking about things like, 'God, my feet hurt,' or 'I gotta pay the rent,' or 'Why can't I get my guitar in tune; it doesn't sound quite right'—I never get past the trivial little bullshit, so I never see the audience, I never see anybody in the band, I'm just locked up in a little private hell—heh, really, man. But sometimes on those nights people will come up to me and say, 'God, that was the most incredible music you guys have ever played; it sounded—' And I just go, 'What?' I listen to a tape and it sounds amazing and I say, 'I don't remember that; I didn't play that,' and it's those moments that I realize that my conscious will, the me I know of as the day-to-day me, is just really not very involved in this whole thing in a way that can interfere with it substantially or cause it. It's something that occurs in a mediumistic way, something involuntary. I trust it because I know it's *not* me. If it was me, I wouldn't trust it because I couldn't dig it; I know myself too well.

"I go to science quite a lot, in trying to figure this out, because science has the best consensus. I also go to astrology and the *I Ching* and random input—you know, people stop you on the street and say, 'Hey, man, there's a big flood coming next week and look out your car's got four flat tires.' Prophecies. You learn to just let things happen to you because it's random input. You've got science with its world of structure and legitimacy, you know, and the intuitive and the occult with their nonlinear relations to primal questions, and philosophy, and religion—they're all addressing the same thing in a lot of ways and we're addressing it in another way, which has to do with getting a lot of people together and playing music and having energy of some invisible kind that's nonetheless real for everybody involved with it.

"I've been reading a lot about probability and quantum mechanics, because all that stuff contains clues about what we're doing and what the importance of it is and why people feel involved with it. There seems to be a lot of evidence coming to the fore now that ideation is an *in*ductive process rather than deductive, which means that what consciousness can imagine, it can achieve. My favorite story is the one about boron. The element, you know, in the periodic table? It used to be an inert material, which meant that chemically speaking it didn't interact with anything. Then a mathematician postulated a situation in which it would interact, created a number as a model, so from that point on it was no longer inert. I mean, he *changed* the physical properties of a substance; once they created the model the material followed suit. That's pretty dramatic. You dig? Pretty far out. The consequence of that is that whatever we can imagine is what's real.

"Then, the idea of probability—we play randomly. We don't have signals. While there are various tip-offs that we're all aware of, we also know from our own experience that enough things happen that *aren't* the result of signals or planning or communication that we're aware of, but that are miraculous manifestations, that keep proving it out, that there's no way to deny it. We're just involved in something that has a very high incidence of synchronicity. You know, the Jungian idea of synchronicity? Well, shit, that's day-to-day *reality* for us."

He does a couple of lines and lights another cigarette. "We're looking in a nonlinear way for clues to try and further this idea, from Mickey going out in the desert with a tape recorder to me poring through quantum mechanics and Alfred North Whitehead. We're all just poking around. So where are you going next?"

"I'm going to have dinner with Phil Lesh," I say.

"Oh," Garcia says. "That'll be a *good* experience."

Let Him Cast a Stone at Me for Playing in the Band

Phil Lesh lives in a small house in the Marin County hamlet of Fairfax, with a red Lotus and a large library of classical records (Bruckner is on the turntable when I arrive). Lesh, who studied composition with Luciano Berio before he started hanging out at the fringes of Ken Kesey's Stanford acid scene with Garcia, was a prolific songwriter for the Dead during the *Aoxomoxoa-American Beauty* period—arguably the height of their musical creativity. He has had several formal music projects on hold for the past few years.

"I have a project in the back of my head. A symphonic poem. You're familiar with the form? Invented by Liszt in the nineteenth century. Mine is based on Coleridge's 'Kubla Khan.' You know the poem? An opium dream, or so they say. It's for percussion, synthesizer and voices. That's one project, and there are others, but the rehearsal time for all the players is so expensive...Right now I'm just playing the bass. I'm kind of bored with trying to write for the Grateful Dead, because I tend to write some pretty dense shit, and it's almost antithetical to rock 'n' roll skill. It's hard to get them to play it. That period around *Live/Dead*, when the music was a little more complex—that was the peak for me. Now we've gotten into a format.

"But I don't get bored with being *in* the Grateful Dead. To me, the Grateful Dead is life—the life of the spirit, and the life of the mind, as opposed to standing in line and marking time in the twentieth century. I went through the Acid Tests with the Grateful Dead, and all I can say is, you had to be there. That was the *baptismo del fuego*. When you're up there and your *face* is falling off and you've still got to play, and you do this over and over again, spilling your guts in front of thousands of people...you develop a certain *flip* attitude, even toward performing. You begin to believe that you could go out there naked and nobody'd notice, as long as you played loud enough."

Over dinner, Lesh talks about the Dead's trip to Egypt in September of 1978 for a series of concerts at the pyramids. "It sort of became my project, because I was one of the first people in the band who was on the trip of playing at places of power. You know, power that's been preserved from the ancient world. The pyramids are like the obvious number-one choice, because no matter what anyone thinks they might be, there is definitely some kind of *mojo* about the pyramids. And when you get there you find out that there *is* power. The same kind of power you get from the audience, only there's more of it, because it's older and because of what was built into it.

"Ever since the Acid Tests, we've been into that power. That's what powered the Acid Tests, *behind* the acid, and it later became apparent that you didn't need drugs if you had the enthusiasm. It was a rawer order of energy, less information riding on that raw carrier wave of power, but the power was always there. It was a matter of awareness...feeling...intuition...anything but rational thinking. I wonder sometimes if the audience is as aware of that as we are. Obviously, if it's not there, you stroke it and get it up. In that sense it's a traditional show-biz trip: Stroke the audience and get 'em up. Build it up to the point where it's self-sustaining. This is true of all performers, yes? But for some reason especially true of the Grateful Dead. There's a special lock-in with the audience that can occur—it's totally random in a lot of ways, but I do know that we've never been able to really *do* it two nights in a row, including

Egypt. I don't know if we really did it in Egypt or not, musically, but to be there was so deep and so dense and so thick and so impressive that it was almost...I don't know, it changed my life, it was the high point of my life to date. But it still wasn't good enough.

"Now, getting the band into Egypt: Having ascertained that that was a place of power, we started trying to do it around January of 1976. We asked Bill Graham to help us, because we really didn't now how to go about it ourselves. We discussed it with Bill and it was agreed that he would make the first moves because he knew all these people in our government. He was saying, 'I know so-and-so and so-and-so in the White House, rucka rucka,' right? So we call up every day and ask what's happening with Egypt.

"Now, Bill is a busy man. You can imagine how busy he must be. I was him, I'd be busy too. *Buy* them condominiums! Plant shows at the Coliseum! Whatever.

"So we abandoned Bill Graham to the vagaries of his own conscience, and it turned out that we had a contact with Jonathan Wallace, who edits the *Middle Eastern Economic Digest* in London, and *he* knew a guy named Joe Malone, who was president of the American University in Beirut for 25 years and now has a consulting firm. Anything you want to do in the Middle East, he'll help you.

"So in March we go to Washington and meet with Joe Malone and his wife Lois, and they have got the Egyptian thing covered—they know all those people by their first names, from Sadat on *down*. And we plot out a strategy revolving around the fact that we're not going to take any money out of the country. The money will be donated to the Department of Antiquities, which is our idea, and to Madame Sadat's favorite charity, which was Joe's idea. It was slick as hell, man.

"Then we had to go over to our side and deal with the American diplomats. Some of the people we allow to represent us abroad, man—I mean, they're ugly to me, and I'm an American, cross my heart. But Joe was such a wheeler, he talked to these guys about what we wanted to do and how mellow it was, spicing it up with anecdotes about people they all knew from the Middle East—it was priceless; I mean he charmed these guys right out of their *pants*. There they were—shoes, socks, garter belts, yes. Pants, no. You shoulda seen it. So after an hour with these USIA guys in Washington, it turned out that it was cool with our government if it was okay with Egypt's. You know, 'it's okay with me if it's okay with him.' Grateful Dead works a lot that way. So both governments sent their communiqués to Cairo, and we go over there in March with Lois Malone.

"First we had to convince these two guys at the U.S. Embassy, which we did in half an hour, thanks to Lois. Then we went over to see a most remarkable person, Dr. Saad el-Din, who was the Egyptian second deputy minister of culture, I believe. Poet, writer, friend of Lawrence Durrell's and former head of the secret police, all in one person. He was so perceptive that it was amazing. The terms in which he *grasped* it...The report had come in from their embassy in Washington. I saw it. It said: 'P.S. This group is very heavy in the United States. These people are not playing,' in effect. 'They mean it.' So we talk to Dr. Saad el-Din about how we won't make any money except from the record of the performances and the Egyptians have a piece of that too, so there's no feeling of here come the white boys gonna rip us off again.

"About fifteen minutes into it Dr. Saad el-Din turned to me and said, 'Have you ever played any place outside the U.S.?' I said, 'Yeah, we've played in Europe.' He said, 'Have you found that your music changes when you play in different places?' I said, 'Pre*cisely*, and that's why we want to play at the pyramids,' and he said, 'I thought so.' And that was it. That was the fulcrum, right there—those three sentences changed it in their eyes from somebody jacking off to somebody meaning business. Remarkable guy. After that, it went through various government officials, but from that moment on it was essentially a fait accompli."

And the Egyptian Booking of the Dead relieved some of the boredom...?

"It was handy as hell. I'd have been real bored if I had to stay home during that period."

"But you still have musical ideas and impulses that aren't satisfied by the Grateful Dead?"

"Yeah," he says quietly and a little wanly. "There's just things in heaven and earth, Horatio, that are undreamt of by the Grateful Dead. And things that are impossible for the Grateful Dead as a unit, or as a Gestalt..."

"Like what?"

"Anything with more than four chords! Ha ha ha ha ha! Just had to slip that in. Ha. No, there's no way to make it all come out even. When I started with the Dead in 1966, I said, 'Look, guys, I don't want to be doing this when I'm 30.' Well, I'm 38 now, and I'm gonna be doing it when I'm 40. It may turn out that I'll just go gentle into that good night, you know? I may just become a country squire and forget my musical ambition...because I've seen what musical ambition can lead to for people who are incapable of handling success, or failure, or frustration, or whatever. Loneliness. I would love to be able to contribute something to the culture. I don't know whether I can at this point. It remains to be seen. Let's not get too serious."

Head's All Empty and I Don't Care

Time's just a loop, you dig, and here we are back in New York for the second night of the Garden gig. By 5:30 the Long Island Railroad commuter terminal is dotted with these weirded-out high school and junior high school kids, kids who have mastered the one-big-bandana school of fashion that you saw in the East Village twelve years ago. Al, for example, a seventeen-year-old girl from the Island ("Don't put what town I'm from; it's a totally lame town to be from"), is not only wearing a shapeless white peasant blouse and paisley-patched jeans, but also has unearthed one of those cut-glass refraction balls and has it hanging from a ribbon around her neck.

"I would say there's about 80 percent Deadheads at my school," Al says.

"There's too many," says her friend Dave, in an exquisitely faded denim jacket. "It's just getting to be a fad to be a Deadhead now."

"That's 'cause of their new music," Al says. "They're getting disco'd out. I like *Aoxomoxoa*."

"Do you think you missed out on something by not being around in '67 and '68?" I ask.

"God, definitely," says a girl named Leslie. "Those concerts must have been something. Everybody was so into it. Nobody *trusts* anybody anymore. I mean, the attitude then...I think people were doing more drugs."

"This isn't a time when you can have an attitude, though," Al says. "It's just a thing in your head now."

"Do you think that attitude is going to come back?" I ask Leslie.

She answers quickly and indignantly: "Well, God, it *better*."

On the cover of the Grateful Dead's *Europe '72* is a painting of a fried-eyed boy with enormous buck teeth trying to eat an ice cream cone. He has missed his mouth and crash-landed the cone on his forehead with a vivid *splat*.

Rock 'n' roll is a splayed, factional music now, and the junior Grateful Dead faction is roughly coincident with a strange swelling in the high school malcontent army. The kids in question are stoned, and on many of the same agents used by the kids who saw the Dead for free in the park in the sixties, but with none of the guileless optimism attributed to those flower children. Instead there is a cynical contempt for the exhausted present and the querulous future and anyone over *twenty* (there are fifteen-year-old boys with hair down to their shoulders who deal "pyramid acid" and use the word "hippie" to denote a retrograde figure of high comedy and pathos).

It is no coincidence that the Dead repertoire is so threaded with spookadelic images of disaster and treachery, that so many of the songs portray the universe as a tumble-down casino in which all the games are fixed. Train wrecks, shotgun murders, collapsing roofs and hungry wolves: The common ground between the Dead and the young Heads is the belief that the way to meet an impossible circumstance is with voluntary craziness. To get as far out there as the ice cream kid. To go palling around with death's signatures and sandblast the line between what is hopeless and what is just funny.

On the cover of *Shakedown Street* is a drawing of a terminally decayed street scene—cops frisking people, hookers swinging their purses, bums and pimps patrolling the corners. Everyone in the picture is grinning like crazy.

The song that gets the big response on the second night at Madison Square is "U.S. Blues," from the Round Period. From the first stanza—

Red and white,
Blue suede shoes,
I'm Uncle Sam,
How do you do?

—the kids are standing and singing along, partly because, for their purposes, the Grateful Dead *is* America. Not the crypto-optimistic America of Jimmy Carter, but the real America, where the roof is caving in and all concerned are too fucked up to feel it.

"The whole mythos is right there in the name," Phil Lesh says. "The Grateful Dead? I'm glad to be dead? And I'm still walking around?" Just so, like the zoot-suited phantom on the back of *Shakedown Street*, swinging his chain and grinning his Cheshire grin without a body to call his own.

I'm Uncle Sam
That's who I am
Been hidin' out
In a rock 'n' roll band

It's the kids' best guess that they have been born into the sudden-death-overtime of Western Civ—or at least, as Garcia sings in "Shakedown Street," "It's midnight, and the dark of the moon besides," with no guarantees about the dawn—it is time to sew on these skulls—

You can call this song
The United States Blues.

And it will look like Halloween all year *round* pretty soon, is what the kids suspect. What is getting mixed into the Kool-Aid these days is not LSD. The skeletons are asking for the next dance. And if the whole situation is irretrievably warped, as Tennessee Jed and the Deadheads can tell you in a second, it becomes incumbent upon the human to warp himself *into* shape by any means necessary, starting now, and not fade away.

Feature magazine was a short-lived successor to the early rock magazine *Crawdaddy*. Abbott's piece from the March 1979 issue is similar, in some ways, to McClanahan's epic article for *Playboy*, containing, as it does, interview material with Garcia and descriptions of the band in concert and of the audience. But the interview with Garcia includes accounts of two watershed experiences in his life that are revelations. The concert described is from December 17, 1978, at the Fox Theatre in Atlanta, Georgia, part of a rare Southern tour. Abbott is a distinguished fiction writer and has published several books, including *Love Is the Crooked Thing*, published by Alonquin in 1986; *Strangers in Paradise*, published by Putnam in 1986; *Dreams of Distant Lives*, published by Putnam in 1989; *Living After Midnight* published by Putnam in 1991; and *Wet Places at Noon*, published by the University of Iowa Press in 1997.

Dead Reckoning and
Hamburger Metaphysics

Lee Abbott

Interviews about me are boring. I would rather direct attention to things I think are more interesting. It's hard to talk about myself. I'm with myself all the time. In that sense it isn't much fun to be revealing bits of myself to people who don't know me, because I already know me. It's more fun to turn people on to things that may be interesting or useful to them later on. I'm only interesting because of what I'm interested in. I'd rather talk about IT than Me. Me's...old.

—Jerome John Garcia, December, 1978

tlanta, the Monday following the 75th anniversary of Orville and Wilbur Wright's "mad metaphor of flight" at Kill Devil Hills, and allusions to flights of every fancy—mechanical, spiritual, vegetable—are flapping through the Colony Court's Savannah Suite like a circus of dope-weaned hipster crows. *The Cosmic Trigger*, Masons, Knights Templars, pyramid power, Blake, phosphenes, Fortean phenomena and L-Fields—soon one expects to hear of tap-dancing Buddhas, gun-toting fakirs or Tasmanian coconut monks.

The subject for today's Grateful Dead seminar in applied metaphysics: the hamburger, specifically the difference between IT and Steak Tartare. Gone for the nonce is the feverish discussion of the hot dog vs. the frankfurter vs. the weiner vs. the schnitzel. Among the questions raised:

If God is good, why does he permit ground chuck?

When is a burger a burger?

What does one call a resident of Hamburg, Germany? And does that Teutonic burgher dream of special sauce, cheese, pickles on a sesame-seed bun? Imagine his confusion, his paranoia. Suddenly, silence. A presence is felt. It is 36-year-old, father-of-three-girls Jerome John Garcia. Chemically lit Rasputin eyes roll excitedly behind his tinted, rimless glasses. A coptic's black beard and shoulder-length tangle of gray-streaked hair give him the mien of a messiah. In the middle of the room, the Grateful Dead's traveling "secretary," Rock Scully, freezes, tilted forward precariously on tippy-toes, his axe-blade of a face bright with zeal. Slumped in a chair, manager Richard "Zippy" Loren lurches upright in anticipation. Clearly, Garcia is onto something here. What is fat? *Why* is fat? Whither the patty, in the Great Scheme of Things? Whosoever mocketh the lowly patty...

At last, his small hands carving the quintessential burger from the air, Garcia speaks. "To my mind," he says, his voice a kid's squeal of glee, "the *idea* of a burger always has something to do with"— he hangs fire, epiphany but a shout away—"BUNS!"

Buns, burgers and bushwah—it has always been thus for Jerry Garcia and the looney-tune freak-outs of wisdom and woe that are the Grateful Dead. Through drug busts, bum record deals, the death of Ron "Pigpen" McKernan in 1973, the demise of Haight and the rise of straight, it has always been Uncle John by the riverside who had "some things to talk about here beside the rising tide." To their legions of Dead Heads, the band is still mythic. Especially now that the Dead's second album on Arista, *Shakedown Street,* is making uncharacteristic waves on the charts; yes, especially now that the tour is going so well, that the Great Scheme of Things is sorting itself out so expertly and that spokesman and lead guitarist Jerry is in a self-described State of Happiness.

Uncertainty is what's happening to me. Are we living out some predetermined script in which the ending is already known? If so, why are we doing it? What's the purpose? Or is it possible that the gift of consciousness has a direct relationship to the atoms of the sense and purpose in the design of organisms, you know. I mean, we're surrounded by artifacts of the mind,

things we've invented. All these things are metaphors—they're telling me
something about what my mind is. Matter to energy, man, that's the game
here in this universe. It's furious manipulation, man, and it's coming from
my mind. It's what separates us from IT. I'm curious because I've had my
fucking mind blown. What is IT? I can't imagine being alive and not won-
dering about IT. Many don't care, but something cares for them whether
they like IT or not.

—J.J.G.

IT is the voice of an era, the '60s: Owsley acid, Sandoz LSD, DMT, STP, Consciousness III, the Be-In at Golden Gate Park, Wes Wilson posters, the Family
Dog, the Diggers, Tim Leary and Dick Alpert, the *Oracle*, freak-outs, the Fillmore and the Avalon, the Trips Festivals, Ken Kesey and the Merry Pranksters,
black light and "Living thunder." It is, some contend, the voice of Jerry Garcia,
"Captain Trips"—a fuck-up.

"I was a fuck-up in high school," Jerry says, easing himself onto the couch.
Outside, a hard rain threatens. Inside, Garcia is in high animation, giggling
and working over the past with a bantamweight's vigor. "When I was a kid, I
was a juvenile delinquent. My mom even moved me out of the city to get me
away from trouble. It didn't work. I couldn't stand high school 'cause I was
burning my bridges as I went along. But I didn't have any way to go. I don't
think I did any more than anybody else. It's just that I was always getting
caught—for fighting, drinking, all the stuff you're not supposed to do.

"I was involved in more complex ideas. I started reading Schopenhauer,
Heidegger and Kant when I was in the seventh grade. After that, school was
silly. I couldn't relate to it. Not only that, I was a teenager, you know, so I had an
attitude. I kept saying, 'Why should I be doing these dumb things? So I failed
school as a matter of defiance. I just didn't fit in anywhere. I mean, there were
gunfights in the halls, but I didn't fit into that either. I was happening on a different plane entirely. That's one of the reasons I got into drugs. In all that
teenage craziness, it was the only good trip around."

Garcia takes a heavy toke from an unfiltered Camel and studies his right
hand. (The middle finger is missing to the second knuckle. His brother cut it
off in a wood-chopping accident in the Santa Cruz Mountains when Jerry was
four.) After dropping out of school at the end of his junior year, he enlisted in
the pre-Vietnam Army. "It was either that," he says, "or jail."

Again, he screwed up: "Basically the problem with the Army was that they
didn't get me far enough from home. I got stationed in San Francisco [Ft. Winfield Scott in the Presidio], so it was easy for me to skip out. I treated the Army
as though it were school or a bum job. I was in the motor pool and went to a

missile school. Headquarters duty there is like the softest duty, I'm sure, in the United States Army. But I was always, uh, *late*. And no officer there wanted to have a fuck-up. I mean, they didn't want to hear about it. They didn't want to call attention to themselves. Every single person there was there because he was a scammer. It was a company of champion scammers."

He laughs at the memory of butch-cut lifers and ROTC wonders. "I was a nothing," he continues. "I had been court-martialed twice and had tons of extra duty and was restricted to barracks. I was just late all the time. I would miss roll call. I had seven or eight or nine or ten AWOLs, which is a pretty damn serious offense in the Army. So one day I'm called to the CO's office. No heavy trip or anything. He says, 'Private Garcia, how would you like to get out of the Army?' And I said, 'I'd like it just fine.' Two weeks later I was out."

It was a time of indecision for nineteen-year-old Garcia—a time of hanging out in East Palo Alto and Stanford coffeehouses, of playing "dippy folk songs" at Kepler's Book Store, of hearing about people like Paul Kantner.

"I hadn't decided I was *really* going to play music," Garcia recalls. "I was still oscillating between the art world and music. I wasn't committed. I was coasting."

What happened?

"I was in a good automobile accident." Jerry grows anxious. "I was with four other guys in an old Studebaker Golden Hawk—supercharged engine, *terrible* suspension, ninety-plus miles an hour—on a back road and we hit these chatter-bar dividers. It was just *Wham!* We went flying, I guess. All I know is that I was sitting in the car and that there was this...disturbance...and the next thing, I was in a field. I went through the windshield and landed far enough away from the car where I couldn't see it. It was at night. It was very, very quiet, you know. It was like a complete break in continuity—from sitting in the car roaring down the road to lying in a field wondering what had happened—nothing in between."

Anybody get hurt?

"Yeah," Garcia says with genuine awe. "One guy did die. He happened to be the most gifted of our little group. It was like losing the golden boy, someone who had a lot of promise, the person who had the most to offer."

"You were lucky," I suggest.

"Oh, yeah," Garcia agrees. "The car was like a crumpled cigarette pack. It was almost unrecognizable. And there were my shoes in it, dig? I had been thrown out of my shoes and through the windshield." He paused over the memory of a pair of scuffed Army-issues lying on the floorboards of a violence sculpture. "'That's where my life began." He breathes. "Before then I was always living at less than capacity. I was idling. That was the slingshot for the rest of my life. It was like a second chance." He looks at me hard, his expression earnest, grateful, dead. "Then I got serious."

Another toke. A deep suck of mortality. "I dig the affirmation side of death. Death is one of those things that's been taken from us as an experience. We hide it. As a result, it becomes fearful, scary, because it's unknown. Really, man, it's the other side of being born."

For the moment the Fox is churchyard quiet, as quiet as only 4,500 parishioners expecting a miracle can be. It's then that you realize you've been let into some Top Secret vicarage where the Dead are going to whipsaw darkness to light. Angels, demons, UFOnauts, fairies, wood nymphs, succubi—they're all here, sensed but unseen.

Then it starts. You can hear Bob Weir's incantatory whisper count it down—"We are going to heaven, folks..."—and the first notes...Almost immediately there is a maze of movement. Fingers twitch, heads bob, and soon you're shuffling in the aisles, making brothers of strangers and sucking the air of self-renewal. But this is the complete tour; no easy truth on the dark side of town. Pimps, sleazeballs, midnight ramblers, low-riders—in the rectory of the Dead, nobody dies.

Mickey Hart and Bill Kreutzmann work over their enameled drums like a pair of Rev. Ikes throwing up barricades against doomsday, while in front, bassist Phil Lesh, pianist Keith Godchaux and Bob Weir on rhythm guitar are laying curbstones of gold. But it's Garcia, with his clear and tingling lead lines, who will guide you all the way down the road.

Decibels curdle thoughts. Fists shoot in the air—defiant and righteous. The balcony bounces and chests tighten with joy. You've seen the Dead and they, by Jesus, are us.

At last, there it is: the miracle. Everybody's shouting the same hymn, everybody hunkered in the same direction, and everybody fixed on the same lovelight of promise at the end of the street.

Personally, I think the government should spend its money trying to figure out what the fuck we're doing here! We're bright enough to convert matter to energy, but are we bright enough to know why?

—J.J.G.

Garcia is on his knees, praying to the coffee table. The toot is vicious, cut with meth, not quinine, and it's enough to rip your sinuses out. It goes straight to the forebrain—a howling blizzard of Insight and Truth. The first rush is, well, chilling; your scalp tingles, a hospital sourness scours the back of your throat. Then a Con Ed generator of electricity sizzles your synapses and in slow-motion—one unruly muscle, one gristle-covered length of bone at a time—you coil into the couch. Your tea is tepid. Your smoke is tasty. You are ready to Talk.

"I hate to keep relating everything to drugs," Garcia begins, "but my most palpable experiences have all been psychedelics." There was one in particular, the *ne plus ultra* trip, the "apocalypse" at the end of what Jerry describes as his psychedelic period.

"It featured countless—thousands, millions—births and deaths. The phoenix trip, you know. And in my consciousness, it went all the way from, uh, *insects* to *vegetables* to *mammals* to civilizations—to organisms of every sort."

What happened?

"*Everything,*" Garcia barks, drawing closer, the glint of his eyes grave and dear. "For me, my trips began to take a different kind of form. The first ones were visual, you know, patterns, colors, profound revelations. 'Yeah, I get it'—the standard stuff. Then I started going to the Acid Tests and experiences were happening to more than one person at a time. They had this telepathic quality. Then into that stepped another level which was between and amongst the telepathic explosions. Between the flashes and surprises was this 'You're *almost* getting it.' An *urging.*

"Then there was a presence which I think of as the Teacher, which represents a higher order. There would be this feeling of *deja vu.* All these little bits of input—people talking, certain sights—would start to coalesce: 'Damn, You Got It! BOOM!' It took on this teacher-pupil relationship: Me and my other mind! Instead of outside reality, there was a whole other substance—other smells, other sounds, other tastes. Instead of, like, putting on a pair of funny glasses, this reality out here was replaced by a wholly other world."

Garcia teeters on the edge of the couch, his hands drawing wild arabesques in the air—a psychedelic hula story sans grass skirt.

"It scared the shit out of me, man. It was like, 'What do you believe?' It removed everything I was certain of. And in its place was a new set of circumstances. And these circumstances were like pages in a book. They started *moving* until I was living out a whole lifespan with all the intricacy of one's life, all the way up to the moment of one's death. The final realizations, the summation.

"I was simultaneously experiencing all these slightly different versions of my life until they got to be *very* different and finally *completely* and *utterly* different. I remember being a hive of bees. I was the whole damn hive! Instead of hands and fingers and feet and nerve endings, I was little bee bodies. I was a field of wheat. And then I was, like, part of these archetypes that involve everybody. It was like a dream in which you know somebody by their identity, not by their looks. You know, when somebody looks like Father Time but in reality is your mother."

Jerry's hands slash though the air, plucking solar systems like apples.

"There'd be, like, a whole epoch—planetary evolution, starting from nothing and going through the whole life of a planet with all the life forms, all the civilizations, all the consciousness and going all the way until it burns out. And one of them would be, like a pastoral trip. Another would be warlike. Another would be an incredible, multisensory life."

Again the hands make a sweep, this time rubbing out the past.

"Cosmic is the only word for it." he sighs. "Nothing has happened in my life since then, man. Nothing was as climactic, as complete as that."

Is it finished?

"In a way," he avers. "I can go back and visit bits and pieces of it, but it's all here—" Garcia cradles his head like a crystal ball—"in the foreground of my mind."

Fantasy time. Bob Weir's line has come true: "That crowd is angry. It's a hanging crowd!" It's, say, the Cow Palace and the crowd is 16,000 strong—ugly, unruly Dead Heads in army surplus drag. A thunderclap of dope haze moils near the rafters. It's a Scorsese pan shot of meanness, corruption and waste. The show is three hours old but as tight as a drum head. Garcia surveys the scene: balloon headgear, Viet chic, foot-stamping, 16,000 pair of adder eyes—the future is here and it ain't wholesome.

With a roar, the band lunges into "Johnny B. Goode." Gritting his teeth, Garcia throttles the neck of his Travis Bean guitar. Having established a vampire's intimacy with his piano, Keith Godchaux hunches into the music like a strong wind. Behind him, Phil Lesh is blood-pumping bass notes.

But Jerry is not satisfied. He senses something, knows it's there—Yes, it's fear: rocks-in-the-gut, back-brain fear. The skin glistens with an icy sweat, the nerves jangle. Then he spots them, rising like colossi from the sea—six dudes in CIA sharkskin and rep ties, brandishing death-dealing Uzi submachine guns. A hail of lead-tipped bullets rips across the stage. Underneath, there is the sizzle of *plastique*...

"It's an easy fantasy," Garcia says, laughing. "It's something that could happen. Mainly because nobody expects it. In fact, I always thought it was sort of

obvious. I was real paranoid about it before everybody started getting assassinated. Before assassination became a cheap shot."

The fact is, it almost happened once.

"A guy took a knife out in front of the stage," Jerry recalls. "It was a particularly exciting moment. This was a ballroom so it wasn't a seated concert.
Everybody around him was, like, ecstatic. But this guy had a panic-stricken
look on his face. You could tell he was going over, that he was losing it, freaking out on some drug. And he reaches into his coat and pulls out this huge
hunting knife, gleaming. What with the red and blue stage lights, it was just
like a fucking movie."

The promise of rock 'n' roll violence had become real: Death Meets the
Dead.

"I'm playing," Garcia says, "and I spot it. And I think, 'Oh, Jesus God! It's like
I'm the only one who can see it, you know. The people around him don't see it;
they're just boogying. And so I look over at Kreutzmann, and I'm whispering
'Hey, Bill! Hey!' And he looks down and sees this guy standing there in his
moment of indecision. I'm thinking, 'What's he gonna do? Is he gonna grab
this chick next to him and just slash her throat?'

Garcia has an imaginary Bowie knife in his fist. Menacingly, he eyes a
phantom fan to his left.

"So, all of a sudden, I catch his attention. He's looking at me, holding this
blade, so I kinda gesture, use body language to get him to throw it onstage. I'm
really concentrating. 'Please, man, up here', I'm thinking. 'Not here, man. Don't
do it here.' So Kreutzmann darts out and grabs the blade after it's been tossed
up. And then the guy kind of, you know, *relaxed* a little. He'd made contact."

Why does something like that happen?

"Just because of the kind of power, the X-factor that characterizes the
Dead's audience." Garcia gazes out the hotel window, lost in a thought.
Twenty-three stories below, Atlanta weathers another stormy Monday.
"There's something about it which I fundamentally don't trust," Jerry con-
tends.

There's a moral coming, you can feel it. Once a culture hero, always a culture hero. "I have the feeling it's somewhere along the road of losing your will."

Garcia: I'm involved in the Big Questions. I assume every human is. Who
are we? What are we doing? Why? Why all this elaborate hoax? You know,
what is all this stuff? The more I can articulate questions, the easier it is to
find answers.

Q: Have you found any answers?
Garcia: Hundreds, thousands, millions!

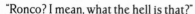

"Ronco? I mean, what the hell is that?"

The scene is the upstairs dressing room of the Fox Theater at 600 Peachtree and Jerry Garcia is busy figuring out the pedigree of the latest miracle of modern science, the smokeless ashtray that sits atop his amplifier. Tomorrow he will worry the precious history of the words Work and Love, but tonight it's all langyap and flapdoodle—the Hula-Ho, the Vegematic, the Egg Scrambler *("Do your children loathe runny egg whites?)*.

Garcia giggles hysterically. "To me this is the stuff that's going to change the world!"

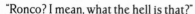

Great? For me, that word is tied into the individual—Michelangelo, Dosto-evsky for example—where one person is the vehicle for a tremendous out-pouring from the creative heavens. But I don't think that's what's called for now. The idea of the unperishable quality of one person's ideas...It's something I don't trust.

—J.J.G

It's encore time in Tampa's Curtis Hixon Auditorium and backstage, Rock Scully, onetime prison mate of Bob Haldeman at Lompoc, is pacing nervously in the grub room. There's lots to do: Feed the band, fend off the local press, make sure Charlie's got his limos warm. Then he nails her. She's curled up under a coatrack, sucking ice and grinning sheepishly.

"What are you doing here?" His briefcase hits the buffet table with a smack.

She is Orlando Beth, seventeen, tanned nut-brown, dressed in a denim shirt and string-tie pants (the cuffs of which are dyed sunshine yellow). She's caught the gig last night in Miami, partied in the bar, and now she's hooked. A friend loaned her $40 plane fare. Follow the Dead anywhere, that's her motto. Follow: Get Loved, Get Free, Get On, get away—Tampa tonight, Birmingham tomorrow, Nashville the next...

"You can't do that," Scully yells, then knocks back a mouthful of Heineken. He doesn't want to be cruel, but this is 1978; the days of easy freedom are over. No more free concerts. No more shuffling off to Big Muir. The moral mission is *kaput*. It's show business now—money, schedules, publicity. It's time to shake down the street and see what tumbles out in the way of...in the way of...

"You gotta tell people what you're doing," Scully shouts. "We can't be responsible for you. Just 'cause you got big tits doesn't mean you can do this kind of shit. You gotta be responsible."

No good; she doesn't hear a word. When it comes, her voice in Wonderland sweet, innocence in every syllable: "Where's Garcia?"

Scully shakes his head mournfully. Another one come to see the Wizard.

"I thought I'd stamped that one out," Garcia says later. "I don't want to be a leader because I don't want to be a mis-leader. I haven't put any safeguards there. I haven't paid the dues to be responsible for leading people. The most I would want to do would be to indicate, using my life as a model, that it's possible for you to, uh, go for it. But following me is like a dead-end street. There's nothing here but me. I can't multiply fishes and loaves and turn water into wine.

"I remember going down to Watts Towers after the Watts Acid Tests. It had been a hard night, I'd gone through a lot of heavy changes, and it was dawn. I remember looking at this stuff. It was just junk. Nobody could tear it down, so they made a monument out of it. I remember thinking that I'd rather have a life that gets me off while I'm living it and leave nothing and not litter the world with concrete relics or ideas or things that will hang you up. Maybe that's why the world is in such trouble. Because ideas that should have died a natural death have outlived their own pertinence."

Nevertheless, Garcia is aware that there are many who see him as a spiritual figure.

"If I think of greatness at all," he says, "it has to be the whole experience. It can't be just me. I can see what I'm missing. I can compare it to my ideal version of myself and see that I'm way short."

And his ideal version?

"Being great, man." He laughs, another day done, IT made flesh: "Being fucking great!"

Late afternoon. In the distance, planes circle like vultures. Sunlight so cold it's depressing. With a true dilettante's delight, Jerry has been through it all this day: Masons, quantum mechanics, pyramidology, conspiracies. Only one more item remains: phantom limbs.

His voice a roller coaster of pitch and volume, Jerry tells it—apocryphal or not—with an actor's urgency, taking all the parts.

There's this woman, see, who's had her right arm amputated to the shoulder. But she has a problem. The phantom limb seems so real, so utterly palpable, that it's become twisted at the wrist and this deformity is causing her shoulder—her real shoulder—to become wrenched. The muscles are wire-tight with pain. She's growing hunched, the afflicted shoulder rolling inward. The pain, though clearly psychosomatic, is incessant, torturous. The doctors are dumbfounded, impotent to help. There's nothing she can do, right? Wrong!

Garcia's eyes twinkle. The air is heavy with anticipation. "Acupuncture," he announces. "An acupuncturist does his thing on the absent arm!"

So what happens?

Well, with much patience and inscrutable understanding, this physician labors over the missing arm, deftly turning the needles, soothing, deadening the illusory nerve. The pain vanishes. The shoulder relaxes. The arm relaxes. Even the invisible wrist becomes normal.

"Right, right," Zippy Loren stutters. "The pain's in the brain anyway."

Garcia nods: Another lesson, another metaphor.

"I mean," he begins, "what holds it together? Fingers to hand, etc.? Why do you still have the same scars even though you've been remade several times? Why do you still have the same features? What holds this all together? What is it, I wonder?" Climactically he throws his hands in the air, as if to test the principle. "Beyond that, why bother?"

Big Questions deserve big answers. Class dismissed.

I met Blair Jackson once, at a Grateful Dead concert in Oakland. He didn't just arrive at the concert and find a seat and sit down, waiting, with everyone else, for the show to start. He *introduced* himself ("Hi, my name's Blair,") to the people around him. He wanted to meet fellow Deadheads and to foster a feeling of good energy, for the sake of the concert, before it started. I appreciated that. It made a difference in our little corner of Grateful Dead land for that evening. Jackson is one of the most, if not *the* most, prolific writer about the band, beginning with his early pieces, such as the one below, for the April 4, 1980, issue of *BAM, The Bay Area Music Magazine,* a free bi-monthly tabloid that ran for over 24 years, and continuing through his book *Grateful Dead: The Music Never Stopped,* published in 1983 by Delilah, and then in his long-running self-published fan magazine, *The Golden Road* (1984-1993). Much of the best of that periodical was collected in Jackson's anthology, *Goin' Down the Road: A Grateful Dead Traveling Companion,* published by Harmony in 1992. His *Garcia: An American Life,* published by Viking in 1999, is a brilliant biography. His writing is that of an insider who can maintain a journalist's professional objectivity, so that we get the best of both worlds, and that is a gift.

Dead Heads: A Strange Tale of

Love, Devotion and Surrender

Blair Jackson

"here was never a possibility that we wouldn't go see the Dead in Egypt. We were going to do whatever it took...and we did." Larry Murcer of Portland, Oregon is sitting on top of a muddy sleeping bag in a park across the street from the Oakland Auditorium, where the Grateful Dead will ring in the New Year—1980—in about three hours. With his girlfriend Judy Schweiger, Larry hitched down to Oakland the day after Christmas and had been camping out in the park ever since with about 50 other Dead Heads, as the group's fans are known. The Grateful Dead were playing five shows at the Auditorium, and Larry and Judy were not about to let inconveniences like torrential winter rains and no money for food keep them from missing a single note of any of the performances. "I've been to every West Coast Dead show since mid-'77," Larry beams, the white of his teeth suddenly dominating his overwhelmingly furry countenance. "But Egypt was IT!" Judy—a diminutive but attractive woman dressed in a traditional Dead "skull and roses" T-shirt and a faded denim skirt adorned with an odd assortment of calico and paisley patches—chuckles and nods in agreement. "THE DEAD IN EGYPT!" Larry exclaims, as if that particular combination of words in itself has some sort of obvious cosmic significance.

When Larry first heard the reliable rumors that the Dead were going to play a series of concerts at the foot of the Great Pyramid in September 1978, he quit his job as a part-time postal employee, sold all of his records ("even my Dead records—*that's* how important this was"), his stereo and his ten-speed bike, and, with Judy, started hitching across the country. In Montana, he and Judy hooked up with two Dead Heads they had met at a Dead concert in San Francisco the previous year, and by the time they arrived in New York, their group had grown to eight—eight people, none of whom really had any money to speak of, five of whom had full or part-time jobs, who decided, basically on a whim, to chuck it all and go see the Grateful Dead perform in the shadow of Cheops' tomb. Two of the eight never even made it to New York's Kennedy Airport, though: they were arrested carrying a stereo system out of a West Village apartment, "to earn enough bread to make the BIG TRIP," Larry explains. "I never heard if they got out of prison or not. They were pretty cagey guys. They *might* have made it," he adds, grinning at the prospect that a pair of dedicated Dead Heads might have somehow outwitted the best brains of the N.Y.P.D. to boogie in the Egyptian night.

Larry, Judy and four traveling companions flew to Cairo three days before the concerts, "scored THE BEST HASHISH I'VE *EVER* SMOKED," Larry bubbles, and managed to find a reasonably clean room in a private home, where the six of them stayed for the equivalent of 25 cents a day. By the day of the first show, Larry and the group had encountered dozens of other Americans, many of whom had gone to similarly extreme lengths to make the Egypt trip. "One guy from Chicago figured out how to embezzle money from his *father's* business to get there," Larry claims.

"I'm not saying the Egypt shows were the *best* Grateful Dead concerts I've been to," Larry says, "They weren't. But they were definitely the *highest!* C'MON, man! THE DEAD...in *EGYPT!* He breaks into a staccato laugh, and Judy hugs him. The Dead in Egypt. Be there or be square.

Most of the people in line at the Auditorium this New Year's Eve didn't make it to Egypt, which doesn't make them squares necessarily, or even imply that they're anything less than hardcore Dead Heads. After all, many were lined up to see their fifth Dead show in six days (*the band* took a day off) and many of them were attending their 30th, 40th, 80th, 150th, *225th* Dead concert, and if that's not hardcore, nothing is. Some of them undoubtedly staged bizarre rituals of their own those three nights the Dead were shattering the desert calm in Giza—listening to favorite Grateful Dead concert tapes in their homes in San Francisco, Seattle, Syosset, Long Island or wherever, filling rooms with suspicious-smelling smoke, and perhaps ingesting mysterious chemicals as they invoked the spirits of Osiris, Keb, Ra, Ptah, Anubis and all the other deities awoken from their slumber by the Good Ol' Grateful Dead. Perhaps what the Dead Heads who didn't go to Egypt lacked was that *crazed* edge that separates the faithful from the *obsessed*—those poor souls who *had* to go, who seemingly had no choice in the matter because they were pulled by forces far too powerful to control. They're the Dead Heads whose eyes look right through you, who grin a toothy, just-this-side-of-diabolical smile that says, "I *know* something you can't even imagine." And they probably do.

"Being a true Dead Head involves a commitment to surrender your soul to the music," comments a remarkably articulate 17-year-old San Rafael girl named Anne, as she sits in a circle with three friends outside the Auditorium passing a joint and a Bota Bag filled with white wine. "When the music starts, you just let it take you completely. If you don't surrender, you don't get what you can from the music. You should open yourself up, empty yourself, and let the music fill you from head to toe—as if it were water filling an empty vessel."

"It's like a pact," adds one of her friends. "We show up and give the Dead our good energy, and they fill us up in return." The circle erupts into self-conscious laughter. "It sounds kinda stupid when you talk about it," Anne says.

If this pre-concert scene has taken on the appearance of some strange metaphysical service station, that's not too far off the mark. Dead Heads flock to Grateful Dead concerts like cripples to Lourdes for a spiritual shot in the chakras, and few leave disappointed. A Dead concert is symbiosis on a grand scale: the Dead Heads feeding positive energy and—dare we speak the phrase?—"good vibes" to the stage and to each other, while the band tries to fuse that energy with their own creativity to synthesize an entertainment that, at its best, transcends every notion of what a "rock concert" is or "should" be. Together, the Dead and their fans form a peculiarly amorphous organism that is completely unlike anything that lives and breathes in this world; but then the nature of this animal is that it soars, hovers, *sprawls* in some undefined space midway between planet Earth and the Twilight Zone.

Dead Heads are a strange lot. There's no way around it, and they're the first to admit it. In fact, most of them openly flaunt their nonconformity—just as the Dead themselves have remained fiercely independent of popular musical trends over the years. The cliche about Dead Heads is that they are the last survivors of late-'60s hippiedom, an army of LSD casualties truckin' to the grave in concert halls and auditoriums coast-to-coast. It is not a completely inaccurate stereotype. You will see more scruffy-looking refugees of the '60s at Dead concerts than just about anywhere else. But what that simple sketch doesn't allow for is the thousands of *young* Dead Heads, kids who were playing with GI Joe and Barbie dolls when the Dead, Kesey, the Merry Pranksters and the other original hippies were giggling up a psychedelic storm at Muir Beach and La Honda. In fact, the majority of people who go to Dead concerts these days are teenagers, youths who probably had to *learn* the peculiarities of the hippie lifestyle from older brothers and sisters, or even parents, who had originally embraced that free-living spirit. It is a little strange, unsettling even, to see a 15-year-old boy with long hair wearing a head band and torn, patched jeans: it is a sight rarely seen outside of an arena where the Grateful Dead are playing. Culturally, at least, going to a Grateful Dead concert is a bit like entering a time warp. The look, even on the youngest fans, is late-'60s San Francisco. The atmosphere, friendly, even carnival-like, is late-'60s San Francisco. Even the drugs are late-'60s San Francisco—Dead concerts still lead all others in per capita consumption of LSD and other psychedelics.

Dead Heads are understandably defensive about charges that they are trapped in an anachronistic fantasy world that is hopelessly out of step with 1980s America, that they are living testimony against Darwin's Theory of Evolution.

"People who say shit like that are full of crap," says a feisty Long Islander who had flown to the Bay Area to see the Dead's Oakland shows. "They're the people who are insecure about their own hipness. They're the people who are slaves to fashion, who think that by being 'up to date' other people won't think they're lame."

"The only thing the Dead have to do with the '60s," says another, "is that they got their start then. They're an '80s band. They're going to be around—and all of us will be following them—as long as they keep doing something that no one else is doing."

"It's futile to analyze the Dead or Dead Heads," comments a third. "You can't explain it. It *is*. And what it is, is a *party*...and not everyone is invited, or can go."

There is unquestionably a certain elitism that is common to many Dead Heads, as if they are all members of an exclusive club. Entry is not difficult—merely opening up and enjoying the Grateful Dead is all that's required—but keeping up that "membership," staying "on the bus," as Tom Wolfe wrote,

involves varying degrees of passionate commitment...not to mention toler-
ance of some of the biggest nonsense-spouting zealots this side of Sun
Myung Moon. Dead Heads at their worst are insufferable bores who seem literally incapable of carrying on any sort of intelligent conversation without
somehow relating everything back to the Grateful Dead. There are probably
as many people who have been permanently turned *off* to the Dead because
of the incoherent ramblings of some maniacal Dead Head who thinks the
song "Sugar Magnolia" should be the National Anthem, as have been con-
verted to the cause. Somewhere along the line there is a leap of faith to be
made, when the whole Dead Head experience *clicks*—and that's why there are
very few people who "sort of" like the Grateful Dead. If, as the bumper stickers
claim, "There's nothing like a Grateful Dead concert!" then there most *certainly* is nothing like a Grateful Dead fan, either. They are simply the most
rabid fans in the rock world.

If that last statement smacks of hyperbole, think for a minute. How many
people do you know who would follow Led Zeppelin, Cheap Trick, or, God-
help-us, Journey, from city-to-city on a tour? Or who would concoct schemes
straight out of *Mission Impossible* to smuggle expensive tape decks into halls
and stadiums to record Aerosmith or Ted Nugent? Or who would rather *give*
an extra ticket to another Styx fan rather than selling it to a scalper? Or who
cannot imagine a world without Donna Summer and The Eagles? Not many,
most likely. Yet those sorts of attitudes and actions are relatively common in
the admittedly unusual universe in which Dead Heads thrive. Why?

"Because seeing the Dead is completely different than anything else I do,"
offers an 18-year-old San Francisco boy wearing a home-made T-shirt with
heat-transfer letters that spell out "Grateful-Fucking-Dead." "I go see other
groups sometimes but they just put on a show. You watch it, dig it, go home.
With the Dead, we start partying the afternoon of the show. Everybody hangs
out together outside the theater and inside, too. We get high together. We
dance together. The party goes on all night. That doesn't happen anywhere
else."

Another Dead Head, this one with his brown beard streaked with Day-glo
paint to celebrate the New Year, puts it more succinctly: "It's all in the music.
It's magic. You can look for this kind of magic at other shows, but I'd bet you
everything I own...everything I'll *ever* own, you won't find it anywhere else."

Few words are as integral a part of the Dead Head lexicon as "magic." It is
the one term—with all its implications of Merlin, *brujos*, shamen, and psychic
legerdemain—that almost every Dead Head will arrive at eventually to
explain what it is that separates the Grateful Dead from other bands. Fans and
band members alike imbue the concept with a virtual life of its own.

"On a very good night," comments Dead drummer Mickey Hart, "the magic will visit us. On other nights, for whatever reasons, it stays away. All we can do, as musicians, is be true to ourselves and play as well as we can and hope that it all meshes and the magic finds us."

It is precisely this notion that "the magic" only visits Dead concerts occasionally that leads so many Dead Heads to go to every show of a run in a given city, or follow the Dead as they tour entire regions of the U.S., or give up everything to go to Egypt in hopes the aura of the Sphinx will somehow coax the magic to appear.

"There are two things I've learned from years of going to Dead shows," says Dan Aniello, a Dead Head from Pennsylvania. "The Dead will almost never play *great* two nights in a row; and you never know which night will be the hot one, so you've got to see them *all*! Hitting that one fantastic show makes going to the others essential."

"Dead Heads are very patient and very forgiving," acknowledges Mickey Hart. "They let us do what we want musically, knowing that it's not always going to be great. A lot of times we're fishing when we're up there on stage, and that means sometimes we're going to come up with clams, and sometimes we're going to come up with pearls.

"Dead Heads will wait out the storm. They don't boo us, *ever*. They won't yell out stuff like 'BOOGIE!' or 'ROCK AND ROLL!' when we're trying to play quietly or spacey. They're there to hear what we have to say. And that's the best thing an audience can give me: the freedom to play what I feel. It's that way for the entire band. Our strength is in their numbers and their openness."

What the Dead offer their fans—and this, more than anything explains their tremendous appeal—is a style of music they literally can hear nowhere else. The Grateful Dead are the last great experimental rock and roll band. Other groups from the Outlaws to Led Zeppelin indulge in lengthy instrumental solos that are improvised, but the Dead are the only rock band that is willing to completely abandon all musical structures to go completely "outside," in the jazz sense. When the Dead enter the marathon jam that inevitably comes in the second set of one of their shows (and which more often than not rears its unpredictable head near the end of the first set, as well) there are *no rules*: the band paints on a blank canvas. There are nights when the jamming leads quite naturally from one song to the next, as if the jigsaw puzzle has been figured out and it's just a matter of linking the pieces together. Other nights, rhythms break down, each member of the band seems to be drifting out on his own tangent, and chaos reigns for much of the evening. The minutes tick by and you can hear the band trying to feel its way back to safer ground, trying to build some sort of identifiable structure out of the free-form dissonance they have quite deliberately immersed themselves in. Sometimes the disparate elements coalesce smoothly, coming together brick by brick until the madness *explodes* into a familiar riff or song; other times it never quite gels, so the structure is uprooted again, new avenues are explored, perhaps shifting the entire weight of the jam in a new direction.

The key is that *chances are taken*. The Grateful Dead dare to fail. And they often do—there are evenings when the group simply does not play well; when the ideas seem scattered and disjointed and the players never quite get on track. But by taking the risk, by putting themselves out on the edge of the precipice as it were, they open their concerts to exciting possibilities—to the fabled "magic." Because on those good nights, when the chemistry between the players is obvious in every note, and the audience, as one, feeds its energy to the stage to nourish the developing organism, Dead Heads are privileged to experience the creation of a totally new music—music so tied to the moment, so rooted in the ever-changing elements that went into its genesis, that it can never be repeated, because the conditions that allowed for its germination will never be identical.

"You can't make it happen by acts of will or addressing it in a direct way," lead guitarist Jerry Garcia to *New West*'s Charlie Haas a year ago, "so you look for devious ways. It's like dialing a combination: 'Let's see, I remember that night I had two glasses of brandy, smoked a little hash and took a snort or two, and I felt just perfect and the band played beautifully, so maybe if I repeat that combination...' but it never works that way, so that automatically keeps it interesting, because it isn't a matter of will. The fact that things work out as well as they do as often as they do is like on the level of the miraculous; I mean it's way outside of chance."

"I think what we have that is *required* if we're ever to succeed musically on a given night is a sense of *daring*, a certain amount of recklessness," Hart says. "It takes daring to go up in front of 20,000 people and not know what you're going to play; when you haven't even really thought of what you *might* play, and for a reason have tried *not* to think about it, but to instead be open, move with the feeling of that night, maybe fall under a spell and spin a web. That's the fun for me, 'cause I could memorize a solo, or play so fast and so *bad* it would rock your socks off. But I refuse to do it.

"We're always looking for something else, something that you don't find in rigid structures. That's why our music is always in a state of flux. It's like a river; always moving and always changing. We don't even try to keep tabs on it, really. We let it change. And for that reason we have on and off nights. The more you experiment, the more you leave up to the fates and the lower your percentage of being able to pull off the experimentation successfully. But the rate of return is *worth* it. That's why the Dead Heads come back time and again. They can get regular rock and roll much *better* from other bands. That's not what we give them. We're a different animal."

Or as Garcia commented once, "I think basically the Grateful Dead is *not* for cranking out rock and roll...I think it's to get high."

And so it has always been. Not just in the drug sense, mind you (though it is a rare Dead Head who does not dabble in consciousness-altering agents of some sort), but "getting high" from being part of a continuing experiment and stepping, if only for a few hours at a time, off *terra firma* and onto a world of uncertain consistency.

A typical Dead concert (if, indeed, there is such a thing) assaults the senses with so many different musical forms and styles that the diversity itself can be somewhat disorienting. On any given night, you might hear Bob Weir of the Dead singing country classics like Marty Robbins' "El Paso" or Merle Haggard's "Mama Tried"; Garcia playing cutting Motown R&B riffs on a version of Martha & the Vandellas' "Dancin' in the Streets"; seminal rock and roll tunes like Chuck Berry's "Promised Land" or "Johnny B. Goode"; a fast blues or two; jazzy rhythms and chord progressions; extended solos featuring exotic African and Asian percussion; cacophonous feedback and electronic rumblings that shake every molecule in your body; and more. Much more. And the great majority of the tunes are Dead originals.

The Dead have perhaps the largest active repertoire of any major rock band. It is so extensive that the band can easily play three or four consecutive nights and never repeat a song (though there *are* usually a few carryovers from night to night, particularly if they are testing new material). The Dead never play the same set of songs twice; they never work from a set list, choosing instead to play whatever seems right for the moment; and the huge list of songs that the Dead perform on any given tour changes from year to year, sometimes drastically. Because the Dead have no "hits" to speak of, they never feel *bound* to play any particular songs. Certainly there are perennial Dead favorites—"St. Stephen," "Dark Star," "China Cat Sunflower," "Playin' in the Band," and "Truckin'" to name just a few—but rarely will you hear more than mild disappointment expressed if this or that song was not played. Dead Heads know the rules of the game: if you don't get "Scarlet Begonias" tonight, maybe tomorrow night, and if not this tour, next tour. Certainly the attitude of the Dead Head is a far cry from, say, the average Led Zeppelin fan, who likely would try to bomb Jimmy Page's limousine if the Zep refused to play "Stairway to Heaven."

Songs drop out of the Dead repertoire for long periods sometimes, surfacing after a few years like a long, lost friend, or occasionally in radically altered form. For example, the spry country tune "Friend of the Devil," a staple at Dead shows in 1970, was resurrected in the late '70s as a plodding dirge which was virtually unrecognizable from the original. More recently, the song "Don't Ease Me In" has undergone an interesting revival—originally a favorite of Garcia's and Weir's pre-Grateful Dead country-bluegrass band, Mother McCree's Uptown Jug Champions, the tune popped up in the Dead's occasional acoustic sets in '69 and '70, and now just in the past year, in a rocking, electric arrangement. And before it can metamorphose a fourth time, it has been captured on vinyl at last: it appears on the Dead's new album, *Go to Heaven*.

It is the Dead's own sense of history and continuity that constantly reinforces the notion that there is a grand and noble tradition being carried on every time the group steps on a stage. It is a tradition which, ostensibly, dates back to the now-legendary Acid Tests (which were so influential in shaping the band's attitudes toward playing, and their relationship to their audience), and snakes up through the years to include inspired nights at the Avalon, Family Dog, the Fillmores, Monterey, Woodstock, Watkins Glen, Egypt, and a billion other points along the way where the Dead practiced their sorcery. The Dead Heads, much more so than the Dead themselves, are the caretakers of this book of memories. They know the dates, the names, the particulars. As if the information is somehow genetically encoded in them, Dead Heads can reel off amazing tales about Dead concerts through the years, regardless of whether they happened to attend those concerts or not. They can describe to you in vivid detail the show at the Fillmore West the night Janis Joplin died; or the nights in April of '71 when Duane Allman and the Beach Boys jammed with the Dead on successive nights at New York's Fillmore East; or the time Pig Pen (the late Ron McKernan) warbled "Hey Jude." And don't forget the February '71 show at the Capitol Theater in Portchester, New York where the Dead enlisted the entire audience in a rather unusual experiment: as the band played a loose jam, the crowd put all of its concentration on a slide that was projected on a screen above the stage depicting a man sitting in a lotus position. Fifty miles away, at the Maimonedes Dream Lab in Brooklyn, a sleeping subject hooked up to an EEG was bombarded with energy unleashed by the Dead Heads in Portchester. Sure enough, the EEG jumped furiously.

These kinds of stories—and much wilder ones, to be sure—are told and retold in Dead Head circles, changed a little here, embellished a little there. Those are the perils of the oral tradition (after all, if the Apostles couldn't quite get the Christ story straight between them, what can you expect from a bunch of LSD freaks swapping tales about the Grateful Dead?), but in the long run the mangled yarns only add another gossamer-thin layer to the Dead's already highly mythologized history.

Although the Dead's legacy is firmly rooted in the late '60s, in terms of mass popularity, they are strictly a '70s, and now '80s phenomenon. The Grateful Dead's following is the largest it has ever been today. The group routinely sells out concerts in large halls in most major American cities. Their last two records, *Terrapin Station* and *Shakedown Street*, were the fastest sellers in the group's history. And all of this is happening despite the fact that they are constantly pilloried by the cynical rock press, which tends to view the Dead as old geezers who *still* can't sing; despite the fact that they have never had a *smash* album or an AM hit; despite the fact that because of the tighter FM radio formats nationwide these days, the Dead probably get less airplay now then they did ten years ago. To defer to Stephen Stills momentarily, "There's somethin' happening' here. What it is ain't exactly clear."

Traditionally, the Dead's popularity has spread by word-of-mouth mainly, confirmed Dead Heads dragging their friends to concerts and playing their records until the grooves wore out. That situation changed slightly in 1970 when the Dead put out two highly melodic, song-oriented (rather than jam-oriented) LPs that definitely had a light, country-rock feel to them. *Workingman's Dead* and *American Beauty* became FM radio favorites on both coasts, and a new breed of Dead fans started showing up at concerts. These Dead Heads were younger, by and large, than the crowds who had followed the Dead from their very early days as an almost exclusively psychedelic band, and many of those charter Dead Heads did not hide their disgust when they encountered people who came *only* to hear the FM "hits" from those albums, like "Uncle John's Band" and "Casey Jones," and who couldn't begin to fathom a 56-minute medley of "St. Stephen" and "Turn on Your Lovelight." For most Dead Heads, though, it was not an either/or proposition—they ate it *all* up, and viewed the changes for what they were: evidence of the band's increased sophistication.

"Before that, we were an experimental music band in almost every sense," comments Mickey Hart. "We were improvisationalists. We'd play for two or three hours, sing for 45 seconds—off key—and play for another hour. We were not one of your better vocal groups," he chuckles. "Then Crosby, Stills & Nash came along and changed us tremendously. Stills lived with me here at the ranch for three months around the time of their first record, and he and Crosby really turned Jerry and Bobby onto the voice as the holy instrument. You know, 'Hey, is *that* what a voice can do?' That turned us away from pure improvisation and more toward songs. In the old days we used to play all this *really* strange stuff hour after hour and we'd leave the Fillmore laughing: 'I wonder if they can whistle any of *those* songs? Nooooooo!' Well, with *Workingman's Dead*, that changed, you could whistle our songs. And we were real happy that we could attract that new and different audience."

In 1971, the Dead, obviously intrigued by the quick growth of their following, established an official Dead Heads organization for the first time, urging
fans to write them at a post office box in San Rafael. The initial plea ("Dead
Heads Unite!") appeared on the inside gatefold of the Dead's enormously
popular double LP called simply *Grateful Dead*. (It was initially supposed to
be called *Skullfuck* but Warner Bros. nixed that idea. Most people call it the
"skull and roses" album, after its cover graphic of a skeleton crowned with a
halo of roses.)

The response from Dead Heads was quick and tremendous. Mary Ann
Mayer of the Dead organization was initially in charge of assembling the mailing list, but by early '72, the volume of mail pouring into the Dead's small
downtown San Rafael offices was so heavy that a second person was brought
in to help—Eileen Law, who took over the Dead Heads job completely soon
after, and remains the Head Dead Head to this day.

"I've never really considered Dead Heads a fan club," she comments,
"because we don't send out the standard promo pack with glossy pictures and
the offers to buy all sorts of merchandise. Also, we've never charged any
money to be in Dead Heads, because if we did we'd feel obligated to put out a
newsletter often, and we just don't work that way."

The infamous Dead Heads newsletter was started in the fall of '71 but came
of age in '72 and '73 when Garcia and his songwriting partner Robert Hunter
would design elaborate four- and eight-page flyers littered with poems;
bizarre, post-psychedelic doodles that made the drawings of the French sur-
realist Bresson look normal by comparison; utterly undecipherable smatter-
ings of a pseudo-philosophy called "Hypnocracy," the teachings of a fictional
sage named St. Dilbert (who was sort of a combination of Henny Youngman
and the Buddha); and, oh yes, tour information and hot scoops on all the latest
doings within the band. The newsletter came out sporadically up through
1974, after which the organization was temporarily shut down when the band
went into a one year "retirement." At that point, Eileen had about 40,000
names in her files. Today, the Dead Heads list contains more than 85,000
names and it's still free...for everyone but the Dead. To mail a four page circu-
lar today costs the Dead nearly $15,000, and they are not (and never have
been) a wealthy organization. In addition to the newsletter, which just started
again after a three-year absence while Eileen updated her files and caught up
on back correspondence, the Grateful Dead organization has also set up two
telephone hot-lines Dead Heads can phone to get tour information—one in
San Rafael, and one in New Jersey—that one for the insatiable hordes of Dead
Heads on the East Coast (which remains the band's strongest area).

The Dead have saved practically every letter they've received since the days of the original Grateful Dead Fan Club ('67-'68). Boxes of letters, cards, and original poems and drawings sent in by Dead Heads fill much of Eileen's office, and she says there are thousands more stashed away in some mysterious hiding place. One box of what looked to be about 1,000 pieces of mail consisted entirely of get-well cards sent to Garcia when he was hospitalized with throat problems a year ago.

A perusal of a few hundred random letters from Eileen's boxes reveals Dead Heads to be a far more literate lot than many people have given them credit for. Instead of the expected litany of "far-outs" couched in stoned prose, most of the letters are quite well-written and cover a broad range of topics. Many are sincere testimonials to the power of the Dead's music ("your music speaks from the soul, not from the pocketbook"), with lengthy explanations of why the Dead moved them. Others offer suggestions of where to play and where *not* to play in various cities ("the band really pays attention to those," Eileen comments), and suggestions of what songs they'd like to hear. And believe it or not, there are even a few complaints—"Please change your repertoire. It's become rather boring in the last few years hearing the same songs all the time," wrote one. "They've gone from a dismal three nights of material to an almost unforgivable *two* nights worth of material: a never-ending nightmare of 'Mama Tried' / 'Mexicali Blues' / 'Estimated Prophet' / 'Eyes of the World'," wrote another. And a third: "I'd much rather just hang out with Dead Heads than see the current Dead."

Most interesting, though, is the incredible artwork and handicrafts that are sent in, and occasionally even given to the band out on the road. Most offer unique graphic interpretations of the traditional Grateful Dead symbols. There are skeletons on horse-back, skeletons with wings, infinite variations on the skull-and-roses motif, and the "white lightning man" (the famous skull with a lightning bolt through it, a variation of which appears on the cover of this magazine). No other group has been the inspiration for folk art to the degree that the Dead has. There are literally thousands of hand-painted, drawn, -sewn, -crayoned, -appliqued Grateful Dead T-shirts, jackets, patches, hats and other clothing in Dead Head closets and on Dead Head bodies. At a given Grateful Dead show, you can probably spot upwards of 100 different Dead shirts, some homemade, others officially licensed by the Dead, or by Kelley & Mouse, the two brilliant Marin County artists responsible for the bulk of the Dead's album covers and, by extension, most of the Grateful Dead iconography.

Although there are now popular bands who sell more T-shirts than the Grateful Dead, the Dead were *first*. They started the trend of marketing band paraphernalia. (Of course it could be argued that there were Beatles T-shirts and Elvis T-shirts sold, but the Dead, Kelley & Mouse in particular, turned the production of T-shirts into a high art, no pun intended.) In one of the first Dead Head newsletters, T-shirts were offered through a company called Kumquat Mae, described as "the Deads' old ladies' store." That eventually folded and was absorbed by The Monster Company, Kelley & Mouse's T-shirt concern. According to Jim Welch, who acts as personal manager and agent for the two artists, Kelley and Mouse were the first people to utilize the four color silkscreen process currently in vogue in T-shirts.

"They made unbelievably beautiful T-shirts of really high quality," Welch says. "Unfortunately, though, they didn't understand how to merchandise this great product they had. They didn't understand marketing."

The Monster Company went under finally, but under Welch's efficient guidance, Kelley & Mouse are doing well with their lines of different Grateful Dead T-shirts (not to mention their current hot sellers, Journey's various logo T-shirts, which they designed). And since Welch has entered the picture, Kelley & Mouse have also started going after non-licensed T-shirt makers: a recent injunction against T-shirt Barn, an Eastern operation that was printing up its own Grateful Dead and other band T-shirts, effectively stopped a $1,000,000 scam. Welch says he has no interest in bothering the thousands of Dead Heads who make their *own* shirts. "The Dead love it. So do *all* of us. They're not hurting anybody; they're not out to make any huge profit on the Dead's name."

The Dead likewise offer no discouragement to the thousands of Dead Heads who are part of what is likely the largest co-operative taping network in the music world (underworld bootleggers excluded, of course). The Tapers, as they are commonly known, have been recording Grateful Dead concerts since the very early '70s, initially sneaking cheap portable cassette recorders into auditoriums and making mediocre mono tapes. They would trade tapes by mail, using publications like *Dead Relix*, a N.Y.-based Dead fan mag (now a general rock publication called *Relix*) to spread the word. Today, taping Dead shows has become remarkably sophisticated, and surprisingly easy. At Bay Area Dead shows it is not at all uncommon to see 20 or more expensive tape decks piled up behind the sound board, with microphones attached to poles that are anywhere from 3 to 18 feet tall, rising from the mass of decks. Not only is the taping not discouraged, some of the tapers have Grateful Dead sound wizard Dan Healy's tacit cooperation—he occasionally lets Tapers use power from the board.

"Healy's interested in the tapes we make because in a sense, we reflect how well he does his job," says Bob Menke, among the most obsessive of all The Tapers. Menke has been addicted to taping since 1971 and has amassed a collection of over 400 Grateful Dead concert tapes, believed to be the highest number on the West Coast. "In 1978," he continues, "we gave Healy copies of some tapes we'd made in '77. He heard some weakness in his mixing through our tapes and in early '78 he re-arranged the stage and developed a new mix." Menke says that the lax attitude toward the tapers has *made* problems for Healy, too: "Back East there was a show where there were so many microphone poles between Healy and the stage he could barely see the band!"

A neurotic and paranoid lot for the most part, The Tapers worry endlessly about smuggling their decks into halls and arenas, and they've been known to go to great lengths to accomplish their goals. Tapers have hidden decks on motorized wheelchairs, tossed their machines (which can cost hundreds of dollars) over fences into the arms of friends, and even bribed security men. Menke uses a small Sony D-5 recorder these days—the $700 machine is small enough to fit inside a hollowed-out book or down the front of his pants.

Most of the tapers are scrupulously honest folks—they will only *trade* tapes to one another. Profiting from Dead tapes is strictly *verboten*. They are *not* bootleggers.

"It's come a long, long way," Menke says. "It's gotten to the point now where I don't think the Dead can do a concert anywhere in the U. S. without somebody making a good, high quality tape of it." Menke can usually get a tape of any Dead show within a few days—that's how well developed and extensive the taping network is. The hardcore tapers are Grateful Dead junkies in the truest sense of that term: taping, to them, is almost like a drug.

"I've got some tapes that are absolutely painful to listen to, the playing is so bad," Menke says, "but on the other hand I've got lots of great stuff, too. A lot of the shows I taped myself are special to me because the good nights were some of the finest moments of my life—and they're preserved for me. Twenty years from now I'll *still* be able to relive those nights."

They were good nights for many people, which is why *the next one* becomes a topic of conversation the minute the last one ends. In between the concerts, those weeks and sometimes months of no live Dead fix, there are memories to keep the spirit alive. There are stories to be swapped, tapes to be listened to, and with any luck at all, perhaps one or more members of the Dead will come through town with his own band. Dead Heads are loyal to the point that they will support anything that is even remotely connected to the Grateful Dead. They have kept the New Riders—the first Dead spin-off—afloat all these years. They flocked to see Garcia's various bands, Weir's Kingfish; even Dan Healy's group drew large crowds on the East Coast club circuit recently. They religiously buy magazines that give space to the band. And if the Dead's movie comes to town they pack the theater.

But still, it all comes together at the concerts. Friendships are renewed, the sacraments are passed, the rituals explained to newcomers. The lights go down, deafening war-whoops fill the air. The crowd, giddy with excitement before the first note is played, moves toward the stage as a single undulating mass. One last hit. One last snort. One last swig. Lights! And the four-hour Dead Head orgasm begins. Will the magic visit tonight? Maybe, maybe not. Don't worry. There's always Portland, and Seattle, and Denver, and St. Loo...*wherever*.

"It's *funny* sometimes, isn't it?" Mickey Hart asks. He smiles. "It's just musical appreciation that's gotten *a little out of hand.*"

Dennis McNally, these days, is the Grateful Dead organization's publicist and the band's official historian. When he wrote this article for the Sunday *San Francisco Examiner & Chronicle* magazine, *California Living*, September 28, 1980, he did not yet work for the band, but was known to them as the author of *Desolate Angel: Jack Kerouac, the Beat Generation, and America* (Random House, 1979), his doctoral dissertation that was published as a commercial biography of Jack Kerouac. His view of the band harkens back to the Beats, and he sees them as part of a continuous thread of American thought that in turn crosses back over the Atlantic to William Blake, and further back.

Meditations on the Grateful Dead

Dennis McNally

akland Auditorium, December 26, 27, 28, 30, 31, 1979: "Bill Graham Presents The Grateful Dead." Rock and roll's most extraordinary tribe gathers.

Drive across the Bay Bridge and you see the vans and VW's and the odd Mercedes with "There is Nothing Like a Grateful Dead Concert" bumperstickers. Get on the BART in San Francisco or Richmond or Concord and watch the Dead Heads trickle in, longhaired and bearded young men with Dead emblems—a grinning skull wreathed in roses or cut by a thunderbolt, a mad fiddler skeleton in sunglasses, an Uncle Sam skeleton in sneakers—embroidered with exquisite detail on the back of their denim jackets by the women who accompany them, often dressed in long skirts and beads, crowns of roses in their hair. There is an even easier way to spot them; look for the smiles. If you have ever wanted to see 6,400 people as deliriously happy as they know how to be, truck on down to the show, because, the Dead are home to play. (They're currently performing through October 10 at the Warfield in San Francisco.)

As we walked from the BART station the first night of the stand, my friend Dan laughed, "You know, once we get there we won't even be in Oakland anymore." Another Dead Head added, "Hell, for the next week this isn't even in the U.S.A." These two square blocks are not only out of place, but in a sense out of time, for this event is a continuation, a functional evolution of Haight -

Ashbury in the sixties. San Francisco poet Michael McClure once said that the Haight scene ended when people stopped dancing at concerts, and that is the point: people have never stopped dancing at Dead concerts.

Out of place, out of time—a Dead concert has little to do with the popular image of a rock and roll show. There are no hit songs from the radio, no flashy costumes, no dry ice fog nor smoke bombs, no sexy vocalist taunting an adolescent crowd with his or her limber pelvis; in fact, there are almost none of the conventional accoutrements of entertainment. As well, the distinction between performer and audience is blurred here, because to a remarkable extent this audience is part of the act. When the Dead play there is a family—an inner family of band and staff and crew, and an extended family of "audience"—all come together for a ritual that most closely resembles a stoned religious proceeding.

It is the festival of Dionysus in downtown Oakland. For nearly a week, the Auditorium and the park in front of it will be a temple for a tribe whose values have little to do with the Top 40 entertainment mentality that is modern corporate rock and roll. It is the church of hypnocracy (a private Dead joke centering on the adventures of one St. Dilbert), and the players—Jerry Garcia (lead guitar), Phil Lesh (bass), Bob Weir (rhythm guitar), Bill Kreutzmann (drums), Mickey Hart (drums), and Brent Mydland (keyboards)—are only the choir that leads the congregation. Nothing to take too seriously, though—the primary thing is, as Garcia once sang, that they "can show you a high time." It's fun.

The medieval alchemists called the first stage of their transformations the *Caput Mortuam*, the Dead Head. It is slightly more than a good pun, for the Dead (first named the Warlocks—i.e., wizards) are out for a music that can transform the mind, that can make you high. They are consciously part of a transcendental tradition in the arts, a tradition that reaches back through the Beat poets and writers Jack Kerouac, Allen Ginsberg, Gary Snyder and Michael McClure to William Blake, the romantic poets, and beyond.

The tradition resurfaced fifteen years ago in the Bay Area in a social rather than literary way with the Merry Pranksters, a group of friends whose most famous members were the writers Ken Kesey, Robert Stone and Stewart Brand, and Kerouac and Ginsberg's closest friend, Neal Cassady. The Dead served as "house band" when the Pranksters put on Acid Tests, adventures in creative chaos, in formlessness and the acceptance of an LSD-inspired swirl of generally benign madness that made even the later glory days of the Haight—the Be-In and the free concerts in Golden Gate Park—look tame. Yet the substance of that odyssey remains.

As Garcia told Charles Reich in 1972, "I think basically the Grateful Dead is not for cranking out rock and roll, it's not for going out and doing concerts or any of that stuff, I think it's to get high...To get really high is to forget yourself. And to forget yourself is to see everything else. And to see everything else is to become an understanding molecule in evolution, a conscious tool of the universe. And I think every human being should be a conscious tool of the universe. That's why I think it's important to get high." Dead Heads usually have various drugs along for the ride, but what brings them to Oakland Auditorium is the opportunity to get high on the Grateful Dead.

They will do anything to get there. Dead Head, in fact, is a rock journalism metaphor for the fan who will climb any mountain, swim any river to get to a concert. People come for thousands of miles for every show, but New Year's Eve is special. The first person in line for last year's New Year's Eve concert to close Winterland arrived on Christmas Eve. At the Cow Palace on New Year's Eve three years ago, I gave a spare ticket to a woman who had just hitchhiked from Long Island in seventy two hours, arriving three hours before concert time.

They are fans so passionate that Bill Graham's organization took care of them this year in advance, and arranged to let them—some penniless after spare-changing their way into the hall—sleep in the concession tent or pitch their own in the park in front of the Auditorium. Graham's front-of-stage director Bob Barsotti explained, "We got the park because we knew people would be there regardless...We've gotten to know a lot of them over the years, and they're real reasonable people who just love the Dead—if you take care of them, things will go real well." Of the arrangement for this year, he remarked, "We promised the Oakland Auditorium people we'd keep twenty-four-hour security in the park, and at night we had one guy, but I think he mostly slept. So we just told the folks, you can have the tent and just watch our stuff. There were maybe twenty-five the first night, maybe 150 the night before New Year's Eve, plus lots of people in campers and vans around the neighborhood."

It is, as Bill Graham later said, "a pilgrimage." On the night Winterland closed, Scoop Nisker asked a young woman from Long Island how she'd gotten to the concert: "My mother gave me the plane ticket." "Your mom?" asked a surprised Scoop. "Yeah, my mom," she smiled. "She'd rather I'd be a Dead Head than a Moonie."

Except for the fact that there is no hierarchy or manipulation here, the juxtaposition is not so far off. We have in Oakland 6,400 people whose gathering has every earmark of a religious festival: there is the scripture of the records and bootleg tapes, often made with the tacit cooperation of the Dead sound crew (by New Year's Eve some thirty microphones will sprout like a small forest behind the sound mixing board). There is the arcane symbolism of the graphics worked into t-shirts or more personally by hand embroidery, painting, or tattoos. There is the familial feeling of a cult, the friendships among people who live thousands of miles apart but which spring up instantly at every concert and create the most amazing grapevine I've ever encountered—the first night of the stand, word seeped out that the band would tour Europe in July, and within hours most of the crowd knew about it and were making plans to save money for a charter. On their 1978 return from playing the Pyramids, the band accompanied their shows with a giant slide show of the visit. It struck me perfectly as "How we spent our summer vacation," in a family that happens to play music and have 5,000 cousins.

But the music is—always—what counts. There is a shared, essentially spiritual purpose, not to worship Jerry Garcia or the Dead, for this is not a cult of personality, but a cult based on an idea—to dance and confront the moment and get as high on the music as one possibly can.

A majority of Dead Heads are the middle class white male students who comprise the bulk of most rock and roll audiences. Brian is twenty-three, a sometime student—"it's hard for me to go to school or hold a job when the Dead play"—in New Jersey who had seen the band forty-five times as of late December 1979. Tonight is his 123rd concert. He has little income, financing his travels by selling bumperstickers, and is glad to sleep in the park. Thoughtful, he said of his passion, "it's not just the music but the people involved. There's just so much love generated at a concert, people looking out for each other—it gets crowded, but there's no crunch...you know, some nights I don't even smoke a joint and I get so high—they get you high."

In the course of the week I interviewed perhaps forty Dead Heads, and reached several impressionistic conclusions. Probably 1,000 of every night's audience came from the East Coast. Virtually all came for all five nights. Though generally young, they have a deep sense of history and the Dead's presence in the sixties, often sounding as though they were ten years older than they are. Though they love to boogie, they are also proudly aware that Lesh once composed complex serial symphonies, or that Garcia reads Wittgenstein and quantum mechanics. The three main points of the Dead Head worldview were close to unanimous: the warm sharing of a family; the hippie contempt for commerciality that makes them stubbornly condescending to most other rock bands, as when they silently ignored a hyped Warren Zevon some two years ago when he had the misfortune to open a Dead concert; and a noisy but peaceful determination to have a good time.

Their backgrounds vary considerably. One of the people with whom I spoke attended his first Dead concert in Golden Gate Park at age four, then

became a real devotee two years ago at seventeen, and now spends half of his time in school and half with the Dead. I was introduced to the group by a man who is now an assistant professor of mathematics at Harvard—and still a Dead Head. The people with whom I attended New Year's Eve had several advanced degrees and included lawyers and a young man in management at Dinner-Levinson. Along with the hippies sleeping in the park, I met several people who stayed at the Hyatt-Regency.

The Dead may play Madison Square Garden, but they never went commercial; they remain committed to improvisation and spontaneity in their music, and never do they go out on tour with the rehearsed-to-the-last-note perfection of the Stones or the Eagles or Fleetwood Mac. I asked Christopher about spontaneity. He is fourteen, and has been a Dead Head since the fifth grade. Shy and not overtly articulate, he said, "It would take a long time to write down what they do to a song in a given performance—it's never the same, the variations and changes—and yet they do it—different—every night, as unique musical compositions, and that's just incredible."

On another end of the age scale, Tim is thirty-one, a successful and hard working lawyer in Southern California, and describes himself as a "conservative anarchist." He takes no drugs, practices a great deal of yoga, and is patient and good humored, the last two characteristics basic to all Dead audiences. He and his wife Lois are as "straight" in appearance as one could imagine, attend every Dead concert west of the Rockies and own perhaps 1,000 hours of concert tapes. Tim suggested that the music be called "alternate reality rock," or "transcendental rock," that it wasn't earth music, but a search for a spiritual/alchemical transfiguration.

Then there's Erin, a seventeen-year-old Marin high school student. I was startled when she interrupted herself to remark, "You should talk to my father—he's great and you'd like him." I agreed, and she added, "Great, he's in the balcony, let's go!" Lee is forty-two and a manager at a Bay Area television station who attended a Dead concert in 1970 and was hooked: "There was this live broadcast of New Year's 1970-71 and we carried it," he recalled. "I was there as management supervisor. I was able to move backstage and onstage— in amongst the paraphernalia—and I heard sounds I'd never heard before. Somebody told me, 'Oh, that's the Grateful Dead'—it was about two and a half seconds of unbelievable sound, and I've loved them ever since."

And it spreads. Lee continued, "We've gotten lots of friends our age turned on, too...one summer afternoon at a party at our house—lots of Mexican food and tequila—my wife said 'I feel like dancing.' Our friend Norman, who's a high school librarian here in Marin, said, 'No, I never dance.' My wife turned on a tape of the Dead, and sure enough, he danced. Now he has tapes of them in his car."

New Year's Eve 1979, 11:58 p.m. A tape comes on of the Dead song *Truckin'* and curtains fall away from a shape in the rear of the hall to reveal a truck marked "Dead Ahead Trucking." It moves forward a few feet, and then stops; the top flies off the truck and into the air soars the biggest Dead Head of them all, Bill Graham, dressed in a bright green butterfly costume complete with Dead skulls and thunderbolts painted on its wings, arms flapping and anten-nae bobbing, a beatific grin on the face of this fifty-year-old businessman who is terrified of heights. The crowd is spellbound with delight as he reaches the ceiling and glides toward the stage.

Later Graham would reveal that it hadn't been perfect: "Unbeknownst to anybody except two people, I'd rented a lavalier mike that I had on me," and patted his shoulder. "And at the top of the hall, there was going to be this voice," and Graham slips into a French/Bronx accent: " 'Ello, 'ello, zis ees Roger But-terfly. Oh, zis mus' be zee place – la la, Monsieur Philip Lesh on zee bass—I was going to introduce the band while flying through the air—Zis ees zee night, zis ees zee place, zis ees zee music, zee Grateful Dead—but I got so messed up with the helmet, which had been pushed down by the halo of roses I wear every New Year's, that I forgot about it until I started coming down."

It was a minor loss. Graham continued, "But even with that, I know how awesome it is. I cannot describe to you what it's like to be a butterfly over an audience feeling first of all not like a butterfly—I felt like an eagle—I moved my wings, and I saw these hands and these faces going up to—heaven—not me, I'm not saying Bill, they love me, or they love the butterfly. But for the moment, I was the Grateful Dead"—with a broad grin he smacks his hands together boom!—"and then they got *them.*"

Garcia stands to the left, usually still but for his fingers, Weir bounces enthusiastically about the middle, Lesh paces elegantly to the right. Alto-gether, there is little for the eye to catch; yet there are moments when being at a Grateful Dead concert closely resembles being at ground zero in a nuclear explosion. Lesh slams giant chords out of his bass and you suddenly realize that you can no longer hear the bass line as holes, but it's a vibration inside your chest cavity, a steady roll that you sense as a tactile presence even as the floors and walls begin literally to shake. A wave rolls through the crowd as heads stretch an inch or two higher when Garcia answers with a piercing wail of electronic sound, hollow and filtered through the computer like whale songs crossed with the sound of stone tearing in an earthquake, or perhaps a run that if visible would be endless pinpoints of light, or possibly a different sound that might come out as giant silver globes streaming off into the air above the crowd.

The improvisations are so endlessly involved, so sophisticated and com-

plex, that you can see the pattern and its filigrees, its shape and texture and color, feel it in your skin and in your bones, almost understand. Something happens, deep in the mind and spirit, and one is lost the way voodoo dancers or the drummers of the Moroccan goat god ceremonies (Bou-Jeloud) or the riotous worshipers of Dionysus were. The most sophisticated electronic technology in the world—analog computers, phasers and gizmos of every description—produce an elemental reaction as old as the human experience. You are very, very high, "high as the Zen master is high when his arrow hits a target in the dark," as William Burroughs once said, and the music flows on, your awareness with it. Kreutzmann and Hart build a wall of sound behind the apparent chaos, Weir's rhythm guitar and Mydland's piano fill in, and the band leaves the "space" segment and slinks into the crunching rhythm of "Not Fade Away."

Your mind is tossed like a ping pong ball in the surf and you let it go and realize that there is far more here than just music. There is a level of communication here that constitutes a true communion.

A few years ago, Garcia told a reporter, "Really, we have a relationship with our audience, and we're only interested in keeping that straight—independent of what the rest of the rock and roll world is doing." He was then speaking of the band's 1974 sound system, a behemoth composed of forty-eight amplifiers, 641 speakers, 26,400 watts of continuous power, and seventy-five tons of you-name-it designed for musical quality, not flash. That is a commitment.

Judged by rock and roll business standards, the Dead are failures. They've never had a major hit single, and their albums sell modestly. They tour not to flog records, but to *play*—which is not normal. Clem Burke of the group Blondie recently referred to the Dead's low profit cultiness when he jabbed, "We want to be one of the great bands, not like the Grateful Dead." Most critics dismiss their admittedly erratic singing, and reject the long cosmic jams as boring, content to see the band as anachronisms, leftover hippies irrelevant to the current scene. That attitude resurfaced in a *Rolling Stone* article about the highly profitable Fleetwood Mac: "The idea that a rock and roll band (much less its audience!) can be community, an extended family, seems faintly silly in 1980..."

On meeting someone like Eileen Law, the Dead ethos impresses me as more remarkable than silly. A lovely woman who communicates a tranquil warmth, she is a major link between the band and the audience, having run the Dead Head mailing list for nearly ten years. In that time she has watched it grow from 3,000 to over 90,000 (7,000 foreign addresses), retaining throughout an esteem for her correspondents that is the essence of the operation. Like every other "employee" of the band, she is first of all a Dead Head.

The informal organization called Dead Heads is not, she is quick to point out, a "fan club," which in the music business usually means a convenient method for merchandising p.r. packages. Rather, it was established at Jerry Garcia's suggestion in 1971 as a method for channeling communication from audience to performers. "I read every letter that comes in," Eileen said, "and if it's to a specific band member I put it in his box. But specific complaints about producers or a hall's acoustics or maybe just general comments about the direction of the band, I pass those on, too, and they really do listen."

As we talked we were joined by Nicki Scully, a staff member, and Alan Trist, the business manager. Considering the *Genus Deadheadus* came easy, surrounded as we were by pinned-up letters clamoring for information of every sort. One letter simply reads, "I am a new Dead Head. Please teach me." Others ask for history lessons, or the type of strings Garcia and Weir use; they come from a theological seminary, a U.S. Senate office, doctors and lawyers. Having seen the side-door antics of fans lusting to get backstage, acid casualties babbling, "I gotta talk to Garcia," I asked about the over-enthusiastic fans, the borderline lunatics. "There aren't really all that many," Nicki said, "and it's rare out here. It gets a little weird on the East Coast sometimes. There *are* people who get too high, lost in egolessness, and start believing that Garcia is literally speaking to them...but most of the people who want to talk to Jerry do so because they want to know that he sees the trip the same way they do, not to make the final connection—it's already there—but to substantiate it."

Alan Trist, a professional looking gent with an English accent, added, "I consider all of us fans." He went on to comment that most fans send letters to groups expecting them to be thrown away or handled by faceless automatons, "when actually it's the feedback, the letters, that makes this work. We spread them out on a table and use them as the basis for many of the decisions we make—halls, producers—and send relevant complaints to producers. For instance, with the *Grateful Dead Anthology* [a recently published songbook of over fifty tunes], the songs we chose to include were the ones most requested by the letters—Eileen kept track, and that's what we did."

The affection is mutual: the office reception area is graced with an enormous and beautifully done stained glass portrait of the *Blues for Allah* album cover, a mad fiddler skeleton in sunglasses, given them by a fan who didn't even leave his name. Conversely, a considerable part of the recent documentary produced by Jerry Garcia, *The Grateful Dead Movie*, focuses on the audience.

Or consider the opinion of Bill Graham, not only one of the most successful of rock producers, but arguably the best. One of the champion screaming wheeler dealers of all time and a wildly busy man, he personally runs a ticket-sales-by-mail program for faraway Dead Heads at New Year's Eve, tickets he could far more easily sell through BASS. It is a labor of love.

"The Dead are not my best friends," he remarked in a recent interview. "We don't have the same lifestyle or socialize, but the unit the Grateful Dead, and for what they represent, will always have my affection, will always—they have *me*, whatever they need from me—because they do something so wonder-ful...they make their fans feel good! And I've always felt that I voluntarily owed them and their fans the extent of my ability, and I put out more—not for the Dead's gain, the fans are going to come anyway if I had rubber carrots so stale...but because [the fans] come so open hearted, so ready to receive, that we have in the Dead Head the most precious patron—he has an overt heart, and overt mind, open to all that you put out. He will taste the fruits of your labor."

As Nicki Scully would later observe, "Graham discovered that with the Dead, the ambience is the whole thing; you can't do it partway. You can't take care of the band and not the audience, because it's all one group—and you need it all."

Pointing at thank you letters from the file on his desk, Graham's face melts from a politely friendly smile into a reverie that is—believe me—love. "It's a labor of concern, toward preservation," he continues. "Even if they came to me and said, 'Bill, we don't want you to do our shows anymore,' I'd say—'Please find someone who cares...'"

"Now, if people would understand that I understand how lucky I am to be involved in that position, then they would understand that if it were to be done for nothing, I *would* do it..." Graham tells how the Dead decided to give the proceeds of the first night, December 26, to Wavy Gravy's organization combating blindness in Nepal, and relates a story that neatly illustrates the band's influence on him.

"When the night started, I said to myself, this is the first time I've ever done a benefit where the group decided at the last minute to give their share, and I haven't been asked. Isn't that great!—now wait a minute, what's so good about it? If the Dead are doing it...it just doesn't feel right. Now they haven't asked me—they've planned it this way! They're gonna make me feel guilty—no, they didn't make me feel guilty, nobody said anything to me, and at the end of the night, I went over to Wavy and said, 'Do me favor, have somebody stop by the office tomorrow, I'd like to make a contribution...'"

The mirrorball sprays light over the crowd as the band comes back to "Sugar Magnolia" four hours and two sets after they began playing it at mid-night, driving to a spectacular finish. Slowly, oh-so-slowly, the crowd dis-perses after five nights together. A buxom young woman dances about nude, but few pay her any mind, having seen far more exciting things that night. Smiling, tired, people trickle out and drift home. Graham shares Dom Perignon with his family in the hot tub set up backstage for the band—it was made available to Dead Heads camping in the park on the open date during the week—before going out to dish fifty gallons of minestrone and 300 loaves of French bread to the hard core left at dawn. Later he'll vow, *"not one—not one, oh my children*—complaint or problem in five nights."

"It all rolls into one," wrote the Dead's lyricist Robert Hunter, "and nothing comes for free; there's nothing you can hold for very long." But one can hold on to an idea, an idea shared by nearly all those in the Auditorium—that life can have infinite possibilities, that it can be a high dance rather than a lonely plodding. More succinctly, the idea is captured in the single word painted in the destination slot of the fabled Merry Prankster's "Magic Bus": FURTHER.

Milton Mayer's somewhat oversympathetic portrait of the Deadheads, published in the May 1983 *Progressive*, as peace-loving rebels against a materialistic society is a poignant reminder of those ideas that lay beneath the entire phenomenon of the band and many of its followers. "My son the manager" is Rock Scully, himself the author of a book about his experiences, *Living with the Dead* (1995). Mayer was a rare creature in twentieth-century writing, a philosopher of humanity and of education and politics in the most wide-ranging sense. Among his many books are *They Thought They Were Free: The Germans, 1933-35*, published by the University of Chicago Press in 1958; *The Revolution in Education* (with Mortimer J. Adler), published by the University of Chicago Press in 1958; *What Can a Man Do? A Selection of His Most Challenging Writings*, published by the University of Chicago Press in 1964; *If Men Were Angels*, published by Atheneum in 1972; and *Biodegradable Man: Selected Essays*, published by University of Georgia Press in 1990.

An Aged Deadhead

Milton Mayer

It was the end of the wretched '60s and I was the speaker at a Quaker college in southern Indiana. I expected an audience of half a dozen—the students had done away with compulsory attendance—but the place was mobbed. When I asked the dean afterward how come, he showed me a poster and said the campus had been covered with them. The poster read:

COME AND HEAR

Milton Mayer

Father of the Manager of

THE GRATEFUL DEAD

The Dead had packed them in at a Quaker college in southern Indiana.

I had heard all the rock-'n'-roll I wanted to—and more, much more—on records, since Ms. Baby Mayer, the companion of my sorrows, was a true-blue Deadhead. (My son the manager.) I didn't cotton to the thunderous tom-tom of the music. I was the genteel Dixieland/Mozart type.

Ms. Baby said that you had to hear the Dead live, in the flesh, to under-

Twentieth-anniversary press conference at the Greek Theatre, Berkeley, 1985.
Photo by Susana Millman

stand, not them, but the hundreds of thousands of Deadheads who followed them everywhere with an unparalleled fidelity. So I heard them live.

I go on hearing them live. I don't cotton to the music, but I cotton to what it evokes (or responds to) in the auditorium, the stadium, the amphitheatre, the playing field in the park. I see, and hear, and feel, a whole second generation now of young people carried up and away by the mystique of rock-'n'-roll and by the unique mystic of the Dead. Inhaling the marijuana, I wander around the half-jumping half-hushed hall and raise the average age of the audience by fifty years or so.

They are having a good time in a bad-time world. They are having a good-natured hour—three hours—on a bad-natured planet. They are having the nearest thing we see these parlous days to good clean fun. They are able to let themselves go, and not just harmlessly. Their friendliness is consummate. Their openness is consummate. Their acceptance is consummate. Their whole social behavior is consummate, if reeling and writhing (but not arithmetic) doesn't bother you.

They are marching to a different tom-tom.

I've talked to the swarms of police, in Springfield, MA, in Santa Cruz, CA, and in between, who are sent out by the Fearful Fathers (fathers like me) on riot control at the concerts, and they are amazed to tell me uniformly in their uniforms that there is nothing to control. Rock-'n'-roll—at least the Dead's rock-'n'-roll—is a shining instant in a painful passage. The Dead family band, the family band that plays together and stays together, have somehow captured and transmitted the devotion and constancy that characterizes their changeless personnel.

The family Dead and their family extended around the world are what is left of the counterculture that was turned off in the '50s and the '60s, turned off by a patriotism that turned out to be a bloody, bullying battle-rag, by a winners-vs.-losers free-enterprise system that tightened the chains on the already enchained, by the ideal of thrift that turned out to be greed, by the ideal of frugality that turned out to be meanness, by a work ethic that turned out to be rapacity and a coronary, by a faith that became a hard sell, by a purpose that became a trample.

(And by having to crawl under school desks to be saved from the atomic bombs that only a barbarous people like the Russians would think of dropping.)

When they began, the Dead were going to be finished when they got to be, well, thirty-five. But they grew, and grow, no older. They grew, and grow, no different. They communicate to the second generation of Deadheads the same innocence they communicated when they drifted together in the Hashbury. Innocence of having bought the counterfeits and the forgeries and the phonies their elders were selling the natives.

The Dead have marshaled the truants, piping them, if to no lasting good, at least to no immediate wickedness—and that, in an immediately wicked world, is super-great stuff. The Deadheads are the part-time grasshoppers, dancing while the full-time ants, here, there, everywhere, make industrious headway making bigger and better means of inflicting indiscriminate pain. The truants are not dropouts from the rat race, they are non-droppers-in.

They are white. Why are they white? Is it because the blacks already know how to reel and writhe? They are white-collar. Why are they white-collar? Is it because the blue-collars are busy buying the American counterfeits and forgeries and phonies? The Deadheads, oh, my, have no social doctrine. In a pig's eye they have no social doctrine: Without proclaiming one, they exude anti-materialism, anti-militarism, anti-nationalism, anti-intolerance.

The Grateful Dead are the band that wears no costumes when it plays.

Look, mom, no sequins.

Why are the Deadheads different from all hordes that ever were? Why don't they fight and brawl and trash and tear the place apart and make miserable mischief in the streets? Why do they do nothing at a Dead concert but enjoy themselves unconfined? Why are they mannerly? Harmless? Innocent? The answer has got to be a magic chemistry that produced the Grateful

Dead and says something to a world stoned on suspicion, hostility, war, and woe.

A reader-into like me doesn't want to read too much into this perennially astonishing phenomenon. Maybe—like phenomena generally—it goes nowhere and goes to seed and leaves its alumni indistinguishable from the buttoned-down alumni of the junior establishment.

But for the nonce I'm a sort of wrong-side-of-the-blanket Deadhead, an old square who doesn't cotton to the thunderous thumping—though I have come to recognize the masterful and hardwrought musicianship.

I'm a Deadhead despite my dread of seeing ten, twenty, or fifty thousand people assembled anywhere, any time. I'm a Deadhead because I've seen ten, twenty, or fifty thousand people assembled to shout no curses, see no one beaten, howl no one down.

Mary Eisenhart has a particular affinity for Hunter's entire body of work, which shows in her perceptive questions during the following interview published in *Golden Road*, Fall 1984. Although the interview precedes the top-ten success of "Touch of Grey" by three years, Hunter does talk about that song and about the "new album" that was even then in process, which would include the song. And Hunter conveys a sense of a band in a period of stagnation that is coming to an end. Eisenhart is the co-founder of the Grateful Dead conference (and many of its spinoffs, including the literary conference "Deadlit") on the WELL, as well as the Grateful Dead Forum on AOL. She is the former editor of *MicroTimes* magazine and she is presently the editor/webmaster of *valleypeople.com*, an on-line magazine for and about people in the high-tech industry.

Robert Hunter: Songs of Innocence, Songs of Experience

Mary Eisenhart

If you were there, you probably haven't forgotten. But get a good audience tape of New Year's '81-'82 and listen to "Terrapin." Picture, if you will, 8,000 people, many still soaking wet (it rained a lot that day, and took a long time to get in), jammed into the Oakland Auditorium. Listen to the band blazing, Garcia belting out the lyrics with exceptional fervor—and the rumble. By the time he gets to the "Counting stars by candlelight" line, 8000 people are roaring along, matching him syllable for syllable through the crickets and cicadas, the end and the beginning, the train putting its brakes on and the whistle screaming TERRAPIN! Not one of us has ever laid eyes on Terrapin Station, and we'd be hard pressed to define exactly what it was, but for that moment there was not the slightest doubt that if we listened hard enough, sang loud enough, and just hung in there, we could collectively lift that decrepit hall off its foundations and *get there*.

Chances are, if you're reading this magazine, Robert Hunter's lyrics have had a profound effect on your life. Whether you're the scholarly type who pores over words and songlists with cabalistic intensity, or a more carefree soul who (as Hunter himself notes with a certain chagrin) hears "We can share

the women, we can share the wine" and never notices that that attitude culmi-
nates in treachery and death, his songs have influenced your perception of
the world and indeed shaped that world itself. (Consider, if nothing else,
"What a long strange trip it's been.") Hence it is more than a little interesting
to check out *his* perceptions of the world from a non-lyrical standpoint.

This interview took place on May 23, 1984. Hunter was in a cheerful frame
of mind, having completed his new album, *Amagamalin Street*, to his own satisfaction and being about to embark on a host of new projects. He willingly
discussed not only *Amagamalin* (a gritty urban tale that represents a considerable departure from, say, "Terrapin," and is a tour de force of thematic and
character development), but his life and work in general. The discussion was
much punctuated with trips to the bookshelf to demonstrate this or that point
(to convince me that *Jack o' Roses* contains "the wrong 'Terrapin,'" Hunter
pulled out the recently completed suite), and he made many a foray into esoteric tangents (while reluctantly submitting to having his picture taken, he
read excerpts from his "Sister Joseph of Arimathea," a wildly surreal work
loosely based on the dubious joys of pre-Vatican II Catholic education). Since
Hunter's lyrics are supremely literate and his solo performances feature
everything from quotations of John Donne to full-blown renditions of the Get-
tysburg Address, it seemed only reasonable to ask, "What do you read?"

HUNTER: There's my collection over there [he points to a shelf filled with
most of the great works of Western literature], and I hope to have most of that
read before I kick off. I was raised around books. My father was in the book
business with McGraw-Hill, and so we had a splendid library around the
house, and I've grown up reading. I'm just about through Proust finally—I've
been digging at Proust for about six years, and I'm *finally* on *Time Regained.*

EISENHART: I'm impressed.

HUNTER: [Laughs] Well you should be. I'm impressed myself. I'm going to
finish it this year.

Proust and Spenser, *The Faerie Queene*, those are the two biggies. I've
wanted to be one of the people who have read The *Faerie Queene*. I have a
beautiful edition of it up here, but I'm afraid that a certain amount of Spenser
is about all I can take, and then—

EISENHART: Being an 18-year-old brat at the time, I had a pretty bad introduction to Spenser.

HUNTER: Even a worse introduction than reading Spenser himself? It's
so hard. There was this long poetry piece I was writing [gets up, pulls a book
off the shelf and starts flipping pages] a couple of years ago called "Idiot's
Delight." I wrote about 100 verses in this short scan here, and then for the next
200 I was going to write them all in Spenserian stanzas. First I had to figure

out the Spenserian stanza by reading it, then away I went. And these are all Spenserian stanzas, properly rhymed. I don't know how many I went through until I realized that it was limited.

I've got a giant book there that I'm deathly pleased about and want to pub- lish. These are all real long poems, "Idiot's Delight"; then I've got another long poem called "The Brass Axis," in which I just wanted to work with a certain form called a constricting quadrangle, each stanza is one less. What I'm writ- ing about in this is the state of mind you have to be in to do this.

EISENHART: Metapoetics.

HUNTER: Yeah, precisely. And then the R-rated Brer Rabbit, "Raggedy Remus," is completely in this form, and rhymed as well. After doing this, I feel that it was a waste of time, but what it did do was force me to use poetic devices that just wouldn't occur to me normally, uses of metaphor.

Anyway, I finally threw the whole idea away and went into this thing here, which is my *masterpiece,* "Evald and Fanteon."

EISENHART: What's it about?

HUNTER: It's about the fall of the perfect proud spirit into matter, more or less.

EISENHART: Blakean ?

HUNTER: Well, unfortunately it is a bit Blakean in places. There is cer- tainly one scene in it that's Blakean to the extreme. It's a description of Boston—

EISENHART: What does Boston have to do with the basically mythic character of all this?

HUNTER: Well, this mythic character comes to Boston and tips his hat to some ladies and is immediately busted for being insane, and thrown into an asylum, although he's come to save the world. And in the asylum he meets his match. The godlike powers in him are destroyed one by one—his vision, everything is destroyed, until finally he's considered cured and ejected, like almost a paraplegic, onto the street. But then what he's done is become true humanity, so now he can understand what's going on, which, as a god, he could not. So what seems to be a tragic ending in it, I hope is allegorically a rebirth into the human condition.

EISENHART: When do those of us in the outside world get to read this?

HUNTER: Soon as I get this tour done—the album's done now—and do some work with Jerry, then get a month or two by myself, I'm going to go through this and correct it for taste basically. And I think I will go through those other things and take that stupid squareness out of it, and if they stand on their own without it, I'll use 'em. And if they don't, I'll just consider them a very curious exercise in writing.

EISENHART: Is all the old stuff you read English?

HUNTER: I've been trying to brush up on my French because I'm getting interested in the French Symbolist poets again, and I want to read them in French. I've done a little bit of translation, some Mallarmé and Verlaine.

I was trying to learn a little Italian, because I wanted to read Dante in the original. I have got through the first canto in Italian.

I have eyes to do at least one Wagner translation. I would love to. I think I would do something simple like *Flying Dutchman*, or something to get my teeth into. I've got a good feeling for Wagner, I'd like to bring some of it properly in English. The sounds of the German in Wagner are too hard for the American ear.

This is one of those projects that you dream about doing and probably never get around to. Especially since it involves getting the German to do it, though it's possible to use comparative translations and one's own ear, I suppose.

EISENHART: Did you take Latin in school? Because German is a piece of cake after Latin.

HUNTER: No, I just have the church Latin. *Introibo ad altare Dei.* My Latin is extremely weak, it's a shame. I wish I'd had that Greek and Latin background right now. It's just a pain not to have it if you're trying to read widely. There's so much to read in Greek, and the translations are so miserable.

But everything just dropped for the making of this record. When I have time, with nothing to do, then I do this kind of weird stuff. I'm looking forward to getting back to my poetry, because there's something it fulfills in me that nothing else does.

EISENHART: Where does the name *Amagamalin Street* come from?

HUNTER: It just came out of my head, the way "Terrapin Station" did. I sit down, I write *something* on a piece of paper—"The title of this is—la di dah. OK—what's *that* about?" And then I just start exploring it and find out what it's about. I'm one who feels that vowels and consonant combinations have power sounds, they evoke stuff. "Amagamalin" evokes something. It's got a flavor, a spice, a taste to it—it will then sort of let you know what it's about.

In this case, it's a place where boy meets girl, boy beats crap out of girl, boy leaves girl, boy picks up another girl, boy beats crap out of this girl, best friend takes girl away from boy, is very nice to her, she goes back to boy A who beats the crap out of her again, and then splits on all of them. Boy A dies and girl A meets Boy B. Just a simple boy-meets-girl scene strained through "Amagamalin." The first record is all one guy talking, and the second is another guy.

What a piece of work that was, getting it all synched up. Those people were inhabiting my brain for some time. I feel I know them really well, and by the time I got into the recording studio with them, the appropriate voices were singing out of those two guys. Record Two's got a different voice than Record One does.

EISENHART: On the song "Amagamalin Street," isn't that a third-person narrator and not the character?

HUNTER: That is the only third person in it. I thought I might put on the album that the first record is Chet's story with an interjection by the narrator, and then the second record is all Murphy. But then I figured, why give 'em any clues at all?

EISENHART: Well, they'd probably appreciate it...And besides, sometime in the last 18 years you must have heard some exotic interpretations of your lyrics that have nothing to do with anything you ever thought about.

HUNTER: That is one reason I don't print the lyrics. You know, very definitely people hear their own songs, and if you can kind of cue them into their own thought processes that way, then later when they find out what the words really were, they hopefully realize that was their own song they were listening to, or their own interpretation. I like that. That's why I don't print the lyrics.

But I believe the lyrics on *Amagamalin Street* can be heard; there's no reason to print them.

EISENHART: How many attentive listeners do you think you have?

HUNTER: If they're not attentive, I hope they'll just like the songs. 'Cause I hope most of them stand just as a collection of songs, and that the fact that there's a thread in it is secondary. It's a structure to build around, and the songs really must stand by themselves.

I hope there's some value in *Amagamalin Street*, because doing a solo thing is such an ego trip, frankly, and to justify this ego trip—I was talking to Jerry about it the other day, and he says, "Well, you don't have to justify yourself, man." And I said, "Whaddya mean? I'm a double-Cancer Roman Catholic, I have to justify myself." [Laughs] "*Oh*," he said, "in that case, right..."

What I'm hoping to achieve in this, from my 40-plus point of view, is to say the run of these things, of these disastrous relationships of a certain sort involving violence and a very laissez-faire attitude...what sort of characters have these things, and what comes of it in the way of human degradation and eventual unhappiness. Just to paint a picture of this whole hell, how it works, the interactions in it, what it comes to, just give an older man's point of view. And maybe some kid can flash on this and be spared the kind of hell that this all leads to.

And hopefully that's the good that *Amagamalin Street's* going to do, to justify almost the terrible egocentricity of just putting my voice forward rather than giving it to the Dead so it's part of a group thing. I feel scot free in group things; I feel no need to justify—there's a great thing happening just in that a group of people is working together. More justification is needed for soloing in the manner that I'm doing. It's got to amount to something. Somebody has got to get some more good out of it, other than saying, "Oh, Hunter sure strings words together nice."

EISENHART: But nowadays the music business seems much more oriented toward cranking out product than to saying something.

HUNTER: Oh, we know this out front, that content doesn't sell. And I've just made the decision somewhere along the line—this music business is so tacky that I don't think you can really have any gentlemanly pretensions and partake of it unless you can turn it to some sort of use. And so I just say a big no to any kind of commercial thing, that way, and I feel *very* comfortable. And that allows me to perceive myself as a poet, and to continue on with my poetry writing, which I consider every bit as important—to me anyway—as my lyrical work. I'm able to arrive at this advanced age and not feel like a sellout. I couldn't live with myself if I was doing that other thing. I would've burned out a long time ago. I think the Dead would've too. All of us partake of this to some degree. It's our ethic.

I look at it as a wide-open field. Nobody is much interested in what doesn't directly lead to fortune or overwhelming fame. If you have what it takes and want to try to say something, you don't have any competition. Of course, you may have trouble finding a record company—in my case, I'm just using an independent distributor. And of course I've got a good foundation in the Dead aficionados, so that I assume I can sell a couple of copies of it. Hopefully it'll pay for itself.

It's a wide-open field. Everybody's busy trying to express what the market would like them to express. And they're going to lose themselves somewhere along the way. You know that. Just follow it year after year. It's the same old story over and over and over again—Duran Duran will take the dive next. You know, it's—Get all the way to the dizzying top of that thing and then try and dive into a wet washrag. And while you're diving there's lots of applause and everything, and then you hit the washrag. Well, I want to take a dive from a smaller tower in a *great big* bathtub, at least, you know. [Laughs] I want to come out alive.

EISENHART: Do you have any sense of a non-Deadhead audience? Other than my mother, who gets your stuff quoted to her all the time.

HUNTER: I don't have much sense of that. There's *my* mother. [Laughs] I would like to move beyond a strict cult following, which is certainly what the Deadheads are. They're wonderful, but it's always been a bit miffing, that you have to identify yourself as part of this group in order to appreciate this thing, and if you're not one you don't even listen to it or even consider it. That doesn't seem exactly fair. But I do have that stamp on my head, for a fact.

It'd be very nice to expand into a more varied listening public. I would like to speak to people my own age, many of whom have just turned their Grateful Dead thing off. They don't come to concerts 'cause they don't want to go for the crowds, and perhaps the records have not been so great in the last bunch of years. Yeah, I would like to address people my own age as well as younger people. I don't have pretensions to addressing anyone older.

EISENHART: Why not?

HUNTER: I'm just a kid to them, they've had more experience. I just know what a 42-year-old knows. I don't know what a 45-year-old knows, necessarily.

EISENHART: Do you think it's entirely a function of age?

HUNTER: Not entirely. I'm just speaking in the broadest category, giving everybody the benefit of the doubt. Pretending that people really do mature. I'm certainly not sold on that proposition.

I think basically maturity is just being able to step outside yourself and judge or look at your actions and their effects as though you were somebody else, rather than always from the inside, all arrows coming in.

EISENHART: Where did the story come from for *Amagamalin Street*?

HUNTER: In the original, the version I had done with The Dinosaurs, there was no Chet and Murphy. And I was just walking down Fifth Avenue and all of a sudden the idea struck me, and I just leaned up against a building and watched the crowd go by and got into it and realized who the characters on *Amagamalin Street* were. They gave the focus to it. From there it was a short step to doing the whole cycle. These characters were alive to me then, and I wanted to tell their story.

EISENHART: Were all the songs written specifically for the album, or had some of it been around for a while, and just fit in?

HUNTER: "Where Did You Go?" was a song that I'd had for some years, the changes for it, and some of the lines for it, but I rewrote it to go in. It happened to be exactly right—as things that come from my head do tend to be exactly right for other things that come out of my head. I couldn't *not* write a Grateful Dead song if I tried. [Laughs]

I don't have to sit down and try. I expect damn near everything I've ever written interconnects, and I'm starting to see what the grand patterns are in it all now. I don't want to do any overt interconnections. I don't want to do like Lennon did and say, "I told you about the walrus."

It's too pat. There are connections in one's own head about this, but you make those connections in your own head and you just present the tunes, and if people see the connections, that's fine. But what have I written?—200 or 300 songs—and they're all coming from the same body of experience in me, so they're going to connect. That's just the way it is if you remain fairly true to your own experience and don't try to assume someone else's, something that happens to be popular, or try to be the sort of person that you aren't or don't know.

EISENHART: From that standpoint, did you have any problem with the characters of Chet and Murphy? Was either of them harder to do than the other?

HUNTER: Well, Chet and Murphy are both aspects of myself, these are all attitudes that I have had. There's nowhere else to go for such experiences. If you want to make them believable and real, you've got to get in the way Freud did when he wrote his books. He went to his own experience and—I think rather fearlessly—presented it in order to give his things credibility.

I did a lot of thinking about the characters. I wanted to be sure everybody was being true to his own weaknesses.

It's a simple plot. I think that people can piece it together. That was another thing: If you're going to do it, don't get it too complex. I always thought maybe Roseanne goes to Italy and has an illegitimate child by the Pope and the last album'll take place on a space station. I was digging, I wasn't quite sure.

Then I thought to myself, Well, what would really happen to these characters? What *would* happen to somebody like Chet? Obviously he'd drop in the gutter at some point, and Murphy is able to predict this because he couldn't really end any other way. Murphy's another case himself. He's much more complex a character than Chet. I kind of hated to have Maggie walk out on him, but she would, you know, given the situation. 'Cause he's her rescuer, he's not her lover. She's in love with this guy, Chet, who's got *something* to talk a girl like Roseanne into what's he's talked her into. He's got a persuasive charm, whereas Murphy is more or less just a good, righteous street cat.

EISENHART: And protective and honorable.

HUNTER: All the things that a girl like Maggie eventually can't hack. I mean, here he is saying, "We'll move out to the Catskills, away from the city life" and everything. I mean, she's just lived 20-some years in Ithaca, for Chrissakes, she doesn't want to move to the Catskills. [Laughs] But she wants to get away from Chet before he kills her, or at least Murphy convinces her that she does. For a while.

I hope that anybody who can identify with this story will just fill in pieces of their own lives to the parts I didn't put in. That's one reason for leaving little gaps in between, putting results rather than exactly what happened, thing after thing.

I hope I'm getting into an area that everyone has had some experience in. A lot of people have had experience with violence in their upbringing. I think in this day and age a lot of that stuff is covered very frankly in television and movies. *Streetcar Named Desire* was a big flash when it first came out, that this sort of material should be presented. Now I would say that it's damn near passé—oh, not that Tennessee Williams' writing would ever be passé, but that once he opened it up for inspection, a lot of people followed suit. Those themes have been explored now, and people do know about them. Perhaps 20 years ago it was not such common knowledge.

EISENHART: When I was in high school, *Catcher in the Rye* was considered real racy stuff, and now I keep running into high school students who bitch and moan, "Oh God, we have to read *Catcher in the Rye.*"

HUNTER: [Laughs] They'd be bored with Erica Jong, I suppose.

EISENHART: They're bored with reading. The average American kid doesn't seem to be into reading at all.

HUNTER: Well, let's give 'em their literature through the ears, then, with a rock beat. See if that happens. There is a great joy in good literature, but if you're not getting that great joy out of it, there's no point in pushing your nose in it.

Dylan opened up pop music as a literary form, I think, and then Lennon was very influenced by him and followed suit. Robbie Robertson was trying to do things that way, and several of the people in San Francisco. It went its way, and now it seems to be a very dated form. I refuse to think that it's dated. I want to keep it moving. I think we can get our literature and our rock and roll and make it like one massive assault on the sheer idiocy of the '80s. I hope.

One of the reasons I would like to see *Amagamalin Street* successful, other than egotistical or monetary reasons, is that if it were successful, then people would do it: try and put some meaning and some thought in what they're doing, maybe on a larger than one-song level. I'd like to revivify this whole song-cycle idea—Townshend did it with *Tommy*, a thematic idea. With "Terrapin" I was trying to develop a thematic idea, and unfortunately only a certain amount of it got onto the record. It's a much longer thematic piece.

I think some of the frustration of not really getting "Terrapin" properly done has been lessened by getting *Amagamalin Street* done. Finally, one whole coherent idea that I had is out. This is the form I want to pursue. I mean, I still want to write individual songs, songs by themselves, but I think for the time being I'm very much on the idea of—I'm a novelist. I've got novels tucked away up here that I've been writing. I don't think I'm a very good novelist. I think I've got a lyric gift more than I have a prose gift. But I have a novelist mentality. I like plot and whatnot. I think this may be how I do my novels, rock and roll.

EISENHART: I was really crushed at a show a while back when you said you didn't like *Jack o' Roses*, because I think it's a tremendous album.

HUNTER: The only reason is that I didn't feel I did the right "Terrapin." The "Terrapin" that is on there, all the additional material, is not the *right* material. What I had done was lost my original drafts of it, and then I just rediscovered them in my trunks last year. And my original inspiration for it was something entirely different than the "Terrapin" I ended up with on *Jack o' Roses*. And so I've subsequently finished it up, and have it all written and corrected and presentable as a complete piece, and it's better. I never felt that my "Terrapin" on *Jack o' Roses* worked.

EISENHART: But it fit really well with everything else on the album .

HUNTER: I'll have to listen to it one day and see if it's good. Les [Kippel, whose Relix Records distributes Hunter's recent solo albums] tells me it is. He wants to keep it in release. I was saying I thought I'd like to just let it sleep. In fact, I've got the idea that all my albums are not so good up to *Amagamalin Street*, and why don't we just let it sleep and kind of start all over? But he assures me that a couple of them are decent.

EISENHART: I tend to find Rum Runners a little inaccessible.

HUNTER: I didn't have any idea what I was doing when I was producing that. It was my first crack at the studio, and the rhythms are all off and it's rough and ready. As one critic said, it sounds like it was recorded in a bathroom.

And *Tiger Rose* has those terrible vocals on it. One, because I couldn't sing very well there; and two, because [his son] Leroy was being born in England and I had to hop on a plane and dash over there and leave the album with these kind of make-do vocals on it, which all go out of range. They're not really well done. I couldn't stay around to finish it, and we had a production schedule, so it just went out with the vocals I had on it.

I've been thinking of taking *Tiger Rose* back in the studio and redoing the vocals on it, 'cause I think I have some good songs on it, they're just *pitifully* sung. I like Garcia's arrangements and production on it, and I like the songs. The only thing I can't stand is the vocals on it. I played it for the first time in years the other day and I was just *horrified*.

EISENHART: Don't change a note of "Yellow Moon."

HUNTER: That would be a hard one to change, because Garcia and I sat down in the studio one morning and just played it. There's no tracks on that; it's just a live thing with a microphone set up, so it couldn't be changed. I just played it through for him a couple of times. "Here's how it goes," I said. "OK, now you play lead on it." We turned on the microphones and that's what we came out with. I think it was the first take. I'd just written the song the night before. I needed another song for the album.

EISENHART:You lived in England for a while?

HUNTER: Yeah, for a couple of years. On the West Coast, near Bristol. Then I just decided I was letting my Grateful Dead duties slip too much, so I winged it on back. But that was at a point where I felt that life being the Grateful Dead lyricist and all that was getting to be too much of a bag and I was missing *life* outside of that closed circle. So I just moved off to England and— then I came back. [Laughs]

EISENHART: Have you ever found the Grateful Dead lyricist thing claustrophobic?

HUNTER: Very. Very. It put me through years of more or less retreat. I was a little frightened about what had been wrought there, and I wasn't sure how soon it might turn nasty. And I very much kept myself out of the public eye. I didn't want photos out or anything like that. I had some idea that I might get shot or something. And I wanted to keep my own identity. I just knew, I had a feeling, an intuition, that you lose your identity from too much public exposure.

I think at my age now I can take that sort of thing. I think I was right in what I did back then, in keeping my profile very low and trying to concentrate on my work, rather than on my persona. And now I feel in a way that I've got my chops together as a writer, and the persona and stuff has to be put out. I'm still a bit reluctant to do it because I do feel safe. I can walk down the street and nobody recognizes me, whereas Jerry certainly can't do that. And he's pretty much confined to quarters, 'cause anyplace he goes—"Heeyyy! There's Jerry Garcia!"

EISENHART: And he's mobbed by crazy people.

HUNTER: If not mobbed, at least *noticed hard.* And it makes you damn self-conscious. And most people tend to retreat under those conditions. Whereas it wasn't necessary so much for me to retreat, although in a way I did anyway. I don't know why. It was such an overwhelming experience when the Dead first started hitting the charts and happening. It was deeply frightening to me in a way. I don't know if it was a failure wish or whatever it was, but I just kept myself back from it. I guess it scared me a bit.

EISENHART:What was going on that was scary?

HUNTER: Those were the radical days, the political radicalism days, and the Grateful Dead was not a political band. And a lot of people would take exception to such a thing. And I just had a feeling that if you got prominent enough, somebody was likely to pop you anyway, just for the hell of it. And I know that we attracted an odder-than-usual audience because of the heavy drug use. I just wasn't—it made me nervous.

I'm not nervous about it anymore. I'm not crazy about the idea of putting my picture out, but I've confronted it, realized that it's a necessity. OK, I'm onstage now, people are taking pictures, I might as well accept it. Although I'm starting to get recognized down at the local store and things like that because of Dinosaurs posters.

I don't get the feeling that everywhere I go I'm being watched. I'm a walker, too. I like to get out and walk all around for hours, and, oh, I'd *hate* to have that taken away from me. I don't like the idea of losing my personal identity into a mass consumption somehow, but I'm not scared either.

EISENHART:Do you feel a big difference between your private self and your public self? Are you aware of becoming a different person onstage?

HUNTER: Oh, Lord. Boy is that a complex question.

I think that anybody who gets onstage becomes somebody different to a degree. There are things—like the way I'm talking right now, back and forth, I can make some kind of coherent sense. When I get onstage and open my mouth it falters, because there's no one person I'm talking to, who I have some suss on their intellectual level, or their acceptance level. When you're talking to a crowd...I'll open my mouth as though I'm going to address you, for example—and I'm not. I'm addressing this monsterous being, which is a crowd. And what you have to remember is that there is no such thing as a crowd, they are just a collection of individuals. But there won't be any feedback from what I say, or any—"Oh yeah, we understand what you mean, and how about this point of view?" All you get is either a "Yea!" or a "Hey, he's spaced!" or something like that. And so I tend to have learned to more or less keep my mouth shut onstage, unless I really feel moved to make a statement about something, which is rare enough.

I wish it were otherwise. I wish I had the gift of patter onstage. I did have it about 15 to 20 years ago. When Garcia and Nelson and I were playing in the Wildwood Boys, I did the stagemanship. But back in those days, that's what was done. You had to have a line of patter when you were onstage. Nobody was *allowed* to just stand up there and be silent, so I used to drink a lot of beer and rave away.

EISENHART: Are your musical roots basically folk?

HUNTER: I considered myself a folksinger, and then we all became blue-grass musicians, which was a logical extension of that. When it turned rock and roll, I turned to my typewriter. I wasn't really interested in rock and roll, and it still strikes me as odd that I really even did get into it. I thought of myself as a Serious Novelist before I first started writing for the Dead. But, you know, Jerry said, "Look, you're the writer, you write." And...OK!

EISENHART: So you never just sat down and decided to be a lyricist.

[Negative noises]

EISENHART: But you did sit down and decide to be a writer.

[Affirmative noises]

EISENHART: What brought that on?

HUNTER: Oh, I've been writing since I was a tad. Always have written.

EISENHART: Did it run in your family?

HUNTER: No, but my father certainly didn't discourage it, being in the book business and everything. Although he told me there was no money to be made in that profession, I wasn't as discouraged from that as I was from my trumpet and violin. [Laughs] Which, after a hard day at work, he would tolerate but not encourage.

EISENHART: Are you from around here?

HUNTER: I'm from up and down the West Coast. I've lived in Portland, Seattle, San Francisco, Palo Alto, Los Angeles, Long Beach, all that, a couple of years in Connecticut, in my growing-up period. Never in one place too long. I think Palo Alto about the longest of all—I spent between 8th and 11th grade there. Up till then I think I went to a different school every year, which certainly helped to develop my outsider feelings, always the new-kid-in-school stuff. I grew up defensive that way, I think.

EISENHART: Is that what made you take up music?

HUNTER: It made me take up books more than anything else. I always had my nose in a book. I was getting away from it.

EISENHART: Did you mostly think that people were bozos when you were that age?

HUNTER: No, I don't think I did. I thought that a lot of them were just better than me. I didn't feel that I was particularly smart, and I felt that they didn't like me for some reason. I think the reason that they didn't like me was that I was too defensive and I would strike first. But I'd just forget it all and bury my nose in *Robin Hood* or something like that, you know. I think my real life was books, in my growing up. So it was only natural that I started writing. I started my first novel when I was 11.

EISENHART: Did you ever get to the point of realizing that people don't act like they do in books?

HUNTER: [Laughs] They don't? Maybe I haven't realized that yet. It depends on which books. A lot of them act like Madame Bovary. Of course, Flaubert has human nature down. And a lot of the great writers do write the way people are, like Thomas Mann in *The Magic Mountain*. This is the way people really *are*. So it depends on the book you're talking about. *Robin Hood*, no.

I became terribly disillusioned through my early 30s about people. And then I think I came to the realization that what I was disappointed in was the way they treated *me*, that they didn't give me what I wanted, the appreciation or whatever that I wanted. And then I began wondering just how much of it I wasn't giving *them*. And there was this sort of turnaround point where I realized that the world is not oriented around me. And then things got easier from that point on.

I haven't fully realized this yet. I can sit down and think it real hard and then go out and direct myself to realize this, but then you get sloppy, and once again it becomes, "they're not very nice to *me*." And it's a totally reactive world that way.

EISENHART: Or else you get to the point where you're really on a roll, and everything is falling into place, and you think it's going to go on like that forever, and then, POW!

HUNTER: Yeah. Pride rideth before a fall. It's a fact. Right now, with all these projects I have going—I'm working on a movie too, *Armageddon Rag*, by George R.R. Martin, a very good science fiction book, which I recommend; I'm doing some soundtrack work for it and making some comments on the scriptwriting process—and opening shows for Garcia, having my album out, having a bunch of my books finished, and things like that—I really have this sitting-on-top-of-the-world feeling. I'm trying to remember, in this flush-of-success feeling I'm having right now, to keep things in proportion, 'cause boy, that fall is bad. That balloon gets deflated as surely as you blow it up.

But right now I feel so positive. It's almost frightening. Things seem to be going my way this week, after about 42 years of preparatory work. We shall see.

EISENHART: Are you still Catholic?

HUNTER: Oh, that's just my upbringing. I think that there's a bit of the Catholic that remains in anybody with the upbringing. It is a certain way of looking at the world—lots of guilt. [Laughs] It doesn't leave you just because you understand it; it's conditioning, and it just behooves you to know that you have it, I think, and to not make too many of your decisions based on known nun-inflicted guilt. The words that'll ring in my head forever: "We don't wear engineer boots at St. Ignatius, Robert." [Laughs]

There just came a point when it no longer was right and I stopped subscribing to it. And then not until 20 years later did I realize that I had the conditioning, because I read some books, like James Joyce's *Portrait of the Artist As a Young Man*. I understand Stephen Daedalus.

EISENHART: Do you feel much sense of being part of a particular literary tradition?

HUNTER: Nothing pops into my mind. I used to say to that question, Robert Burns and Sir Walter Scott, but I don't say that anymore.

EISENHART: Not Beat stuff like Kerouac and Ginsberg?

HUNTER: I don't think my stuff has much resonance with that, does it? It might, I don't know.

EISENHART: Your idiom is completely different.

HUNTER: That's all I meant. I'm certainly simpatico with Kerouac. I think he's one of the finest American writers. Still undiscovered, as far as I'm concerned. Undiscovered for good reasons—I mean, amongst the jewels that Kerouac has come up with you have to go through wheelbarrows of slop. But they're there. *Visions of Cody*, it's there.

But I can understand not liking Kerouac. As a writer, there are things in him that just turn my stomach. How can a guy just slop over a page like this? The urge to reach for the blue pencil is almost irresistible at times. Oh, with Proust too, I've blue-pencilled Proust—I said, "Wait a minute. Dangling subjunctive clauses [Laughs], just whip those things out, and get this in order..." Oh yes, I'm an editor, I love to edit. Adjectives, passive voice. Slice, cut.

The best teacher I ever had—at the end of my senior year my English teacher said, "You've got a real gift for the language, Hunter. Trouble is, you never *say* anything." I've got her voice still ringing in my ears. And over the years, that critique applies when I'm writing something. Like, OK, sure, these words are fancy and everything like that. Have you *said* anything? Oh, all right. Say something, huh? Skip the adverbs and the adjectives. They don't *make* color of themselves. Substance makes color.

EISENHART: What are you going to do next?

HUNTER: What I want to do next is work on some material with Garcia. I kind of would like to interest him in doing a song cycle too. And if he goes for it, I'd love to do some collaboration with him on it. He is so much fun to collaborate with.

EISENHART: How does it work?

HUNTER: Well, today, for example, I went over with a song I'd written for him. Of course, we have worked a hundred different ways, but this is a pretty good example of how it works. Today I brought a song over, and then he looked at it and said, "How does this go?" And so I reached for his guitar to show him some chords, and he said, "That's a little bit out of tune, there's an acoustic over there." And I was going for that, and he said, "Wait, wait, wait, on second thought, don't play it for me, because when you do it takes a couple of weeks for your changes to get out of my mind so I can get to business with it."

He generally prefers to be just given the lyrics. I generally write a *song*. And with something like "Touch of Grey," which is a bit difficult, he may say, "Well, how do you do this?" to get an idea of how it rolls as a song. But as he says, then it might take him months to get my musical impressions out of his head, because he doesn't use my impressions. He's a creator, and he wants to create his own thing around that. And that's kind of how it works.

And then what he doesn't like in the lyrics, or if he wants more, or less, or different, or something like that, then he expresses his objections about it. And I'll rewrite to specifications. Or argue.

EISENHART: Does he have a deep understanding of the lyrics?

HUNTER: Yeah. Yeah. That's why I can work with him. He does understand what he sings. There's no two ways about that. When I write for him—It's like I told him today. I said, "Your muse visited me last night and said, 'Here's a song for Garcia. Now if he doesn't appreciate it or do something with it, then you can have it, but you've got to give him first choice on it.'" It kind of works that way.

I write differently for Garcia than I write for myself. I write it with the intention of him singing it, and I write things other than I would write with the intention of me singing it. I know the kind of—in a way, through long experience—the sorts of things that he doesn't like to sing about, the sorts of things that don't express *him*. And, like there are attitudes in *Amagamalin Street*, songs that Jerry wouldn't express, and so I skirt those.

EISENHART: Like what?

HUNTER: Oh, just the "'Taking Maggie home / She don't wanna stay / We're walking out of here peaceful / Don't stand in our way"—That doesn't fit Garcia's persona, it's not *him*. And I just have to get a suss on—which we do conversationally—what he likes, what he doesn't like. There's a whole kind of revolutionary rhetoric, sort of things like that, that he just finds *distasteful*. And I've tried on revolutionary songs, everything else, and he says, "Oh, that's great," puts it away, and totally forgets about it.

I see what it is that he does, and what it is that he doesn't do of what I've given him over the years, and I get a bit of a suss of what he feels that he can speak comfortably. There's a range of motions he doesn't like to talk about, and certain ways of relating, whatever, that aren't his ways. And you just have to know the cat to some degree to feel what he would express and what he feels comfortable doing.

EISENHART: So in a way it's like writing a different character?

HUNTER: I couldn't write for Garcia: "I'm comin' to getcha, honey, I'm gonna getcha, I'm gonna getcha, yeah, yeah, yeah!" I wouldn't write that for Garcia, right? I wouldn't do that. You can't imagine him singing that, can you?

Whereas if I were tunesmithing for somebody who I respected who would sing such a thing...For the *Armageddon Rag* I'm writing some stuff that I wouldn't write for myself *or* for Garcia, but the character in the movie who's going to be singing this stuff, this is the kind of stuff he'd sing. Some of it's pretty down and dirty, heavy revolutionary punky sort of stuff, some of it.

Which is interesting to take a hand at. Plus some '60s-type songs that I'm enjoying writing, knowing what I know now. It's a kind of chance to return.

Right now I think we [the GD] are starting to blossom again. I think there's going to be interesting tidbits flowing out in the next year. The record'll be getting done. It may be the first real high in three years. It's been a slump.

EISENHART: There are people who basically maintain that the Grateful Dead ceased to exist in 1974 and never came back.

HUNTER: [Pugnacious] We'll see about that. We'll just see, huh? See about that. People put expectations on us, they want us to remain what we were, and no human being can do that without becoming totally crystallized. Maybe we're bad, maybe we're not giving them what they expected, but...

EISENHART: But that's not what you're for.

HUNTER: No, we're for ourselves, more than anything else, for our own musical development. If it goes through a slump, it goes through a slump. But I think we've made a bit of a career of meeting different expectations than are had of us, starting with *Workingman's Dead*, which *was just a joy* [big grin] to drop on them after the psychedelia, and to see how their heads would explode on that one. And maybe we'll do it again.

The only explanation for all of this, and the length of time it's taking to make the album, and all the years like that is just *phenomenal* untogetherness. We've been in a slump, we haven't been together, except onstage, I suppose. I think it's a natural change, and I believe that with enough good will among the members that it is coming together again. I get the feeling it is. I do hope so. We shall see.

Alice Kahn contributed distinctive humorous essays for years to the *East Bay Express* and, subsequently, *The San Francisco Chronicle*, where her column was nationally syndicated through 1994. The following piece on Garcia published in the *San Jose Mercury's West Magazine* on December 30, 1984, is unusual for its focus on his formative years in the Bay Area. Kahn has published three collections of her work, *Multiple Sarcasm*, published by the Ten Speed Press in 1985; *My Life As a Gal*, published by Delacorte in 1987; which includes the excerpt below; and *Luncheon at the Cafe Ridiculous*, published by Poseidon in 1990. In 1998, she published (with John Dobby Boe) *Your Joke Is in the E-Mail: Cyberlaffs from Mousepotatoes*, published by the Ten Speed Press. She is now back to her previous career, working as a nurse practitioner in the Kaiser Permanente Chemical Dependency Recovery Program and at the Kaiser Division of Research.

Jerry Garcia
and the
Call of the Weird

Alice Kahn

He came out of suburban California twenty years ago with his latter-day beatnik, proto-hippie buddies and started playing music. And for Jerry Garcia the music's never stopped. The band was once known as the Zodiacs, then as Mother McCree's Uptown Jug Champions, then as the Warlocks. Finally it became the Grateful Dead. It's been a long, strange trip for Jerry and the boys from the bars of San Carlos and the pizza parlors of San Jose to the ballrooms of America, the concert halls of Europe, and the hearts and minds of two generations of devoted fans. Garcia remains a cult figure within a subculture.

This subculture is most apparent at a Grateful Dead concert. It may be the 1980s out there, where troops of entrepreneur-worshiping young Reaganites eat to win, dress for success, jazzercise for life, and work hard for the money.

But inside of the Grateful Dead's New Year's Eve concert—an annual ritual for Deadheads—it's National Hippie Preservation Park.

The adoring sea of tie-dyed, Day-Glo Deadheads distinguishes the band's concerts from just another rock 'n' roll show. Remarkably, Dead concerts sell out without any advertising: the Deadheads find the band through organized phone trees. This year I was included. In the great tradition of "the first one's free," I was contacted by a Deadhead and treated to my first night of the living Dead.

Outside the concert, hundreds were walking around, vying for the twelve-dollar tickets, some offering up ten times that amount, some promising things they did not have. Others held up signs reading I NEED A MIRACLE—Deadhead code for "I want a free ticket." Two girls came down the street outside the theater, doing a Tweedledee-tweedledum dance and chanting:

"One ticket is all we need.

"Trade you a ticket for a bag of weed."

Estimates of the number of Deadheads vary. Dennis McNally, the Dead's publicist, places it at somewhere between 20,000 and 250,000. The lower number refers to the hardcore Deadheads who follow the band on tours, traveling until their money runs out. The higher number indicates the usual album sales and the fans who attend at least one concert a year.

Another take on the number of Deadheads comes from Eileen Law, the liaison between the Grateful Dead organization and the Deadheads. In an interview with *The Golden Road*, a Bay Area quarterly exclusively for Deadheads, Law said that the official Deadhead mailing list (now computerized for efficiency) contains 90,000 names—up from 10,000 in 1972. Proudly, Law adds that she carefully guards these names from exploitation, having refused requests this year from both the Mondale and the Hart campaigns for access. Law also maintains the phones in the organization's San Rafael (Marin County) office. This phone hotline is generally the only way Grateful Dead concerts are publicized. Devoted Deadheads phone in weekly for news of ticket sales. Most concerts sell out quickly. Last Halloween, a six-day run in Berkeley sold out completely within forty-eight hours of being announced on the hotlines.

The Grateful Dead are an anomaly in the world of rock 'n' roll because they are a performing band—making most of their money from extensive road tours rather than record sales. Deadheads will tell you that the band can't be recorded in the studio because the mysterious flirtation between Dead and Deadheads is missing.

It is a strange mutual dependency, resulting in an improvisational style that sometimes leaves the band sounding like amateurs but at other times

carries them to the kind of ecstasy more often associated with jazz performances. And some Deadheads talk about the night they heard the Dead perform "Dark Star" or "St. Stephen" the way earlier generations of music
aficionados might recall hearing Caruso in *Aida*. At times, however, the multi-
tudes screaming for songs like "Truckin'" or "Casey Jones" or "Uncle John's
Band" resemble nothing so much as the piano-bar drunk who relentlessly
demands "Melancholy Baby."

When I attended my first Dead concert, the experience took on an extraordinary quality only when Jerry Garcia began one of his plaintive, improvised
guitar solos. Through the electronic equipment I could almost hear the ban-
jos and tambourines of a minstrel show. Was there anything more American, I
thought, than this psychedelic waif, picking and singing?

The Deadhead who guided me to "my first time" was Shelley, a Ph.D. candi-
date in demographics. At the concert she introduced me to her friends—
lawyers, doctors, an economics professor from Yale, a software genius. Other
than the hippie veneer, there was really no way to characterize the Deadheads I met, including as they did military officers, clerk-typists, and gay men.
They were generally of the white-middle-class persuasion and grouped at the
high and low ends of the IQ scale. There were plenty of 165's in the crowd and
plenty of 94's (perhaps self-induced 94's). Your 110's were probably watching
Springsteen.

There were women who appeared to have oozed out of caves in the California mountains, scantily clad hippie mommas who seem to exist on nothing
but Spirulina, megadose vitamins, and cocaine. One, dressed only in a tiger-
skin, performed a sacrificial version of the frug. During her four-hour nonstop
frenzy, she would occasionally hold out her breasts as a kind of offering for
the Dead.

Also in attendance were the entire United Farmers of Humboldt and Men-
docino counties wearing shirts with unabashed marijuana ads like "This
Bud's for You," "Sense and Sinsemilla" and "Humboldt: the Ultimate Smoke."
They stood right next to their more urban brothers who wore stylish haircuts
and treated the event like a hippie aerobics class, wildly bopping in place for
hours, doing a revved-up pelvic tilt that would surely surprise the guys back
at the office. One could almost imagine these day-job yuppies shouting
"Good workout, Jerry!" Outside the concert, where many supported their
Dead habit by selling skull-and-roses shirts and decals, one fellow hawked a T-
shirt that showed two teddy bears dancing. It read, "Jerrycise." Another shirt
on sale showed skeletons dancing and was emblazoned with the motto
"Deadercize for Life."

At the concert, I was surprised to see an acquaintance, a fairly conventional woman. She told me she'd been a Deadhead for twelve years. She had attended seventy concerts, owned and played the concert tapes that are traded underground through national magazines like *Dead Relix*, and papered her house with skull-and-roses posters. Why, I wondered, would this forty-year-old mother of two teenagers, who had risen in the ranks of a major research laboratory, live a secret life as a Deadhead? "You've never worked for NASA-Ames," she replied.

Individual band members have their own constituencies. Bobby Weir, the preppie-next-door from prosperous Atherton in the purple Lacoste shirt, has a teenybopper following (although many of these boppers are women in their thirties). Other fans are drawn to the more ambitious musicologist Phil Lesh, the bass player with a classical academic background. For some, the highlight of a Dead show is the weird extensive drum duo performed by Bill Kreutzmann and Mickey Hart. The least mythologized member is relative newcomer Brent Mydland, who plays keyboard and must compete with the memory of Ron "Pigpen" McKernan, the wild organ and harmonica player who was part of the original band and died in the '70s of liver failure. Deadheads talk about Bobby or Phil or Bill on a first-name basis. But they especially talk about Jerry.

Perhaps none of it would have come about if a young man named Jerry Garcia hadn't been kicked out of the army in 1960 and headed back home to the San Francisco peninsula. The son of a Spanish musician and an Irish-Swedish nurse, Garcia spent his childhood, after his father died, moving through the apartments and suburban tracts of the Bay Area.

Today, Garcia shares a Marin hillside home with other members of his organization. It's a perfectly ordinary suburban house, the kind of place where middle management might live. Getting a message from Garcia proved no simple task. After several canceled appointments I was told Garcia had selected me over the *Today* show for a rare interview. That's how I happen to be seated before the fire (at 10:00 p.m.) as Garcia appears in the same unceremonious way he appears onstage—he's just there. His shaggy graying hair and large, round body suggest a creature somewhere between Father Time and Big Bird's mythological friend, the Snuffleupagus. He gives off a strange mixture of warmth and remoteness.

"I'm from San Francisco," Garcia begins, "but in a larger sense I feel like a Bay Area person. We moved to the peninsula in that furious rush people had in the '50s to get the kids out of the city. At ten, I was becoming a hoodlum so my mom moved us from San Francisco to this new, ranch-style '50s house in Menlo Park, a real nice place that was just bursting out of the ground. My mom made a lot of money, and the thrust of her thinking was to get us out of the city."

Marshall Leicester, a University of California-Santa Cruz English professor, has known Garcia since junior high in Menlo Park and even played with him in an early jug band. He recalls Garcia's "great head for words and word-play. There was a lot of wit-play between us, that old *Mad* magazine satirical outlook that was so liberating for American kids in the '50s."

"I was a reader because I was a sickly kid," Garcia recalls. "I had asthma and spent a lot of time home in bed, so I read—that was my entertainment. This separated me a lot from everyone else.

"When I moved to the suburbs, I was hungry, really hungry to know, and I had a couple teachers who were very radical—far out. They opened the world for me. Being close to Stanford turned out to be a boon because they had all these educational experiments and they used the public schools. I had the advantage of elaborate and accelerated programs.

"That period gave me a sense that there are radical possibilities and other life-styles. Teachers always responded to me because I could draw well. I was encouraged to be an artist, and my time on the peninsula nailed that down real well." Ironically, in her quest for suburban safety, Garcia's mother may have confirmed his future as someone who would belong only up on the stage or out in the streets.

His feeling of being different, however, probably dates back to age five, when his father died suddenly in a fishing accident. Garcia was sent to live with his grandparents, who raised him for the next five years. "I think that probably ruined me for everything. It made me what I am today. I mean, they were great people but they were both working and grandparently and had no stomach for discipline." A lifelong pattern of doing as he pleased was set for Garcia.

His father's death, Garcia says, "emotionally crippled me for a long time. I couldn't even stand to hear about it until I was ten or eleven. I didn't start to get over it till then maybe because of the way it affected my mother. Also, it wasn't something I was allowed to participate in. I think it was a real problem that they tried to protect me from it. That's why I was sent to live with my grandparents."

Garcia doesn't remember his father, but he recalls hearing him play. "Sounds linger and I can recall them, you know, the way some people can recall smells. I can hear a sound and all of a sudden it will transport me. I remember him breaking out the clarinet."

Garcia chooses his words thoughtfully, carefully, as he talks about his father's music. "I remember the sound of the clarinet more than the tunes—the clarinet has that lovely, woody quality, especially in the relaxed middle register. That sound is very present in my ear. I can hear that clarinet right now. I don't know what the tunes were, but I do remember Stephen Foster kind of tunes. You know, nice little melodies." I thought about "Brokedown Palace," the Dead's farewell song at concerts, a Foster-like tune with lyrics that tell of leaving one home and looking for another.

"I wish I could have a better picture of my father as a musician. He was a jazz musician, hip for his day, apparently. I remember poking around, looking at some of the arrangements his band used to play, and I thought they were pretty hip. He was a genre player like I am, an idiom player."

Garcia's first leap into his father's footsteps came in 1957 when he hocked the accordion his mother gave him for his fifteenth birthday and got an electric guitar. "When I got that guitar, a Danelectro, a good cheap pawnshop guitar—very cheap but nice and loud—I was beside myself. I was so happy to get it. I wanted to be an artist but I fell in love with rock 'n' roll—Chuck Berry, Little Richard...I lean more to the rhythm and blues, the black music, because that's what I listened to first.

"Later, I listened to the crossover guys, the rockabilly guys, the white guys—Elvis Presley, Jerry Lee Lewis, Carl Perkins—those kind of guys. I loved them, too. You know, the stuff. The real stuff." He giggles. "I came right to the surface for that. Yeah. Yeah. Me. Me. That's for me!"

By seventeen, Garcia was fed up with high school and dropped out. He joined the army, hoping to see the world, to go to Germany or Japan or Korea. He was sent to Fort Winfield Scott, the majestic old structure just beneath the Golden Gate Bridge. There he saw others guys like himself, bigger "screw-ups," boys with "Live Fast, Die Young" tattoos. After almost a year of being involved in "all these soap opera scenes" and going AWOL to be with a friend who was threatening to commit suicide, Garcia was dishonorably discharged. "These things piled up and I was out. So I went to Palo Alto and hung out.

"I met Hunter there—Bob Hunter—the guy I write music with. I moved into my car. He just got out of the National Guard. He also bought this old car like I did and it broke down just like mine did and we were both living in this empty lot in East Palo Alto in these broken-down cars. So I had a pal. We were the beginning of this little community. We started going to the local coffeehouse, St. Michael's Alley, and pretty soon that became our social life. Actually, that became the ground floor for the Grateful Dead." Garcia recalls this period in his life as "just enormous fun"—hanging out at St. Michael's Alley at night and Kepler's bookstore during the day. "That was my day job: I practiced guitar and read books at Kepler's. You can think of the inside of Kepler's as the Greenwich Village part of it and the parking lot to the beach as the California Experience."

During the early '60s, Garcia began to play acoustic guitar at various

South Bay clubs, forming different bands with his friends. A friend of mine, who was Garcia's girlfriend in 1961, recalls sitting with him in the front row of Joan Baez's concert at Palo Alto High that summer. He watched Baez intently, saying, "I can do that! I can beat her technique." But slowly he moved from folk songs to rock 'n' roll. He played the Tangent in Palo Alto, the Boar's Head in San Carlos and the Off Stage in San Jose. All of which, he says, "was part of the networking of what became the hippie world—what became the Haight-Ashbury eventually."

Garcia and friends moved into a large house behind Stanford, not far from writer Ken Kesey's Perry Lane house where, Garcia says, "Kesey lived with older people, a college scene. We were all the young total freaks and we were into drugs heavy. Kesey's scene was a little more adult and not so drug-oriented. This is before acid. I didn't like to drink ever, and drugs were much more fun for me. I loved pot. Pot was right up my alley. Anything that makes you laugh and makes it so that you love to eat—to me, that's fun." Garcia, who does not appear to need help in the appetite department, laughs heartily. Garcia views drug use as a very personal matter, "more personal than a person's sex life." But he has also seen people like Janis Joplin and Pigpen die of drug- and alcohol-related problems, and says, "it's not for everyone."

A sobering moment occurred in 1961 when he was in an automobile accident that killed a friend, Paul Speegle. The incident is part of Grateful Dead lore: some claim the group's name comes from this accident because Garcia supposedly traded places with Speegle in the car right before the crash. "Something like that happened," he recalls, "but that wasn't the important part for me. At that time I wasn't going anywhere. I was playing acoustic guitar and thinking of myself as an artist but not going to art school. This accident put some focus, some intensity and desire, into our life. It's like somebody important was gone from our little scene, someone who had real talent and who might have been great—it was necessary now to fill in, to take up the slack. Three of us survived and we were all profoundly affected."

Eventually, Garcia, Weir, Kreutzmann, Lesh, and Pigpen would form the Warlocks. One night Ken Kesey, who had discovered LSD as a volunteer in a Menlo Park Veterans Administration hospital experiment, invited them to play at a strange party. "The first Acid Test was in San Jose," Garcia recalls. "We were freshly unemployed, burned out on bar gigs, so we brought all our gear down there. We set up our snazzy rock 'n' roll stuff on one side of the room and Kesey and the Pranksters had all their funky weird stuff on the other side of the living room. We cranked up, went completely hog bananas wild and then we packed up and went home. We had this tremendous purpose—a completely organized rock 'n' roll band in the middle of their formless party." The Warlocks took their new acid-rock sound to Magoo's, a pizza parlor in Menlo Park. "There was pandemonium that very first show and it really hasn't changed much. It was like one of those old rock 'n' roll movies from the '50s."

If it hasn't changed much, is it going anywhere? How is Jerry Garcia fitting into Reagan's America? "Very poorly," Garcia says. "I've often had the horrible suspicion that those of us who are out here on this fringe going 'Huuuuuuuuh-hhh' are creating the Moral Majority over there going 'Huuuuuuuhhhh.' I know there must be some connection because we represent the poles and the pendulum swings between. But I just don't like that guy Reagan. I didn't like his movies and I don't like his politics. I like things wide open, with question marks hanging over it, everything changing—nothing settled.

"I've never been that uncomfortable with the world. I've always had my stuff to do and that always seemed more important to me than paying attention to what the world was doing. I feel part of a small, tight, long-lived community that is similarly purposeful. I don't see us formed that much by the world or contributing dissidence to it. We're not that important. We could drop out and they wouldn't miss us, or they could drop out and we wouldn't miss them. It's just too bad we all have to live on the same planet."

Garcia is currently at work on a script for a movie about outer space. He says he belongs with those who heed "the call of the weird." So space is the place, I think where Jerry Garcia will finally be at home.

Brent Mydland's death in 1990 came at the height of the band's popularity as a concert draw, fueled by a huge influx of new fans following the release of the album *In the Dark* in 1987 and the subsequent top-ten success of the single "Touch of Grey." Mydland, ironically, did not survive. The keyboard slot was filled, initially, by Vince Welnick and Bruce Hornsby, but Hornsby eventually dropped out and left Welnick in the "hot seat"–so called because three keyboard players had now died: Pigpen, Keith Godchaux, and Mydland.

Besides *In the Dark*, the band released the albums *Built to Last* (1989), *Without a Net* (1990), *One from the Vault* (1991), *Infrared Roses* (1991), *Two from the Vault* (1992), and *Dick's Picks, Volume 1* (1993). Of these, only *Built to Last* was a studio album containing new songs. The band continued, as always, to work up new material on the road, and a new studio album was anticipated for a number of years, but was never finished.

By 1987, drug-assisted mental explo[...] had been under fierce attack for so long that Jack Britton's article on the natural affinity between Gratef[...] music and psychedelic drugs seemed foolish and brave. But Britton, in this piece for *High Frontiers* [...], makes it clear that he is aware of the dangers of being too open about the connection. As far as can b[...] certained, the following is the only piece of writing Britton ever did!

The *Swirl* According to Carp
A Meditation on the Grateful Dead

Jack Britton

It was vintage Carp all the way. Rich Carpenter danced around my living room doing his best Mick Jagger—even down to the long scarf, which he periodically flung across his left shoulder as "Sweet Black Angel" blasted out of the hi-fi. He had the pouting lips, the affected arrogance, and he slurred the words juuuu-ust right. I've listened to the Stones' *Exile on Main Street* a thousand times since it came out in '72, and I'm no closer to being able to decipher the words to "Sweet Black Angel" than I was when I bought the record. And Carp's delivery wasn't helping things. But I wasn't about to stop him, because when Carp gets going you just want to sit back and watch. Carp *not* on psychedelics is a trip in itself, but Carp on two hits of Bloom County blotter acid—with Mr. P. Opus staring out at you from each little square—is really something. Especially if the Dead show he'd dropped for was a good one. And the one that evening at the Greek Theater in Berkeley was a hot one indeed. Sometimes, when the concert is only so-so, you get the introspective Carp at th[...] evening—not bad if you're in the mood to watch a guy sit in a chai[...] four hours saying almost nothing. We have a saying: "The Dead giveth and the Dead taketh away." And when you feel the paper slowly dissolving in your saliva, or the liquid drop sort of slides across your tongue like mercury, or the mushroom fragments form into a foul mush in the back of your throat, or the clear, powder-filled capsule shoots down your gullet like a toboggan, it's anybody's guess what kind of night you're in for. But nine times out of ten it's a great ride; if it wasn't you wouldn't come back. Carp and I always go back. It's not tempting the fates, really. More like going with a proven winner. If the Dead are playing West of the Rockies, we're there, psychedelics in tow.

"What is it about the Dead?" I was wondering that night, watching Carp in his delirious dance. His belt was off now, and he whipped the ground in an uncanny mime of Mick's sadism routine for "Midnight Rambler" from the Stones' '69 tour. "Mind the vase!" I shouted as the leather swooshed through the air with the rumble of some oversized Jules Verne bumblebee. "What is it about the Dead?" I asked, this time aloud, more or less in Carp's direction. "Why is it that the Dead's music is so perfect for psychedelics?" I was coasting in the final hours of another great mushroom high, a grin plastered on my puss. I didn't really expect Carp to reply. After all the answer was in my grin and I knew it. But the query stopped Carp's demon dance in its tracks. Without uttering a word, he tore the Stones album off the turntable and started fingering through a stack of discs before him. No point in protesting, I thought. There's usually a method to Carp's madness—better to go with it and see where we end up.

Mere moments later, Carp's eyes—all glint and twinkle—met mine. He raised an eyebrow in a mock-sinister arch, turned the stereo up another three notches, dropped the needle on the record and then shouted: "Here's why!" Instantly I recognized that we'd been blasted into the middle of "The Eleven," an incendiary jam off *Live Dead*. Guitars slashed against each other in heroic battle, seemingly ascending into the air above my very living room. The bass line roiled across the fiery musical landscape and drums chug-a-chugged, spit-crashed and cracked, propelled, it seemed, by some mysterious force. And wheedling in and out of the lava flow was the birdsong of a diamond-bright organ. The music bubbled and undulated, the lead guitar repeating a riff again and again until it burst with supernova force onto the next octave plane and the rest of the band followed to start building it all again. I was breathless. And Carp was laughing, his eyes blazing.

"That's why!" he said triumphantly. "THE SWIRL! THE SWIRL!"

And I knew exactly what he meant. Things calmed down over the course of the next hour or so and that's when Carp, now coming down into that glistening end-of-L crystalspace, just started talking.

"The Dead are the only ones who play the swirl," he began, as a mellow Ry Cooder record bip-bopped in the background, its choruses of gospel singers occasionally punctuating our talk with little "Ooo-ooos." "In a regular band, the bass, drum and rhythm guitar move forward through the song in the same relationship to each other, as if they were three little trains on parallel tracks. The Dead's music doesn't travel that straight line. Instead, all the players move inside and outside of each other in an intuitive dance. No one is playing pure rhythm because they're all playing a rhythm. The melody might be primarily stated on lead guitar, but everything that everyone is playing at any given time is, in a way, an embellishment on the melody plus a rhythm. What I'm saying is that it's pure melody and pure rhythm. Get it?"

"Sort of," I said tentatively, knowing full well he was just getting into his rap.

"Lemme draw you a picture," he said, picking up a purple pen. "Think of the band like a little solar system, except, instead of the planets revolving around a fixed sun, they revolved around each other in random ways, swinging out of each orbit and into new ones, either around a single planet or even a couple of planets at a time. "Sounds like you're describing an out of control square dance," I offered. "That's not too far off," he said. "When it's all going smoothly—when they're really at their peak—it melts together into a big ball of sound. You can still hear each element clearly, but overall, it's that swirl." He said the word reverentially, almost in a whisper. "And when they don't quite have it together you hear a lot of banging around, musical collisions ranging from little fender benders to 100 mph head-ons, and that can build the swirl in itself!"

"Now, sometimes the music they're playin' is pretty straightforward and it's not really too hard to grab some kind of handles and just bronc-ride it, but when they're off the planet in a jam and the energy is flying every which way, you're out there on your own—no sail, no rudder. It's completely unpredictable, and therefore there's no predicting your response to it, either. It's the thrill of spontaneous creation and total propulsion into the unknown. And where do you find that in this day and age?

"What psychedelics do is let you participate in the swirl. You can jump from planet to planet at your own speed in your own swirl, leaving thought behind. Because psychedelics both stretch and compress time—obliterate it really, if you're lucky and it's really happening—you become the swirl with the band. Now I'm not saying you can't get hints of that space without psychedelics ..." His voice trailed off as if he'd lost his train of thought. Then he brightened: "But why would you want to?!"

He cackled that sharp Carp cackle and continued on his rave without missing beat. "Do I have to give you the standard rap about the Dead?"

"Well," I said, "what if I were trying to explain this to a non-Deadhead, non-initiate audience, say for a magazine piece?"

Suddenly, the door across the room slammed shut, and standing under the Moorish arch was big, bearded Tom Alyasso, resplendent in a black and white University of Zimbabwe T-shirt. "What are you doing an article on?" he asked as he drew a spliff out of a silver cigarette case. "Well, I wanted to try to explain why the Dead's music is so perfectly suited to psychedelics," I told him.

"Oh great. That's all we need," T.A. said, his characteristic cynicism coming to the fore. "An article that brings cops into the scene. How many times do I have to say it,"—Carp and I jumped on his sentence laughing 'cause we knew what was coming next: "IT ISN'T COOL TO TALK ABOUT IT!"

"Yeah, yeah, we know," I said. "Like the DEA has no idea that there's still a psychedelics scene surrounding the Dead! When was the last time you looked around you at a Dead show? Narc-city, man!" OK, I was exaggerating a little. OK, a lot. But he knew what I was saying. If you're cool, if you're discreet, you'll be all right. They can't get in to see your brain ...yet.

"C'mon Carp," I said finally. "Give me the rap—in layman's terms."

"*The Rap* by Rich Carpenter," he intoned solemnly, and then accelerated his speech so that it was almost a blur. I could see the speed lines coming off every "W," every "P," every word that raced by as he laid it down:

"Because-every-show-is-different-and-they-never-play-a-song-the-same-way-twice-and-their-lyrics-are-open-ended-and-time-becomes-suspended-and-you-never-quite-know-where-it's-all-going-or-where-it's-been-'cause-one-second-you're-riding-in-a-Western-movie-and-the-next-you're-in-outer-space-and-now-we're-'Goin'-down-the-road-feelin'-bad'-and-then-you're-butt-rockin'-to-Chuck-Berry-and-swinging-on-some-comet-tail-near-Andromeda-and-then-before-your-synapses-have-a-chance-to-cry-'uncle'-or-a-chance-to-say-'more'-it's-over-and-you've-laughed-you've-cried-but-daddy-o-I'm-here-to-tell-ya-you've-lived. Is that any clearer, Jack."

"Indubitably," I said sheepishly, doing my best Stan Laurel. The record party went on for a couple of hours more—a glorious succession of Jimi, the Allmans, the White Album and even Laurie Anderson as dawn approached. We dropped the subject, 'cause actually T.A. was right. It isn't cool to talk about it. Not because it's going to bring a plague of cops on us, but because, if you're talking' about it, you're not doin' it. And if that sounds like 79-cent Zen, you're right, but it also happens to be true. I guess, in the end, what it comes down to is this: the Dead's music was born in the swirl and over the course of 22 years, it's never really stopped. It's there to grab hold of, jump on to, dive inside of or gawk at in slack-jawed wonderment. It's trippier some days than others, more together some days than others. There are days when the swirl never quite gets up the steam to suck you in. And there are days when I don't have the energy to do any more than let it pass by ...let it pass by. But the world is a better place for having the swirl—specifically for having an accessible and communal swirl. And whether you know what I'm talking about or not, whether you've seen it in action or not, you have to believe me that it's true. And the proof is that contented smile that seems to live permanently on Rich Carpenter's face. Carp knows.

Silberman has set himself the task of a nutshell "explanation" of the Dead's music, and he succeeds admirably. The following piece was published in the *San Francisco Sentinel*, a primarily gay alternative publication, on November 6, 1987.

Transformative Mysteries
the Wholly Uninformed

A Primer on the Grateful Dead for Aficionados, Initiates and

Steve Silberman

fter 22 years on the road, suddenly the Grateful Dead are a marketable entity. Lead guitarist Jerry Garcia's avuncular visage smiles from newspaper photographs, the cover of *Rolling Stone*, and glossy promotional materials for the Dead's new single, "Touch of Grey," which broke unexpectedly into *Billboard*'s Top 10. MTV recently devoted an entire day to the band, which once would have seemed as remote a possibility as an MTV special on Sun Ra.

The Dead managed to mature from a modest inception as a free-form neighborhood rock band, to global cult status, and now unto the very thrones of multiplatinum establishmenthood, with only cursory, uncomprehending, and frequently derogatory media notice. The attention the band has received lately is barely more informed, casting the band as a hippie nostalgia act, or conversely, reinventing Garcia as one of the ubiquitous Betty Ford Center alumni—the "new" Grateful Dead for the '80s, "sounding better than they have in years," finally worthy of ink and airplay. What the Dead actually do—the historical context of their music, its diverse influences, the implications of their method—is almost never discussed, in favor of more *People* magazine-fodder about tie-dye and incense.

The Grateful Dead is, in drummer Mickey Hart's words, "a dance band ...playing simple chord changes," but that is only one mask the Dead wears—a band with so many faces like a Hindu goddess: the polyrhythmic dance band, the electrified folk combo playing original melodies with the haunting archetypal quality of traditional ballads, the atonal chamber sextet improvising through a Jovian sound system, the sleek bluegrass locomotive at full throttle.

The Dead boast an active repertoire of over 100 tunes, but the compositions are only rough sets of coordinates to facilitate excursions into *terra incognita*. Built into the band's arrangements are points of release, places of de-composition that allow the players to expand or ignore the melody, alter the time, shift timbres, or even modulate into a different tune. This is nothing new in jazz, but is nearly unheard-of in rock and roll. In high school, listening to a live recording of the Dead charging from "China Cat Sunflower" into "I Know You Rider," I noticed that the band sang the verses well enough, but what went on between the verses, and especially between the songs, was much more interesting: melodic themes and counterthemes were elaborated, and the rhythm became elastic, but the players always remained precisely together, as if a kind of telepathy was occurring.

The band's delight in perpetrating any infectious rhythm—from reggae to an effervescent calypso riff to a Nubian wedding song to "Johnny B. Goode," *all in one night*—makes the metrical resources of any other rock band seem spare. Precision is the quickest way to ecstasy, and whatever mode the Dead kick into—from the most abstract to basic four-four—the band cooks with fearsome heat.

Who's Dead

The band's ability to authoritatively interpret divergent strains of American song reflects the diverse musical interests and backgrounds of its members. The Dead arose out of a community of Bay Area musicians in the mid-60's that encouraged eclecticism and experimentation. Given the protean nature of the local scene, it was not improbable that a seasoned bluegrass banjo player named after Jerome Kern (Jerry Garcia) should join forces with a young folksinger (Bob Weir), an aspiring avant-garde composer (Phil Lesh), a drummer inspired by Elvin Jones' polyrhythms and Motown (Billy Kreutzmann), another young drummer paying his dues in local big-bands (Mickey Hart), and a blues rapper (the late "Pigpen" McKernan) to form a rock-and-roll band.

Garcia is an exceptionally versatile improvisor capable of incisive blues playing, inexhaustible melodic excursions worthy of the young Wes Montgomery, and sensitive ballad work. There is an inimitable "cry" in his tone, and his compositions are distinguished by a highly individual sense of grandeur, wit, and consolation.

The contributions of rhythm guitarist Weir are sometimes overlooked in Garcia's shadow, but his ringing etched-in-glass chords often provoke the band to proceed in more challenging "outside" directions.

Bassist Lesh is the most enigmatic of the band's personnel, seemingly frustrated at times with the limitations of playing in a rock-and-roll band. Lesh has millions of watts of digitized wallop in his arsenal: he is capable of deploying subsonic depth-charges felt in the huge halls more as wind, or an earthquake, than sound.

Kreutzmann is the backbone of the Dead's rhythm section, dealing out the complex time signatures that are the Dead's bread and butter across a broad range of voices, from Rototoms to timbales to talking drums. Kreutzmann's rock-solid anchoring frees Hart to accent off-beats and embellish cross-rhythms. Hart is a collector of world folk instruments, and owns a battery of acoustic and electric instruments custom-built for him. Midway through the second half of the show, Kreutzmann and Hart engage in a percussive dialogue, known as the "Rhythm Devils," that goes far beyond the traditional, predictable rock drum solo—a hair-raising amalgam of primal drum shamanism and state-of-the-art silicon wizardry.

Keyboardist Brent Mydland is the greenest member of the band, having joined in 1979. One feels sometimes that he would be more at home hollering and pumping away during a blues workout than finding a sonic footing in deep space, but the enhanced tone-color capabilities of his keyboards—including a sampling rig that allows him to, say, patch a down-home fiddle riff over "Maggie's Farm," lends the Dead's pop outings a bright sheen.

A Peculiar Waveform

Though the very soul of the band is unpredictability, a great measure of the power of a Dead show is inherent in the two-set structure, or "waveform" in Garcia-ese, that has remained relatively constant since 1970. The first half, or set, typically consists of short up-tempo numbers played with little improvisational expansion. The majority of the tunes on the new album will find a home in the first set, alongside the usual blues shuffles, cowboy songs and chestnuts like "Friend of the Devil" that have been in first-set rotation for years. Often during the first set the music feels tentative, as if the band is searching for a common timbral language. The penultimate song—"Bird Song" perhaps, or "Let It Grow"—offers a glimpse of what's to come, stretching into a lyrical inventory of the band's resources and imagination.

Visualize the following scene, which took place at the Greek Theater in Berkeley on the 20th of last June, but has repeated itself with the constancy of ritual in hundreds of venues for the last two decades. The break between the

first and second sets, at last, is over: a surreal limbo-time wherein psychedelicized spirits of all persuasions and aspects mingle and schmooze, some brav-
ing it to the refreshment windows, others resting on the grass observing the
transits of cloud and wind with eyes widened enough to see the new in what
is most familiar.

Now there is a settling-in as the bandmembers walk casually onstage and
adjust their instruments and equipment. Maybe somebody shouts a greeting,
maybe a ripple of applause passes over the crowd but subsides quickly.
Throughout the stadium there is a pervasive, singular feeling of *event-
quality*—that almost everyone here would rather *be* here, at this moment, than
anywhere on Earth.

The better part of the audience is civil and considerate of the common wel-
fare because each person feels they are among friends, and that even the people on stage are, in a way, intimate comrades. What is about to happen will
happen to everyone present, including the Dead themselves, who by stretching the boundaries of the known, in Ezra Pound's words, "make it new."

As they tune their instruments, a weird whistling chord escapes from an
amplifier, and instead of ignoring it, the band chases it as a rogue harbinger, a
vector of possibility. Soon the guitarists are bending and scraping strings,
and Healy, the Dead's longtime sound expert, is taking obvious pleasure in
framing each gust of strangeness in crystalline sonic transparency.

Even given the experimental nature of the second set, it is unusual for a set
to *begin* with this free blowing, which Deadheads have affectionately chris-
tened "space." Garcia commences plucking the sprightly, syncopated opening of "Iko Iko" and, for a while anyway, overtly structured playing reigns.
After the Rhythm Devils, the Dead will venture into space in earnest, and
some of the newer fans in the audience may shake their heads, venture to the
bathroom, or attempt to out-shout the cacophony swirling out of the speaker
stacks. A few will listen attentively to the Dead doing what they do best, and,
smiling, will keep on dancing.

Space is the Place

*In the rear of the thundering auditorium, far from the crush in front of the bright
stage, two women are dancing together. The music envelops them, the cascading, nearly mathematical permutations of the rhythm completing itself in their
bodies. Their long hair is damp; they have been dancing for hours, but when
their muscles begin to fatigue, they hear in the music an uplifting force that does
not tire, that could hardly be coming from only the six men working at the other
end of the hall.*

This great energy makes limbs light—they float and spin effortlessly in a feel-

ing of complete aliveness and permission. After the concert has ended, the two women will carry this freshness and vitality back into the day-world, their work and life together.

The Dead are the archetypal cult band, a secular entertainment that generates so much pleasure and intensity for Deadheads they are willing to travel thousands of miles to attend a show, and their adoration approaches a religion. The word *religion* grew out of the Latin *religio*, "To bind strongly," and cult derives from *colere*, "to till and cultivate." The Dead and their audience are bound strongly together in the cultivation of a field of mystery.

It is no secret that psychedelic drugs are utilized in vast quantities at Dead shows. In other cultures where psychedelics are imbibed sacramentally, rituals exist that guide and inform the content of the experience, making it a vehicle of cultural meaning and identity. Psychedelics are cultural orphans in America. It's illuminating to regard the "wave form" of a Dead show—moving from familiarity in the first set to the unknown in the second, in the hope of arriving at a *transformative moment*—as an *ad hoc* attempt to derive the home-grown equivalent of a peyote meeting from good old American rock and roll.

The Dead claim both improvisational freedom and virtuosity as the parameters of their music. The close listening and vigilance this music asks of those who help create it have kept the Dead's music vital when nearly all of their peers have surrendered to excess, self-parody or lame degeneracy. The Dead are, you could say, in the business of cultivating new thought-forms. If God is in their music, it is because God has been invited by their method, like Elijah at the Passover seder—a place has been set at the table.

We Are Everywhere

It is not surprising Deadheads have appropriated the proclamation originally set forth by gay people, "We are everywhere." Ultimately, the act of identifying oneself as gay, and the act of identifying oneself as a Deadhead, are efforts to communicate and forge a community of meaning.

There is a kind of existential freedom available at Dead shows difficult to access elsewhere in Jesse Helms' America, outside of gathering of radical fairies in the wilderness. Gay people and Deadheads are orphaned tribes that grew out of the ground like beautiful flowers of otherness—not merely to challenge the straight world, but to grow into their own true forms.

Gay people subvert the social behaviors expected of them and engage the mystery of gender in order to uncover unique, powerful identities. The Dead, and other partisans of the "outside" tradition in music, subvert the limitations of pre-planned performance and rote riffing to sing the unheard and give birth to a music that is wholly their own.

The grinning skeleton with roses twining through the stark cage of ribs that adorns millions of T-shirts is a reminder that we are together a brief time. Let it be in a dance that reaches all the way downward to mystery and fertile darkness, and up to bright joy.

The previous piece by the ardently gay Deadhead journalist Steve Silberman alluded to a similarity between the world of gay people and the world of Deadheads; Edward Guthmann's January 3, 1989, article for *The Advocate* makes it explicit and includes a sidebar interview with Silberman. Guthmann is a staff writer and film critic at the *San Francisco Chronicle*, where he has worked since 1984. He is also the producer and director of "Return to Cameroun," a documentary about his missionary grandparents that appeared on cable TV and several PBS stations.

A Tale of Two Tribes
A Gay Man's Adventure in the World of Deadheads

Edward Guthmann

f anyone had told me three years ago that I was about to turn on to the Grateful Dead, I'd have told him he was nuts. Me a "Deadhead"? Grooving to warmed-over acid rock with a bunch of scruffy, unreconstructed hippies? Hailing about in tie-dyes, bare feet, and nose rings? *Get real.*

Well, it happened. In February 1986, after sharing office space for two years with a friendly Deadhead and listening to her rhapsodize about life among the Dead, I got curious. My initiation was the band's annual Chinese New Year's concert at Oakland's Henry J. Kaiser Convention Center, an occasion I approached with bemused if not jaundiced detachment—like a weekend ethnographer probing uncharted land.

Well, I got zapped. The music, the lights, and the midshow procession with gongs, cymbals, polychromatic dancers, and a human-powered dragon with steaming nostrils were wonderful. But what really startled me was how *nice* everybody was—there was none of the snarling and pushing you get in most large-scale rock concert—and how avidly involved they were in the music. At the highest moments, the crowd's intensity was reflected in the playing; performers and audience seemed to coalesce, to spark each other and erupt, creating the kind of spontaneous magic that vinyl never delivers.

Unlike their contemporaries from San Francisco's psychedelic heyday—the Jefferson Airplane, Country Joe and the Fish, et al.—the Grateful Dead are still going strong after 23 years. In the 1960s, the band made a name for itself by playing free gigs in San Francisco's Golden Gate Park and jamming at the Merry Pranksters' infamous Acid Tests. The Dead joined the massive rock festivals at Woodstock and Altamont, toured extensively, and cut two classic albums, *Workingman's Dead* and *American Beauty*, in 1970.

Although they didn't score a major mainstream success until last year, when the album *In the Dark* and the single "Touch of Grey" sold in the millions, the Dead have generated one of the most loyal followings in entertainment history.

Contrary to the standard line on the Dead—that they're mere nostalgia mongers, recycling hoary licks from a bygone era—I found that the band is actually one of the most innovative musical groups around, incorporating blues, jazz, and country with get-down, ballsy rock and roll.

A really good Dead concert, I discovered, was a lesson in reciprocity and shared experience. It was potent and stirring, at its very best a shamanistic ritual from which the participants emerged cleansed and revived. Even today, 18 concerts and nearly three years later, it's not the music alone that draws me to the scene—although the music is far more inventive, infectious, and muscular than I ever imagined. The real payoff is the community of people at Dead shows, their extraordinary rapport with the band, and the sense of joy and giddiness that results from that alchemy.

Given the diversity and openness to new experience that characterize the great Deadhead family, it used to surprise me that the Dead scene was overwhelmingly straight. The gay world and the Dead world, it seemed, had so much in common: both stretched accepted boundaries, were populated by mainstream exiles, both offered a sense of community in an increasingly numb and unfriendly world. (A friend calls the two groups "orphaned tribes that grew out of the ground like beautiful flowers of otherness.")

As happy as I felt at the shows and as much as I enjoyed my new Deadhead friends, all of whom were straight, I kept wondering why gay people were so scarce. Although I didn't recognize them in the crowd of swirling bodies—what I like to call the great, pulsing fabric—I later learned there were dozens, maybe hundreds who had that same feeling of belonging and yet not belonging. I'd heard about gay Deadheads, but I never met one until I read a letter to *Relix*, an East Coast magazine for Deadheads. The author was Steve Silberman, a San Francisco poet and journalist. *(See sidebar, p. 223.)*

"One of the more delightful aspects of the Dead environment," he wrote, "*is* the free-floating sexual charge: Our hearts open, bodies electric and blissful, so many young spirits riding the waves of music! Hugs everywhere and looks of deep longing. I learned quickly, however, to stifle my own interested gaze, my own delight in the attractiveness of other guys in the crowd, even when the looks were initiated by others. Even if nothing was said, I could feel it: The Dead crowd is a straight crowd."

Although he had turned on to the Dead a lot earlier than I had and was more devoutly a Deadhead than I was or ever will be, I knew what Silberman was talking about. So I called him up. We met for coffee at San Francisco's Cafe Flore, and slowly we became friends. Eventually, Silberman was instrumental in forming the first organization of gay and lesbian Deadheads—a still untitled, very loosely attached alliance that functions basically as an occasional social network.

In many ways, my fondness for the Dead scene surprises me as much now as it did in the beginning. I'm not that much of a rock-and-roll fan. I've never been a joiner. I detest crowds. Also, it's my nature to stand outside things—observing, scrutinizing, musing—instead of diving in. I guess that's why I'm a journalist. And I think that's also why I tapped into the Dead experience: the fact that it releases me from my insulated, objective self, giving me a time and place to act silly, be transformed, and express affection.

I think it also has a lot to do with AIDS: After years of grieving for lost friends, a process that certainly hasn't stopped, I really needed a dose of joy in my life. I needed an earth-daddy guru to experience the kind of collective bliss that the Grateful Dead and their brethren often deliver. I never expected I'd be writing these words, but they're true.

There's really no way to adequately describe a good Dead show; you just have to go and feel it for yourself. The late mythologist Joseph Campbell (*A Hero's Journey*) once said that Deadheads are "doing the dance of life." Impressed by the high spirits he saw at Dead concerts, he remarked, "This, I would say, is the answer to the atom bomb."

So does this make me a Deadhead? Mind you, I haven't become the slack-jawed, babble-spouting freak in a time warp that the media depict as your typical Deadhead. In fact, I do all the things I did before I started seeing the band: I live and work and struggle and aspire to greater understanding. I basically see the world in the same way. I even dress the same. I just have a little bit more fun now.

Deadheads, I've discovered, are a very diverse lot. There are hard-core "tourheads," a ragtag lot who follow the band coast to coast, seeing up to 70 shows per year; middle-aged, graying hippies who've been digging the Dead since the mid 1960s; very young, apple-checked Deadheads ("Jerry's kids") who've made an earthdaddy guru out of guitarist-songwriter Jerry Garcia; and professional Deadheads (engineers, journalists, pharmacists, you name it) who shed their work drag and "Deadercise" every chance they get.

The strongest unifying factor among the "heads" is loyalty to the band. In *Rolling Stone*, writer Mikal Gilmore wrote, "The Dead have forged a symbiosis with their audience that, no matter how naive some may find it, is simply unequaled and probably unshakable. In fact, the Dead and their audience practically form their own self-sufficient fellowship—an alternative pop commonwealth."

I confess that I don't always get a perfect hit off the Dead. Sometimes the band is off; sometimes I'm preoccupied and don't connect. On the occasions when it works, though, it's magic. I've never been to a radical faeries' nature gathering, but I'd guess that a Grateful Dead rapture experience is the closest you could get to that kind of high in a crowded, urban, largely heterosexual environment.

A year ago, when I first made plans to write this piece, Silberman was delighted. "For ten years, I thought this was my trip," he told me. "It's almost like masturbation. You do it for so long and then discover everybody else enjoys it too."

Sidebar: A Grateful Secret: In Search of Gay Deadheads
Steve Silberman isn't the only gay Deadhead I've met in the past three years, but he's probably the most articulate and the best equipped to discuss those points where gay culture and Dead culture intersect. A New Jersey native, he graduated from Oberlin College in Ohio and moved to San Francisco nine years ago.

Today, he works part-time as a waiter, writes for a variety of publications, and lives with his lover of seven years in a Haight-Ashbury flat. For our interview, Silberman and I drove to San Gregorio, a beautiful beach 40 minutes south of San FrancisCompany. It was a warm, shimmering day, so we spread out our blankets, got high, and gabbed the afternoon away.

"In 1974—I guess I was about 17—my best friend, Mark, invited me to see the Dead at Roosevelt Stadium in Jersey City. I remember looking around and thinking that the crowd was different from any other rock-concert crowd I'd ever seen: They were much more into the music, and it was also a much more diverse crowd.

"The thing that impressed me about their playing—which I take for granted now—was that their sets, especially their second sets, almost had a kind of narrative. So if the set was really good and you were tripping, it could be used as an almost shamanistic journey of initiation. It was not just a sequence of their hits; there was a structure.

"It was probably ten years before I met another gay Deadhead. How did it make me feel? Well, I was used to having a compartmentalized life from growing up gay in heterosexual suburbia, so I was used to having areas of profundity or sacredness in my life that I could not share with the people in my immediate surroundings. I carried the secret of being a Deadhead into the work world and the gay world, and I felt that I carried the secret of being gay into the Grateful Dead world.

"The Dead were my chosen universe, my chosen tribe. It was great ...But there was something missing. I mean, there I would be, with my pupils wide open from LSD, having thoughts of cosmic tenderness, and I'd think, *Well, if my boyfriend were here ...*

"For all the sexual juice that's flowing around at Grateful Dead shows, I think that the gay trip is still very 'closety'—even in Northern California. Mountain Girl [wife of band leader Jerry Garcia] said that when she goes to the Haight [district] now, it seems completely dead. She said, 'Well, there probably are sensitive souls living there, but they have to figure out a new signaling system for weirdness.' And I think gay Deadheads have to figure out some kind of signaling system. A friend of mine has thought of making some kind of shirt that would be discreet [that] only gay Deadheads would have. Somehow, gay people have to find a way of coming out within the freaky Grateful Dead subculture, the same way that we had to figure a way of coming out in mainstream culture.

"A couple of years ago, I went to a party for gay Deadheads in the Haight. The epiphanous moment for me happened during 'Scarlet/Fire,' when I was dancing in this room with painted stars on the ceiling. Everybody was really into dancing at that point, and I realized, *Here I am—doing what I usually do at home in my room or at a show—with a roomful of queers.* And it was great. I loved it. It was fantastic.

"I think that ecstatic happiness is profoundly healing: It generates community, and it's profoundly overlooked in the Christian tradition. The beating heart of Christianity is a guilty one. The central metaphor is one of obligation, whereas the central metaphor in the Grateful Dead world is one of fulfillment."

David Gans is an unusual mix: a dedicated musician and an adept journalist who makes his living producing work about the Dead, primarily in the form of a nationally syndicated radio show called *The Grateful Dead Hour*. Each week, as well, Gans takes the helm of the venerable Berkeley, California, radio station KPFA for an adventure in free-form radio that rivals the experience of a Grateful Dead concert in its own right: anything can happen on Gans's show. He gives his audience the benefit of the doubt when it comes to their willingness to listen to many different types of music, with the sole unifying factor that each example can be tied somehow to the Dead band. This leaves the field wide open, given the variety of musical interests and influences of the band and its various members over the years. The following piece is the only representation of Gans's writing in the anthology, mainly because his own excellent books about the Dead are readily available, and I encourage you to seek them out. Here he writes for the in-house magazine published by KPFA for its subscribers in the July 1990 issue. Gans's books include *Playing in the Band: An Oral and Visual Portrait of the Grateful Dead* (with Peter Simon), published by St. Martin's Griffin in 1985 and 1996; *Conversations with the Dead: The Grateful Dead Interview Book*, published by Citadel Underground in 1991; *Not Fade Away: The Online World Remembers Jerry Garcia*, published by Thunder's Mouth Press in 1995; and *Talking Heads: The Band and Their Music*, published by Avon in 1985. He performs frequently in a variety of musical aggregations, including his own band, The Broken Angels, with whom he recorded a single, "Monica Lewinsky," in 1998. He also released an acoustic CD with Eric Rawlins, *Home by Morning* (1997).

Reporting Live
from Deadland

David Gans

I'm dancing with my notebook in my hand at the Shoreline Amphitheater on Friday, June 15, 1990. I've been avoiding this *Folio* article for two months, but now, awash in this music and collective consciousness, I know what I want to say. I get a lot of good thinking done at Grateful Dead shows.

Of the three dozen people in my row, I know about 12 by name and another 12 are nodding acquaintances from my eighteen years of attending these concerts. The number of people I know is unremarkable, given my job, but the number of my acquaintances who know each other is phenomenal. This is a reserved-seat show, so the number of strangers is a little higher than normal; last week at Cal Expo in Sacramento I probably could have told you the names of three quarters of the people within a hundred feet of me.

Following an excellent one-hour opening set and a 45-minute interval full of visiting and shopping and eating, the second set opened with "Scarlet Begonias," a brisk song with a powerhouse rhythm track, provocative lyrics and jazzy tonality. It's a great dancing song and a great jamming song. I was at the Cow Palace in 1974 when they played it for the first time, and I was at Winterland in March 1977 when they plunked "Fire on the Mountain" full-grown into the middle of the Scarlet Begonias jam; the two songs have been inseparable for the most part ever since. I wasn't in Portland when "Fire on the Mountain" and Mt. St. Helens erupted simultaneously, but the story is often told by those who were.

Not far from me I see a feature writer from the *Examiner*, probably not here on assignment but rather, as always, for the sheer boogie magic of the Dead's music. He has written eloquently and accurately about the Dead many times—like me, and other professionals in the crowd, he likes to put his day job together with his fun wherever possible.

In the spot where drummers Bill Kreutzmann and Mickey Hart are usually left alone onstage with their huge array of world percussion instruments and digital sampling devices, guitarist Jerry Garcia stays out there with them for a while. This is unusual and exciting! I am one of the Deadheads who really loves it when they do something entirely new. Others of my acquaintance experience the music more viscerally, less concerned with the intellectual nuances; this music appeals to people who dance, people who play (I'd wager that a quarter of the men in attendance are guitar players or otherwise involved in hands-on musicianship; I'm not sure about the women), people who listen intently to the lyrics and to the sequence of songs, etc. Right around now I'd say I'm a listener who is learning to be a dancer.

Now the drummers have left the stage and Garcia, Bob Weir (guitar) and Phil Lesh (bass) are involved in an unstructured improvisation. It's a mordant concoction of mutated samples, recordings of real instruments which are manipulated using ultra-modern digital technology and triggered by the "real" instruments. Jerry's "flute" becomes a sort of trumpet that twangs like a sitar. Some Transylvanian pipe organ moods are interposed, and then the drummers and keyboardist Brent Mydland return to the stage and the beat begins to sift itself into the breathless 12/8 of "The Other One." This is the Dead's most durable vehicle, in the repertoire since 1967, and it has never once failed to satisfy. This is scary/joyful music, with heart-pounding urgency in every beat: "Escaping through the lily field, I came across an empty space," Weir sings. "It trembled and exploded, left a bus stop in its place / The bus come by and I got on, that's when it all began ..."—the Dead at their most thrilling, pumping out energy and emotion and conviction.

Now they're easing out of the jam, winding down into one of Garcia's rueful ballads. Tonight it's "Wharf Rat," a story within a story, with two narrators—one a little deeper in the Slough of Despond than the other, probably, but little is said of the first speaker's circumstances. That is the source of much of lyricist Robert Hunter's power: his songs are rich in detail and characterization but also sketchy, leaving large unpainted spaces for the beholder to interpolate ideas from his own mental landscape. In "Wharf Rat," we are given to ponder the similarities and differences between these two narrators in the face of the bleakness and redemption at the song's climax.

We ride out on a grand, arching Jerry Garcia guitar solo—no mutant instruments here—and then the band shifts smartly into a moderate-tempo reading of Chuck Berry's "Around and Around." This song fell out of the rotation for a few years and recently returned with a nicely indeterminate set of ending possibilities. The last time I heard them do this song they tacked on a crisp instrumental coda; tonight Weir brings the chord progression back with a smoky, intimate beat, but before long they've brought it all the way back up, rocking the fullness. It's a great way to end the set, a novel musical extension brilliantly played. To top it off, they add a James Brown-style false ending and take it through one more time.

The encore is "Knockin' on Heaven's Door," the second Bob Dylan song of the evening (the first was "Desolation Row," one of those bitter, big-screen ballads with a little something for every occasion). The Dead's repertoire includes many Dylan songs; "When I Paint My Masterpiece" has been a favorite lately, like last week when it was the perfect accompaniment to a gorgeous sunset over Sacramento. The story of the sunset will accompany the tapes of the show from Deadhead to Deadhead across the country and around the world.

A couple in their seventies, one of several such pairs I know who attend most of the Dead shows in the Bay Area, are in the row in front of me. Behind me is Sharon, who I rarely see at shows but with whom I work every year at the Bammies. She is visiting with Michael, a friend of an old friend of mine. I didn't know they knew each other, but nothing surprises me about the friendships and connections in this community.

The Grateful Dead scene—at concerts and between tours—teems with energy, intrigue, commitment, crime, obituaries, recipes, literature, childbirth and—most of all—music. It is music that binds the lives of these thousands to the fortunes of some hundreds of workers and entrepreneurs and to the inspiration of half a dozen musicians and their respective collaborators. My friends took me to my first Grateful Dead concert in March 1972, and it was the music that brought me back again and again. I have been attending—in the company of many of those same friends—more than half of my life. I long ago lost track of how many Grateful Dead concerts I've attended, but it's well over 300 by now. Along the way I have wandered from the upper reaches of Winterland to a comfortable spot by the onstage monitor mixer, with many stops in between. The relationship between the band and crew and the Deadheads is sometimes pretty strange, and since I prefer to identify myself as a member of the audience that's usually where I hang out. I'm happiest these days in that audio sweet spot between the stage and the sound board, but I usually don't pay the dues to get there so I often watch from reasonable seats in the "Phil Zone" (stage right). I used to sit stock still, listening with my musician's head, but not any more. Now I try to keep moving through the fiery bubble of it, solving riddles and posing thoughts as I wander among the various elements: the music, the lyrics, the onstage interactions, the audience, my companions, and my internal dialogs on a variety of subjects. I've gotten some of my best ideas at Dead shows, cried some of my best tears, solved some of my knottiest problems, received some of my most productive inspirations.

It is a privilege to serve the Deadhead community across America and a strong hit of genuine freedom to do so on KPFA every week (after an unsettling year in commercial syndication, I brought the program to public/community radio where diversity is acceptable and ratings are not the primary measure of success). I respectfully submit that the Deadheads are a mindful lot and a worthwhile addition to the cultural mix of the station.

I take the freedom of KPFA very seriously, I must add. I am required by political necessity to bleep the word "fucker" from "Wharf Rat"; in a world that is capable of punching such random holes in the fabric of liberty, we all have a lot of defending and celebrating to do. The Deadheads are for the most part a white, well-educated and well-heeled lot, but that does not exempt us from the shadow of oppression that creeps across the landscape. I sincerely hope that we are able to spend the lion's share of our time here celebrating rather than defending the truth and fun of American life.

I know there are more significant things I could be doing in this world, but I have the privilege of working closely with the music of the Grateful Dead. I have been speaking this musical language nearly as long as I have been hearing it, and my hands-on knowledge of its workings informs my appreciation of the music as listening matter. I put the Dead's best foot forward on the radio every week; with apologies to the late Joseph Campbell and Madge the manicurist, I'm not just following my bliss, I'm soaking in it!

The concert described here was at Wembley Arena, London, Wednesday, October 31, 1990, the next-to-the-last show of the brief European tour that fall. The following piece appeared anonymously in the *New Yorker's* "Talk of the Town" section, November, 26, 1990. Alvarez is the author of *Night: Night Life, Night Language, Sleep and Dreams,* published by Norton in 1995.

Good Use

Al Alvarez

e've also heard from a man who lives in London:

A friend from Las Vegas called up last week asking if I would like to meet the Grateful Dead, who were in town at the end of a European tour that had taken them to Sweden, Germany, and France. I am not much interested in pop or rock and roll, but the Grateful Dead are special. As Keats might have said, the very name is like a bell to toll me back to my youth and that wild vanished time. I found it hard to imagine those mellow, spaced-out San Franciscans in gloomy London, but the opportunity was not one to pass up.

The backstage of the vast Wembley auditorium looked like a combination of Houston Mission Control and a shantytown: towering banks of electronic consoles with digital readouts and flickering lights, and behind the consoles a row of little shelters cobbled together from the metal-bound travelling cases in which the group's gear is transported from gig to gig. The shelters had folding chairs and trestle tables, and the members of the band and the crew used them, between numbers, for R and R. The space between the high tech and the shanties swarmed with technicians, stagehands, wives, girlfriends, and an astonishing number of small blond children, most of them wearing earmuffs to protect them from the overwhelming din of the amplified music.

*Wembley Stadium, London, October 30, 1990, second set. © Susana Millman,
1999*

The performance was set to start at seven-thirty, and a couple of hours
before that Bob Weir, the rhythm guitarist, and Phil Lesh, the bass guitarist,
were out on the front of the stage playing riffs and fiddling obsessively with
the controls of their instruments. Jerry Garcia, the lead guitarist, was lounging
in the back, beside one of the consoles. "I always have bad nerves before a
show," he said. "How would you like to get up there in front of ten thousand
people and make a fool of yourself? What we do is kinda precarious, and we
don't always succeed. In fact, many times we fail. Maybe that's what keeps the
audience interested. They know we're taking a chance, and no matter how
many times they come to a show it's never going to be the same twice in a row.
I mean, I've been to every show we've done—right?—and I can't say I'm bored.
I can never predict what anyone else in the band is going to play. They always
surprise me. We surprise each other. It's like throwing logs on the fire. I guess
we're still developing, still working at it. In that sense, we're all students of the
same phenomenon. It has the effect of permanently renewing youth."

As it happened, Garcia did not look nervous, but neither did he look
youthful. He looked, instead, like a benign, slightly raffish college professor:

white beard and thick white hair, spectacles, expansive waistline. He is forty-eight years old—two years younger than Phil Lesh, and five years older than Bob Weir, who is the youngest of the five musicians who got together in 1965 and became the Grateful Dead. Four of them are left—the fifth, Ron (Pigpen) McKernan died of drink in 1973—and apart from Weir, who has a ponytail and a face with a lot of mileage on it, none of them look much like pop stars. Lesh looks as if he would be more at home with a soldering iron in his hand than with a bass guitar: he has a clever, bespectacled face, a receding chin, and the vaguely puzzled air of what the English call a "boffin"—a backroom scientist. One of the two percussionists, Bill Kreutzmann, with silver hair, a silver mustache, and a spreading belly, might have stepped out of a Western movie. The other, Mickey Hart, joined the band in 1967; he is small and intense, with a deep chest and heavy forearms. The only one in the band who looks the part is the pianist, Bruce Hornsby, but he's a recent recruit, and still in his thirties. "I'm trying to bring some of that teen-age-idol thing to the Dead," he said.

"I'd be glad to be teen-age anything at this point," Garcia replied. "I've got to where things are beginning to fall apart, but what's comforting about age is everyone's falling apart with you. I don't see anyone getting any younger."

"Yeah, but some are falling apart slower," Hornsby said.

Garcia did not seem disconcerted. "It's a matter of use, man—good use," he said. "I enjoyed it when I had it, whatever it was. It all went to a good cause."

The Dead have been playing together for a quarter of a century—an eternity in the pop-music business. Back in the sixties, the Dead were kids playing to other kids. Now they are middle-aged and they are still playing to the kids. That is what is most remarkable about them—even more than the music. The Dead are a touring band—they play seventy or eighty concerts a year—and everywhere they go their fans, who call themselves Deadheads, go with them. A few of the Deadheads are relics of the sixties (there are said to be perhaps a thousand people who catch forty or fifty shows a year), but most of them are in their teens or twenties. What unites the Deadheads is not nostalgia for a period when few of them were alive but companionship, fervor for the band, and a sense of shared adventure. Before each concert, they set up a bazaar outside the auditorium and barter or sometimes sell memorabilia, tie-dye clothing, psychedelic T-shirts, tapes, drugs, and, above all, tickets. (The concerts sell out in advance, and, although the Dead try to cut out the scalpers by running their own ticket-sales office, not all Deadheads are lucky with their applications.) But the real purpose of the bazaars is sodality: they are places where the fans can meet and exchange Grateful Dead arcana and talk about what has happened along the way.

"The people who are our audience now are the same sort of people who were our audience originally," Jerry Garcia said. "They are looking for something different, something to enlarge their own personal myth. Touring with us becomes, like, their war stories: 'Remember that time we were travelling with the Dead and had three flat tires in Des Moines and had to wake up a farmer in the middle of the night?' That kinda thing. It's part of the adventure of finding yourself, of moving through life. It used to be there were a lot of ways of finding out about yourself: join the circus, hop a freight train, hit the road with Jack Kerouac. Now there are only a few ways left, and we're one of them."

When the concert starts, the sense of community is overwhelming. "The audience is a nation unto itself," Bob Weir had said, and what a large segment of that nation does is dance. That night, the Dead played for four hours, with only one break, and the audience danced with them from start to finish. I noticed one figure in particular, who swayed and gyrated, coiled and uncoiled himself ecstatically and without pause. He looked like a blond John the Baptist—tall and gaunt, with his hair down to his shoulders, and a straggly beard. But the oddest thing about him was that he was wearing a printed cotton skirt. "A lot of Deadheads do that," I was told. "It's not a sexual statement. They just prefer dancing in a skirt."

An Oxford undergraduate I know told me later that he had gone along to the concert expecting to meet a lot of middle-aged hippies and to be bored. "But it was nothing like what I expected," he said. "Sure, there were plenty of beards and long hair and tie-dyes. Also huge numbers of Americans. You could pick out the English types: they were the spotty guys in glasses, wearing parkas. But no one was there to see pop stars. What counted was the atmosphere, the friendly attitudes, the good humor. The guy next to me, whom I'd never set eyes on before, swung round to me in the middle of it with a beatific smile and said, 'I'm going bald, man. I feel genuine at last.'"

From where I sat, in the shadows at the back of the stage, where the technicians monitored the winking control panels and the vibrations from the giant speakers came up from the floor, I could see the band in the dazzling spotlights and, beyond them, the huge, packed auditorium. The Dead were singing "Truckin'," one of the songs that have made them famous, and the audience was singing along with them. They were not quite in unison, yet the understanding and the flow of affection between the kids out front and the aging, genial figures onstage was unmistakable. Despite the decibels, the Dead seemed curiously relaxed. They smiled at each other, or to themselves, when the music really got to them; they smiled at the smiling faces beyond the lights. "What a long, strange trip it's been," they sang.

Jackson wrote the following piece in Spring, 1990 as an editorial for *Golden Road*, the magazine he co-edited, as a labor of love, with his wife, Regan McMahon, and it's a typically thoughtful piece assessing the State of the Dead Union, which at the time was wobbly at best.

This Darkness *Got to Give*

Some Thoughts on Problems in the Dead Scene

Blair Jackson

ell, the Dead have just about made it to their 25th anniversary milestone! Wa-hoo! We should all be cheering, slapping high-fives, singing Beethoven's "Ode to Joy" and generally celebrating this momentous occasion. Instead, our joy is tempered by the sobering realization that the fragile Grateful Dead eco-system is still perilously threatened. There have been improvements on some fronts, regression on others, but the sum total of all the tweaking and adjustments is that it's not enough—the Dead are still unwelcome many places and the wretched excesses of Deadheads coast to coast continue to generate bad publicity and bad feelings. What's being done? What's to be done? Who's going to do it? And is it already too late? Let's take a few moments to examine a few of the issues and areas of concern.

Last fall was the first time the Dead banned camping and vending outside their shows, and the feedback we've received from Deadheads tell us that this definitely cut down on the number of people hanging out in the parking lots before shows. Cameron Sears, the Dead's road manager, had this to say about the situation when we spoke to him recently:

"I felt that aspect of it was a success, by and large, and by a 'success' I mean that most people were fairly cooperative with us. There was a strong amount of resistance from some people, and a strong amount of resistance from some communities, too. Some communities think it's better to have it all contained [in a campground, etc.] than to have everyone wandering around municipalities looking for parking spots or hotels or whatever. I can understand that, too, but I think this [no camping/vending] is something we have to stick with for a while to see what difference it makes. It's still early, and it didn't eliminate all the problems by any means."

Unfortunately, many of the really serious problems in the scene are connected in some way to drugs—specifically to the flagrant selling of drugs and the inability of large numbers of mainly younger Heads to handle the drugs they take.

On the first of those two points, it should be clear to anyone who's paying attention at all that it is time to *cool out* when it comes to openly selling drugs outside Dead shows. People are getting busted left and right by police and undercover narcs dressed as Deadheads. At this point, the Drug Enforcement Agency makes no secret about the fact that they view the Dead scene as the single greatest source of psychedelic drugs in the country. Whether they're right or wrong, this is the *perception*, and that bearded fellow playing the wooden flute over there could be a government agent. Paranoia, anyone?

Every month brings new letters to *The Golden Road* from low-level dealers—kids 17 and 18 years old—who are doing time in federal prisons because they were careless enough to sell to undercover cops. In years past, there were relatively few people who were dealing to stay on tour, and those folks wisely tended to be discreet about their activities. But somewhere along the line two things happened: the number of dealers increased significantly (hasn't *everything* in this scene increased significantly?); and more and more people came to believe that somehow we'd all pulled a fast one on society and that we could all do whatever we wanted within our Grateful Dead world, and everyone would look away. In fact, that *was* pretty much the case until the numbers of people outside shows got so large in the late '80s. All of a sudden, "Just Say No" America took notice of this snowballing phenomenon, and it didn't like what it saw.

The huge number of busts outside Dead shows has made civic officials nationwide wary of the Dead and Deadheads, a situation that really has jeopardized the Dead's ability to get bookings.

"A lot of fans probably think that the people who run these facilities will forget that there was trouble at Dead shows, but they don't," says Cameron Sears. "You've got to realize that most of these buildings stay busy 350 days a year. It's not as though they rely on us to come and play there to make their money. We as an organization try to cooperate with them as much as we can, but it's getting to the point where a lot of them are thinking, 'Hey, it's not worth the hassle. We can do Billy Joel for six nights and his fans go home at the end of the night and aren't dealing in the parking lots.' Who do you think they're going to pick if there's a choice?"

You want a couple of concrete examples that should make you weep? There will be no Frost or Greek shows this year—and perhaps ever again—because of drug arrests and open drug peddling. In the case of Frost, Palo Alto police, in cooperation with DEA types, did extensive surveillance of the crowd outside last year's Frost shows, capturing numerous instances of dealing and consumption on video. This reportedly influenced Stanford University not to allow the band back at Frost this year. As for Berkeley's Greek Theater, the university sought to make the Dead financially liable for all legal and adminis-trative fees associated with busts of their fans—a ludicrous bit of extortion, perhaps, but there it is.

Personally, I think that whether the band likes it or not, drugs are always going to be part of the Dead scene. This is a band that was born out of psyche-delic experimentation and that continues to exist for many people as a sort of living metaphor for the range of psychedelic experience. While no one in the group has discouraged the use of pot and psychedelics, some band members *have* been vocal in their disapproval of hard drugs like cocaine and heroin, and they have specifically asked that people not sell nitrous oxide in the park-ing lots outside shows. Unfortunately, the venal profiteers with their shame-fully high-priced balloons are among the most intransigent of vendors. And talk about stupid: there's never been a drug that made noise before! "Right this way, officer! Follow the hissing tank."

"I've walked out in the parking lot with security people and watched them politely ask the nitrous vendors, 'Hey, the band has asked that this not take place,' and their response is, 'Well, fuck you,'" Cameron says. "So then it becomes, 'Well, if you're going to say that to me, what're you going to say to the next guy who comes along, who's gonna have a blue shirt and a badge and who's gonna cart you off to jail?' Then the next day the beat reporter at the police department picks up that 50 people were arrested at our show and that's headlines across the country. Whose fault is that?"

The tragic, much-publicized deaths last fall of Deadheads Adam Katz at the Brendan Byrne Arena and Patrick Shanahan outside the Forum in Ingle-wood, California, underscore the gravity of the situation we find ourselves in. Brutish police and security forces, already disdainful of Deadheads for their apparent lawlessness, unwilling and ill-equipped to deal with the unusual sit-uations that Dead shows present, overreact and people get hurt and killed.

In the case of Adam Katz, exactly what happened is still a mystery—whether he was, as many (including his father) believe, beaten to death by security goons who then dumped his body outside the facility; or whether he died in a fall or some other way. The Byrne security forces are notorious for their brutality, and indeed several guards were indicted for battery in separate incidents not connected with Katz's death. Their reprehensible behavior isn't limited to Dead shows, either: in February, a Byrne security thug was accused of raping a fan at a concert there.

The Patrick Shanahan affair is a little more cut-and-dried, because there were numerous witnesses who saw Shanahan being manhandled by the Inglewood Police. The youth died in a patrol car in police custody, the result, the coroner said, of a police chokehold with a nightstick. The police position on this is that Shanahan was completely out of his head on LSD, he was hostile and uncontrollable, and that they used the force necessary to subdue him. Even sympathetic witnesses agree that Shanahan was behaving very erratically.

The link in these two cases is that, according to reports from the victims' friends, both Katz and Shanahan were extremely high on hallucinogens at the time of the incidents. Psychedelics are tricky, of course, and different people react differently to them depending on the size of the dose and a hundred other environmental factors.

So what can we do to prevent these sorts of episodes? Well, short of not taking drugs, the most reasonable solution seems to be for all of us to watch out for each other more carefully. If you're at a show with someone who seems to be having a little trouble clinging to reality, take the time to help out; keep an eye on him or her. If you're in a parking lot after a show and you see someone who is obviously in need of some assistance—folks wandering around naked when it's 40 degrees out, or lying in the roadway staring at the sky; we've all seen it—ask if he or she is OK, and if you don't get an answer, maybe it's time to see if you can't find some sort of responsible rock med-type to help get the person out of harm's way. The last thing you want is for someone in that state to have to deal with police or security people *alone*.

"It's a fact of life that we're playing in big places with large security forces these days," Cameron says. "It's just a big scene. Everything is multiplied from what it was in 1967 or '68, as we're all aware.

"Security is the toughest job at any rock 'n' roll show, whether it's Barry Manilow or the Rolling Stones or the Grateful Dead. And when you have a security force of 200 people who are getting paid $6 an hour, you can't expect to find someone with a Ph.D. in psychology to help you through the night. They're not going to be there. You can *hope* for the best people to be working at your show, but the reality is there are always going to be people there who are not top-flight. You're lucky if some of these people have graduated from high school.

"When I go [to a venue] I try to explain to them in advance, 'Look, these people may look different and seem different, but they're basically a peaceful crowd.' Yet they then encounter someone who is flipping out and they don't know what to do. Situations get distorted. Granted, some security forces are better than others, but it's still a tough job—you're meeting resistance at every turn from people who don't want to do what you want them to do. You're getting shit thrown in your face the whole time and you're expected to keep your cool. An intelligent, thoughtful person is capable of doing that—*most* of the time. You take someone who doesn't have the patience or understanding and you're asking for trouble. I don't know what the answer is."

Many Deadheads believe the answer is for the Grateful Dead to be more careful in their choice of venues. Brendan Byrne, for instance, has been a trouble spot for the Dead just about every time they've played there. The Forum, on the other hand, was relatively trouble-free when the band played there in February of last year, and actually, with the exception of the Shanahan incident, wasn't that problematic in the fall, either.

The fact is, because of their popularity right now, there is a finite number of places that the band can play—*before* you factor in such intangibles as civic resistance and venues in settings too sensitive to accommodate Deadheads. So the Dead must constantly do advance work to defuse potentially volatile situations with civic authorities and local police. When there was trouble in Providence and Hartford a few years ago, the Dead's tour managers had extensive talks with police in those towns before the band went back to either city. More recently, every attempt was made months in advance to make sure that Nassau Coliseum, so notorious for its busts in the past, would deal more humanely with Deadheads this spring. (Still, in light of Garcia's comments in *Rolling Stone* that the band would never play there again, many Heads were outraged to see it included on the '90 spring tour.)

"A couple of things happened there," Cameron explains. "Back when it was almost famous for having so many busts, it was a county-owned and –run facility. It's still owned by the county, but it's run by Spectracorp, which is a well-known facility management group. Jon McIntire and I went back and met with the chief of police [in Uniondale, L.I.], we met with the guy in charge at the show, we met with the building people and the promoter there. And we said, 'Look, we're not anxious to come back here because we've had bad experiences in the past.' And they knew that; they acknowledged it.

"I really believe it will be improved, but at the same time, people can't go in there and expect it to be a free-for-all. When Jerry played there over the summer it went OK. There were 40 arrests, but that's an *average* at this point. We had good meetings with them and they seemed sincere. We'll see. It's as much on our audience as it is on the police to do the right thing. That's the way I see it."

In the case of Nassau, the Dead tried another experiment, which, as usual, raised the ire of many Deadheads. Mail-orders for tickets were only accepted from a relatively limited geographical area, in an effort to cut down on the usual flood of Deadheads who stay overnight and give conservative towns-folk unwanted heartburn. Another variation on this theme is what we've been calling "guerrilla" shows—where the band announces it will play a facility a week or so in advance, and tickets are available only locally.

"I think it's a good alternative for places that are so volatile for us that's the only way we can go there," Cameron offers. "I'm hoping that people might pick up on the fact that the reason we don't announce the show and the rea-son tickets aren't always available through the normal ways is we want to have a cool gig; we don't want problems. And if you don't have a ticket, don't come to the show. Hampton [last fall] was great. Hartford [this spring] will be harder to pull off successfully." (The Dead didn't help things by playing two of the best shows of 1989 at Hampton. Now the "guerrilla" show has attained a real mystique.)

Yes, these shows exclude a lot of people—tourheads mainly—who might want to be there, but I think the Dead should be applauded for at least trying a few creative options—for not simply giving up on a place like Hartford, and for giving Nassau another try after the debacle at Brendan Byrne. Because what's the alternative? No New York-area shows? *That* would go over really well.

Beyond these sorts of imaginative solutions, it's hard to see what the Dead can do on their end. They're already playing more stadium shows than most of us would like. And it's certainly not their job to police the Dead scene per-sonally or to lay out some *Robert's Rules of Order* for Deadheads. No, much as we'd like the Dead to bail us out of this mess, the onus is still on all of us.

I think part of what we're all having to deal with in these troubled times is the long-standing myth that the people who attend Dead shows are a giant unified group, when in fact we are a rainbow of different people—and that includes selfish people, irresponsible people, people who don't care about so-called '60s values, people who just want to *party down*. "Deadiquette" be damned. A lot of these people won't respond to a well-worded suggestion from a concerned stranger, much less a flyer from the band. The "language" they understand is visible security.

Cops and rules are anathema to most of us, but if we're thoughtful and dis-creet and we treat others with respect, it shouldn't be a problem; it shouldn't even be an issue.

Paddy Ladd can lay claim to writing from two unusual perspectives about the Dead: first, he is British; and second, he is deaf. Both factors have made him acutely attentive to certain kinds of details that escape the scrutiny of other writers–and his writing displays a propensity for psychological speculation that is rewarding for its own sake, simply because Ladd thought to write about it. The following article by Ladd published in a slightly different form in the October 1992 issue of *Spiral Light*, is somewhat prescient, which makes me wonder if we shouldn't all pay attention in the way Ladd does. Ladd conceived of and organized the special section for Deaf Deadheads at concerts, the Deaf Zone. He recently completed his doctoral dissertation, *In Search of Deafhood–Towards an Understanding of Deaf Culture.* The British Deadhead-oriented fanzine *Spiral Light*, ceased publication shortly after Garcia's death.

Paddy Ladd

Spent a Little Time on the Mountain

mong the qualities which mark Spiral Light out from the other Dead magazines, apart from a certain mordant British humour and a similarly British reluctance to let go and simply enjoy (which results in a sometime cynical edge to our writing), is the desire to look at the current overall health of the Deadbeast itself, that cranky old dragon that flaps around bumping into trees and occasionally letting rip with some serious fire. In fact this might even be the magazine's raison d'etre, linked as it is with tour reviews and setlists, because the rest could be written when the band were no more.

Why does this seem to be our obsession? Perhaps because we don't have the shows to go to, and a network of Heads around us in our daily life to chew

Berkeley Schools benefit, September 24, 1994. Acoustic set by Lesh, Garcia, Weir, and Welnick to benefit the music program in Berkeley public schools. © *Susana Millman, 1999*

them all over with (not to mention the free local phone calls that Americans seem to have!). At any rate, we seem to take things for granted less, and reflect more. For those that do fly over, anxiety about the Beast's health seems intensified by the distance—each time we leave, we never know if it will be the last time, for us with our limited British wages, or for them.

Thus frustrating it is when *Golden Road* closes and *Relix* fails to pick up the slack (although in fairness they have never set themselves that particular aim). *Unbroken Chain* is starting to expand into a mag with that wider vision, but apart from that only *Dupree's* (which you should also be subscribing to!) even attempts to give us the raw materials for analysis. Tapes being so slow to come across the ocean, and videos even more so, those materials are hard enough to claw out as it is.

All this is a long way round from stating my main theme, but I'm sure the reasons for such an opening will emerge in a while!

After an almost unbelievable 1990 recovery via Bruce and Vince, one year later it seemed some cracks were showing. I wrote in #25 about the Madison and Boston shows, about life after Brent, about how that affected our attempts to define what this whole Dead thing is and so on. If you recall, my fears then about Garcia's strength and morale, about the roles and place of Vince and Bruce, were allayed by (a) the promised 6 month break, and (b) the sheer fairytale of the successful effort they made to scale the mountain in front of them at Boston and bring that tired ole Jerrybear home.

Takes All You Got Just to Stay on the Beat

And then, with some sort of crisis thrumming away underneath it all, Uncle Bill died, reinforcing the feeling that the end of something was coming. They pulled it off again heroically with the shows for Bill, but by that pallid, depressing New Years Eve 91 tape, it sounded quite obviously Time To Stop Awhile. And then—and then...they backed down on their layoff plans! Aaagh! How could they be so stupid?!

Yet by Spring Tour 1992 the situation had become less clear. Four new songs at last—with more in the pipeline, showed clear proof of their determination. And the remarkable Devils/Space developments, the exciting potential of the sounds behind "Corrina," as well as a few pretty good shows, all suggested an improvement in the Beast over Spring 1991. To me (though not to others here) it sounded like Bruce was really becoming one of the band, yet the fact remained that *the actual Grateful Dead still had not come back into being.*

Finally, almost two years after losing Brent, Bruce finally announced his retirement from his utterly essential bridge-building role, and the GD began anew. All would be revealed on the Summer Tour, it seemed.

Got Two Good Eyes But Still We Don't See

But alas, we were still not getting the full picture from across the Atlantic. Almost zilch coverage of the spring tour from the US magazines. And no first-hand reports of either tour from our readers (smacked wrists especially to our exiles who moved to the US and should have known better). All this meant that it was only fairly recently that we began to see that it wasn't much of a summer tour; the least impressive since...fill in your own date. They appeared close to playing that "cold music on the bar room floor."

Then a video of Hampton 92 came through. It was a big shock to put it mildly. Jerry not only looked large and unwell, but his onstage demeanour had become as taciturn as we hadn't seen since...well 1985 for sure, the time of "Trouble Ahead, Jerry in Red," and lots of "Black Peter" and "Comes a Time." But this time, how come no-one, but no-one reported what this video seemed to show. Where were you all at, US mags and SL show-goers?! Is it that you're too far back at shows to be able to read the onstage body language? Or is it that this deaf lad just focuses on this to compensate for what he doesn't hear? Or is it that it's not cool to be downbeat (that seems a US/Deadhead characteristic at times)? If so, it's a very real danger, because in trying to pretend that the world is as you want it to be, which may be liberating in terms of freeing you to act as admirably as you do, you may also be afraid of accepting that sometimes the world is a dark and dangerous place. Likewise, focusing on the glow of beauty, truth and community is how you've all made this amazing scene what it is. But negative energy isn't transitory either. So all in all you may not get round to certain critically important acts until it's too late.

You Say It's a Living; We All Gotta Eat
Sounds like that could apply to the band too, though the Billy interview we did should have warned us. Yet we know from our own experience that there are 2 yearly cycles in the Beast's health since the 1980s. Maybe we forgot that pattern after it was broken when the 1990 performances built on 1989 and went up instead of down? (And what an amazing human achievement that will seem when we look back on it...)

No, what was really disturbing were the reasons for not stopping which were emanating from San Rafael; that they had a large family to support and that the Heads wanted them out there. Just why these are considered valid I don't know, since if Jerry goes, there ain't no more bread in the breadbox for the family anyway, and speaking for most of us here, we would rather they rested than chum it out and decline. Really, you would think it was in their interests to have Jerry alive and well first and foremost!

The More That You Give, the More It Will Take
All this prevaricating is just making it harder for Garcia. Even if you're too far back to see him, surely the recent turn of lyric, both in new songs and old choices, is him telling us how he is really feeling? Now I know some scoff at my inclination to study this aspect of Dead-dom, and I agree you have to do it carefully (for example, not taking "Patience runs out on the junkie" to be "Bob talking to Jerry, man," but rather Bob debating his/his character's "tom-cat heart"). But surely there's a place in our scene for some intelligent intellectual exercise of this kind? Deadheads love their lyrics, though as my "Song Cheers" article showed, there's an awful lot of dumbing down going on out there (Jerry, mournfully—"Seems like this night could last forever." Audience, huge cheers "Yayyy!").

I mean, here we are, being told "This could be the Last Time" with renewed frequency (and out of Space, normally a positive emotional slot). And, for the first time in 20 years hearing "One way or another, this darkness got to give," rendered not as a chirpy stoic philosophy, but as a despairing cry. Or the end of "Standing on the Moon," where it seems that the cry "I wanna be with you" has become "I gotta be with you no matter how bad I'm feeling 'cos that's my fate." Not to mention "Casey Jones" back from the bad old days of 1984—"Trouble ahead!"

However, the most significant pointer is "So Many Roads." How can you not get a tremendously strong visual image of poor ole Jer singing, almost every other night, "So many roads to ride." Singing it after Drums. Singing it before. And even singing it in the first set several times. Imagine "Black Muddy River" being treated thus, and you'll get a glimpse of what sort of a statement is being quietly made. "New York to San Francisco, so many roads I know. All I want is one to take me home." How clear does it need to be for us to realise it? And that's without the heart-rending final section, with Jerry trying to ease his soul by howling his refrain.

It could be argued that Jerry's "trapped on the road again" blues here is just a character role, like "Black Peter" or "Wharf Rat" (and we don't want to fall into what Richard Thompson describes as the fundamental trap of thinking the singer is the protagonist of the song). But what I hear is someone trying desperately to achieve catharsis, exorcising his pain by naming it and trying to transcend it. And, even more sad, sometimes seeming to communicate "the road's the only home I will ever have, and I have to ride it till I die."

Given all that, what are we to make of being told very softly "You don't seem to hear me when I call"? For are we hearing him? He's surely calling.

Who Do You Wanna Be?

Before I move on, a related digression. Have you noticed how since *Built to Last*, Hunter has been writing a completely new dimension into the Dead experience? It's as if the last hiatus really got him thinking about mortality and the GD, and for the first time he's overtly expressing the current, up-to-the-minute burning issues for the band, being their Zeitgeist. From the title song, to being alone on the moon, to this obsession with road and home, both in Vince and Phil's new songs, Hunter is trying to tell us something too. And isn't he someone we think we are listening to? Is there after all, any more important collective topic for them to focus on except what is needed for the GD to find a philosophy that will energise them to carry on. Yes things *are* as serious as that.

OK—back to the summer tour situation. We could argue that it will take time to break themselves in with Vince, not to mention the new monitors. And since nobody sees all the shows, it takes a while to build a consensus from friends, tapes etc. But just as the summer ended and we prepared to fly out to either Shoreline or the East coast, me pretty much rehearsing all the above for the next article on how they pulled the chestnuts out of the fire yet again at Boston when...Blam! It all blew up in our faces.

Boy, was I angry! Not with Jerry but with the rest of the family. It must be bad for him to miss that Kesey reunion gig. How bad? Well all that Phil talk about Elvis on the hotline was alarming, and even though close sources say he will recover, it's obviously time to Take a Step Back and finally have that major rethink. My anger has abated somewhat—after all we don't have, can't have, the full picture. But my heart aches for those poor Brits who lost their two years worth of savings on non-refundable air and hotel bills—they spent this on you, GD, and you could have avoided this!

So OK then. Let's start doing this major re-think in the magazine, and really focus on the health of this Beast. We know They get the magazine, so perhaps we can get through that way. Someone has to stick their neck out—I guess it must be up to me.

That Thin Line Beyond Which...
Let's go back to the first public evidence, that *Rolling Stone* (and *Boston Globe*) interview in fall 1991. What a cry from the heart *that* was—Jerry hasn't been so clear and so public ever before. What really rang alarm bells for me was his desire to have a band with Bruce, Branford and Rob. That was the first time I felt him seriously tempted by a musical entity other than the GD. Now if you go back to the book with Reich in 1972 you find him agonising over whether he wanted to be in the band, stating that he'd felt that way for years (and finally deciding "Yes"). But this has probably continued to eat away at him over the years since, until finally he could hold it in no more. And finally too, he had an idea for a band that could stretch him as much as the GD, in a whole new direction for music. Imagine then, the feelings of the rest of the band about all this. Maybe they began to think "If we stop for a break now, we may never get Jerry fired up to start again"? If that's so, family alarm would be understandable.

You Put the Load Right on Me
We've always had the image that the core of the band's philosophy has been that "I don't do nothing I don't wanna do"—in music or life, and of course Heads have absorbed the "go for it" aspect of that philosophy. Yet more and more I realise that band interviews generally rationalise to us, like putting a determinedly brave face on "what ought to be," which is admirable to me they're putting the GD collective entity ahead of them-selves as individuals.

But that's a rather different philosophy; one that resonates more with my British cultural perspective, but won't really play that well with many Americans.

I say "they." But maybe I mean "Jerry." I'm guessing here but I would place my money on Garcia wanting to quit but being too much the gentleman to do so. Papa Bear has a large family to feed and an entity to pacify, this GD entity which they've often admitted has a life of its own. Is "service" in this form so unusual to Americans that it's hard to recognise? It may be so, for the first statement of Dylan's Christian era was "You gotta serve somebody," no matter who it is, like the idea was kind of unamerican. Such blasphemy eh? "Don't tread on me" indeed!

You Remind Myself of Me....

Hey guys, it's important to recognise this in the time we have now to review things. Because for years now we've had continual moaning about Jerry's drug use, that amounts to an angry or exasperated blaming, when in fact this may be caused by the inner division of having to do something you don't want to do for years on end. Imagine him looking out on that unique love-fest that is the GD community and feeling like he's the only one not getting off on it, despite being seen as the fount of that loving spirit! What would that do to you, year after year? I think this whole "I've got an addictive personality" bit is just not the whole picture. Unless it's "addicted to service."

Yes, I know some point the finger differently. "Huh, Jerry says he wants time off, yet he goes straight off and plays with his other bands." But this surely misses the point. GD music isn't about running through cover songs with some guitar breaks. It's about *transformation*—going out on the edge in order to try and take an audience to a spiritual place, otherwise unobtainable in modem life. ("If you don't, who else will" indeed). It's a huge responsibility— no wonder he wants to bury it under some good-time playing. You can be the JGB forever. But you can't keep lifting people to this huge awesome place easily. It's "a lot less than a prison, but it's more than a jail," eh, Jerry?

In The Heat of the Sun a Man Died of Cold

Third point then. If there's any truth in the above, then it follows that Brent's death really knocked him to the floor. It was one thing for him to be consoled by the fact that this new momentum had emerged since the comeback of 1986, up and up each year till 1990. It's quite another to try to pick it all up and start over. In that Boston 1991 article I tried to explain this musically, that they needed to know each other's rhythmic patterns inside out, so that they could lose the "one," the downbeat and take off for the "outside." After years of working up to that with Brent emerging more and more, they reached the plateau of summer 1990 and—wham—the carpet was yanked out from under them. What that must have done to an aging Jerrybear—after all he is the one who seems to feel most *responsible* for the band and the scene.

But now I feel it went even deeper than that—that much of that momentum came from the special relationship between Jerry and Brent, one they had built out of their mutual problems to help each other through. How could all those Brent-haters miss the constant loving looks they gave each other (or their choice of the lines they sang whilst looking at each other, which deserve a whole article in themselves). Re-listening to Essen 1990 which at the time felt like a show sung to Brent, I found in the "High Time" what I thought I got wrong at the time—"I told you goodbye. How was I to know?" Yes, the pronouns reversed...sob...Garcia—under your rough guy language, you hide such a beautiful soul!

Recently several of sat round and almost everyone sort of said "The Dead died with Brent." I was amazed—I didn't wanna be the one to say it, 'cos people would say "Oh that's Paddy on his Brent love-trip again." But something deeper than music has left with his passing, some elemental reality of the fundamental pain of real life and the possibility of transcending it by facing it, at least onstage. The odds on getting in touch with that again will lengthen each time they back off from their crises or stay imprisoned in a hippie cool.

Maybe it can't be replaced. But this long strange trip ain't over yet. It's important to notice that Jerry isn't happy with Vince at some level—that's in stark contrast with Bruce (pace Boston 1991). But it took time with Brent too, so maybe the two of them can get there, musically if not real-life-pain wise. We need to keep up the good job done so far of encouraging Vince—we did learn something from our treatment of poor Brent at any rate. (Maybe if we had done some more plain talking like this about the Brent-Jerry situation we could have gotten the audience to show more love to him). Anyway, count me in—I'm not trying to compare them. It's just time for straight words is all.

Gonna Jump-Start My Life or Go Down Trying

Of course I'm still hopeful. He should get his 6 month layoff now—provided they wait till next spring, eh boys—and they have songs they want to write. (Maybe even Bobby has woken up to that). So we might get a *Blues for Allah* type scenario of stuff produced whilst holed up together. Vince, bless him, has new energy (and insight into the GD spirit if "Tomorrow Never Knows" is anything to go by), as does Bralove—he's in the band too you know! Phil steps out and gets better year by year, and the Devils have already shown the way. So there's plenty to play for yet.

Maybe too the shock will jolt them. The excellent Bruce interview in

Unbroken Chain contains a good description of his frustration, one that we recognise ourselves over the years. He talks of the jams he was involved in with them (e.g., Madison 1990) and his bemusement as to why they quit such an exciting possibility. Well, maybe they'll stop pulling back from such exciting new areas and go for it!

In the meantime we'll have to wait and see if the strength's there to carry that weight again. My gut says, for 2 more years at most. "I don't know whose back's that strong; maybe find out before too long," indeed!

If Mercy's in Business I Wish It for You

But we can all do something—don't kid yourself that we can't. The band could start by taking some of that responsibility off the old guy's shoulders, and step out more. And we can do what some of us did in 1986 which is to pray in the sense of sending healing energies to Jerry, setting aside a few minutes when we can. Maybe pick a song to focus on while we do it, like Attics. Let him know "Jerry, it's all right for you to stop. Take as long as you need." It worked in 1986, so it's worth a shot now.

Don't be fooled into thinking "We-ell, he's not in a coma, so...." because if it all ends you'll only be wishing you could have done something. Visualise those old lungs healing, that old heart working smoothly. Then mentally re-enact the triumphant resurrection of Spring 1987 right on through to the encores of those stunning summer shows with Dylan, and our man standing there strong after 4 hours onstage, roaring "I will survive" to 100,000 people in the sweltering New York stadium night-light.

And from here on in let's be thankful for what we get and play our part in showing it. If the horse can't pull, you got to carry that load! Weirder things have happened, you know. How else could the Beast still be alive in its 27th year? You know it's gonna get stranger, so let's get on with the show!

The two following pieces by Blair Jackson work well as an examination of Phil Lash's place in the band. The first piece is Jackson's introduction to a Lash interview that appeared in the Summer 1990 *Golden Road*. The second is an interview from Spring 1994, published in *Dupree's Diamond News*.

Introduction to
We Want Phil!
An Interview

Blair Jackson

It seemed somehow appropriate that on the morning of the day I was to interview Phil Lesh, I was jolted from a sound sleep at 6:54 a.m. by a rumbling 5.4 magnitude earthquake. Talk about a rattling bass sound—Phil's got a ways to go before he matches that one! To make matters weirder, it was also the 84th anniversary of San Francisco's '06 quake; I instantly thought of Phil's famous "Earthquake Space" during a Hartford Civic show April 18, 1982, the 76th anniversary: "SAN FRANCISCO IN RUINS!!"—*Bwonnnnnnnngg!!—thuddddd-thud-thud!!*

Actually, through the years there have been times during "space" at a show when I've been sitting there with my eyes dosed, and Phil's bass emitted such a ground-shaking low note that I honestly wondered if the ceiling above might start to crumble. Crushed at a Grateful Dead show—what a way to go! These fantasies are rare, however, and more often I associate Phil's bass sound with less threatening natural forces: I keep thinking of that line in "Crazy Fingers"—"Peals of fragile thunder, keeping time."

The thunder analogy is obvious, but apt. (And in part of "Let It Grow," it's even literal.) His playing conjures other images, too: There've been "Other One" jams where the bass line reminds me of some jungle beast chasing its prey; others where it's our very cosmos spiraling out of control. Are Phil's sonic booms on "Morning Dew" the end of the world, or a prayer for redemption? Maybe they're just notes in a musical piece. Depends on the listener and the moment, I suppose, like everything else.

The point is. it isn't *just* bass; some solid rhythmic anchor married musically to the drums. In a band where no one player is setting the rhythm. and in fact *all* the musicians are setting the rhythm all the time. Phil's bass is able to dance through the music with peerless fluidity and grace. (Would anyone be offended if I fondly compared it to the hippo ballet dancers in *Fantasia?)* To say that his playing owes more to jazz bass than rock 'n' roll or R&B bass doesn't exactly capture it. either. Yes. it's rooted in continual improvisation. like Mingus or Scott La Faro or Charlie Haden. but there's the matter of *electricity*—Phil's style and touch are rooted to his mastery of the possibilities of his electronic instrument. Indeed. he's been a true innovator in this area. involved with aspects of the design of nearly every instrument he's used since the halcyon days of his gargantuan Alembic axes.

Unlike most bassists who came up during the mid-'60s. Phil didn't learn his instrument by copping James Jamerson licks off Motown singles. or Paul McCartney riffs off Beatles records. Rather. he learned on the job. playing with the Grateful Dead in bars and ballrooms. At the same time he was building his chops. the band was getting high and experimenting with *demolishing* conventional musical structures. The group's eclectic approach forced him to continually explore new areas as he grew: It's an R&B band! No. it's a cowboy band! Wait. it's a space band! No wonder he doesn't sound like anyone else.

Though he's adept at every style the band plays. Phil shines brightest when the music is most open and challenging. Quickly tripping through the years in my mind. I hear Phil lending a fluttering accompaniment on a jam at the end of "New Potato Caboose"; rumbling like a Harley over the other instruments as Pigpen raves during a hot "Lovelight" rap; moving determinedly through musical asteroid fields and gaseous clouds en route to a distant "Dark Star"; prying open the jam in "Playin' in the Band"; darting around. under. *through* Garcia's leads on "The Other One"; cascading in a Baroque waterfall of notes at the tail end of "Crazy Fingers"; twisting in a unison downward spiral with Garcia and Weir in a late '70s "Dancin' in the Streets" jam. I love that counterpoint that sounds like a Latin motet progression he sometimes plays at the end of Garcia's solo on "Friend of the Devil"; that high. dramatic descending figure he plugs in before "Maybe I'll meet you on the run" in "Sugaree"; his snaky lead over the opening bars of "Help on the Way"; the air he leaves between notes on the quietest parts of "Stella Blue"; and on and on.

For a while there in the early and mid-'80s. I wondered if Phil was going to stick it out with the Dead. Onstage he often looked positively bored. and his playing frequently lacked both the crispness and assertiveness that characterizes his best work. I think it's no coincidence that this was also the period when Garcia was struggling hardest with his personal demons. becoming

insular both musically and socially. So much of the Dead's power depends on the special musical camaraderie between Garcia and Lesh, yet there were shows—*tours*, even—when they didn't seem to connect onstage. As Garcia slowly emerged from his addiction during the second half of '85 and early '86, though, Phil perked up noticeably, too, and all of a sudden you could see them interacting again. It's been a steady climb back for both of them since Garcia's near-death in the summer of '86.

These days it really does seem like we're hearing the Phil Lesh of old at most shows. (As the bumpersticker says, LESH IS MORE!) Sure, he still has his crabby nights, where he spends much of the show scowling at his amps and yelling at the crew. I can assure you that *all* the members have those kind of nights; Phil's moods are just more transparent. But lately, more often than not he's been downright frisky onstage. He looks more relaxed than he has in years, his voice is stronger, he's obviously in great physical shape, and I'd argue that he has reasserted his role as one of the band's musical leaders. He's even out onstage for "space" most of the time; always a good omen. Evidently a happy family life and his (and the band's) relatively clean living agree with him.

As proof of his renewed commitment to the band, Phil has even taken on the production chores (with engineer John Cutler) for the Dead's upcoming live album—the first time Phil has taken an active role in production since *Steal Your Face*. (Uh, we won't hold that against him this far down the road.) In fact, it was after a session of listening to tapes from the spring tour that I caught up with Phil at the Dead's Club Front recording studio. Sitting around the giant Neve mixing console there, we chatted about what he's up to, in and out of the band.

In Phil We Trust

A Conversation

Blair Jackson

t's great to see Phil Lesh so involved in so many aspects of the Grateful Dead these days. Of course, we expect him to be a force and presence onstage, unleashing thunderous clusters of notes and even the occasional gossamer sinew as he fearlessly tried to steer the band into the great beyond. There's a truism in the Grateful Dead world that if Phil is happening, the band is happening. Although that's obviously an oversimplification (there's not really much he can do to elevate another band member having an off-night), it is true that when Phil is "on" the music hits a different level; it's always been that way. My own view is that Phil's been on a roll for the past several years, individually transcending the occasional dips and valleys that periodically appear in Deadland (don't be alarmed—it happens to everybody) and providing a much-needed kick in the ass to everybody when the going gets slooooooow. He's obviously in great physical and mental shape, and his attitude is good, too. Whether or not you like "Wave to the Wind," or any new tunes he has coming down the pike, it's great to see him putting himself out there and asserting his role as a dominant player in the group.

What's been somewhat surprising is seeing his emergence the last few years in ancillary areas of the Dead world. He's reportedly been somewhat involved on the merchandising end of things, he's shown the greatest interest of any band member in the Dead archival CD series and he's even written the occasional official memo to Deadheads to clarify the band's position on this issue or that.

I last interviewed Phil four years ago, for Issue #23 of *The Golden Road* (that interview is available in my 1992 book, *Goin' Down the Road: A Grateful Dead Traveling Companion*). So this interview was more a case of catching up than dealing with big, general topics about his playing. We met at Grateful Dead headquarters in San Rafael on April 25 and sequestered ourselves (along with his very well-behaved four-year-old son, Brian) in a small office for about an hour. Phil sat directly under his own portrait by Stanley Mouse from the back cover of *Workingman's Dead*. It's amazing how little he's changed in the 24 years since then. As always, he proved to be both thoughtful and articulate. He measures his words carefully and, nice guy that he is, steers away from controversy (rats!).

JACKSON: What's been your level of involvement with Dick's Picks?

LESH: None really, except that I had them cut a bass solo I didn't like. I think I played two bass solos during that period, and one was okay and the other wasn't, and this is the one that wasn't. It was *not* usable. There was absolutely nothing to it; nothing happened in it. It was just a bunch of strumming. The other I remember being much more interesting, though I haven't heard it in a long time.

[Jackson] How do you feel about the whole archival end of the Dead trip?

LESH: I love it. We're hoping to get some kind of idea of the response we can get on these releases by using only mail order. I don't have the latest figures, but I think [*Dick's Picks*] has done pretty well. It sold 20,000 in one month and I know the people in GD Merchandising were very happy about that. I assume that's a good rate for mail order.

JACKSON: Is it true that you were the one who essentially nixed the last pick for the From the Vault series [2/19/71, Capitol Theater, Port Chester, NY]?

LESH: Yes. I didn't care for the performance. Somebody else had chosen it; in fact Dick [Latvala] wasn't even that involved with that choice. It was a situation where it was desired that it be a multitrack, and it was one of the multitracks from that period we'd already mined for the *Skull & Roses* album. So aside from the fact that that performance wasn't that good, we had already been through it years ago and gotten what we could out of it then. I don't recall if we actually used anything from that performance on the record. But the bottom line was the performance wasn't up to my standards.

JACKSON: And everyone in the band has that power over releases?

LESH: Yes, exactly.

JACKSON: Is it fair to say so far you've shown the most interest in the archives?

LESH: It's fair to say that I'm the only one who's listened to a lot of it, I think. Actually I don't know that anyone else in the band has a particular interest in making a decision about these thing, so it's sort of fallen to me. Since everyone can trust me to be pretty cold about it, I think they feel safe that I won't let a sloppy performance or a lousy performance or a meaningless performance get by.

JACKSON: *Once you excised that hideous bass solo from* Dick's Picks, *what did you think of the rest of the show?*

LESH: The rest of it is amazing. In fact, I can't imagine how I managed to play such a bad bass solo in the middle of it! [Laughs]

JACKSON: What does the '73-'74 Grateful Dead sound like to you today?

LESH: It sounds pretty good; pretty interesting. My kids are starting to get into the band a little. We have a random selection of Grateful Dead CDs at our house, and they've been getting into *Dead Set* [from 1980]. I've noticed there's some stuff on there that's kind of nice. We played "Fire on the Mountain" and didn't rush. So we know it can be done. [Laughs]

The '73-'74 period was interesting to me because we were so together. Frankly, I don't remember us being so together musically. The other thing that really blew my mind was Billy's drumming.

JACKSON: Me, too. It swings so much on the cd—all those great cymbal splashes and quick little rhythms. Amazing!

LESH: Yeah. I'd forgotten he played like that. Since we have two drummers now, I suppose he doesn't need to play that way anymore.

JACKSON: Also, Keith was really in his prime then.

LESH: Yes, he was a fine player. He was the perfect guy for our music at that time. It's like he came forth fully grown. He didn't have to work his way into it.

JACKSON: Of course, the fans all want to know why you don't put out more CDs, and why you don't put them out faster. And of course, they all claim to know what's great, etc. How do you deal with that level of intensity?

LESH: I ignore it. [Laughs] We'll put it out at our own speed. I'm really glad there's a demand for it out there, because that's our old age insurance in a way. We're going to keep putting it out, and personally I'm always interested in having people tell me what they think are the great shows. That's one reason Dick is involved with this—he's so deeply steeped in the shows, he gets other people's input, and he has opinions of his own as well. That's invaluable in dealing with this, because nobody in the band wants to go through and listen to all of that.

JACKSON: Living through some of them was probably bad enough.

LESH: Yeah, that's true. [Laughs]

JACKSON: Sometimes I'll run into Dick and he'll ask me, "Did that show on Thursday night really suck, or is it just me?" I'll say, "No Dick, it was really cool—check it out!"

LESH: [Laughs] Well, sometimes they do suck.

JACKSON: An analogy I've heard from Deadheads is that everything John

Coltrane ever played that was recorded is going to come out, so why not the Dead? Of course, not as many Coltrane shows were recorded, to say the least, and Coltrane isn't alive to say "Nope, that one sucked!"

LESH: Same with Hendrix or any of those guys. On the other hand, there is probably some value to everything that Coltrane ever played. I don't know if that's true of the Grateful Dead, but in terms of Coltrane, I think somebody could learn something from every note he played.

JACKSON: Certainly in the case of the Dead, there's value in studying the evolution over time.

LESH: Sure, if that's what people want to see.

JACKSON: The other thing about Coltrane is, like the Dead, that there are tapes from different sources, ranging from professional two-tracks to little homemade recordings done with a recorder sitting on a table in a club.

LESH: I haven't heard any of those [homemade recordings] of Coltrane, but I have a Charlie Parker one done by this guy Dean Benedetti who went to a club with a wire recorder and only taped Bird's solos!

JACKSON: Well, Deadheads are already attuned to that sort of thing because of years of listening to high generation audience tapes.

LESH: That's true, but getting back to Dick's Picks for a minute, I was really impressed by the sound quality. I couldn't believe that Kidd [Bill Candelario, of the gd crew] had mixed it at the same time he was doing Keith's keyboards and whatever else he had to do onstage. In a way it's the ideal mix for our music because if you set it and forget it, we'll play the dynamics. I think it's an excellent document of the Grateful Dead.

JACKSON: Are you a person who tends to go into the vault to check things out from time to time?

LESH: No, not unless it's time to do a live record or something. Eventually there will be a Three from the Vault, and I'll probably end up mixing it. But I'll let Dick and the committee give me the options. Hopefully it'll be multitrack, but we're not even sure there's enough multitrack to even continue the premium Vault series because, like I said, we've been mining our multitrack recordings for live albums ever since 1968.

JACKSON: That's true, but one could argue that the criteria you used for choosing track for *Europe '72* was affected by the kind of stuff that had already come out on *Skull & Roses* and *Live Dead* before it. So at that time you weren't looking at the hot version of "Dark Star" from the Europe tour, or "Not Fade Away/Goin' Down the Road." There's some great stuff on those Europe tapes.

LESH: That's true. Those are the kinds of things that slip my mind. That's why I'm glad I have Dick and other people to remind me.

JACKSON: The level of minutiae surrounding the Grateful Dead is unparalleled *in* popular culture—no band has been documented as thoroughly and with the kind of detail as the Dead.

LESH: You mean Deadbase and that sort of thing?

JACKSON: Yeah, that whole level of anal retentiveness [Phil laughs] to which I must confess I occasionally succumb.

LESH: Well, some of that stuff is neat, like tracing the roots and sources of songs.

JACKSON: What do you make of the fact that people are into the band on so many different levels?

LESH: I ignore that, too.

JACKSON: Is it scary?

LESH: No. Actually it can be when copies of address lists and phone numbers start popping up out in the real world, but I guess there's no way to avoid that happening from time to time. If somebody wants to know something about you they can find it out.

JACKSON: Do you feel like you're under a microscope?

LESH: Not particularly. In fact, I don't feel that at all. I don't get harassed on the street. People don't come to my house.

JACKSON: What kind of mail do you get?

LESH: Birthday greetings. "Hey, I've loved your music for years, keep up the good work." Nice stuff mainly. There's the occasional weirdo who wants to tell you about everything that's going on in his or her life. But I tend not to get much of that.

JACKSON: I know that from time to time you've looked at what goes on in the Grateful Dead conference on The WELL. What are your impressions of that?

LESH: I use The WELL now for electronic mail pretty much, and I don't really hang out much in the Deadhead area. Occasionally I'll log on to see what the response is to new material or something like that. They seem to have a whole world of their own going there.

JACKSON: Does it bother you that a lot of hardcore Deadheads seem to have this proprietary attitude that they should have a vote in the way things go with the band?

LESH: Well, they do and they don't. They have a vote psychically when we're performing, when the link is there, when there's a circuit that's been closed—then they do have input. But it's not the kind of concrete input that many people would like to have. As far as the way we run our scene, the decisions that we make, we make on our own. Any input is always welcome, but they're always our decisions. Are you referring to anything in particular?

JACKSON: Not really.

LESH: There was a guy who wrote a letter in *The New Republic* saying that the Grateful Dead is not doing enough against mandatory minimums. That's something we are working on, but we're not working on it because this guy says we should. We're working on it because we think it's wrong. We just haven't quite figured out exactly what we should try to do about it. It's the kind of thing we all have to agree on.

JACKSON: Do you have a good sense of what kind of people make up the Dead's fan base at this point?

LESH: All I know is what I see at the shows, and that seems to be a tremendous variety of people, and there's a tremendous range of ages in our audience. But I couldn't tell you what proportion of them are gypsies who follow us around and who are the locals. But it seems like a pretty diverse bunch.

JACKSON: Do they feel like "your people"?

LESH: Yeah, I've gotta say, I really love and admire Deadheads, because without them we wouldn't be anywhere.

JACKSON: Do you think you would be a Deadhead if you went to your first show at the Omni on April 1 and checked it all out? You went early, you hung out in the parking lot with your buddies...

LESH: That's like asking me, "What do you think the band sounds like out front?" How can I answer that? I'm already there, and I can't dissociate myself from already being there. It's like, we can't listen to older music with the same ears that listened to it when it was first performed, because we've listened to everything that's happened since then.

JACKSON: I guess I'm really asking if the current Grateful Dead Experience seems like the kind of thing you would like if you were 22 and just getting out of college.

LESH: Oh yeah! Because it's the last holdout, the last piece of that culture that really exists in this era. It's history, and for some, I suppose, it's nostalgia, but it's still very much alive—that's the key.

JACKSON: I have a hard time explaining to people why it's not primarily a nostalgia thing.

LESH: That is hard to explain.

JACKSON: It's certainly has a lot of the signposts of '60s culture.

LESH: There's nothing else like that in the world today. If it is the only remnant of the '60s, thank goodness there's something left! Because there really isn't much else that survived the '60s intact.

JACKSON: Have you checked out any of the so-called neo-psychedelic bands—Phish or the Spin Doctors or whoever.

LESH: A little, though I've got to say, those bands don't sound very psychedelic to me, because I haven't heard any of them really stretch out much, jam out. I haven't heard enough to really make a judgment, though. I just got a magazine from England that says there are dozens or hundreds of psychedelic bands there. And they've got this "traveller" culture there.

JACKSON: Right, the government there has really cracked down on the hippie gypsies, even more so than here, where most of the government attention seems to be focused exclusively on drugs, rather than the gypsy aspect of it.

LESH: Right. Over there it's a flourishing little culture that's sort of a replay of the '60s in a way.

JACKSON: Any general impressions of the last tour?

LESH: Yeah, there was a new transparency to everything for me.

JACKSON: You mean sound-wise?

LESH: Partly because of the sound, and partly because four of the guys in the band [Phil, Mickey, Billy, Bob] are now doing yoga. Billy and I agreed that it made a big change in our perceptions.

JACKSON: Can you pinpoint it more?

LESH: It's a question of your perception, of where you're coming from—where you're perceiving the music from. It's hard to describe, but there were points where I had a very centered feeling, which is rare—usually I'm more scattered because I'm not just myself onstage; I'm also those five other guys, and I'm concentrating so hard on what everyone is doing. This was a new experience. I was able to balance that perception with a new feeling of centeredness. Whatever caused it, it allowed Billy and me, in particular, to lock in a lot better.

JACKSON: What got you into yoga?

LESH: I needed something, some basic kind of physical discipline, and regular exercise wasn't enough. I thought of trying Tai Chi or something. But this has opened up a whole new world to me.

JACKSON: Do you have a teacher and everything?

LESH: Yes, his name is Larry Schultz. I think he was Sting's teacher, or something. I know Sting does the same kind of yoga, and hey, he goes around with his shirt off all the time. [Laughs]

Anyway, I think both yoga and the new soundspace had a real effect on the music this tour. On the very first night [in Chicago], the beginning of the second set, on "Scarlet Begonias" and "Fire on the Mountain" everyone was playing different stuff—placing their notes differently. Also on this tour there was some really amazing space music. Three nights in a row we did some great stuff—in Atlanta, I think.

JACKSON: Over the course of those three nights of *Space* in Atlanta, are there connections night to night that you can detect?

LESH: Occasionally. Sometimes I'll just leave the last setting on my midi bass where it was and then start there again the next night, so the tone or timbre of whatever preset I was using will carry over. But I don't know if the other guys do that. And then there's always a thread through all Space, jams, and that's Jerry's "I Love New York" bassoon-kind of tone. That's what I call it. [Laughs]

JACKSON: How do you like the way the more recent material has developed?

LESH: I think "Corrina," in particular, has gotten pretty interesting. It's been a long time coming, but the feeling, the groove, is starting to happen.

JACKSON: Are you more attracted to something that has a definable pulse like that than, say, a song like "Days Between," which is interesting in a whole other way?

LESH: No, I'm not attracted to any particular way of presenting music. I enjoy playing a tune like "Days Between," for instance, because it's a song that really stretches your capability to play in time because it's so slow. It makes the whole feeling of the presentation of it more legato, if you will; it's less chopped up. You can think in larger units, as it were. On the other hand, playing something like "Corrina," it's really nice to get into that pulse and work off the different subdivisions you can agree on.

JACKSON: The jams after "Terrapin" frequently get into those interesting pulses, too. And real floaty. It sounds very '60s to me for some reason.

LESH: There's an ethnic music it sort of reminds me of—

JACKSON: Indian raga?

LESH: Sort of, but it's nowhere near as complex or subtle as raga because we don't really use microtones in a systematic way. With the thing out of "Terrapin," it was interesting to have Jerry play the melody [of the end-jam] over a drone; that's how that started. Instead of making chord changes along that. That then suggested other possibilities.

JACKSON: What's become of "Wave to the Wind"? It seems to disappear for tours at a time, then come back.

LESH: We just need to run it down more. When we first started trying to play it, it was too fast and it had too many verses. So the next year we slowed it down. I cut a verse out of it and reworked the lyrics a little, and it was working a lot better that way. That's the form in which it's going to continue to develop. Actually, it was getting good, and for some reason it just didn't come up, we didn't play it, whatever; maybe I wasn't pushy enough about it.

JACKSON: As someone who doesn't write much, or hasn't written in awhile, is it odd to go through the experience of seeing what the other members of the band do to your songs?

LESH: Yeah. In the case of "Wave to the Wind," I think I put too much into it to begin with. I made a MIDI demo of it, which was probably a mistake in retrospect. I think maybe my ideas about it were too fixed. On the demo I designed a drum pattern, I put on two midi keyboards, horns and a bass and a vocal. So there was all kinds of stuff on there. I've just written a couple of new songs. We've only gotten to work on one.

JACKSON: Is that "Red," which appears as one of your "new gd songs" in Hunter's Box of Rain book?

LESH: No, that one's not going to come out at all. I wasn't satisfied with how that was going musically. There's one called "If the Shoe Fits," and another called "Childhood's End."

JACKSON: Like the Arthur C. Clarke novel Childhood's End?

LESH: Yeah, although it has nothing to do with that. With both of those songs, all I did was make a tape of me playing guitar and singing—real simple.

JACKSON: Are you a good guitarist?

LESH: No. This is just chunka-chunka-chunka simple stuff. Part of the charm of it is that because I'm not a good guitarist, it leaves everything to the imagination of the other guys [in the band]. Really, the only things there are the melody line and the chord changes.

JACKSON: What are they like stylistically?

LESH: "Shoe Fits" is kind of a rocker, and "Childhood's End" is a slower tune.

JACKSON: Really? Have you written lyrics before?

LESH: Only once, but this came out a lot better than that one.

JACKSON: Which was...

LESH: "No Left Turn Unstoned." [Laughs] It was a truly awful song I wrote for the Grateful Dead during the Matrix era—I think it was '67, maybe '68. It's on a couple of tapes I think. It's God-awful. It's so awful I can't even listen to it to find out what it was like. [Laughs]

JACKSON: What's it going to take to get the Grateful Dead to rehearse?

LESH: I don't know—how about a bonus or something? Somebody always seems to be out of town or not in the mood, or both.

JACKSON: I feel like whenever I've interviewed band members, independently you all say you want to rehearse, but then it still doesn't happen.

LESH: Have you actually heard everybody say that?

JACKSON: Actually, I guess Jerry's line is, "We don't rehearse."

LESH: [Laughs] Well, there you have it!

JACKSON: Any chance that "Passenger" will come back? One of your finer efforts in my opinion.

LESH: Bob's made some noises about bringing that back. I don't care—if he wants to do it, I'll play it, but I'm not going to push for it.

What's weird about that song is I sort of did it as a joke. It's a take on a Fleetwood Mac tune called "Station Man." I just sort of sped it up and put some different chord changes in there, but the feeling is similar. It's a little short of plagiarism, but not much.

JACKSON: Last year you guys had the honor of sharing your stage with three of the best saxophonists in the world—Ornette Coleman, Branford Marsalis, and David Murray. Can you contrast what each one brings to the music?

LESH: Whew, that's a tough one. Branford is like an encyclopedist. He's a repository of all sorts of different ways of looking at music.

Ornette is like [he whispers] the fringe. Even his pitches are like the fringe of tonalities, the microtones and stuff like that. It's so different from most of what we do. We're pretty much 12 notes to the octave; everything is pretty much equal temperament, especially with the keyboards. Except for Jerry's solos when he bends his strings for inflection and things like that. But Ornette really plays in the cracks. It was so wonderful to hear the integration of that kind of thinking with our stuff. At Mardi Gras ['93] when we played "Lovelight," boy, some of the stuff he came up with—it was like honky-tonk, but filtered through the strangest sense of melody.

David plays like a volcano. His music erupts from the core of his heart. The power and fluency of it astonishes me. I really want him to play on "Wave to the Wind."

They're all different and I feel honored that each has chosen to play with us at one time or another.

JACKSON: Is it fair to say that Murray fits in somewhere between Ornette and Branford stylistically?

LESH: No, I'd say it's more like they're points of a triangle.

JACKSON: In last year's Guitar Player Grateful Dead issue, Jerry and Bobby had some things to say about your playing that I found really eye-opening. I wonder if I could get you to comment about a couple of points in there. Here's Bob: "Phil's unimaginably angular. His own little specialty. After nearly 30 years of playing with him, you learn not to intuit what he's going to do because it's not possible. He can hear you thinking and make sure he's not supplying what you're expecting."

LESH: [Laughs] That's great. I'm glad my playing affects him that way, because that makes him respond in a more creative way, maybe. But hey, I don't consider myself angular really, because everything I do is built on scales.

JACKSON: Bob's been playing some cool stuff recently—more sustain and feedback.

LESH: Yeah, he has sort of been in that bag recently.

JACKSON: What does that do to what you play in relation to him?

LESH: It makes me think about the rhythm more, for one thing.

JACKSON: Because he's no longer supplying the rhythm?

LESH: No, he still is, because when he stops one note and starts another that's where the rhythm lives—in that hole. So I can either put something in the hole, or put an accent where he stops, if I can figure out where that's going to be, or I can play around it in different ways. It's equally interesting. Pretty much anything Bob does is interesting to me, because it gives me something to hook onto.

JACKSON: I feel like I've never been able to figure out who his influences are.

LESH: Well, he doesn't play like anyone. First of all, he's got those enormous hands. I don't know how many frets he can stretch, but it's certainly more than I can. And his voicings are unique.

JACKSON: And he builds all his songs out of such unusual chords.

LESH: To say the least. Although "Easy Answers" does remind me a bit of "Victim or the Crime."

JACKSON: Let me read you one of Jerry's quotes about you from the Guitar Player interview: "Instead of playing figures or patterns or connective tissue like regular bass players do, Phil might actually do a line that's the length of the song. He plays long ideas. When the time comes to do what the bass has to do, like hit the root on a key chord or whatever, Phil is usually there for the important stuff. There's the required stuff and the elective stuff. For Phil, the required stuff is about one percent of what he plays. [Phil chuckles] You have to have faith in what Phil is playing; that's the key. He plays the bass as though he invented the instrument and nobody ever played it before him."

LESH: I'm not exactly sure how he meant it, but I consider that all very perceptive.

JACKSON: Is that true that you'll play lines that long? He said you can sometimes hear it better if you speed up the tape.

LESH: Yeah, he told me that once. I think he said that on one of the songs on *Reflections* [Garcia's '75 album], by some freak accident, he heard it sped up, and he realized that what I was playing was all one melody.

The way I think about it is, I just try to do something different all the time, because most of the songs we play are strophic—in other words, sections repeat—so I just try to develop what I'm playing through those many repetitions to the greatest extent I can. In other words, it might start out simple and then take off from there. But I want it to change the whole time. Literally, I cannot play the same thing for every verse. It's not in me.

JACKSON: Is it something you can pre-plot? Can you have an agenda for what you want to do on a tune?

LESH: No, because of course it depends on what can happen on that particular night. It depends on my fantasy, on my caprice. And what the others are playing.

JACKSON: Is it harder to pull that off on a tune that's more repetitive, like "Women Are Smarter," than on a tune with more obvious timbral choices?

LESH: No, none of it's particularly hard. It's just that the context is more or less receptive depending on what everyone else is playing on that given occasion.

JACKSON: How do you like your midi bass these days? You're out there every night during Space...

LESH: Like I said, on this last tour, it's become very interesting. After a year or so of having a real MIDI instrument, I've found a few key pre-sets that I can use in practically any context.

JACKSON: What are some of your favorite tones? It's hard for us in the audience to tell who's playing what sometimes.

LESH: That's the way we like it. [Laughs] I couldn't tell you what the names are of any of my presets.

JACKSON: You essentially dial up a number that represents a sound?

LESH: Yeah, it'll be something like 01 Synthesizer 2. And I have an octave shifter, too, so I can play anything in any one of three octaves.

JACKSON: How are you enjoying Vince's playing lately?

LESH: Very much. Vince and I were able to connect a whole lot on this last tour. What I enjoy is he seems to understand that on the jammin'-out portions of tunes like "Playing in the Band" and "Terrapin," I'll change the roots of the tonality—say on "Playing" we're going out on a D. I'll take that D and that scale we use to play it and I'll take it to A-minor, I'll take it to F, I'll even take it to B-flat, which is really out there. I'll take it to G. And Vince has picked up on that, and now he's using components of those keys to trigger me, to say, "Okay, let's go there now! Here's a little A-minor to stick in there."

JACKSON: I sense he's got a pretty good jamming head.

LESH: Oh, yeah. He does.

JACKSON: And of course, he's the guy who's always talking about bringing back weird stuff like "Born Cross-Eyed."

LESH: Right, he wants to dig up all that stuff, and we could, of course, if we ever rehearsed. I'd love to do "Born Cross-Eyed." Hell, I could get a pair of timpani out there!

JACKSON: Get the trumpet out!

LESH: [He mimics his horn line from the record.] I don't know, my lip is pretty flaccid these days.

JACKSON: Anything happening with the fabled new album?

LESH: I haven't heard anything about it. We've actually discussed it a couple of times, but nothing's happening. I don't think there's enough material to choose from. I'd like to have more choices. What I really mean is I want to get more of my tunes on. And since we can't rehearse, for whatever reason, I don't feel like making an album until some of my tunes are worked up enough.

JACKSON: I guess you can't teach them songs at some soundcheck on the road, eh?

LESH: Actually, everybody but the drummers came up to my house and worked on "Shoe Fits," and we sort of had enough of it to do it at a soundcheck, but something always came up—late to the soundcheck, doors had to open, Bob's guitar was messed up, Jerry's guitar was messed up; something always happened. One day [on the last tour] Jerry actually suggested, "Why don't we try your new tune?" So I ran off to get the lyrics and the chord sheets, and when I got back Bob's guitar wasn't working. It's just one of those things; I'm not blaming anybody. On this tour there was always something.

JACKSON: Well, I hope it's not another seven-year wait, like it was between Go to Heaven and In the Dark, where everyone's heard all the "new" stuff for years.

LESH: Well, that happened with In the Dark and look how that record did! I still don't know why that record did so well. It wasn't that different from any of our other records.

JACKSON: How does it sound to you today?

LESH: I don't know, I haven't listened to it in a long time. I guess the feeling of it was a little different than some of our records because we did the basic tracks all at the same time.

JACKSON: Whereas on Built to Last it was more of an instrument by instrument construction over time.

LESH: I really believe if we hadn't had a deadline imposed on us by the record company [Arista] on Built to Last, we probably would've gone back and done the whole thing over again more in line with how we did In the Dark.

JACKSON: The Grateful Dead intimidated by a deadline? Since when?

LESH: Well, we took a big advance on that, which gave them the power.

JACKSON: How about the next one. Any deadlines hanging over your head?

LESH: No. We're making 'em wait. [Laughs]

JACKSON: Is the general mood of the band pretty good right now?

LESH: As far as I can tell, it was pretty good coming off the road.

JACKSON: Are you ready for what is sure to be a fair amount of hoopla next year surrounding the 30th Anniversary? You can't avoid it. It's going to happen.

LESH: I'll ignore it as much as I can. I mean, we've already had 20, then we had 25, now we're going to have 30. So what! We're still goin' on.

Philip Baruth's hypnotic novel *The Millennium Shows*, published by Albion in 1994, traces the concert-going existence of a "tourhead" named Story, whose identity is the mystery of the narrative. The band is a shadowy presence throughout the novel, and Garcia and Weir are referred to as "the older one" and "the younger voice." The novel leads up to a series of concerts planned for New Year's Eve 1999. Baruth wrote the book in 1994, and he foretells a millennium concert's taking place after the death of the "older one." He teaches fiction writing and 18th-century English Literature at the University of Vermont. He is also the author of *The Dream of the White Village*, published by RNM Press in 1998.

The Millennium Shows

Philip E. Baruth

y life is a set-list. Sometimes I think that there have been *more shows than there are possible memory configurations in the brain. Certainly I've lived more concerts than I can remember. There is no question of that, no question. I guess I need to assume at least one twin of every show I've seen, so close to the one I do remember that I've found it necessary to silently reduce the overlap. Maybe even twins is just a manageable illusion.*

Assume quintuplets.

I imagine that my mind has found very ingenious methods for shaping, thinning, making my remembered geography light, plastic, portable. It feels fine, though. I feel as though—more than most people—I carry just enough in the way of the past. I can remember music with digital precision. I can hear any song I've ever heard, exactly as it was played. Even songs from shows I didn't see flicker to consciousness, out of the descriptions I've heard from people in roadside diners and campgrounds. My mind interpolates what must have been played. I can remember the various, sweet groups of deadheads I've traveled with from city to city. I can remember the distinct feel and character of each of those groups. Memories like a small rack of bootleg tapes, a partial plastic testament to the live and unknowable whole.

Everything I remember has happened at a show, on the way to a show, after a show, or in long, rare intervals when there were no shows, such as December to June of 1974, when the Dead became Eastern mystics and spent months in Punjab, in seclusion, foreheads touching mats at daybreak. In my mind there is nothing else. What came before me? The musical roots of the Dead, which, when they had shot from the ground, matured and blossomed, flowered into concerts in every major auditorium in every major city of every state in this very large country. I appear, like a sea-green aphid, on one of the leaves of one of those shows. My memories begin with a ticket in my hand, years ago, years ago. I was in an extremely long line. Dead music played invitingly. It was a Friday show. There is no question of that.

Of the more than thirty shows in or outside Denver, Colorado, one will never be collapsed or excized for lack of space: I am up on the top of a Winnebago, a top-of-the-line model, big as an aircraft carrier. Many people are on the top of this Winnebago. We sit like dark fighter jets on top of it. It is late in the evening, and we are all facing a huge band shell some three-quarters of a mile away. There are mountains in the distance, brooding, bullying. It is blue-dark, and there is enough of the taste of summer lightning in the air to feel like the end of the world. A light desert breeze is blowing. The music falls and rises, changing moods and temperatures and outlooks. It shifts as invisibly and absolutely as atmospheric pressure. There is the sweet, floating smell of marijuana. Some of the people on the Winnebago are dancing, but many are huddled in blankets. I am huddled in a blanket. Little pinpoints of lighter fire go up, burn and then go down, in small, disposable tributes.

There is a couple sitting next to me, kissing intermittently, wrapped together in their own thin green Army surplus blanket. They are very young, and everything else is lost on them. They touch one another's faces, turn occasionally to stare off in the distance toward the bandstand. I can tell that they are not supposed to be here; they've told their parents that they're going to the movies.

He is seventeen, thin, with untameable curly black hair, rimless glass, bad skin, and a start at a beard. It covers his chin and certain parts of his cheeks, it does not join with his wisp of moustache. His green jacket is Army surplus too, but covered with left-wing pins to dilute the militancy of it. He sees the jacket as an aggressive and manifest contradiction, but it isn't; it's a very coherent statement of his desire to belong, to the right, or the left, or whatever fringe will have him. He wants what we all want. He is very happy to be with the girl.

She is fifteen. Her parents don't allow her to car-date. She is only just beginning to realize that she is very pretty, that she will be sought after. She is waking up to a sense of her own force in the world.

But now she is still content. He is content. A half an hour ago they smoked a joint which he produced with an exquisitely studied lack of ceremony. He has his arm firmly around her, as much like an oversized, flesh-and-bone engagement ring as he can make it.

I like them. The beauty and the pain of them sitting there is almost enough to distract me from the music washing up from the bandstand.

And as I watch the small lighter fires blink on and off, an almost coded randomness, an intelligible sequence of lights and absences of lights, a helicopter passes over us in a chopping wash of rotor noise. One helicopter, almost invisible except for its running lights. You can see just the moving outline of it, thrashing above us like a dark fish. Many in the crowd don't even look up. But I look up, and see the belly of it, the flashing lights there, and I feel the ordering intelligence there as well. And suddenly those lights tumble in my mind into the lights of the lighters in the hands of the crowd, and I turn to the couple and put my hand on the young man's shoulder. I feel the bone of his shoulder under my hand. He turns. His girlfriend turns.

And I tell them this story. It is the first time I have ever told it. It pushes its way up out of me, I almost vomit it up. The Providence story of Edward and Sonjee and myself, and as I am telling it I am listening too, stunned and listening. It is a story I have never heard before. The memories restore themselves only as I speak them aloud.

Listen. It's important.

The Inglewood Shows

And it was so, that Sonjee saw me dying quietly. Curled in a blanket and in fever, between a Jaguar and a bronco in the parking lot of the Great Western Forum in Inglewood, California. I had my temple against the blacktop, and I lay watching the small silver ornaments on the cars above me war with one another, the jaguar raking the horse's silver-white underbelly. The fighting animals would disperse as a helicopter passed over, pouring colored spots down into my eyes in long white showers. Then lope out of the colors and the confusion and recommence, the stallion driving its steel hoof into the jaguar's skull, shattering its sleek head into small blue sunbursts. Sonjee touched my head and told Edward I was on fire, and I woke in the back of their tired, clothes-scattered limousine with Tiger Balm burning at my temples. They left the limousine in that back row of the lot, until I could ride without being sick. Four hours: they played bootleg Dead and waited, and the music came out a speaker next to my ear and crawled inside it, guitar somehow Asian in movement, at that rarified octave where guitar meets mandolin and sitar.

They asked me what had happened to me, and it took four hours to tell them that I had eaten something, and that the Great Western Forum seemed a huge single organism, perfect, respiring through a system of fans, defecating in subterranean white-tile chambers where water continually flowed. That I had felt the group will of eighteen-thousand people, felt them and their stares as a hive intelligence, fainted and felt them cast me out in my weakness and eliminate me from within them through a gentle knot of men in tan and black who placed me outside under the helicopter lights. That I had fallen between an expensive car and a large truck, seen their murderous hood ornaments, and that I was just twenty-six years old that day.

The Long Beach Shows

They took me on with them, to Long Beach, the Arena Shows, and I paid my way with a credit card that I had in my wallet. I never looked in the wallet other than to pull out that credit card when I needed it, at a cheap restaurant or a ticket window. The wallet was thick with other things, but I never allowed Sonjee to peek inside it, though she once asked. When they would ask me about myself, I would show them the credit card, use it to buy something, and that would be the end of it. I learned that fifty-one-year-old Edward hated the music of the Dead, that he refused to go inside to see the shows. He would remain in the driver's seat, brooding, or leaning against the hood of the square-back limousine, the ornament poking up his windbreaker. From a row of cars away his thick, florid face drew stares. I learned the history of their attendance, the number of their concerts, the geography they pursued in season with the Dead.

Sonjee was picked up by friends she called from a Denny's on the highway, her Long Beach friends, and they came with fringe hanging from their elbows, and with their hair unwashed, approximating homelessness, joblessness. They hugged her and were familiar with her. And there was a hint of deference also, to the sort of woman who shines at gatherings of the Dead, to a sexuality breathing both paganism and naivete. To her blond hair shining in calfskin-tied braids. To the freshness of her body in a print stitched in Guatemala, and sandals purchased from a Rastafarian outside of San Francisco, two years ago at the New Year's Shows. To the prisms she wore in her ears. She was twenty-three. I saw them take her from the parking lot full of buses with cooking stoves and tin chimneys and hand-wrought silver, and I would have followed but for the fact that the Arena brought back images of long lines of bodies passing into deep white-tiled cells and the sounds of air ducts, and the intelligence of a municipal complex. And but for the fact of Edward's possession of her, its savor of the falsest hope.

He was a retired plumber who had met Sonjee at a time when a large cash offer for his business was pending, met her outside a supermarket near Fairfax, California, where she had rolled herself in her sleeping bag beside a hot air vent. The leads of a portable cassette player were in her ears, and Edward heard small, tinny sounds from where he stood. Bootlegged sounds like tabors and tambourines and chanting but infinitely smaller. He drove her to the Shows in Golden Gate Park, and attended the first one with her. The music baffled him with its way of climbing half a peak and then settling for half a fall back, its refusal of climax and its tendency to trail off rather than finish. He was vaguely disgusted by the undulations of the dancers, the uniform and grubby vegetarianism, the colors that stabbed his eyes from shirts, pants, banners. He never saw another show, but always waited for her in the parking lots that were strange bazaars with milling bodies, homemade stalls filled with artwork offered up to the glory of the Dead.

When the Sunday show was over, he would drive her to his two-bedroom house outside Anaheim. Where he kept a collection of World War II souvenirs, but did not keep a single picture of his first wife in any of the drawers or closets, and where they played gin in endless tournaments. Where they would live together until the next shows, she cleaning house and playing tapes.

All of this he told me the during three nights of the Long Beach shows, and I wondered that Sonjee, unmarked, desirable, lived with this man and slept with him in his Anaheim house, took him inside herself and put herself inside of him.

But I asked him only whether he thought plumbing of a sufficient vastness might not develop the resonance of intelligence, especially when controlled in sequence with climate and bodies. I talked of Shows that we would cross the country to see, outdoor shows in the Saratoga Performing Arts Center of Upstate New York, where he would not be separated from Sonjee and I would be able to see the Dead under an open sky. Edward looked pessimistic, dubious. He would scan the crowd bleakly, and then stare in the distance, across a chain-link fence and a loud city-street, at the Arena, the moon full over it like an incandescent bulb. His distaste included everything laid out before him, a patient, slow repugnance.

I left and came back with an old plastic bag full of cooked brown rice and held it out to him. He looked at it hanging in my hand like Medusa's head and looked back at the Arena, and I knew that in his mind Sonjee was on a cool marble slab, her tanned arms drawn up behind her head and her unshaven ankles held by the strong hands of college men who carpenter in Aspen and in Virginia and sink swimming pool foundations in Carmel. As the Dead played over her.

The Steamboat Springs Shows

Of the Long Beach friends, Rebecca and James went on with us to Colorado, after James and I had helped Edward to disconnect the wet bar that stood between the crushed velvet back seat and the Captain's chair behind the driver's seat. Edward worked with smoldering irritation, confused anger that part of the vehicle which he had purchased for Sonjee should be cast off so that strangers might ride to another state to hear the Dead play three nights in a row of music undeniably the same as that they had heard for three nights in Long Beach. But his shoulders and back showed the enjoyment he had in twisting a wrench again, and he heaved the wet bar out of the limo door with a single grunt and thrust like passing a medicine ball. Rust flakes and water trickled from the interior fitting to the maroon carpet, soaking the fiber, and Edward smoothly threaded a brass piece to it, sealed it almost absentmindedly.

I traded the bar to a Cooperative, twenty-six men and women, camped in a bus behind us; I got twelve cassette tapes, bootleg Dead recordings from 1981 to 1986, a French bayonet which I gave to Edward, and a huge skin of a bear which one of the women in the Cooperative had shot through the heart near the Canadian border in the state of Washington. Rebecca and James found the music of the Dead an aphrodisiac and while we traveled they were very free in their touching of one another beneath the bearskin rug. I rode in the hollow left by the wet bar, watching Edward and Sonjee argue wordlessly by the light of an occasional overpass.

Just inside Colorado, she lay her head in his lap and he caught my open eye in the mirror before looking away. Palpable as the heat from Rebecca and James beneath the bearskin, I felt Edward's silent, resolute desire to jettison everything behind the driver's seat, everything unconnected to the gold head under his fingers, the pallid eyelid beneath his thumb. I finally slept, and bumped awake with a sick fear that he had taken the bayonet from beneath his seat and sawed the motor-half of the limousine free, leaving my bearskin-half to slow and wedge in sand, open to the night wind.

And it was so, that the Colorado Shows were the Shows at which I kissed Sonjee. Touched my tongue to hers, feeling something as cold as novocaine in my chest and a displeased, outer awareness of my hand coming to circle the back of her neck, her head moving forward with such subtlety that I could see her tongue glisten with reflected lights beneath the plum of her lower lip. Edward was gone to buy her mushrooms; she had a few hours earlier eaten the last dry caps, sharing out all that remained with Rebecca and James and me in a fit of Saturday night jubilation.

When she came limping back to the limo only one hour into the Saturday show, I had on a tape of November 1985 from the Meadowlands of New Jersey and I put her shivering body under the bearskin rug and started the motor, turned the heat dial to a picture of a genderless figure lying with an arrow pointed at its chest. Hot air filled the car, and she and I might have been in the Meadowlands, stuck out in the cold post-development waste of New Jersey, in a box seat. She was lying beside the captain's chair under the skin, her feet curled up so as not to trail in the cold well left by the wet bar. Only her face showed above the bulk of black bear fur. The moment was an outcropping of immediacy: we were both alive, both shivering.

She knew the concert playing on the cassette deck, and began to repeat the place and date over to herself, driving it like a piton into her mind, to hold on to. She reached out and grasped my arm just below the elbow.

I kissed her and as her tongue passed from her softly freckled mouth into my own, I knew that she was the daughter of a wealthy suburban contractor who finished kitchen cabinets with stain-proof linoleum, that she had thrown her virginity away like a graduation cap, that she would fly a second time to Egypt if the Dead chose again to play before the Pyramids, that at my age she would be married to a man other than Edward, someone nonchalant who would tell company of the years during which Sonjee pursued a musical group across the country and lived with an old plumber. She would leave Edward by plane, after a Sunday show on the other side of the country from his house, leave him with the used limousine. It was pressing your lips against a cold crystal ball, more a reading of chilled tea leaves than a kiss. Never repeated.

She shivered and slept. I climbed forward into the driver's seat and looked out the wrap-around windshield, searching for Edward's blunt, round body among the people selling crystals, and the artists boring into the antlers of deer to make pipes. Finally, I got out of the car and walked the lot looking for him. The colors I saw were profound, but no one that I asked had seen Edward.

I found him hours later on a small dusthill at the edge of the lot, overlooking the bright white circle of the auditorium, intent, saddened, uncomprehending. He stood looking at the security guards and cruising helicopters, the banners tied from column to column, snapping taut in the wind. Like some savage peering through pre-England trees at the high, closed culture of the Romans. The music played from inside, faintly, never cresting and never finishing. No one would sell him mushrooms; they were suspicious of his age and of his blue, bellied-out windbreaker, the sort that policemen wear...I wanted to take his head in my hands and press my lips to the cold baldness of it and pass on the vision I had from the lips of the young woman in the back of his used limousine. Instead, I took the three twenties he gave me and looked around until I found a small bag for the money, so as not to shame him with both a score and a bargain.

Late, confusingly late that night and halfway across Colorado, Sonjee threw up on the black vinyl mat lining the passenger compartment. Edward pulled over immediately, and his door struck a sign reading *Open Range Cattle Grazing Next 50 Miles*. Rebecca and James never came out from beneath the skin. Edward held her head, in the weeds off the road, and I cleaned the mess in the front seat with the napkins Sonjee kept in the glovebox beneath piles of condiments. Dead music filtered out of the speakers. I took the dripping napkin clumps fifty or sixty feet out into the scrub and threw them down behind a thorn bush, and thought about the vomit that Sonjee said she had left on the concrete walks approaching the Great Pyramid at Giza, and about how similar must have been the Egyptian reactions to my own, despite the fact that altogether different versions of the same songs were playing then and now.

The Chicago Shows

Just before the Friday show Rebecca and James bought an entire library of bootleg recordings from a slick-haired boy of sixteen or seventeen. I could look at his see-through eyes and know that he had stolen the recordings from some couple nearly twice his age who lived near or on the campus of the University of Chicago. There were rows and rows of tapes, in custom-built crates that had once held fruit and produce. All neatly labeled, first in a male script and then in alternating male and female, their romance beginning sometime after the Virginia Beach shows of 1989. Rebecca and James paid with starchy bills that they had teased from a large machine, as an advance against Rebecca's MasterCard, earlier that day.

Sonjee and Rebecca and James spent almost an hour, after having eaten their caps, pointing to the small plastic boxes and asking one another if they remembered the shows inside them. Edward was outside, leaning into the grill of the limo. His back was straight, and I could see that he was pointedly ignoring the nods of passing deadheads. He and Sonjee had fought openly the night before, in the parking lot of a Chicago polish sausage stand. Edward always backing off from the ultimatums that burst from his thick chest, always reaching out for her with his pipefitter's hands.

I got out and told him that I was going to try to see the show that night, told him I felt good about the Stadium. He looked at me, down at my tie-dyed shin, looked away. I was just another of the lame followers to him then, and I could see he hated me for paying my way with a credit card with only one name on it, a name he thought untrue, and for the fact that I could leave and chose to stay. We left him standing and smoking, like a chauffeur.

The stadium was no problem for me. The dancers twirling level upon level, up to the artificial sky of the dome, seemed individually motivated and I felt no fear of the air ducts or the concessions spilling out simple foods in perfect, bland order, or the lines of men and women standing in line to use a tiled stall in the lower levels. But I pictured Edward alone at the limo surrounded by people he did not understand, listening to strains of music he knew by heart but had never respected enough to learn the titles or the words. I left Sonjee and Rebecca and James dancing, all of them dancing with their eyes closed and their arms looping.

When I got back to the car, Edward looked up from a map he was studying by flashlight. A fugitive look of welcome before he went back to tracing the complex veins and arteries that connect Chicago with the next stop. I clambered up on the roof of the limo, and he gave me a glance, not seeming to mind. I asked him if he'd eaten yet. At the other edge of the lot, somebody aimed a flare gun at the moon. A bass Thomp! and the sky over us was a red noon. I said that I was anxious to get to the summer shows, the outdoor shows, when the five of us could stay together.

And then suddenly he had the flashlight pointed at my eyes, and was shouting up questions: "Who the hell are you? Did you faint at the sight of a big stadium again? What do you do in your life, boy, do you work, do you have a wife you son of a bitch, or do you just eat rice and listen to that goddamn music?" He was trying for friendly bullying, but there was a tight, frantic note in it as well. As though he'd had too much confusion, too many givens he couldn't understand. The light from his hand came straight at me like a needle, and as it grew brighter with the fading of the overhead flare, I took the credit card from my wallet, held it out in front of me to shield my eyes.

He yelled up for me to hand down my wallet, he was sick to death of driving around somebody he didn't know from Adam and who would only show a credit card. I moved away from his reaching hands, scooting back and forth on the roof as he circled the car. He was a fairly short man and after a minute or two he began to jump beside the car, adding a few inches to his reach. Even so his hands never grazed me. Dust rose thinly around us. It was a frustrating game for him, and he was winded in a few minutes, bent over with his hands on his thighs. He shut himself into the driver's seat with a strong slam of the door. I jumped into the stream of colored clothing passing behind the car.

Not long after, I came back with a plastic bag full of pork-fried rice, and got into the passenger seat. Edward still looked surly, but when he saw that there was meat in the offering, he accepted a pair of chopsticks and began scissoring it into his mouth, the bag resting damply on the leather seat. He told me that he had learned to use chopsticks in the Philippines while he was in the Air Force. He told me that he had been there for six years, and that in the Philippines there were some weird goddamn things, but nothing like the tribe outside the car. I giggled. There was plenty of room in the front seat for us to turn and face one another. It was a casual moment. He asked me where I lived, lightly, amiably. I took out the credit card, and snapped on the small directional map light above us so that there would be no mistake.

Later, when Edward and I were standing and sculling our shoes in the dust of the lot, Sonjee came back with Sunday night passes for Providence. Two of them, astonishingly simple documents, admitting one each to spend the concert behind the stage, and later to drink champagne and to carry fine cheeses about on crackers with the Dead. I wondered not how she got them, but why she didn't have them every night. They were like silk and Swiss chocolate during the last World War, fine rare lures. I took the passes from her, to look at closely, and in their stiff stamped lengths I could feel the offer that had been made to her through them, by some man who had seen her dancing and had danced with her, watching the gentle rippling of her paisley skirt. But also ringing those backstage passes was her refusal, her true innocent surprise when they were given to her anyway.

She offered the second pass to Edward first, sliding her arms about his neck and then jumping unexpectedly up to twine her skirt-wrapped legs around his big waist. He hugged her quickly to keep her from falling, without bothering to look at the deadheads milling and staring all around him. He was happy. He hadn't expected to be offered his chance to refuse.

The Providence Shows

Sonjee and Rebecca sat cross-legged in the back of the limo, facing one another, anointing one another, threading gold and copper chains through the shining braids they made of one another's hair. Their smiles were vague and expectant, and the whole interior compartment took on the smugness of brides. They were mystically precise in selecting tapes for the stereo: this year, that month, in this town set down before this mountain, the Friday night show. They had told some people in our row about the passes. People brought small, bound messages for them to deliver, and flowers. A coffee-skinned man in a turban brought them mushrooms with the bulbous heads and attenuated stems of a daddy-longlegs spider.

When they followed the crowd out under the dusk, James squiring them, I watched from the top of the limo. I watched them cross fences and a wide city street. Edward was in the driver's seat, sunk in a detective novel. Night fell, and cooking fires came up. I ate three tail-stemmed mushrooms as though they were candy canes, breaking them piece by long piece. We could hear the music from the concert over the noise of traffic. Skyscrapers leaned over the Civic Center, and helicopters moved between them with the quickness and the rapacity of locusts. Edward called to me from the cab of the limo. I hung my head down into his window. He had the map light on, and was studying a white, Xeroxed poster with a dark picture on it. He held it up toward his open window, toward my hanging face. *Missing. Last Seen Forum, Inglewood, California, Five Foot Eleven, Blond Hair, Brown Eyes, Please Forward Information Concerning This Man.* There was a Los Angeles number to call. This is you, Edward said.

I slid off the roof and came around to the passenger side. I leaned over the seat and reached my duffel bag from behind the captain's chair. I piled my clothes on the carpet until I came to the pile of posters at the bottom of the bag. Found at the odd show here or there, stuck to a camper, posted by unseen hands on a concrete auditorium wall. I handed the stack to him, and he shuffled through them, reading my small notations on their blank backs, which days of which shows I had found each. He handed them back to me calmly. These are all you, he said, and he might have been my high school principal the way he laid them on the seat between us. A tired, good man.

I snapped off the maplight. A black, almost confessional second. Edward, I whispered, there is something I have to tell you. At some Sunday show Sonjee will leave you, she'll board a plane with no luggage, but with tapes in her pockets. She will play those tapes on the plane back across the country, on the same small portable tape player that she wore the day you met her. That will be her last concert. She will marry a young man with black, black brows that match the blackness of a beard he allows to grow from Friday morning until seven o'clock the following Monday. He will be athletic and have a temper. Her marriage to him will face 180 degrees from the part of her life where you drive this limousine and wait for her to come back.

Edward looked at me for a moment, and then he hunched forward and turned the key in the ignition. The dash display began to glow. Dead music played from the Spring of 1977. He reached around his back and thumbed a switch. My door lock shot down.

"Now you show me that wallet, or we will go to war, the two of us," Edward said softly. He uncrossed his thick arms. The small fires burned in the lot outside the windshield. I handed him the wallet. He opened it, stretched its thick leather folds, taking out ripped ticket after ticket, small piles of them in each compartment, pulling them out with a certain disgust. He filled the seat between us with them. I reached for one of the moisture-smudged stubs and he slapped my hand back, knocking a small pile to the vinyl mat where it separated in the dark, an invisible geography. There was only the credit card, finally, and the wallet resting stupid and empty on the seat.

"These are me," I began to say and James was suddenly beating heavily on the driver's-side window with one fist and holding up Sonjee's bruised face and Rebecca wouldn't wait but pulled the door open, driving in the smell of the campfires and the staring of the crowd. Edward thrust forward his hands to receive Sonjee's small head and unmoving torso. He pulled her carefully up over his lap, gathering up her legs. Between the two of us we passed her body to the rear compartment, and laid her on the cigarette-burned carpet, covered her with the heavy bearskin, while James and Rebecca talked hysterically, jabbering like parrots: *One of the bouncers, a big man, the man who had given Sonjee the passes in Chicago, he said that there was a room just behind the stage where the music would be so close, so very close, where they would wait for the Dead, the Dead wanted to meet Sonjee, not Rebecca, just her, just the room next door where they would wait for the Dead to finish, Sonjee was to go and meet the Dead.*

We could still hear the drifting music from across the street, competing with our own sounds in the dark space. Sonjee slept, her small teeth chattering at the level of a whisper. I had my head on the carpet, listening to Rebecca still talking about the big man who had brought Sonjee back, who had taken the two of them to a rear exit and pushed them out among a throng of autograph seekers, and wrenched the door shut behind him, when I heard the front door of the limo open and smelled the fires. I pushed my face to the fogged rear window and saw Edward close with the crowd, pass into it.

I crawled to the front seat, I followed him. His blue windbreaker would appear in a break in the crowd and then someone would push a sign in my face *Kind Veggie Sandwiches* or *I Need a Miracle* and I would lose him, his stocky form thrusting quickly through the vendors and the colors like a bulldog. My balance was somehow hurt, and I kicked jewelry from spread blankets. I saw him waiting with a crowd for the light at the six lane street fronting the auditorium. I yelled his name and my voice sounded flat and recorded and odd in my own ears. You don't even know his name! I screamed at him. You don't know at what level he works, in which row! Which entrance does he work! Young people stood in T-shirts all around me and stared, first at me, then at Edward. Cars flowed in front of me in perfect synch, without interval, at forty miles an hour. And then Edward forced a break on the other side and sprinted heavily across. He ran up to the concrete ramps that led to the entrance. My knees felt as though they would buckle, and I passed my arms around the smooth pole which supported the light.

And it was so, that when the light signaled green for me to go, and the six lanes of cars had braked in a perfect row before me, I saw a large van with a warning light pass and a helicopter drop toward the entrances, both moving calmly and directly and both with radios playing the same garbled voice out of the same static. Both had loudspeakers from which they requested the crowd to part, and this parting was smooth and economical, a neat halving of the bright colors of the crowd. Vans and helicopters and partings of the crowd such as I had seen in civic organisms endlessly configured. In municipal complexes strung out on a national tour like the irregular spotting of a bacterial culture, with every attribute of life, that of breathing, those of irritability and of evacuating waste, that of reproducing themselves through endless cultural stirrings that ended always in growth. And this van and this helicopter of Providence were converging on a spot where identical large men in security T-shirts were holding something small between them. Then the spotlight from the helicopter shone down as knowingly as a dentist's lamp, and black-and-white policemen merged with the security men and they passed the small figure between them, and a tinier reflected flash that must have been the bayonet which rested for a year beneath the driver's seat of a used limousine and was destined to become a part of a private collection of war souvenirs. I saw the figure passed into the van, followed by two men as stiff as centurions with visored helmets, and I saw the doors of the van close and the van move to the six lane street, where an emergency light began to flash yellow, smoothly stopping the flow of automobiles, and I fell to the concrete sidewalk. As my head touched the coldness, I could see Sonjee's plane leaving the airport in the morning, queuing up with other oversized aircraft on a lighted concrete strip, perfectly on schedule, with Sonjee stunned and cradled within it, cool air spraying from a plastic nipple onto her face.

There was no inside for me to fear anymore. I saw that clear as colors. Because there was no outside, and had not been for many years, and I continue to walk among you to tell you without ceasing that this is so, my brothers and sisters in the Dead.

The final summer tour preceding Garcia's death on August 9, 1995, was a chaotic and dark series of events, which included a near-riot and gate crashing incident, some fans being struck by lightning, and the collapse of a structure in a campground occupied by Deadheads. There were rumors of threats on Garcia's life. When the inevitable happened, the press weighed in heavily, with columnists like George Will adamantly insisting that Garcia got what he had coming to him, even as many in the political arena suddenly professed to be closet Deadheads. I like to think that Garcia would have been amused.

Much of the resulting writing, though, turned out to be very insightful, giving writers an opportunity to summarize both Garcia's career, and the career of the band as a whole, often from a very personal standpoint.

The *New Yorker*'s coverage of the Grateful Dead, over the years, amounted to no more than six articles. Three of them appear in this anthology–an indication of the generally high quality of writing in that venerable institution of a magazine. Hal Espen's pithy and on-target eulogy for Garcia from the August 21, 1995, issue, gets at the heart of the contradictions of the guitarist's life, and is both affectionate and dispassionate. Espen was born in San Francisco and graduated from the University of California at Berkeley. He attended a number of Grateful Dead concerts in the 1970s before decamping to New York in 1980 and joining the staff of the *New Yorker*, where he eventually became a fiction editor, senior editor, and frequent contributor. Since 1996, he has worked at Santa Fe–based *Outside* magazine, and in 1999 he was appointed editor.

American Beauty

The Grateful Dead's Burly, Beatific Alchemist

Hal Espen

As word of the death of Jerry Garcia spread last Wednesday, via news reports and phone calls and E-mail, the scale of the reaction and the depth of the response quickly surpassed what anyone might have expected. It was suddenly obvious that Garcia had become, against all odds, an American icon: by Thursday morning, the avuncular old reprobate had smuggled his way onto the front pages of newspapers around the world. That his battered, ruined body had finally given out was somehow less surprising than the abrupt recognition of how much he had meant to so many. He was eulogized as a rock star and as a guitar god, of course; he was praised as a businessman who marketed his mystique both shrewdly and generously; and, in the obituaries that recounted the intermittent struggles with addiction that preceded his demise, at the age of fifty-three, in a Marin County drug-rehabilitation center, he was inevitably, and with some justice, pronounced a casualty of drug abuse. But Jerry Garcia was a more graceful and complicated figure than those categories can encompass: he transcended show business, and it's impossible, even now, to think of him as a victim or a sad case. The choices he made in life, whatever their ultimate cost to him, command respect. He was a lyrical hipster, an outlaw with a sense of humor, a fount of profound pleasure for tens of millions of people.

He started his extraordinary career as a bad boy in the classroom ("I was a wise guy, I talked too much, I spoke out of turn, and I was a notorious underachiever," he told an interviewer in 1989) and graduated to become a hood on the streets of San Francisco. In the late fifties, he joined the Army to avoid jail (the reverse of what some of his fans would do a decade later), was discharged after a few months, and wound up living in a car and playing low-end folk gigs in clubs and coffeehouses around Palo Alto. It was a fateful place and time: Beat culture was mixing with pop culture, and the Bay Area's perpetual party was on the verge of being hijacked by the novelist-provocateur Ken Kesey and his band of Merry Pranksters, who spiked the punch with a stash of LSD that had been liberated from local research laboratories. Garcia and his friends went to see "A Hard Day's Night" and metamorphosed from a jug band into a rock band. In 1965, the newly psychedelicized Garcia opened a dictionary of folklore and alighted on the phrase "grateful dead," and his group, having adopted the name, began playing at a series of Acid Test gatherings: wild, euphoric, Dadaist affairs that celebrated noise, nonsense, and open-ended improvisation. Those acid-fuelled evenings became the inspiration and the model for the next three decades of Grateful Dead concerts, each of which sought to invoke, in some measure, the crazed, beatific spirit of the Acid Tests.

Amid the chaos, Garcia managed to project a casual authority, and his crystalline lead guitar enhanced the alchemist's aura that he gradually acquired. (For a long time, Deadheads called him Captain Trips, a title he disliked.) Onstage, he was a stolid, impassive, faintly Buddha-like presence, but in conversation he turned out to be a street philosopher with a keen wit and a taste for the absurd. Despite, or because of, all the drugs, he was a lucid, articulate raconteur and spokesman. What he was a spokesman *for* was not exactly clear (and, in any case, he disavowed the role). The Grateful Dead seemed to be the ultimate hippie band, but its members, and Garcia in particular, were far more sardonic and tough-minded than the flower children who wafted into their concerts. The Dead were independent, apolitical, and free of self-dramatizing posturing, and their ornery edge was one of the secrets of their longevity.

Garcia was both starry-eyed and impish about the first blush of the psychedelic subculture he helped bring into being, but there was also a touch of cruelty in his outlook. He loved to tell stories about the first Trips Festival, which was held in San Francisco's Longshoremen's Hall in 1966. It took place "right down on Fisherman's Wharf, near where all the tourists are," Garcia once told a radio interviewer. "People came in total drag—the parking lot was full of cars painted Day-Glo colors, and all kinds of crazy things. Nobody had seen any of this stuff before, this was all *brand-new*. One of my vivid recollections is seeing this old friend of mine, who was stoned out of his head on God knows how many tabs of acid, and he was running down the street stopping tourists and sticking tabs of acid into their mouths, making them take acid, forcing them to take it." He laughed his smoker's half-choked laugh at the memory. "It was crazy, outrageous. There were women running around naked, and Hell's Angels, and every kind of weird thing. Nobody had ever seen this stuff before. The straight people had not seen it. It was like taking Martians and dropping them right into 1957."

It *is* funny, but the slightly chilly indifference to the reality that some people did not (and do not) survive the Acid Test was a characteristic that persisted throughout the history of the Grateful Dead. Yet it was an honest indifference: the imagery of death's-heads and skeletons and matter-of-fact mortality ("If the thunder don't get you then the lighting will," as Garcia's song "The Wheel" puts it) was right on the surface, and the band carried on with a minimum of angst through the passing of three earlier members. Garcia was unwilling to condemn even heroin. "It's tough for me to adopt a totally anti-drug stance," he said in 1989. "For me, it was like taking a vacation while I was still working, in a way. I was on for eight years. It was long enough to find out everything I needed to know about it, and that was it." Evidently Garcia was unable to maintain that kind of detachment until the end.

In spite of these dark tints, Jerry Garcia's legacy is overwhelmingly positive. Grateful Dead tours became an American institution, a travelling Chautauqua of eclectic musicianship and communal, cross-generational joy. For every show that fizzled out into noodling mediocrity, there were two or three that sheltered the audience in a beneficent rainbow of great rock and roll. In the future, those who will come to know the Grateful Dead only through their recordings may wonder what all the fuss was about; the Dead's most original creation, after all, was the gestalt of their concerts—the belongingness that enveloped their audience and made it as central to their music as their very voices and instruments. If something so evanescent could be put in a museum, an evening with the Grateful Dead would warrant a place of honor in the Smithsonian. But what was best about the band cannot, by its nature, be preserved, and that gives Garcia's passing a special sting. With his death, only the gratefulness remains.

Trying to select which of the many obituaries to include in this reader was a difficult task. Perhaps someday someone should just go and put together an entire book of the articles written about Garcia in the two months following August 9, 1995. Mary Eisenhart's obituary published in *BAM*, August 25, 1995, set as it is in the context of the Golden Gate Park memorial, is particularly appropriate, and bittersweet.

Obituary

Jerry Garcia

1942-1995

Mary Eisenhart

The phone rang a little after dawn this morning. Fred, an English Deadhead I hadn't seen in eight years, was calling to convey the Brits' condolences to the Yanks. I told him the memorial in Golden Gate Park had been beautiful, but that once Bob Weir started weeping in mid-eulogy, the truth was inescapable.

In England, Fred said, they'd gathered for their regularly scheduled monthly Deadfest. They'd played the newly arrived tapes of Garcia's last show with the Dead, at Chicago's Soldier Field on July 9th. They'd shared their memories. And then they'd played "Ripple," Garcia's voice sweet and strong:

> You who choose to lead must follow
> But if you fall, you fall alone
> If you should stand, then who's to guide you?
> If I knew the way, I would take you home.

Whatever you say about Jerry Garcia—and the next months are sure to bring Rashomon-like tales of love, brilliance, generosity, and self-destruction—he wasn't interested in following anyone, and he wasn't about to be anybody's leader. Not the Grateful Dead's, and not the Deadheads'. There was a big crazy universe out there and he was too busy checking it out.

True, he could convince you in about six notes that jumping off this musical cliff with him and the guys was the best possible thing you could do. True, a few hours with him and the guys could leave you questioning the entire course of your life to that point and revising it drastically. But you had to figure it out for yourself: nobody could do it for you. And if Jerry Garcia couldn't stop his adoring audience from making him an icon in absentia, he made it clear that he was nobody's guru.

"I know better, you know?" he laughed when we did an interview in 1987. "You know yourself for the asshole that you are; you know yourself for the person who makes mistakes, and that's capable of being *really stupid*, and doing stupid things. I don't know who you'd have to be to believe that kind of stuff about yourself, to believe that you were somehow special. If I start believing that kind of stuff, everybody's going to just turn around and walk away from me. Nobody would let me get away with it, not for a minute. That's the strength of having a group.

"For me it's easier to believe a group than it is a person. Certainly one of the things that makes the Grateful Dead interesting, from my point of view, is that it's a *group* of people. The dynamics of the group is the part that I trust."

Garcia's death on August 9th was surely the worst blow the group has sustained in its 30-year history, and the Dead's future—to say nothing of the future of the Deadheads—remains an open question. But, as Garcia said in 1987, "Remember who we are? We are in reality a group of misfits, crazy people, who have voluntarily come together to work this stuff out and do the best we can, and try to be as fair as we possibly can with each other. And just struggle through life."

Drummer Mickey Hart drew wild applause from the assembled Golden Gate Park mourners, when he said, "If the Grateful Dead did anything, we gave you the power. You take it home and do something with it. We didn't do this for nothing."

But when Garcia's daughter Annabelle added that as we move through life's trials we should ask ourselves "What would Jerry do?" the guy next to me muttered, "Yeah, and do the opposite!"

No point turning the man into a role model now that he's not here to defend himself.

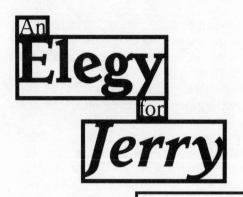

An Elegy for Jerry

Robert Hunter

Jerry, my friend,
you've done it again,
even in your silence
the familiar pressure
comes to bear, demanding
I pull words from the air
with only this morning
and part of the afternoon
to compose an ode worthy
of one so particular
about every turn of phrase,
demanding it hit home
in a thousand ways
before making it his own,
and this I can't do alone.
Now that the singer is gone,
where shall I go for the song?

Without your melody and taste
to lend an attitude of grace
a lyric is an orphan thing,
a hive with neither honey's taste
nor power to truly sting.

What choice have I but to dare and
call your muse who thought to rest
out of the thin blue air

that out of the field of shared time,
a line or two might chance to shine—

As ever when we called,
in hope if not in words,
the muse descends.

How should she desert us now?
Scars of battle on her brow,
bedraggled feathers on her wings,
and yet she sings, she sings!

May she bear thee to thy rest,
the ancient bower of flowers
beyond the solitude of days,
the tyranny of hours—
the wreath of shining laurel lie
upon your shaggy head
bestowing power to play the lyre
to legions of the dead.

If some part of that music
is heard in deepest dream,
or on some breeze of Summer
a snatch of golden theme,
we'll know you live inside us
with love that never parts
our good old Jack O'Diamonds
become the King of Hearts.

I feel your silent laughter
at sentiments so bold
that dare to step across the line
to tell what must be told,
so I'll just say I love you,
which I never said before
and let it go at that old friend
the rest you may ignore.

Blair Jackson's excellent biography of Jerry Garcia appeared in August 1999. What is clear from this article, which documents Garcia's career as a guitarist specifically, is that Jackson's overview of Garcia as an artist is sweeping, and at the same time very attentive to detail. Certainly the following piece, which appeared in *Guitar World*, November 1995, amidst a plethora of articles in the months immediately following Garcia's death, is a succinct, enlightening tribute to a man who said he only hoped to be remembered as "a competent guitarist."

American Beauty

Blair Jackson

orget for a moment the dilapidated vw vans plastered with colorful decals and bumper stickers. Forget the legions of long-haired, tie-dye-wearing, pot- and patchouli-scented fans lost in that formless, serpentine dance-trance. Forget the smiling picture of "Captain Trips," resplendent in an American flag hat and paisley velour shirt. Instead, *listen*.

Listen to the crystalline notes as they ascend in a bright spiral, then blast into deep space, scattering like cosmic debris. Listen to the melancholy cry of six strings singing about life and death, love and loss, memory and regret. Listen to the joyous dance of life in a thousand buoyant strums and bright melodic filigrees. Ten years, 20 years, 50 years from now, it's going to be Jerry Garcia's music—and not the day-glo Deadhead sideshow—that most people will remember.

The clichés come so easily: "counter-culture guru," "rock legend," "Pied Piper of the Haight," "tragic outlaw figure," etc. There is truth in all of these. But when the day is done, Jerry Garcia was really just a working guy who loved to play music. Celebrity and deification were unfortunate byproducts and distractions for this gentle, self-effacing man whose strongest addiction was music, not drugs, and whose legacy is a body of music that is breathtaking in its scope.

The Grateful Dead's music was a crazy-quilt of different styles and influences: They drew from folk, bluegrass, old-timey, blues, r&b, ragtime, rock and roll, modern classical, jazz, Indian, electronic and just about any other style you'd care to name. Their musical heroes were people like the Beatles, Bach, Bob Dylan, John Coltrane, Bill Monroe, Howlin' Wolf, Merle Haggard, Ornette Coleman, Stravinsky, Chuck Berry, Edgar Varese and Willie Dixon, and they wore their influences proudly—at the same time as they assimilated those influences, improvised around them, and magically blended them into their own thoroughly original amalgam. Where does a song like "Help on the Way" come from? "Tennessee Jed"? "China Doll"? "Days Between"? These are unique slices of the Dead's peculiar oeuvre, impossible to categorize precisely except to say that they are Grateful Dead Music, with all that implies.

Even outside of the Dead, Garcia's appetite for music was voracious and all-consuming. The Jerry Garcia Band's repertoire came from Motown and Trenchtown, Chicago blues and Southern gospel, Irving Berlin and Mick Jagger, Hoagy Carmichael and Van Morrison. Then there was the acoustic music he played with mandolinist David Grisman: old mountain tunes, sea shanties, ageless ballads, a few Dead tunes and cool jazz numbers like Miles Davis' "So What" and Milt Jackson's "Bags' Groove." In the last year of his life alone, Garcia's studio work included adding guitar to a song on fellow-traveler and occasional GD member Bruce Hornsby's latest album (*Hot House*), cutting a version of the venerable pop standard "Smoke Gets in Your Eyes" with the Garcia Band for the superb film *Smoke* (directed by Wayne Wang, a one-time Garcia roadie); incomplete tracking on a new Dead album, and, in what was his last session, laying down "Blue Yodel #9" for an upcoming Jimmie Rodgers tribute album. Who knows what other irons were in the fire at the time of Garcia's sad demise?

Garcia grew up in San Francisco and lived his entire life in Northern California. He was named after composer Jerome Kern and was the son of a clarinetist and band leader, Joe Garcia, whose drowning death during a family vacation was witnessed by a five-year-old Jerry. Around the same time, he lost part of the middle finger on his right hand when his older brother Clifford accidentally hit it with an axe. His mother Ruth remarried and tried to pick up the pieces for Jerry and Clifford, running a San Francisco bar frequented primarily by sailors and soldiers.

"I grew up in a musical household and took piano lessons as far back as I can remember," Garcia said in a 1993 interview. "The first time I decided that music was something I wanted to do, apart from just being surrounded by it,

Giants Stadium, June 18, 1995. © Susana Millman, 1999

was when I was about 15. I developed this deep craving to play the electric guitar.

"I fell madly in love with rock and roll. Chuck Berry was happening big. Elvis Presley...I really liked Gene Vincent; the *other* rock guys, the guys that played guitar good: Eddie Cochran, Buddy Holly, Bo Diddley. At the same time, the r&b stations were playing stuff like Lightnin' Hopkins and Frankie Lee Sims, these funky blues guys. Jimmy McCracklin, the Chicago-style blues guys, the T-Bone Walker-influenced guys, that older style, pre-B.B. King. Jimmy Reed actually had *hits* back in those days. You listen to that and it's so funky. It's just a beautiful sound, but I had no idea how to go about learning it.

"When I first heard electric guitar, when I was 15, that's what I wanted to play. I petitioned my mom to get me one, so she finally did for my birthday. Actually, she got me an accordion and I went nuts—'Agggghh, no, no, no!' I railed and raved, and she finally turned it in, and I got a pawnshop [Dan-electro] electric guitar and an amplifier. I was beside myself with joy.

"I started banging away on it without having the slightest idea of *anything*. I didn't know how to tune it up; I had no idea. My stepfather tuned it in some weird way, like an open chord...I played it that way for about a year before I finally ran into a kid at school who could actually play a little. He showed me a few basic chords, and that was it. I never took any lessons. I don't even think there was anybody teaching around the Bay Area. The electric guitar was like from Mars, you know. You didn't see 'em even."

While still in high school, Garcia decided to pursue his interest in drawing and painting, and this indirectly led to a shift in his musical interests. "I was an art student at the California School of Fine Art, which is now the San Francisco Art Institute, and I was taking a Saturday class, and my teacher played a four-string banjo and a little guitar," Garcia said in 1991. "[One day] he was playing a Big Bill Broonzy record. I was 16 or 17...I knew what it was but I'd never heard anyone play blues on an acoustic guitar, and it knocked me out."

Garcia dropped out of high school and enlisted in the Army, hoping to perhaps see more of the world. Instead he was stationed at San Francisco's Presidio, where he quickly learned that heavy discipline and regimentation were not for him: he went AWOL several times, and felt more at home hanging out in San Francisco's North Beach area—then still the center for the once-thriving Beat culture—than in his barracks. About the only positive aspect of being in the Army for him was that he met a few people who turned him onto country guitar styles.

"After I got out of the Army," he said in 1990, "I fell in with [future songwriting partner Robert] Hunter, and we were influenced by the folk scare—the Kingston Trio and that kind of stuff. I didn't know how to find my way into that kind of music 'til I met some people who were more involved with it, like Marshall Lester, who was a friend of mine from when I was 10 to 13. By now he was a college guy, and he turned me on to bluegrass music and old-time string band music. He played a little frailing banjo and introduced me to the [blues fingerstylist] Reverend Gary Davis. I heard that sound and I just had to be able to make it."

Garcia moved to the Peninsula (south of San Francisco) and lived hand-to-mouth a few years, practicing the banjo and guitar night and day and playing in a succession of local string bands with fanciful names like the Thunder Mountain Tub Thumpers, the Sleepy Hollow Hog Stompers and the Black Mountain Boys. The endless hours of woodshedding in this wholly acoustic musical environment paid dividends that served Garcia for the rest of his career. His lifelong love of the clearly articulated note came in part from his passion for the banjo. And his devotion to improvisation was fueled by watching great country and bluegrass players.

"I get my improvisational approach from Scotty Stoneman, the fiddle player, who is the first guy who first set me on fire—where I just stood there and don't remember breathing," Garcia recalled in 1991. "He was just an incredible fiddler. He grew up in bars and was a total alcoholic wreck by the time I heard him, playing with the Kentucky Colonels [*featuring noted flat-picker Clarence White—later to play with the Byrds—and mandolinist Roland White*]. I went down to hear him the first time at the Ash Grove in L.A. They did a medium-tempo fiddle tune, and it's going along, and pretty soon Scotty starts taking these longer and longer phrases—10 bars, 14 bars, 17 bars—and the guys in the band are just watching him! They're barely playing—going ding, ding, ding—while he's burning. The place was transfixed. They played this tune for like 20 minutes, which is unheard of in bluegrass.

"I'd never heard anything like it. I asked him later, 'How do you do that?' and he said, 'Man, I just play lonesome.' He probably died of drinking hair tonic; he was another one of those guys...But his playing on the records he appears on—is this incredible blaze. He's like the bluegrass Charlie Parker."

Garcia was so deep into bluegrass that he spent a month in 1964 traveling through the South and Midwest with his Black Mountain Boys bandmate Sandy Rothman, recording various bluegrass bands. When Garcia returned to the Bay Area, however, he joined together with a bunch of his musical friends and formed what was actually a less serious group than many he'd been involved with: Mother McCree's Uptown Jug Champions, which included a scary-looking but soulful teenage blues singer and harmonica player named Ron McKernan—who'd already been dubbed "Pigpen" for his unkempt appearance—and a 16-year old novice guitar player (actually a student of Garcia's at Dana Morgan's Palo Alto Music Shop) named Bob Weir. Also playing with the group from time to time were future Grateful Dead soundman Bob Matthews and David Parker, who was to become the group's financial associate. This rag-tag bunch played a cool mixture of folk, blues and jug-band numbers in local clubs, but by 1965 the Beatles had shown what fun being in a rock and roll band could be, Dylan had plugged in, and Pigpen was looking to get down with some amplified Chicago-style blues. Garcia, Weir and Pigpen recruited a young drummer named Bill Kreutzmann to join their new electric band, dubbed The Warlocks, and when Dana Morgan, Jr., son of the music store owner, couldn't quite cut it on bass, they brought in a one-time jazz trumpeter and "serious" music composer named Phil Lesh—even though he'd never played bass before.

The band cut its teeth playing small clubs, bars and even a pizza parlor down on the Peninsula, playing mainly r&b and blues covers, as well as a few amplified folk and jug tunes. They often played five sets a night and built their following slowly—first driving out the regular patrons with their skull-splitting volume and weirdly elongated tunes, then bringing in their own audience of misfits and thrill-seekers. Around the same time, The Warlocks hooked up with *One Flew Over the Cuckoo's Nest* author Ken Kesey and his commune, the Merry Pranksters, becoming the de facto house band at their LSD parties, the infamous Acid Tests. "It wasn't a gig, it was the Acid Test," Garcia once said, "Anything was OK. It was far-out, beautiful magic. We had no reputation and nobody was paying to see us or anything like that. We weren't the headliners, the event was. Anything that happened was part of it. There was always the option to not play...The freedom is what I loved about it. When you're high, you might want to play five hours, but sometimes you might want to stick your head in a bucket of water, or have some Jell-O or something."

The group had already been smoking pot for a while, but LSD, which was legal until October, 1966, is what really blew the doors open and influenced the band to stretch out in weirder directions. Garcia, the guitarist, was being influenced by a number of different artists during this period, from Mike Bloomfield, whose incendiary blues playing fueled the music of Dylan and Paul Butterfield, to saxophonist John Coltrane: "I never copped his licks or sat down, listened to his records and tried to play his stuff," Garcia told an inter-viewer in 1981. "I [*was*] impressed with the idea of flow, of making statements that sound like paragraphs—[*Coltrane would*] play along stylistically with a certain kind of tone, in a certain kind of syntax, for X amount of time, then change the subject and play along with this other personality coming out, perceptually, an idea that's been important to me in playing [*which also derives in part from Coltrane*] has been the whole odyssey idea—journeys, voyages, adventures along the way."

In December 1965, the Warlocks became the Grateful Dead and the group shifted its focus to San Francisco, where like-minded bohemians and psyche-delic pioneers were quickly turning the Haight-Ashbury district into a hip mini-city with its own music, businesses and support services. The Dead were just one of a slew of bands that lived in the area, but from the beginning they were among the most popular—always guaranteed to get the crowds that drifted in and out of the various San Francisco ballrooms up and dancing, whether it was with a 15-minute version of Martha and the Vandellas' Motown smash "Dancing in the Streets," a peppy rendition of Howlin' Wolf's "Sitting on Top of the World," or their half-hour workouts of Wilson Pickett's "Mid-night Hour," with Pigpen leading the charge. During this period and through the recording of the Dead's Warner Bros. debut album in early '67, Garcia played a red Guild Starfire, with a single cutaway and two pickups, through a Fender Twin Reverb amp. From the outset, Garcia's guitar style was marked by active motion in his left-hand fretwork—bending and shaping notes and dancing around the song's melody.

The band started writing its own material in earnest in late '67 and '68: this is the era that produced the ambitious "That's It for the Other One" (from *Anthem of the Sun*) and Garcia's first few collaborations with lyricist Robert Hunter, including "China Cat Sunflower," "Dark Star" and "St. Stephen." In '68 Garcia switched from the Guild to a Les Paul; then in '69 he moved on to a

Gibson SG, which he used to shape the classic Garcia sound heard on what remains the watermark of the Dead's most psychedelic period, 1969's *Live Dead*. This double album (now a single CD) showcases Garcia and the Dead at the height of their improvisational powers, as they boldly navigate through 21 minutes of intense instrumental exploration on "Dark Star"; build to one roiling, explosive climax after another on "The Eleven"; and rip through Bobby Bland's "Turn On Your Love Light" like some crazy, funky bar band on multiple hits of LSD-manufacturer Owsley Stanley's finest.

As the Sixties drew to a close, Garcia added to his already rich sonic palette by playing acoustic guitar with greater regularity (a number of 1970 Dead shows featured an acoustic set, as well as songs that blended acoustic and electric instruments), and tackling the pedal steel guitar (a ZB model) both with the Dead and the country-rock Dead offshoot the New Riders of the Purple Sage.

"What I'm doing with the steel is I'm going after a sound I hear in my head that the steel has come closest to," Garcia noted in 1971. "I'm really a novice at it, but I'm not really trying to become a steel player." Novice though he was, Garcia's sound on the instrument was quite distinctive, and he lent his steel talents to several excellent albums between '69 and '71, including the Jefferson Airplane's *Volunteers* ("The Farm"), Brewer & Shipley's *Tarkio Road*, Paul Kantner's *Blows Against the Empire*, David Crosby's *If I Could Only Remember My Name* and, most famous of all, Crosby, Stills, Nash & Young's *Déjà Vu* ("Teach Your Children").

The fall of '69 through 1972 represents the Golden Era of Garcia's songwriting partnership with Robert Hunter: produced during this period were the studio albums *Workingman's Dead* and *American Beauty*, the solo *Garcia* (on which Garcia played all the instruments, except drums, himself), and the live *Grateful Dead* (better known as "Skull & Roses") and *Europe '72*. Between them, these albums cover a wide cross-section of American song styles, and contain many of the duo's best songs, including "Uncle John's Band," "New Speedway Boogie," "Black Peter," "Ripple," "Brokedown Palace," "Attics of My Life," "Wharf Rat," "Tennessee Jed," to name just a handful. Garcia's guitar work in this era moved easily from twangy countrified picking—showing the influence of such masters of country's "Bakersfield Sound" like Don Rich and Roy Nichols—to completely dissonant wah-wah inflected flights into outer space. Though the early Seventies saw the Dead frequently dubbed a "country rock band," it was also a period when they played some of their spaciest, most "difficult" music. Garcia's guitar of choice in this era was a '59 Fender Strat. He moved away from Gibsons because "I got bored with them" he said in '81. "I felt I really didn't have any place else to go on them. [*The Strat*] was more of a challenge. It wasn't that I wanted to lose the SG part of my playing, but my reasoning was along the lines of, 'I think that no matter what guitar I play, I won't have any trouble getting a sweet sound,' even though the most difficult thing to produce is a sweet sound."

As early as 1971 Garcia had been talking about having a guitar built for him, and by '73 this was a reality. A Northern California luthier named Doug Irwin built Garcia's first custom instrument, which he described as having the best features of both a Strat and an SG. "[*Irwin*] was working for a friend of mine, [*and*] I picked up a guitar that he had built the neck for at a guitar store and said, 'Wow, where did this come from? I gotta have this guitar!'" Garcia remembered a few years ago. "I bought the guitar and [*upon discovering that Irwin had built the neck*] I commissioned him to build me a guitar. He did, and I played this guitar [*nicknamed The Wolf because of its cartoonish hungry wolf inlay design*] for most of the Seventies. When he delivered it to me, I said, 'Now I want you to build me what you think would be the ultimate guitar. I don't care when you deliver it, I don't care how much it's gonna cost or anything else.' A couple months later he told me it would cost about three grand, which at the time was a lot for a guitar, since it was the early Seventies. He delivered the guitar to me in '78, eight years later. I'd forgotten I'd paid for it. Whatever that guitar says to me, I play."

Since he first played The Wolf, Garcia played Irwin's guitars exclusively onstage, except from 1975-'77, when he favored a bone-white Travis Bean. This was another fertile period for Garcia and the Dead—it includes the albums *Blues for Allah* and *Terrapin Station*. Not many changes in his playing style crop up during this era, though the introduction of some new effects (like the envelope filter that's so distinctive on "Estimated Prophet") did color his sound in interesting ways. Garcia's involvement with the insidious and addictive drug known as Persian (a heroin-like opiate that is smoked) began in the late Seventies, and while it's hard to gauge its effects on his playing, his songwriting output nose-dived from '79 until the diabetic coma that nearly killed him in 1986. "For a long time there I sort of lost heart," Garcia told me in 1988. "I thought, 'I don't know if I want to do this. I don't know what I want.' I felt like I wanted to get away from everything, somehow. But I didn't want to just stop playing, or have the Grateful Dead stop because that's what I wanted to do. I didn't even know consciously that's what I wanted."

For most of the Eighties, Garcia played an Irwin guitar nicknamed Tiger (again for its beautiful, distinctive inlay). When he became interested in incorporating a MIDI set-up into his arsenal in the late Eighties, Irwin came up with "Rosebud," and Garcia used that guitar, along with two lighter, graphite-necked models, until his death.

It's not surprising that Garcia embraced MIDI so enthusiastically—he was always an explorer on the lookout for new sounds and new ways of thinking about his instrument. So, beginning in 1989, songs that he'd played a hundred times with a certain tonality suddenly opened up for him in exciting new ways—"Bird Song" might have a "flute" line, "Shakedown Street" a "soprano sax" break, "Standing on the Moon," a breathy, undefinable choral quality and "Let It Grow" a Mexican "horn" part. And he employed a hundred other textural variations, from a light, shimmering musical shadow to full-out MIDI "drums." The famous second-set "space" segment, in particular, became a MIDI playground for Garcia, Weir and Lesh.

Ask most hardcore Deadheads, and they'll probably admit that Garcia's playing during much of the last two years of his life wasn't as strong as it had been in the late Eighties, when he had recovered from the coma and was free of hard drugs. He produced his last great works—"Standing on the Moon" and "Days Between"—during this period. As his habit reasserted itself, from the middle of 1993 until his death, his onstage lapses and musical errors became more frequent, his playing often took on a listless quality for long stretches, and he seemed physically incapable of playing complex passages with any sort of precision. He had ongoing problems with carpal tunnel syndrome and just how much his slow but steady physical deterioration during this period affected his playing can only be guessed at. Still, even on his final tour this past June, he was able to rise to the occasion—particularly on his moody ballads, which were always perhaps his strongest suit—and rip into a solo with an unbridled passion and grace that was something to behold.

Jerry Garcia was never the type of guitarist who topped guitar magazine reader's polls. He was always an ensemble player: a brilliant and distinctive instrumental voice, to be sure, but still just one bright thread in the complex weave of the Grateful Dead's sound. He was the antithesis of the flashy guitar extrovert, choosing to stand stock-still most of the time, letting his fingers do all the dancing and fancy moves. He hit more clams than your average pro, but that's because he was fishing for pearls, always looking around the next corner, following his muse and his bandmates into uncharted realms. Constant improvisation involves higher risk, but the payoff is worth it: the musicians and the audience are witnesses to the birth of music that is completely fresh and new.

Looking around the musical landscape he left behind, we don't see many Garcia imitators per se, but there is now a generation of players who have been at the very least influenced by his and the Dead's way of doing things—staying true to themselves, their music and their fans, record biz be damned.

And, of course, the counterculture the band literally helped create 30 years ago has evolved into a strong and vibrant community. Garcia may be gone—and, as the song says, "nothing's gonna bring him back"—but it's already clear that his sweet song will reverberate forever.

"People need celebration in their lives," Garcia said in 1989, trying to explain the Dead's appeal. "It's part of what it means to be human. I don't know why. We need magic. And bliss. [*We need*] power, myth, and celebration in our lives, and music is a good way to encapsulate a lot of it."

The following piece by Gary Burnett appeared on the World Wide Web, an appropriate medium for the author, who is a visiting faculty member in the School of Information Studies at Florida State University, where he teaches courses relating to innovative means of presenting information and conducts research on web-based educational models and electronically mediated communities. He has written extensively on topics ranging from the poetry of H.D., to trends in urban education.

The Grateful Dead
A Meditation on Music, Meaning, and Memory

Gary Burnett

Though it began as a mode of composition, it rapidly became a kind of architectural metaphor, a way of defining blocks of space with barely controlled fields of sound, the slide from one phrase to another suggesting both walls and a grid within which we can live in the instant before it once again disappears. Only when it stops altogether is it possible to begin looking forward. And it is only in part a question of style, of the creation of a musical universe unique to this particular aggregate of players.

⚡   ⚡   ⚡

There are just too many stories, many of them fragmentary, most of them nothing more than random images laced together by the assimilative forces of memory. When a thread is pulled, an entire skein follows: a slight move-ment made by Phil at the Greek Theatre (palms out toward Bobby in a ges-ture of denial or refusal, combined with a shake of the head) drags along another fragmentary image: Phil pointing out to Bobby that he can't start "Playing in the Band" because Jerry has already retreated to his amp, lit his cigarette, and begun the endless process of tuning up, what Bobby, with his repertoire of three or four bad jokes, calls "Dead Air."

Given such a tangle of memories, little is specific or completely clear. I'm not even sure which shows Phil's two gestures belong to; one, I know, is linked with a memory of oppressive summer heat, another—or maybe it's the same one—with the remembered pressure of the sand below my feet as I stand with the crowd in front of the concrete risers of the Greek Theatre. And more: eucalyptus trees around the Greek; the two mile walk from home to get there; someone in line saying "Yeah, Jerry used to move a lot"; that sense of well-being and accomplishment when I finally move through the gate.

Nor am I convinced of the accuracy of many of my memories. My feet clearly feel the distinctive physical sensation of that sand, called up across the years; but I can't actually recall seeing sand in the pit at the Greek. Still, there it is; it's the way memory—my memory, at least—works; it's a blur, a melange of things that somehow elude any attempt at description and coherent storytelling. But it's the closest I can come to explaining why I'm "on the bus."

How can anyone else possibly understand the real significance of the arc a fluorescent frisbee took as it flew through the smoky air of Winterland and bounced off of Keith's grand piano at a show in late 1973 or early 1974? Or the fact that such an inconsequential image has remained with me, as clear as ever, for nearly twenty years?

The response is often visual: the legs around me as I sit on the floor become saplings, part of a great forest through which the cool winds of space blow.

mirror
      crashes
some
      supposition
inward
      as well

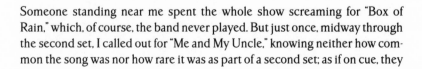

Someone standing near me spent the whole show screaming for "Box of Rain," which, of course, the band never played. But just once, midway through the second set, I called out for "Me and My Uncle," knowing neither how common the song was nor how rare it was as part of a second set; as if on cue, they played it. Everyone turned to stare at me, by now not just "on the bus," but apparently given some kind of strange control over the course of events. That sense of control—that inexplicable command of events—is a cliché, but we've all lived it.

Long, intricate vocal lacework at the end of "He's Gone" and, as second encore, my only "And We Bid You Goodnight."

The next night, when I wasn't there, they played "Dark Star." Of course; the playing of that song is one event I've never—until very recently—been given access to, much less control over.

White t-shirts glow in the black light of Winterland, hair and arms of dancers cutting patterns through space. Distance is meaningless.

> effortlessly lyrical
> > grace
> > mistaken

Two cannabis-laced cookies outside of the Greek Theatre. 1984. Dancing on the small incline near the football stadium where they'd set up speakers for people without tickets.

The year before, they had used the entire baseball field, and hundreds of people came together to enjoy the show for free, with the blessings of all.

The core of my feeling of being on the bus, though, isn't limited by that odd sense of control, any more than it is by the more palpable memories, the tactile, auditory and visual sensations that remain with me. The whole thing is driven by something else: something I'm less certain about, something even less subject to explanation. A poet friend of mine thinks that it has to do with the way the Dead are able to endlessly spin what he calls "musical narrative" out of themselves. And that's true, but it doesn't explain the magic of being at a show.

The continuity (or "narrative") of any good show is part of it, certainly, but only part. The only thing I can say is that each show means something, and that what it means is curiously precise and—at least at the best shows—amazingly coherent.

The Dead build this "meaning"—in its most obvious form—purely out of the actual music they play: sometimes Jerry, or one of the others, will repeat a particular signature riff a number of times throughout the course of a show, turning it into a kind of motif which links songs as different as, say, "Let It Grow" and "Stella Blue." In several 1991 shows, the motif was, unexpectedly, the "Dark Star" theme.

Other instances are more subjective.

At one show—the first time I saw Brent—I felt the air around me being carved by the sheer physical force of the sound, sculpted, constructed. The music created a home, a literal physical space within which I could live. I have no memory of the songs played at that show, but still feel the structure erected, huge, palpable swatches of Brent's organ throwing material walls up all around me, incised with the filigree of Jerry's guitar and buttressed by Phil's bass.

At another show, some invisible force lifted me bodily five feet above my seat and I was blasted with repeated jolts of electricity from the stage. The power of the music took me over, controlling every motion, every surge of energy. I don't know if anyone saw me hovering above the crowd twitching and dancing, but it was the strangest thing I've ever experienced. And there were no drugs involved.

The stage darkens at the end of Drums, and for a moment remains empty as Mickey's last eruption echoes and fades, reverberating from speaker to speaker across the auditorium.

> drums
> simply
> in memory

Alone, Jerry steps out on stage and for about fifteen seconds ethereal arpeggios from his guitar are the only things to be heard. After the violence of Mickey's assault, they are comforting, healing. It's a special moment.

The single most articulate and comprehensible construction of "meaning" I've ever heard came during a second set late in the '80s, sometime after Jerry's coma. The whole set, I could have sworn, was a ritual enactment of the mysteries of death and rebirth, forged in the crucible of "Fire on the Mountain," supplied drama by the terror and chaos of the jam following "Playing in the Band," and given final explication in "Black Peter" and "Knocking on Heaven's Door," both of which dropped through the gates of death and reemerged victorious.

Even the percussion duet faltered, descending at last into silence and nothingness, a dead stop. The silence that night after Mickey and Billy left the stage seemed to last an eternity, carrying with it all the weight of dissolution and insurmountable decay. There seemed to be nowhere left to go, no way the music could possibly continue in the face of that silence, but somehow, miraculously, it did, and everybody in the auditorium shared in that deliverance from the brink.

By the time Jerry sang that he was "knocking on heaven's door—JUST LIKE SO MANY TIMES BEFORE" in the encore that night, carrying the whole ritual into a final enduring celebration, we all, I think, knew what we had been through, and none of us would willingly have done without a single impossible moment of the process.

Those impossible moments of glory and bliss are just too thick in my mental picture of the Dead, now that Jerry is gone, and it's almost impossible not to slip into a nostalgic haze. But this is not—and can't be—just nostalgia, which perverts and distorts everything it touches. The sheer fact that it lasted so long, and was such a deep part of my life, is assurance enough.

And the truth is that, if it were just nostalgia, other kinds of memories would have been obscured. But there they are—Jerry looking green, bloated, and frighteningly frail on stage at so many shows in the early '80s, the hundreds of badly played songs through the years, the increasing ugliness of the scene outside of the shows in the '90s.

It's also true that, like Jerry's, my attentiveness waned at times, sometimes for months or years at a stretch. At one show, I swore that, if I ever heard them play another turgid and lurching version of "Tennessee Jed," I'd never come back. But then, of course, it happened—the next time I caught the song, it was a gem, sparkling and pure.

The grab-bag quality of memory remains—Donna hugely pregnant onstage, Brent counting down "Hey Pocky Way" to begin a show; the muscles in Jerry's left forearm as he worked the fretboard; a jam between Jerry and Bruce Hornsby—the two of them staring, smiling, into each others' eyes—that sounded like a psychedelic reel; moments of 1974 peeking through the interstices in a few shows during the 1990s; the jam in "Eternity" moving into some richly textured and mysterious spaces; "That Would Be Something" suddenly being transformed from a goofy little throw-away into a jammed-out dance tune.

I was fortunate enough to have two final shows, one with Jerry and one with the memory of Jerry. The first, at RFK Stadium, was wonderful. The second, at the memorial service in the Polo Fields, was magic. At the first, Jerry played beautifully with the Grateful Dead, Bob Dylan, and Bruce Hornsby. At the second, he played beautifully with the gods.

I'll never forget either one.

Silberman's eloquent farewell appeared in *Garcia: A Grateful Celebration*, a special edition of *Dupree's Diamond News*, in 1996.

The Only Song of God

Steve Silberman

When there was no ear to hear, you sang to me.
—Robert Hunter

This morning, I walked past the Henry J. Kaiser Auditorium in Oakland for the first time since Jerry Garcia's death.

From 1979 to 1989, the Grateful Dead held forth there 56 times, and I probably saw 40 of those shows.

I had never seen the grass in front of the arena deserted before, with no Deadheads kibitzing on blankets or waiting in line at booths, no wet dogs in bandannas snapping Frisbees out of the air and galloping down to lap from the muddy creek.

Instead of the high archways carved with scenes from Romantic mythology, I remembered milling craziness spilling into the street, and the lines winding around back where the limos came in, growing thicker at the doors near show time as Willie, in his blue security suit, kept everyone honest by preaching the gospel of soul through a megaphone.

I knocked on the front door and a custodian let me in for a few minutes to look around. I walked through the tiled lobby into the main arena, barely longer than it is wide, the light tan planks on the floor marked with black tape, an antique scoreboard dangling from the ceiling.

From the bleachers to the back wall. I counted only 11 rows of wooden flip-up seats. I was so happy to be in that room again.

In the 1950s, gospel groups like the Swan Silvertones, the Mighty Clouds of Joy, the Soul Stirrers, and the James Cleveland Choir used to sing in that room. Smartly dressed ushers walked the aisles wearing white gloves, so that someone who got the spirit in the middle of a number—who might stand up in their Sunday finest, testifying in tongues, and faint dead over—could be carried out into the lobby, fanned back to consciousness, and ushered back in.

In the '80s—the golden years of my life as a Deadhead—I used to think of Kaiser as the living room of the tribe.

The Dead's annual open-air jubilees, in drenching sun, at the Greek Theatre in Berkeley and at the Frost Amphitheatre at Stanford, were more spectacular. But Kaiser—with its midweek shows, and spiral corridors for schmoozing between epiphanies—was for locals. You didn't have to buy a plane ticket or hitchhike a thousand miles to see the band, and many of the people there, you'd know: your neighbors, your dentist, the other Deadhead from your office. For days afterward, you'd recognize faces that you'd seen in the big room, and smile to each other as you passed in the street.

If you weren't from the Bay Area, after three or four shows at Kaiser, eventually, you'd move here. Kaiser was for lifers. It felt like home.

At shows in those years, up at the front on "the rail" where you could observe the musicians at work, the crowds could get so dense on a Saturday night that you would lose your footing. But if you relaxed, you could nearly float, like a cell in a bath of nutrient, the rhythms coming to you as a gentle push in one direction, then another.

If you left your backpack under the bleachers before the lights went out, it would still be there when the applause ended. When the lights came up again, you might see a couple in the middle of the floor who had just made love in the swirling dark, laughing, exhausted, fixing each other's hair.

It was one of the safest places in the world.

I was a suburban kid, the son of agnostic parents who believed in a healing of the world by political, rather than spiritual, means. Still, wherever I looked, the universe seemed animate and mysterious.

The Martian Chronicles, The Science Fiction Hall of Fame, and *The Outer Limits* widened the horizons of my everyday life to include the infinite. In sixth grade, I found a copy of Richard Hittleman's *21-Day Yoga Plan* in the library, lit a candle, and gazed earnestly into the flame.

"Birdsong," June 30, 1995, Three Rivers Stadium, Pittsburgh, Pennsylvania. ©
Rob Cohn, 1995

I remember one afternoon when I was in high school, sitting on my best
friend's bed, listening to *Europe '72*. The music I liked up to that point was
vocal music, like the folk tunes my mother sang to me before I was able to
speak; songs that told stories, like Stephen Stills' alliterative cowboy confess-
ing his love in "Helplessly Hoping."

After the last verse of "China Cat Sunflower," Weir took a lead over Kreutzmann's breathing, elastic time, with Godchaux's piano cascading down like
droplets of silver. But it was Garcia—even out of the spotlight—who added
incisive punctuations that stitched the music into a tale unfolding, and I suddenly had the sensation of riding on a locomotive, surging forward on the
track.

As I grew older, the music of the Dead—especially the restless, exploratory
jams that were Garcia's trademark—often provided the soundtrack for my
introspection.

While the rest of the world was asleep or watching television, I'd shut my
door and put on my headphones, and hear seemingly ancient voices broadcast their truths, listen to each other, and respond; delighted to be part of an
intimate conversation beyond what could be said in words—like eavesdrop-
ping on God's thoughts.

After I started going to see the band in places like Roosevelt Stadium and the Capitol Theatre, I learned that at Dead shows, you could allow the music to go as deeply inside you as it did when you were alone; and you could do it with those who understood, in their own way, how the music felt to you.

Sometimes I liked to turn away from the stage, so I could see how others received it. Some would listen with their eyes shut, swaying; others would gaze toward the men onstage as you would to your oldest friend—who was about to attempt something marvelous and difficult—with a blessing look.

If Deadheads were a tribe that sought collective experience, we were also an aggregation of loners who had learned how not to bruise each other's solitude: that place where our souls, and the music, communed.

If you were tripping, the music would pour forth celestial architectures, quicksilver glistening with might-be's, cities of light at the edge of a sea of chaos, monumental forms that could be partially recollected in tranquillity, and turned into designs in fabric or clay, golden sentences, streams of bits.

And some nights, the hair on the back of your neck would stand on end as a *presence* came into the room, given a body by the magnificent sound system. In the hallways, the Dead's own dervishes, the Spinners, would bow toward the stage, their long hair brushing the floor. Dancers raised one another up like kids in punk clubs, laughing like babies in their father's arms, or weeping.

Startled out of my reflection by some grace-note of primordial majesty, I'd look up and see his fingers...

That furrow of deliberation where all else was left to drift, in the secret place where everything was waiting to be born.

Four days after Garcia's death, my friend Raymond Foye and I picked up a young man hitchhiking by the roadside near Ray's house in Woodstock. The perfume of sweet alcohol filled the car as he climbed in. We asked him where he was going and he said, "To the monastery at the top of the mountain."

We wound up the road to an enormous gate, painted red, and carved with lions.

The monks knew our passenger. "You back for good this time?" one asked.

When the young man offered to guide us to the shrine room, we eagerly accepted. The rooms and hallways leading there had the orderliness of sacred space. There was a rack for shoes, so you'd enter the room barefoot.

Along the walls, *bodhisattvas* glowed in the shadows. I walked slowly, with my hands clasped over my heart, as I'd been taught by my old Zen teacher. With each step, I felt the cool floor against the soles of my feet.

I turned toward the front of the room. There in the dim light, an enormous Buddha, painted gold, sat in the erect, relaxed posture of contemplative alertness, like a mountain in a dream.

I walked up and made a full prostration, my forehead touching the floor, my palms upraised.

On the altar, there was an oil lamp lit, with a white card beside it. It read:

FOR JERRY GARCIA
MAY HE HAVE AN AUSPICIOUS REBIRTH

Sometimes it seems we have little greatness left to us to praise. Our leaders are liars or comedians, and our priests, like teenagers, have a hard time interpreting their own desires, much less the Passion of Christ.

Yet I'm confident the Grateful Dead were truly great, by which I mean, were able to abide some portion of mystery, and allow it to come through them without naming it or taking too much pride in it, or appropriating its surface aspects as a pose or strategy.

Look at the shaman, standing in his once-living robe, holding up a drum, blazed on the walls of caves all over the Earth. The rock and roll fop, pursing his lips under the pastel lights, is a bare flicker over this image, graven in the back of our minds as surely as if it had been carved in the skull-cup of bone by a hand.

The image says: Drums are doors or vehicles, voices bear messages to the threshold of Heaven, and sliding or "flatted" notes are blue highways between this world and the other.

I once asked Garcia how it came to be that a young bluegrass banjo and guitar player with a taste for the blues and R&B had found, in the company of kindred spirits, a road back to the collective experience of music as mystery.

We didn't plan it that way, he said. It just happened, like an escalator appearing in front of our eyes. We had a choice at the beginning, to get on, or not.

That was all.

I remember standing on a train platform after a show, when I heard a freight pass heavy on the rails, the couplings and wheels clattering with a lurching, quirky grandeur that was familiar.

Then I remembered: it was the rhythm of "Ramble on Rose."

For all I know, Garcia might have had the ghost of another tune in mind when he wrote it, or pulled it out of the air—but it was the American air, of boxcars passing (with Jack Kerouac's little St. Theresa hobo shivering inside) through towns with names like Gaviota, Las Cruces, and Wichita.

No pomp and circumstance for us Yankees, but hard luck and a little grace—our own raw melodies sent up with the drafts of a campfire—rippling the moon in the corner of a fiddler's eye.

One night at Kaiser, after a delicate, shimmering jam that threaded out of "Estimated Prophet," the drummers were joined onstage by Willie Green of the Neville Brothers.

Mickey Hart moved from the traps to the *berimbau* to the Beam, an instrument he helped invent: a ten-foot aluminum girder strung with piano wire tuned to extremely low pitches, designed to launch huge standing waves into very large rooms, to shiver bones and make the walls of a coliseum tremble.

As the drummers faced one another, the tidal resonances of the Beam rippled through the floorboards, ebbing in a series of descending pitches that sounded then, to me, like the root of all music.

I felt my knees weaken under me. My palms came together as if of their own volition, and I dropped to the floor.

I didn't need to know or name what called me to make that full prostration. I only needed a place to do it that was safe, a place where I felt *at liberty,* so that inner life and outer life could come together.

The root of the verb "to heal" means "to make whole."

That's why the Grateful Dead were medicine men: the music, and the collective energy of Deadheads, together, helped heal the sickness of existence. To those blinded by habit was conveyed sight, and the lame were made—a little less lame.

In Tibet, the medicine that healed the sickness of existence was called *amrita,* "the strongest poison and medicine of all."

A black muddy river of *amrita* flowed through Grateful Dead land.

Though from the outside, Garcia had an enviable life, he—like all of us—had to learn to make himself at home among many contradictions. (He once said, "I live in a world without a Grateful Dead.")

An intensely humble and private man, his art earned him the kind of fame that plastered his face on bumper stickers. Branded for the duration of his career in the media by the decade in which he came of age, he sometimes seemed most at home picking the tunes Bill Monroe, Doc Watson, and Clarence Ashley played for decades before anyone had heard of the Haight-Ashbury. For someone whose craft helped so many people rediscover the pleasures of having a body, Garcia seemed to only grudgingly acknowledge his own.

And while Deadheads tapped a seemingly inexhaustible wellspring of good news in his music, Garcia himself had endured several of life's great tragedies, including witnessing the death of his father by drowning, and the loss of a finger. (The luminous tracks on *American Beauty* were recorded during a period of daily trips with his brother Tiff to San Francisco General, to visit their mother, Ruth, who had sustained injuries in a car accident that turned out to be fatal.)

A witty and engaging conversationalist, of cosmopolitan interests and encyclopedic reference, Garcia must have realized that his social contacts were becoming increasingly circumscribed by his heroin habit, which he once referred to as a "buffer."

Garcia had made of his instrument a means for direct expression of his soul. In the last year of his life—as his buffer became an adversary to his art, his nimbleness became a thing lost, and the lyrics no longer arrived—the pain was audible in his music.

Last spring, when I asked a mutual friend how the sessions for the new album were going, he said that Jerry was uncommunicative, unkempt, and not playing well. I asked him if Garcia's behavior had any emotional coloration.

"Yeah," he said—'Do Not Disturb.'"

For the last year, I'd been reassuring panicky young Deadheads online that the rumors that were suddenly everywhere—that the Summer Tour would be the Dead's last—were untrue.

The venues for '96, I'd been told, had already been booked.

But the mind-at-large knew better. The universe that set Garcia up as a medicine man in an age thirsting for mystery would not let him exit without the thunderclaps, lightning, and palls of doom that Shakespeare brought down on the heads of a tattered king and his clown.

At four in the morning on August 9th, Maureen Hunter stirred sleepless beside her husband, Robert. Garcia had telephoned the Hunters a day or so earlier, to thank Robert for all the songs they'd written together, and also to say, with unusual explicitness, that he loved him.

Maureen got up and walked into the kitchen, where a breeze was blowing through an open window. She bolted the window, looked in on her daughter, and returned to bed.

A few miles away, a staffer at Serenity Knolls paused outside Garcia's room, not hearing the snoring he'd heard earlier. He entered the room, and found Garcia in bed, his heart stopped, smiling.

⚡   ⚡   ⚡

Part of the joy in being a Deadhead was in wedding yourself to a story that was longer than your life.

When I was writing my essay "Who Was Cowboy Neal?" I began to think of the surging improvised section of *Cassidy* as a place where Neal Cassady's spirit was invited to visit the living. Like Garcia, Neal had been a hero to many, but to himself, a man—fighting a man's struggles beside the titans whose footsteps echoed in those jams that I never wanted to end.

When the chords said "look within," we trusted Garcia to ride point for us, to be the headlight on the northbound train, behind which we were grateful to follow. Each of his discoveries was greeted with recognition. He'd taken us someplace new again, but a place we felt we were fated to go, because Jack's words in *On the Road*—about burning "like fabulous yellow roman candles exploding like spiders across the stars"—had spoken directly to us, the lucky ones; the ones who found the stone, the old stone in the American wilderness that marks the way.

And when we arrived in that place we were born to seek, all our brothers and sisters were there.

Of course.

So now, the story is over.

As prophesied, "Soon you will not hear his voice."

But it is not so.

⚡   ⚡   ⚡

There's an old Zen tale of two patch-robed monks, students of the same master, who meet, years after his death, on a footbridge above a foaming river.

Seeing one another again, the two old friends laugh aloud.

"Do you miss our old teacher?" asks the one.

"No, now I see him everywhere," answers the other.

For it was our love that wedded us to the ancient story, our love the music called to in the words of a poet, Scheherazade's tale of the Many Thousand Nights that included us, in which real moonlight fell on imaginary waters.

The same moon that Neal Cassady saw in the mountain above Denver, shining over the city of the dead.

The last time the Dead played at Cal Expo—a small outdoor venue outside of Sacramento, like Kaiser with no roof—I used a backstage pass and a drop of liquid to peer behind the spectacle, wandering around the picnic tables like a stoned kid at one of my parents' parties.

It was hot and still, but I knew that at the end of the path that runs behind the stage, there was a swimming pool, where you could still hear the music perfectly.

There was no one else there. I stripped, lowered myself into the water, and looked up at the stars, my mind roaming in the constellations as I floated on the music.

Onstage, Garcia had come home to that little place that he and Hunter made, that he loved so much, "Stella Blue." How slowly the world seemed to turn around us in the night as he played it, night after night.

When he came to the line, "I've stayed in every blue-light cheap hotel, can't win for tryin'," I took a breath and plunged, down into the silence, the drifting where once I heard my mother's heart beat.

And back up, breaking the surface just as the moon and stars shone through the strings of a broken angel's guitar.

Friend, when I meet you on the bridge in 10,000 years, please remind me that our teacher's voice is in the wash of muddy river water over the ancient stones, and in the dancing light at the edge, where a fiddler calls the tune and we rejoin the great circle.

For the universe is full of secrets that gradually reveal themselves, but there is not enough time. Barely time for a song to praise this place where we found each other, and pass back into the "transitive nightfall of diamonds," the beautiful melodies and suffering in the meat yearning for transformation—the only song of God.

Credits

"Elegy for Jerry" by Robert Hunter. Used by permission of Ice Nine Publishing Company.

Introduction to "We Want Phil" by Blair Jackson. Originally published in *Golden Road*, Issue 23, Summer 1990. Used by permission.

"Dead Heads: A Strange Tale of Love, Devotion and Surrender" by Blair Jackson. Originally published in *BAM*, April 4, 1980. Used by permission of the author.

"This Darkness Got to Give: Some Thoughts on Problems in the Dead Scene" by Blair Jackson. Originally published in *Golden Road*, Spring 1990. Used by permission.

"In Phil We Trust: A Conversation" by Blair Jackson. Originally published in *Dupree's Diamond News*, Number 28, Spring 1994. Used by permission.

"American Beauty" by Blair Jackson. Originally published in *Guitar World*, November 1995. Used by permission.

"Jerry Garcia and the Call of the Weird" by Alice Kahn. Used by permission.

"You Don't Seem to Hear Me When I Call," by Paddy Ladd. Reprinted by permission of the author.

"Grateful Dead" by Willy Legate. Used by permission of Ice Nine Publishing Company.

"An Aged Deadhead," by Milton Mayer. Reprinted by permission from *The Progressive*.

"Grateful Dead I Have Known," by Ed McClanahan. © 1972 by Ed McClanahan. Originally appeared in *Playboy*, March 1972.

"Meditations on the Grateful Dead" by Dennis McNally. Reprinted by permission.

"St. Stephen Revisited and Beyond" by Richard Meltzer. Used by permission.

"He Was a Friend of Mine" by Robert M. Petersen. Used by permission of Hulogosi Communications.

Index of Song and Album Titles

Index

PML
25'